CliffsNotes®

FTCE General Knowledge Test with CD-ROM, 2nd Edition

CliffsNotes®

FTCE General Knowledge Test with CD-ROM

2ND EDITION

by

Jeffrey S. Kaplan, Ph.D. and Sandra Luna McCune, Ph.D.

WILEY

John Wiley & Sons, Inc.

About the Authors

Jeffrey S. Kaplan, Ph.D. is an Associate Professor and Program Coordinator of English Language Arts Education in the College of Education's School of Teaching, Learning, and Leadership at the University of Central Florida in Orlando, Florida.

Sandra Luna McCune, Ph.D. is formerly a Regents Professor at Stephen F. Austin State University in Nacogdoches, Texas, where she received the Distinguished Professor Award. Dr. McCune is a nationally recognized author of teacher education test preparation review materials.

Authors' Acknowledgments

The authors would like to thank Grace Freedson for bringing us this project. We also want to thank our families for their love and support.

Editorial

Acquisition Editor: Greg Tubach

Project Editor: Suzanne Snyder

Copy Editor: Lynn Northrup

Technical Editors: Barbara Swovelin, Tom Page, Mary Jane Sterling

Composition

Proofreader: Shannon Ramsey

John Wiley & Sons, Inc. Composition Services

CliffsNotes® FTCE General Knowledge Test with CD-ROM, 2nd Edition

Published by:
John Wiley & Sons, Inc.
111 River Street
Hoboken, NJ 07030-5774
www.wiley.com

Copyright © 2011 John Wiley & Sons, Inc., Hoboken, NJ

Published by John Wiley & Sons, Inc., Hoboken, NJ
Published simultaneously in Canada

Library of Congress Control Number: 2011930285
ISBN: 978-1-118-01804-0 (pbk)
ISBN: 978-1-118-09177-7 (ebk); 978-1-118-09178-4 (ebk); 978-1-118-09910-0 (ebk)

Printed in the United States of America

10 9 8 7 6 5 4 3 2

Table of Contents

PART II: TWO FULL-LENGTH PRACTICE TESTS

Introduction

General Description

The Florida Teacher Certification Examination (FTCE) General Knowledge (GK) Test is a computer-based test designed to assess basic skills in reading, writing, and mathematics. The test is composed of four subtests:

- Subtest I—Essay Writing
- Subtest II—English Language Skills
- Subtest III—Mathematics
- Subtest IV—Reading

You will have 3 hours 50 minutes to complete the entire test.

For the essay question, you choose from two prompts. Each multiple-choice question will contain three or four response options. You have to click on your choice to record your answer to a question. No penalty is assessed for wrong answers (you score a zero for that test question). For the Mathematics Subtest, the test center provides a 4-function calculator and a mathematics reference sheet.

Format of the GK Test

Format of the GK Test			
Subtest Competencies and Skills	Number of Multiple-Choice Questions	Number of Essay Questions	Time Allowed
Subtest I: ESSAY			
Essay		1	
Subtest Total		**1**	**50 minutes**
Subtest II: ENGLISH LANGUAGE SKILLS			
Organization and Concept Skills	4		
Word Choice Skills	6		
Sentence Structure Skills	6		
Grammar, Punctuation, and Spelling	24		
Subtest Total	**40**		**40 minutes**
Subtest III: MATHEMATICS			
Numeration and Operations	8		
Measurement	10		
Geometry	9		
Algebraic Reasoning	9		
Probability and Data Analysis	9		
Subtest Total	**45**		**100 minutes**
Subtest IV: READING			
Literal Comprehension Skills			
Inferential Comprehension Skills			
Subtest Total	**40**		**40 minutes**

The Role of the FTCE General Knowledge Test in Teacher Certification

The FTCE GK Test is one of the state-mandated teacher certification tests in Florida. Usually, if you want to teach in a Florida elementary, middle, or secondary public school, you have to take and pass at least three tests: the FTCE GK Test, the FTCE Professional Education Test, and a subject area examination (SAE) in the field in which you want to be certified. The tests and the testing program that goes with them are the result of legislation passed by Florida in 1980. For the FTCE GK Test, you have to demonstrate basic skills in reading, writing, and mathematics—which is what this book is designed to help you do. The FTCE Professional Education Test assesses your knowledge about learning, teaching, and professional conduct. The subject area test covers the content that you are required to teach. Elementary teacher education candidates take the FTCE Elementary Education K-6 test as their subject area test. The purpose of the certification program in Florida is to ensure that certified teachers possess sufficient professional knowledge and skills to perform effectively their roles as teachers in Florida schools.

Statewide committees of subject area specialists identified and validated the content of the FTCE GK Test. The committee members consisted of public school teachers, district supervisors, and college faculty with expertise in the subject areas—with public school teachers comprising the majority of the committees. Selection to committee membership was based on recommendations by professional organizations, subject area experts, and teachers' unions. The test development process involved an extensive literature review, interviews with selected public school teachers, a large-scale survey of teachers, and pilot testing.

Questions Commonly Asked About the FTCE General Knowledge Test

Q. What is the FTCE General Knowledge Test?

A. The FTCE GK Test is the required basic skills test adopted by the Florida Legislature for assessing reading, writing, and mathematics skills of applicants for the Florida Teacher Certification license. It replaces the College Level Academic Skills Test (CLAST).

Q. Who administers the FTCE GK Test?

A. The FTCE GK Test is part of the Florida Teacher Certification program, which is administered by the Florida Department of Education. A committee of experts in teacher education and specialists in specific subject areas draws up the guidelines for the FTCE examinations.

Q. When and where is the FTCE GK Test given?

A. Currently, the FTCE GK Test is 100 percent computer-based. It is offered on computer at flexible times throughout the year at locations throughout the state of Florida and in select cities nationwide. Check www. fl.nesinc.com/FL_TestSites.asp for an up-to-date list of test sites. You also should check the FTCE Bulletin for updated information regarding changes in tests and application procedures (www.fl.nesinc.com/PDFs/ FL_2011RegistrationBulletin.pdf).

Q. How do I register to take the test?

A. Registration is available 24 hours a day, 7 days a week online at www.fl.nesinc.com/FL_InternetReg.asp. There are no deadlines for computer-based testing registrations, but you should register as early as possible before your target test date, because test sites accept registrations on a first-come, first-served basis and seating is limited.

Q. What is the fee for the test?

A. The current registration fee (in 2011) for first attempt testing is $130. The registration fee for second attempt testing is $150. If you have additional questions about fees or need help calculating the total amount you need to pay to register, call FTCE/FELE Customer Service at (413) 256-2893. You must pay your fees for Internet registration using a credit card (VISA or MasterCard only) or a debit or check card that carries the VISA or MasterCard logo and can be used without the entry of a personal identification number (PIN). If you do not have a credit or debit card, contact FTCE/FELE Customer Service at (413) 256-2893.

Q. What should I bring to the test site?

A. You will receive your admission ticket by e-mail after your registration has been processed. Your admission ticket will include your name, the test(s) you are registered to take, the test date, the test site address, the reporting time, and a reminder of what to bring to the test site. Check the information on your admission ticket to make sure that it is correct. You will not be allowed to make changes at the test site.

The day of the test, you must bring your admission ticket and two valid, unexpired identification forms that are printed in English, including one that is government issued with a recent, clear photo and signature, such as a driver's license, state-issued ID card, U.S. military ID with signature, or passport. You may be refused admission to the testing room without your valid admission ticket or proper identification. You are not allowed to bring calculators or calculator watches, watches that beep, photographic or recording devices, audiotapes, highlighters, dictionaries, spell checkers, slide rules, briefcases, backpacks, packages, cellular phones, beepers, notebooks, textbooks, scratch paper, or any other aids inside the testing room—so it is best to not have any such items in your possession when you arrive at the testing site. However, the testing sites do have secure storage in which you may put away personal belongings, including prohibited items. Also, you are not allowed to eat, drink, or smoke inside the testing room.

Q. Can I bring my cell phone into the testing room?

A. Absolutely not! If a cell phone or an electronic prohibited aid is found in your possession (regardless of whether it is turned off or on), you will not be allowed to continue testing. The test site will report this information to the Florida Department of Education, and your score will be invalidated—so, to be safe, you should not bring a cell phone to the testing site.

Q. Are special testing arrangements available?

A. If you have a disabling condition (visual, physical, hearing, or so on), special testing arrangements and test materials can be made available for you. Submit an Alternative Testing Arrangements Request Form (available at www.fl.nesinc.com) stating the specific accommodation(s) you are requesting and send in all required documentation, on official letterhead stationery (including physician name, address, and telephone number), from a medical doctor or licensed psychologist (including license number). When your request has been received and processed, FTCE/FELE Customer Service will contact you about the next steps for scheduling your test with any approved accommodations. You must submit a new form every time you register to test.

Q. May I change or cancel my registration if I need to?

A. Yes, your computer-based testing registration can be canceled or changed online for any reason up until the day before the test date with no additional fees or penalties. Your request to change/cancel must be submitted online, by logging into your account, at least 24 hours before your testing appointment. You will receive a refund for your test fees for cancelation requests submitted 24 hours prior to your testing appointment.

Q. When will I get my score report?

A. When you finish testing, you will receive an unofficial score report on the screen for the multiple-choice subtests: English Language Skills, Mathematics, and Reading. You will not receive an unofficial subscore for the Essay subtest at that time, but you will receive proof of testing that documents your completion of that subtest. Official score reports for the English Language Skills, Mathematics, and Reading subtests will be released approximately 3–4 weeks after your test date. The Essay subtest score will be released approximately 6 weeks after your test date.

Q. **What is the passing score?**

A. The passing score for the FTCE GK Test is a scaled score of 200 or higher. This scaled score was equivalent to the following raw scores on the July 2002 test administration:

- General Knowledge Reading Subtest: 25 correct items.
- General Knowledge English Skills Subtest: 29 correct items.
- General Knowledge English Essay Subtest: A total raw score of six (6).
- General Knowledge Mathematics Subtest: 26 correct items. (Rule 6A-4.0021, Florida Administrative Code)

The maximum percentages needed to earn a passing score on any form of the FTCE GK Test currently being administered are as follows:

- General Knowledge Reading Subtest: 65 percent of items correct.
- General Knowledge English Skills Subtest: 73 percent of items correct.
- General Knowledge Mathematics Subtest: 60 percent of items correct. (www.fldoe.org/asp/ftce/pdf/ percentpass.pdf)

Q. **How long are my subtest scores good?**

A. As a general rule, passing scores must be applied toward a credential within five years of the test date on which the scores are earned.

Q. **What is included in the FTCE GK Test?**

A. The sections of the FTCE GK Test include four subtests: Essay, English Language Skills, Mathematics, and Reading.

Q. **How much time do I have to complete each subtest?**

A. Three hours and 50 minutes are given to complete all four subtests. For the Essay subtest, you are given 50 minutes to prepare, write, and edit your response. The English Language Skills and Reading subtests are each 40 minutes long. The Mathematics subtest is 100 minutes.

Q. **If I pass part of the test, do I have to retake the whole test?**

A. After you pass a subtest, you do not have to retake that subtest. You need to retake only the subtests that you did not pass. However, the second attempt fee for the FTCE GK Test is $150, regardless of the number of subtests you are retaking. Also, you will not be given extra testing time when you are retaking subtests. The time allotted for a subtest is the same as that given when you take the entire test.

Q. **Do I need to take all the subtests at one time?**

A. No. You may take any combination of the subtests at a single appointment on the same day, for a single test fee. However, you must re-register and pay the full fee every time you retake the test or one or more subtests.

Q. **How many times may I retake the test?**

A. You may retake the entire test or a subtest as many times as is necessary to pass, but you must wait 31 calendar days before retaking the test. Also, you must re-register and pay the full fee every time you retake the test or one or more subtests.

Q. **What other tests must teacher candidates take?**

A. Normally, candidates applying for a Professional Teaching Certificate must take the FTCE GK Test and the FTCE Professional Education Test. In addition, candidates applying for a Professional Certificate and those adding a subject area to a Professional Certificate may need to pass a subject area examination (SAE) in a field in which they are seeking certification. The Bureau of Educator Certification at the Department of Education (www.fldoe.org/edcert) in Tallahassee determines individual testing requirements for certification. After your application for certification is on file, the Bureau will issue you an Official Statement of Status of Eligibility, which will tell you your individualized testing requirements.

Q. Can I take all my teacher tests on one day?

A. Not likely. You can register for one test per appointment. Possibly, you might be able to register for multiple appointments on the same day at the same test site; however, there is no guarantee that multiple appointments can be scheduled on the same day.

Q. Should I guess on the test?

A. Yes! Because no penalty is assessed for guessing, guess if you have to. On the multiple-choice section, first try to eliminate some of the choices to increase your chances of choosing the right answer. But don't leave any questions unanswered. On the essay response subtest, be sure to write a complete and logically constructed essay.

Q. Will scratch paper be provided?

A. You will be provided with an erasable noteboard and pen for use during the test.

Q. Can I use a calculator for the math subtest?

A. Yes, but you cannot bring your own calculator. You will be provided with a Casio HS-4A four-function calculator at the test site.

Q. What if I've never taken a computer-based test before?

A. After you are seated for your computer-based test, you will complete a tutorial before you take the actual test. The tutorial shows you how to move from question to question, how to mark and change answers, and how to go back and review previously answered or skipped questions. For the Essay Subtest, you will be shown how to record your response during the actual test.

Q. How should I prepare for the FTCE GK Test?

A. Now that you're ready to begin taking your certification exams, using this test prep book is your best preparation for the FTCE GK Test. This study guide gives you insights, reviews, and strategies for the question types. Some universities offer preparation programs to assist you in attaining a passing score. Check with them for further information.

Q. How do I get more information about the FTCE GK Test?

A. Check the Florida Department of Education Website at www.fldoe.org. As new information on the testing program becomes available, it is posted on this site.

How to Use This Book

This book is organized around the reading, writing, and mathematics competencies and skills of the FTCE GK Test. It includes a thorough review and study strategies for the test and three full-length practice tests (two in the book and three on the CD-ROM). When you read through the list of competencies and skills covered on the FTCE GK Test, you may feel overwhelmed by the task of preparing for the test. Here are some suggestions for developing an effective study program using this book.

1. To help you organize and budget your time, set up a specific schedule of study sessions. Try to set aside approximately 2 hours for each session. If you complete one session per day (including weekends), it should take you about 5 to 6 weeks to work your way through the review and practice material provided in this book. If your test date is coming up soon, you may need to lengthen your study time per day or skip sections that cover topics that you feel you already know fairly well. Nonetheless, be cautious about deciding to skip sections. You could find yourself struggling through material that would be easier to master if previous sections had been reviewed first. Particularly, be wary of skipping math topics, which are usually highly dependent on previously learned skills.

2. Choose a place for studying this book that is free of distractions and undue noise, so that you can concentrate. Make sure you have adequate lighting and a room temperature that is comfortable—not too warm or too cold. Try to have all the necessary study aids (paper, pen, 4-function calculator, and so on)

within easy reach, so that you don't have to interrupt your studying to go get something you need. Ask friends not to call you during your study time.

3. Don't make excuses. Studying for the FTCE GK Test must be a priority. It will require a lot of time and a conscientious commitment on your part. Think of it as a job that you must do. In reality, studying for the FTCE GK Test is one of the most important jobs you will ever do. The outcome of the test can determine your future career opportunities. Do not avoid studying for it by making excuses or procrastinating.

4. Take Practice Test 1 (Chapter 5) as a diagnostic test before you begin your study program. For the essay question, try to see where your answer might have failed to adequately address the given prompt. Of course, you have to judge the quality of your response based on the scoring criteria explained in Chapter 5 and in comparison to the sample response given in the answer explanations. For the multiple-choice questions, carefully study the answer explanations for *all* the questions, not just the ones you missed, because you might have gotten some of your correct answers by guessing or by using an incorrect method. Plan your study program so that you can concentrate first on topics that your Practice Test 1 results indicate are weak areas for you. If you did fairly well in mathematics and writing but poorly in reading, then you should begin your FTCE GK Test preparation with the reading review in Chapter 4.

5. Carefully study the review chapters, being sure to concentrate as you go through the material. Don't let yourself be diverted by extraneous thoughts or outside distractions. Here are some study strategies:

   ■ Monitor yourself by making a check mark on a separate sheet of paper when your concentration wanders. Work on reducing the number of check marks you record each study session.

   ■ Take notes as you study, using your own words to express ideas.

   ■ Leave ample room in the left margin, so that you can revise or make comments when you review your notes. Extract key ideas and write them in the left margin to use as study cues later.

   ■ Make flashcards to aid you in memorizing key ideas and keep them with you at all times. When you have spare moments, take out the flashcards and go over the information you've recorded on them.

   ■ Set aside certain days to review material you have already studied. This strategy will allow you to reinforce what you have learned and identify topics you may need to restudy.

   ■ If possible, set up a regular time to study with one or more classmates or friends. A good way of learning and reinforcing the material is to discuss it with others.

6. When you complete your review, take Practice Test 2 (Chapter 6). Use a timer and take the test under the same conditions you expect for the actual test, being sure to adhere to the time limits for each subtest. When you finish taking the test, as you did for Practice Test 1, carefully study the answer explanations for *all* the questions.

7. Analyze the results of the practice test, then go back and review again any topics in which you performed unsatisfactorily.

8. When you complete your second review, take Practice Test 3 on the CD-ROM under the same conditions you expect for the actual test; adhere to the time limits for each subtest. When you finish taking the test, carefully review the answer explanations for *all* the questions and do additional study, if needed.

After completing your study program, you should find yourself prepared and confident to achieve a passing score on the FTCE GK Test.

How to Prepare for the Day of the Test

There are several things you can do to prepare yourself for the day of the test.

1. Know where the test center is located and how to get there.

2. Make dependable arrangements to get to the test center in plenty of time and know where to park if you plan to go by car.

3. Keep all the materials you will need to bring to the test center—especially, your admission ticket and two forms of identification—in a secure place, so that you easily find them on the day of the test.

4. Go to bed early enough to get a good night's rest. Avoid taking nonprescription drugs or alcohol, as the use of these products may impair your mental faculties on test day.

5. On the day of the test, plan to get to the testing center early.

6. Dress in comfortable clothing and wear comfortable shoes. Even if it is warm outside, wear layers of clothing that can be removed or put on, depending on the temperature in the testing room.

7. Eat a light meal. Select foods that you have found usually give you the most energy and stamina.

8. Drink plenty of water to make sure that your brain remains hydrated during the test for optimal thinking.

9. Make a copy of this list and post it in a strategic location. Check over it before you leave for the testing center.

What to Do during the Test

Here are some general test-taking strategies to help maximize your score on the test. You are given content-specific strategies in the review chapters: Chapters 1, 2, 3, and 4.

1. When you receive the test, take several deep, slow breaths, exhaling slowly while mentally visualizing yourself performing successfully on the test before you begin. Do not get upset if you feel nervous. Most of the people who take the GK Test experience some measure of anxiety.

2. During the test, follow all the directions, including the oral directions of the test administrator and the written directions on the computer screen. If you do not understand something in the directions, ask the test administrator for clarification. The test administrator will indicate how you are to ask for assistance.

3. Move through the test at a steady pace. Work as rapidly as you can without being careless, *but do not rush*.

4. Try to answer the questions in order. However, if a question is taking too much of your time, mark it as one to come back to later and move on.

5. Read each question entirely. Skimming to save time can cause you to misread a question or miss important information.

6. Read all the answer choices before you select an answer. You may find two answers that sound good, but one is a better answer to the question.

7. For multiple-choice questions, try to eliminate at least two answer choices. Before you make your final choice, reread the question (Don't skip doing this!) and select the response that best answers the question.

8. Change an answer only if you have a good reason to do so.

9. If you are trying to recall information during the test, close your eyes and try to visualize yourself in your study place. This may trigger your memory.

10. Remain calm during the test. If you find yourself getting anxious, stop and take several deep, slow breaths and exhale slowly to help you relax. Keep your mind focused on the task at hand—completing your test. Trust yourself. You should not expect to know the correct response to every question on the test. Think only of doing your personal best.

11. Before submitting your test, be sure you have marked an answer for every test question. You are not penalized for a wrong answer (you score a zero for that test question), so even if you have no clue about the correct answer, make a guess.

12. As you work through the practice tests provided in this book, consciously use the strategies suggested in this section as preparation for the actual FTCE GK Test.

You will benefit greatly from this CliffsNotes book. By using the recommendations in this chapter as you complete your study program, you will be prepared to walk into the testing room with confidence. Good luck on the test and on your future career as a teacher!

REVIEW OF EXAM AREAS

Chapter 1

Review for the GK Essay Subtest

The Essay subtest of the FTCE GK Test consists of a choice between two topics, one of which you must select and write an essay about in 50 minutes. The allotted time is for preparing, writing, and editing your essay. Your work will be scored holistically by two judges. "Holistically" means that your essay will receive only one score for both content and mechanics. The personal views you express in your essay are not an issue; you are judged only on the style in which you present your views. Specifically, your essay is evaluated on the logic of your arguments and the degree to which you support your position in a reasonable and coherent manner. The topic may ask you to take a position or develop an argument, but you will be graded on your writing skills, not on your personal beliefs or your knowledge of any particular subject or area. You cannot bring written notes or scratch paper into the testing room.

The Essay Review in This Study Guide

This chapter contains a review of how to write an essay, both in general and for this specific examination. The review sections present writing-skills concepts with examples and explanations, as well as "Test Yourself" exercises. These exercises give you an opportunity to practice what you just learned. When doing the "Test Yourself" exercises, you should write in response to the questions. Then, if possible, have someone proofread your writing for content, style, and grammar. The sample essay questions are similar to what you might expect to see on the FTCE GK Test. A sample essay question and response is provided immediately after the writing-skills review exercises.

Also included in this section are "General Strategies for Writing the Essay for the General Knowledge Test" and the "Scoring Criteria for the General Knowledge Test Essay," as found in the *Competencies and Skills Required for Teacher Certification in Florida, Fifteenth Edition* (www.fldoe.org/asp/ftce).

Essay Skills

As listed in the *Competencies and Skills Required for Teacher Certification in Florida, Fifteenth Edition* (as mentioned above), the Essay competencies/skills you should be able to do are the following:

- Determine the purpose for writing.
- Formulate a thesis or a statement of a main idea.
- Organize ideas and details effectively.
- Provide adequate, relevant supporting material.
- Use effective transitions.
- Demonstrate a mature command of language.
- Avoid inappropriate use of slang, jargon, and clichés.
- Use a variety of sentence patterns effectively.
- Maintain a consistent point-of-view.
- Observe the conventions of Standard American English.

Determine Your Purpose for Writing

Writers write for many reasons. Some write to inform, others to share, and still others to explain. Whatever the reason, you need to determine your purpose for writing before you begin. Knowing your purpose will help clarify your message.

Four common purposes for writing are as follows:

- Self-expression—to express a desire or feeling
- Exposition—to transform information from writer to reader
- Entertainment—to arouse the interest of the reader
- Persuasion—to share a point-of-view

The more clearly you know what you want to accomplish, the better equipped you will be to write your essay. You will be able to make the proper choices to sharpen your writing and perfect your message.

Tip: You also need to know the audience for whom you are writing. Knowing your audience will help you clarify your purpose for writing.

If you are writing to a friend, you might write in an open and informal style. "Hey, Steve! What's up? What are ya doin' this summer? Want to have a blast? I know a great summer camp . . . ."

If you are writing to a general audience, you might write in a more formal style. "The following information is intended to help undecided voters select the candidate who most nearly represents their views and interests."

Finally, if you are writing to a well-defined audience, you might write in a style that reflects their level of expertise. "The high cost of medical insurance reflects the ever-demanding and volatile relationship between the real and actual cost-ratio factors of doing business in the transactional universe of medical liability."

Look at the examples of these following topics and then ask yourself what might be your purpose for writing in each case and what style of writing you might use:

- **A.** The High Cost of Medical Insurance
- **B.** The Decline in Moral Values
- **C.** My Beloved "Talking" Dog
- **D.** Six Easy Ways to Invest Your Money
- **E.** Eat Right! Eat Healthy!

Now that you have had a chance to read these topics, here are some possible reasons or purposes for writing the essays to accompany these titles and also some styles that you might use:

A. The High Cost of Medical Insurance

Your purpose for writing could be to explain how escalating expenses are affecting the individual's ability to receive proper medical care. You might use an exposition style to communicate facts to the reader about the rising cost of medical insurance and expound upon ways this issue can impact the reader's life.

B. The Decline in Moral Values

Your purpose for writing may be to draw attention to what you perceive as a decline of civility and decency in today's confusing and conflicting cultural landscape. You might use a self-expressive style to state your feelings.

C. My Beloved "Talking" Dog

Your purpose for writing might be to share the happy and fun-filled misadventures of your beloved "talking" dog, a pet that seems to have a mind of his own. You might use an entertaining style to delight and amuse your readers.

D. Six Easy Ways to Invest Your Money

Your purpose for writing could be to encourage readers to invest their money in profitable ventures that are reasonably guaranteed to provide a safe return on their investment. You might use a persuasive style in writing this essay.

E. Eat Right! Eat Healthy!

Your purpose for writing might be to encourage your readers to eat a healthful, low-fat diet so that they increase their chances of living a long, illness-free life. You might use a persuasive style to motivate your readers to make this change in their lifestyles.

Formulate a Thesis or a Statement of a Main Idea

Formulating a thesis or statement of a main idea involves two factors: the subject on which you are writing and your attitude or opinion toward that subject. Focusing your attitude or opinion in a single direction gives you a defined purpose for your writing. And since your attitude or opinion may not necessarily be shared by your reader, you need to explain the reasons for your choice.

In all good writing, the readers should know by the end of your first paragraph your thesis statement or main idea. They should have a strong idea of what you are writing about. A good thesis statement not only helps the reader but also helps you, the writer, remain focused on what you are supposed to be writing.

Using the sample topics previously listed, here are some sample thesis statements:

A. The High Cost of Medical Insurance

Something needs to be done about the escalating costs of today's medical care, because the rising price of medical insurance is affecting the individual's ability to receive proper medical treatment.

B. The Decline in Moral Values

As I look around my world, I feel disheartened and disappointed at the lack of real civility and decency in today's confusing and conflicting social arena.

C. My Beloved "Talking" Dog

Believe it or not, I have a dog who manages to get everything he wants by talking in a language all his own.

D. Six Ways to Invest Your Money

Money schemes come and go, but after reading this essay, you will walk away with a clear understanding of how to invest your money in safe, reasonable, and risk-free accounts, guaranteed to yield a modest return.

E. Eat Right! Eat Healthy!

With the variety of foods available to eat, it is more important than ever to know which foods are healthful and which might lead to health problems in years to come.

These five are sample thesis statements. Notice that each thesis statement names the subject of the essay and provides a clear point-of-view or opinion about that subject. These factors are the hallmarks of a strong thesis statement.

Organize Ideas and Details Effectively

After constructing a strong thesis statement, you need to begin organizing ideas and details effectively. With a sharply defined and well-written thesis statement, your ideas and details should flow naturally. You should be able to list fairly rapidly the essential reasons for defending and defining your thesis statement.

Before you begin, it is always best to set up a plan of action. A plan ensures a better finished product, as your ideas will flow with greater logic and clarity. There are several different ways to write an essay, but one of the ways involves the following steps:

1. Write down all the possible ideas you can think of on the essay's topic.
2. Circle the ideas you think are the most important and that you can write about most effectively.
3. Group the ideas that you have circled into possible paragraphs.
4. Organize the groups into possible ways to address the essay's topic.

Most writing projects can be organized into three parts: (1) the introduction, (2) the body, and (3) the conclusion. In the introduction, you briefly state your topic, presenting your reader with a preview of what is to come. The body of the paper—the main and longest portion of your paper—provides the facts and examples that support the main idea expressed in the introduction. The conclusion summarizes and restates the main idea.

The three parts to your essay should work together to make an effective and cohesive whole. Your introduction should be an attention-grabbing device that will "pull" the reader into your essay. In the body of your essay, make sure that every point is relevant to the subject you are discussing. Avoid irrelevant or extraneous information that does not relate to your main topic. Finally, your conclusion should be a strong ending that restates your thesis statement.

A simple technique to remember is to tell the reader what you are going to say, say it, and then, tell the reader what you said. Keeping this rule in mind will help you considerably as you write your impromptu essay. For example, suppose you were asked to write an essay on the following: Choosing a career.

1. Allowing a few minutes to think, you might write something like this:

    Interests, money, location, college, courses, preparation, skills, talents, hobbies, schooling, time, travel, passion, income, standard of living

2. Circle the ideas you think are the most important and that you can write about most effectively. Remember, you cannot write about everything you can imagine; you will only have time to explore a few key points.

3. Group the items you have selected into possible paragraphs. Your essay might look like this:

    - Personal interests
      Talents, hobbies, passion
    - Preparation for career
      Schooling, time, college, courses
    - Financial considerations
      Money, income, standard of living

4. After you have grouped ideas into similar sections, you can organize your groups into an outline. Outlines are an easy way to organize your thoughts and prepare your essay. For example, an outline for an essay on "choosing a career" might look like this:

    I. Introduction—There are many reasons for choosing a career
    II. Personal Interests
       A. Talents
       B. Hobbies
       C. Passion
    III. Preparation for Career
       A. Schooling
       B. Length of study
       C. Practical experience
    IV. Financial Considerations
       A. Potential income
       B. Standard of living
       C. Money to study
    V. Conclusion—Reiterate reasons for choosing a career

When organizing your essay's ideas and details, it is important that you follow a few guidelines:

- **Determine the amount of background information required.** Is your audience familiar with your topic? Do you have to provide background information?
- **Define required terminology.** Does your audience need to know technical terms? If so, which terms?

- **Define the tone of your discussion.** Should you write in a formal or casual style? Which would be most effective?
- **Determine the number of examples required.** Should you include examples to define your thesis? If so, how many? Which ones?
- **Determine the organizational pattern to use.** What organizational pattern should you use to explain your thesis? Which style is most effective?

Organizing your ideas and details to explain your thesis statement takes a good understanding of your subject matter. Thus, when writing an essay, be sure to select a topic that you know much about; otherwise, you will be struggling to add strong details to your writing.

Provide Adequate, Relevant Supporting Material

To develop an effective essay, you must provide your reader with adequate and relevant supporting material. The information that you select to include in your essay must not only meet your needs as the writer, but should directly pertain to the needs of your reader. Otherwise, your writing serves no real purpose.

To make sure that your writing provides strong and relevant supportive material, always be mindful of your reader. Ask yourself some basic questions:

- Do all your sentences help develop your thesis statement?
- Do your sentences follow a logical and clear sequence of ideas?
- Do you include all relevant detail?
- Do you use a consistent style?
- Do you answer all the reader's questions?
- Do you include vivid examples to define your point-of-view?

The following is an example of a passage in which the writer's thoughts are not connected in a coherent, logical, unified, and well-ordered manner:

> I like animals, especially, dogs. Sometimes, I like cats. Most dogs are enjoyable to have as pets, yet sometimes, they can be most difficult, especially when you want to take long trips. I once had a dog who loved to bark all night. Taking a dog on a summer road trip is never easy. You must bring along lots of food and water. I remember a trip we once took in the dead of winter, which made traveling with our family pets exceptionally hard. I do not know what I would do without my favorite dog, Millie.

How much better would the above paragraph be if it were written like the following?

> Keeping animals happy and healthy involves five simple rules. The first rule is to keep your pets' food dishes clean. Wash them thoroughly every day. This will help prevent the spread of bacteria and other diseases from infecting your pets. The second rule is to make sure your pets eat right. A balanced diet is necessary if your pets are to be healthy. If you are unsure what your animals should eat, check with a veterinarian. Also, buy food formulated for your pets' needs. By using these foods, you can be sure that your pets receive the right amounts of vitamins, minerals, and protein for their nourishment. The third rule is to never overfeed your pets. Give your animals as much food as they will eat without leaving any food behind. If your pets leave the dish before emptying it, be sure to take the dish away. This will ensure that your pets do not overeat; and next time, you will know to feed them less. The fourth rule is that all pets must have good houses. Whether the house is a cage or a pet bed, make sure that it is dry, warm, and suitable in size for the animal to use comfortably. Finally, the fifth rule is to make sure pets are checked regularly by a veterinarian and given all the required vaccinations. A sick animal can infect other animals—and even people in some cases. By following these five simple rules, you can help your pets to enjoy good health and a long life.

As you can tell, the second paragraph contains relevant and supporting details presented in a logical, coherent, and organized manner.

Use Effective Transitions

Good writers make use of effective transitions. They use transitional words or phrases to connect ideas and thoughts. Transitional words also provide for a logical sequence of ideas.

Look at the following list of transitional words and phrases. By adopting these words and phrases into your own writing, you can begin to develop a writing style that is clear and unified for your readers.

again	conversely	in any case	namely	therefore
also	finally	in any event	nevertheless	thereupon
as a rule	first of all	in brief	of course	thus
as usual	for example	in essence	rather	to sum up
besides	for instance	in short	secondly	
briefly	furthermore	in the long run	similarly	
by and large	generally	instead	that is	
consequently	however	moreover	then indeed	

Many other transitions are available, but you will find that the preceding list will serve you well. Using these words to connect your thoughts will significantly improve your writing style and fluency.

Look at some examples of how these transitional words can be used:

- Learning to laugh at one's mistakes, therefore, can bring a whole new perspective on one's life.
- Briefly, the three main points of this essay are . . .
- In short, I intend to run for president of the senior class and win.
- Consequently, the politician had little to say when he was indicted on charges of election fraud.
- The construction crew worked tirelessly; however, they did not manage to finish the Robertsons' brand new home in time for the start of the Robertsons' summer vacation.
- The President ignored his own good judgment; therefore, the military mission was an abysmal failure.

Demonstrate a Mature Command of Language

Writing a strong and effective essay requires the ability to demonstrate a mature command of language. Writers must be able to articulate their thoughts in a clear and logical fashion so that all may read and understand their thoughts easily and readily. Any confusion evidenced by a writer's handling of language will result in the reader's misinterpretation of the material. Thus, to avoid such confusion, good writers should do the following:

- Write with a clear and resonant voice. Be sure all your words are chosen to convey the most precise and logical analysis of your argument or thesis statement.
- Use paragraph breaks to divide your thought patterns and make your essay easier to read.
- Use transitions and related word links to connect your thoughts and ideas.
- Provide a sound and logical conclusion to your essay that summarizes your key ideas and thoughts.
- Avoid spelling and grammatical errors. Proofread your work.
- Avoid wordiness. It is always best to use fewer words to express a difficult idea or thought.
- Avoid repetition. Always state enough ideas to make your point but not so much as to bore the reader.
- Avoid oversimplification. It is always wise to clarify your ideas with the words *often, usually,* or *sometimes.*
- Write simply. Often a simpler word is an effective substitute for a more difficult word. By writing simply, you can help clarify your thoughts.

As an example of the need to write simply, examine these two sentences:

1. Joe Smith is the team leader.
2. The undersigned official assumes leadership responsibility for the team.

Which do you prefer? Obviously, the first choice conveys the meaning of the sentence simply and directly. The second choice, however, is obtuse and may imply another agenda other than simply stating the truth.

As an example of a longer passage, examine these two examples.

Passage #1

Bungee jumping was inspired many, many years ago by the celebrated vine jumpers of the world-famous Pentecost Islands in Vanuatu (formerly the New Hebrides) in the vast stretches of the Pacific Ocean, where it is understood by all the inhabitants and natives that bungee jumping is doubly a rite of passage into manhood and a fertility rite performed to ensure a good and plentiful yam harvest. Modern bungee jumping began with four simultaneous jumps off the renowned Clifton Suspension Bridge in Bristol, England, on the very first day of April in 1979. Today, bungee jumping is a sporting event that is practiced all over the world, almost everywhere that people can ever imagine.

Passage #2

Bungee jumping was inspired by the Pentecost Island vine jumpers. There, natives bungee-jumped as a rite of passage into manhood. It was also considered a fertility rite to ensure a strong yam harvest. Modern bungee jumping began with four simultaneous jumps from the Clifton Suspension Bridge in Bristol, England, on April 1, 1979. Today, bungee jumping is practiced worldwide.

As you can see, the second example dispenses with unnecessary wordiness. Following the preceding rules will help you demonstrate a mature command of language and write with proficiency and efficiency.

Avoid Inappropriate Use of Slang, Jargon, and Clichés

When writing an essay, you should avoid the inappropriate use of slang, jargon, and clichés. The use of common sayings and expressions might be appropriate for creative writing; however, such usage is inappropriate for formal essay writing. Thus, it is wise to keep your writing to Standard American English usage and style.

Slang is street language. It is the highly informal language that is acceptable for conversations among friends, but highly inappropriate for formal writing. Slang is sometimes referred to as "colloquial," a word meaning language that is spoken by everyday people.

Some common slang words and their meanings are as follows:

airhead—stupid person
   *Dave is a real **airhead**.*
armpit—dirty, unappealing place
   *His bedroom is a regular **armpit**.*
awesome—great and impressive
   *Hey, man, that roller coaster was **awesome!***
bling-bling—flashy jewelry or expensive possessions
   *Oh, look at Mr. Fancy wearing all his **bling-bling** and driving his new car.*
booze—alcohol
   *Dan is tired because last night he drank too much **booze**.*

cheesy—cheap, outmoded, out of date

> *My boyfriend was wearing such **cheesy** clothes.*

chick flick—a movie primarily of interest to females, often a love story or heavy emotional drama

> *Last night, my wife went to the movies with her girlfriends to see the latest **chick flick**.*

dorky—strange, peculiar (socially weird)

> *Your friend is such a **dork**.*

fab—look grand, fabulous

> *Wow, you are just **fab**.*

flick—movie

> *Hey, wanna see a **flick?***

greenbacks—money

> *Hey, ask your old man if we can borrow some **greenbacks**.*

hairy—difficult

> *Driving super-fast, Arnie took some **hairy** turns.*

idiotsyncrasy—a strange personal mannerism

> *Yeah, he's picking at his ear again; it is just one of his crazy **idiotsyncrasies**.*

lip—fast, cheap talk

> *The students in fourth period always give their substitute teacher **lip**.*

mickey-mouse—unimportant, time-wasting

> *This math exercise is such a **mickey-mouse** assignment.*

paws—hands

> *Get your **paws** off my girlfriend!*

rug rat—child

> *My brother has a couple of **rug rats** running around his house.*

scarf—to eat fast

> *Rushing off to school, I **scarfed** down my breakfast as I headed out the door.*

threads—clothing

> *Willie bought a whole new set of **threads**.*

tie one on—to get drunk

> *In celebration of their last final, the fraternity boys are going to a local bar to **tie one on**.*

turkey—failure

> *The movie was a real **turkey**.*

umpteen—countless times

> *If I have told you once, I have told you **umpteen** times, don't wear your shoes inside the house!*

wheels—car, motor vehicle

> *I took off on the open road in my brand new set of **wheels**.*

whitebread—plain, boring; white, suburban, middle class

> *The TV talk show host had never met a guest who was so **whitebread**.*

> *Outside the inner city, the **whitebread** community of upwardly mobile adults was one of the most affluent communities in the country.*

zero—unimportant person

> *He is such a **zero**!*

Jargon is the specialized language of a discipline or a profession. Individuals involved in a particular discipline, job, or profession use the same words, or jargon, frequently; usually, only the individuals intimately connected to the words know of their meaning. Nothing is wrong with jargon; however, it must be used judiciously so that its meaning is clear to all involved.

> **Tip: When in doubt, always use a simple word. Simplicity breeds understanding, and understanding means clarity in thought and reason.**

Clichés are overused expressions that lack originality. When writing, use clichés when necessary—when they add punch to your writing style—and not when a more apt word or phrase will do. It is always better to use fresh, original expressions to define your writing. Some common examples of clichés are as follows:

A chicken in every pot	*In close quarters*
A penny for your thoughts	*Last but not least*
Agree to disagree	*Life's a long hard climb*
As old as dirt	*No rest for the wicked*
Bug off	*No worse for the wear*
Close only counts in horseshoes and hand grenades	*On the rocks*
Cut bait and run	*Stay the course*
Don't rock the boat	*The ball's in your court*
Easy pickings	*The worm turns*
Exception that proves the rule	*Through thick and thin*
In any way, shape, or form	*Venture a suggestion*

Again, these colorful expressions are fun to say, but avoid them in formal writing.

Use a Variety of Sentence Patterns Effectively

Using a variety of sentence patterns effectively is essential to good writing. A paper that has all the required information but is uninteresting to read will either bore the readers or leave them more confused than when they started to read. Thus, a good technique to improve your writing is to vary your sentence patterns.

Look at the following example of how sentences may be constructed into interesting patterns:

First, a simple sentence, by definition, is an **independent clause.** An independent clause is a group of words that contains a subject and a verb and expresses a complete thought. An example of an independent clause is

I went to the movies.

Second, a sentence can be enhanced by adding a **dependent clause.** A dependent clause is a group of words that contains a subject and a verb but does not express a complete thought. Thus, it is not a sentence. An example of a dependent clause is

When Lauren was done.

Often a dependent clause is marked by a **dependent marker** word. A dependent marker word is added to the beginning of an independent clause. When this occurs, the independent clause becomes a dependent clause. Some common dependent markers are

after, although, as, as if, because, before, even if, even though, if, in order to, since, though, unless, until, whatever, when, whenever, whether, and *while.*

Third, independent and dependent clauses can be connected by **coordinating conjunctions** and **independent markers.** Coordinating conjunctions include

and, but, for, nor, or, so, and *yet.*

Independent markers include

also, consequently, furthermore, however, moreover, nevertheless, and *therefore.*

Also, when the second independent clause in a sentence begins with an independent marker word, a *semicolon* is needed before the independent marker word. For example:

I went to the movies; however, I went when Lauren was finished with her homework.

Knowing this, here are some examples of how two clauses can be written:

I went to the movies. I went when Lauren was finished with her homework.

I went to the movies; I went when Lauren was finished with her homework.

I went to the movies, but I went when Lauren was finished with her homework.

I went to the movies; however, I did not go until Lauren was finished with her homework.

When Lauren was finished with her homework, I went to the movies.

I went to the movies when Lauren was finished with her homework.

Keep these sentence variations in mind when you write your essays.

Maintain a Consistent Point-of-View

Maintaining a consistent point-of-view is a quality of strong writing. A good writer maintains consistency in style, content, and theme throughout a piece. To maintain such consistency, it is best for writers to adopt one voice throughout their work.

As a writer, you can choose from three points-of-view to write your pieces: **first, second,** or **third person.** Each one has specific responsibilities, characteristics, and effects for you, the writer, and the reader as well. Here are examples of how each point-of-view may be used in your essay.

The **first-person point-of-view** is a narrative written with the word "I," which makes it highly personalized. Use this point-of-view when you want to cultivate a sense of closeness with your readers or when you want the readers to identify or sympathize with you. An example of a first-person point-of-view is as follows:

I went home around 2 o'clock yesterday afternoon and checked my refrigerator. Nothing was there to eat. So, hungry, I walked over to my neighbor's apartment and asked whether she would like to go out to grab a snack with me. We knew each other well enough to do those fun things on the spur of the moment, so off we went.

The **second-person point-of-view** is when the narrator addresses the reader as "you." Often, second-person point-of-view is used when the narrator is speaking to a younger or less-experienced reader. Before writing in second person, the narrator should clarify for the reader just who is talking to whom. As you can tell, though, much of the text in this book is written in second person. The reason is that second person is commonly used in technical and reference writing in which a process or technique is being explained. The reader is thought of as a less-experienced version of the author and someone for whom the writer must carefully explain each and every step required to learn a new procedure or method.

Here's our earlier example adapted to second-person point-of-view:

You went home around 2 o'clock yesterday afternoon and checked your refrigerator. You found nothing there to eat. So, being hungry, you walked over to your neighbor's apartment and asked her whether she would like to go out to grab a snack with you. You know each other well enough to do those fun things on the spur of the moment, so off you went.

The **third-person point-of-view** is when the narrative is told by a supposedly objective voice (see discussion below) not directly involved in the story. The narrator is the voice of authority and should be telling the story without noticeable prejudice or bias. Third-person point-of-view is popular in fictional writing and is often present in nonfiction works such as research reports and newspaper articles.

Tip: When writing in the third person, be careful to keep your voice objective. It is very easy to let subjectivity or bias slip into your narrative. See the discussion below of objective and subjective voice.

Here's our earlier example adapted to third-person point-of-view:

> He went home around 2 o'clock yesterday afternoon and checked his refrigerator. He found nothing there to eat. So, being hungry, he walked over to his neighbor's apartment and asked her whether she would like to go out and grab a snack with him. They knew each other well enough to do those fun things on the spur of the moment, so off they went.

Finally, when writing, there are two kinds of voices in which a narrative may be written. They are objective and subjective voice:

- **Objective voice** is when the writer takes an impartial approach to the subject. Objective writing focuses on external things and events, without referring to the personal prejudices or emotions of the writer. News writing is an example of nonfiction objective writing.

- **Subjective voice** is when the writer takes a personal approach to the subject. Subjective writing focuses on internal things and events, presenting reality as the writer sees and interprets it, referring continually to the expression of personal thoughts, impulses, and feelings. Editorials, opinion pieces, and personal narratives are examples of nonfiction subjective writing.

When writing, it is imperative that you select a voice and a point-of-view that is consistent throughout your essay. Knowing what you want to say and how you want to say it are the two key ingredients in any successful writing endeavor. Failure to follow these guidelines will result in poor, unfocused writing.

Observe the Conventions of Standard American English

When writing your essay, you must always observe the conventions of Standard American English. Although this might sound simple to do, it is easy to rush your essays and write poorly.

Here are some tips to follow when writing to observe the conventions of Standard American English:

1. **Use active voice.**

   In sentences written in active voice, the subject performs the action expressed in the verb. For example:

   The dog bit the child. (active voice)

   The child was bitten by the dog. (passive voice)

   Everyone who attended the housewarming party had a great time. (active voice)

   A great time was had by everyone who attended the housewarming party. (passive voice)

2. **Be plain spoken.**

   Say what you mean simply and plainly.

3. **Write in complete sentences.**

   Make sure your sentences have a subject and a verb.

4. **Be sure your subject and verb agree.**

   Make sure your subjects and verbs agree in number.

5. **Be sure your nouns and pronouns agree.**

   Make sure your pronoun references are in agreement with the nouns to which they refer.

6. **Use clear descriptions.**

   Be careful that your nouns and descriptors agree and are connected.

7. **Use proper grammar symbols.**

   Be sure you punctuate your sentences correctly.

8. **Check spelling.**

   Always proofread your writing for common spelling and grammatical errors.

These writing tips will help you adhere to the conventions of Standard American English and avoid common grammatical errors. Also, please note that although you will be composing your essay on the computer, you will not have access to spelling and grammar checkers. Thus, avoid words and phrases that are unfamiliar to you to avoid costly errors and mistakes.

General Strategies for Writing the Essay for the General Knowledge Test

As listed in the *Competencies and Skills Required for Teacher Certification in Florida, Fifteenth Edition* (see the Web address in the first section of this chapter), the General Strategies for Writing the Essay for the General Knowledge Test are the following:

1. **Watch the time.**

   Take a few moments at the beginning of the period to plan your essay and at the end to proofread or revise your work. Use all your time wisely. You should not run out of time before you are done; nor should you write an incomplete essay because you did not use all the time allowed. Note: You do not have time to write a rough draft and then completely rewrite it. Spend your time writing and editing your final essay.

2. **Read the instructions carefully and select one of the topics.**

   Determine what the topic is asking. Think of how the topic relates to what you know, what you have learned, and what experiences you have had so you can provide concrete details rather than vague generalities.

3. **Take a few minutes to prewrite.**

   Jot down your first ideas (some you might like; others you might discard). Sketch a quick outline or group your ideas together with arrows or numbers. By prewriting, you can "see" your essay taking shape—even before you start writing.

4. **Write a thesis statement that provides a clear focus for your essay.**

   State a point-of-view in your thesis that guides the purpose and scope of your essay. Consider the point you are trying to convey to the reader and what you want the reader to understand about the topic. Avoid a thesis statement framed as a statement of fact, a question, or an announcement.

5. **Develop the essay according to your purpose.**

   Develop paragraphs fully to give the reader examples and reasons that support your thesis. Indent each new paragraph. Note that a good essay for the General Knowledge Test might be longer or shorter than the basic five-paragraph format of some short essays. Do not limit yourself to an arbitrary length. The key is to develop a topic by using concrete, informative details.

6. **Tie your main ideas together with a brief conclusion.**

   Provide a concluding paragraph that ties together the essay's points and offers insights about the topic. Avoid a conclusion that merely restates the thesis and repeats the supporting details. Check your time. If the writing period is almost over, wrap up quickly, so you can proofread or revise your essay.

7. **Revise/proofread the essay to conform to Standard American English usage.**

   Look for particular grammatical or spelling errors you tend to make. Read each sentence from the first sentence to the last and make corrections. Look for words, sentences, or even paragraphs that need changing.

Scoring Criteria for the General Knowledge Test Essay

As listed in the *Competencies and Skills Required for Teacher Certification in Florida, Fifteenth Edition* (see the Web address in the first section of this chapter), the Scoring Criteria for the General Knowledge Test Essay are the following:

	Scoring for the FTCE GK Essay
Score of 6	The essay has a clearly established main idea that the writer fully develops with specific details and examples. Organization is notably logical and coherent. Point-of-view is consistently maintained. Vocabulary and sentence structure are varied and effective. Errors in sentence structure, usage, and mechanics are few and insignificant.
Score of 5	The essay has a clearly established main idea that is adequately developed and recognizable through specific details and/or examples. Organization follows a logical and coherent pattern. Point-of-view is mostly maintained. Vocabulary and sentence structure are mostly varied and effective. Occasional errors in sentence structure, usage, and mechanics do not interfere with the writer's ability to communicate.
Score of 4	The essay has an adequately stated main idea that is developed with some specific details and examples. Supporting ideas are presented in a mostly logical and coherent manner. Point-of-view is somewhat maintained. Vocabulary and sentence structure are somewhat varied and effective. Occasional errors in sentence structure, usage, and mechanics may interfere with the writer's ability to communicate.
Score of 3	The essay states a main idea that is developed with generalizations or lists. The essay contains occasional lapses in logic and coherence, and the organization is mechanical. Point-of-view is ambiguous. Vocabulary and sentence structure are repetitive and often ineffective. A variety of errors in sentence structure, usage, and mechanics sometimes interfere with the writer's ability to communicate.
Score of 2	The essay presents an incomplete or ambiguous main idea. Support is developed with generalizations and lists. Organization is mechanical. The essay contains occasional lapses in logic and coherence. Point-of-view is confusing and distracting. Word choice is simplistic, and sentence structure is disjointed. Errors in sentence structure, usage, and mechanics frequently interfere with the writer's ability to communicate.
Score of 1	The essay has no evident main idea. Development is inadequate and/or irrelevant. Organization is illogical and incoherent. Point-of-view has not been established. Vocabulary and sentence structure are garbled and confusing. Significant and numerous errors in sentence structure, usage, and mechanics interfere with the writer's ability to communicate.

Test Yourself—Essay Writing

Directions: This section of the examination involves a written assignment. You are to prepare a written response for *one of the two topics* presented below. Select one of these two topics and prepare a 300–600-word response. Be sure to read both topics very carefully to make sure that you understand the topic for which you are preparing a written response. Use your allotted time to plan, write, review, and edit what you have written for the assignment.

Topic 1

> My teaching philosophy

Topic 2

> A sport I like to watch

Be sure to read the two topics again before attempting to write your response. Remember, you will type your essay on the computer screen. Your essay also must be on only one of the topics presented, and it must provide complete coverage of the topic.

Your essay is graded holistically, meaning only one score is assigned for your writing—taking into consideration both mechanics and organization. *You are not to be scored on the nature of the content or opinions expressed in your work.* Instead, you are graded on your abilities to write complete sentences, to express and support your opinions, and to organize your work.

At least two evaluators will review your work and assign it a score. Special attention is paid to the following more specific indications in your writing:

- Does your writing demonstrate a strong definitive purpose?
- Is there a clear thesis or a statement of a main idea?
- Are your ideas organized?
- Do you support your thesis with clear details?
- Are effective transitions present?
- Do you demonstrate an effective use of language?
- Are a variety of sentence patterns present?
- Is there a consistent point-of-view?
- Are the conventions of Standard American English used?

Before you begin, be sure you plan what you want to say. Organize your thoughts and carefully construct your ideas. This must be your original work and in your own voice.

Sample Answers—Essay Writing

Following are some sample essay answers to the preceding topics. For each topic, there is an example of a poorly written essay and a well-written essay.

Choice 1—My Teaching Philosophy

Weak Response

My Teaching Philosophy

My teaching philosophy? I believe that all children can learn and if you try hard enough, you can teach most everybody. Young children, especially, love to learn and grow and therefore, teachers should try their hardest to make sure that they get all the knowledge and skills that they need to grow and become. Teaching is a tough job and I am sure that I as grow in this worthy profession, I will learn much about what it means to be a good teacher. For now, though, I am happy jt to work with young children, giving them everything they need to know to become successful in their lives.

Strong Response

My Teaching Philosophy

Since I was a youngster, I have always wanted to teach. I want to become a teacher because I love school, and I want to help young children learn and succeed. I want to develop a relationship with the students that I teach that will encourage them to come to me with their problems and concerns. This is my guiding philosophy of education—to nurture others to become the best they can possibly be. This philosophy will guide me in the following ways: (a) to encourage the potential in all young people, (b) to encourage strong study and work habits, and (c) to encourage young people to make wise and purposeful decisions. In the following paragraphs, I will explain further.

First, as an adult, I believe that all young people have the potential to become anything they want. Given the right push and proper conditions, I believe that young people can mature into healthy, responsible adults, capable of figuratively moving mountains and changing seasons. They possess the potential within to blossom into productive and engaged citizens who attack life with a passionate zeal and purpose that defies all expectations. All they need is the gentle guidance and polite push of a respectful and caring educator who will recognize their capabilities and highlight their strengths. And a nudge is often the spark they need to begin their journey. This nudge can come in many shapes and sizes, most notably direct praise for assignments and jobs well done. Teachers who take the time to listen and talk to their students—about their schoolwork and personal lives—can do much to demonstrate to their students that a caring and compassionate hand can alleviate most any burden. Taking time from a busy schedule to attend to students' immediate concerns can do much to inspire them to achieve any goal they can imagine.

Second, as a teacher, I hope to encourage young people to develop smart study and work habits. By providing them with a recognizable routine in our daily class assignments, I intend to model for my students how they too should perceive and organize their own studies. A teacher who demonstrates good work habits and a steady and recognizable routine can do much to improve the lives of often distracted and unfocused youngsters. After all, I know what it is like to be confused and dazed; I was once a kid myself, and I appreciated the many teachers that I had who helped me organize my work and learn my school material. Directly and indirectly, they provided me with many useful suggestions and tips for completing my class assignments and arranging my notes into recognizable and coherent patterns. Once done, I was able to streamline my study time and, thus, learn my material quickly and efficiently. When I teach, I hope to model and inspire my students to do the same.

Finally, as a teacher, I hope to encourage young people to make wise and purposeful decisions. I know, of course, that a teacher cannot save the world. A teacher cannot help every child in the teacher's care make sound choices, but he or she can role model for children how a person does make wise decisions. By providing young people with lessons in decision-making, I intend to demonstrate simple steps that everyone can take when deciding a course of action. Too often, young people make rash choices without thinking about the consequences of their actions. The result is sometimes near-fatal errors that can cause much pain and harm to all involved. Thus, I believe that lessons in decision-making—how best to decide on a course of action, given a set of circumstances and concerns—is the best remedy for helping young people become responsible adults. Whether the decision is as simple as how to behave on the playground or is something more complex like deciding whether to drink and drive, young people need a way to safely and calmly decide how best to behave in a given situation. As a teacher, I can do much to provide lessons in which young people can learn decision-making skills.

Thus, my decision to become a teacher is predicated on the fact that I have always wanted to become a role model for young people. I love school, and I want to continue my life as a public school teacher who inspires young people to become equally responsible adults. As a teacher, I believe it is my duty and responsibility to help all young people to achieve their dreams, no matter how difficult and far away they might initially seem. Once a teacher, I can accomplish my goals by encouraging young people to develop their potential, to improve their study and work habits, and to hone their decision-making skills. By following these precepts, I intend to become the best teacher that I can possibly be.

Choice 2—A Sport I Like to Watch

Weak Response

A Sport I Like to Watch

I like to watch many sports. I especially like to watch basketball, tennis and hockey. Each sport is fun to watch both in person and on TV. In fact, I can spend most of the day in my den just lying on the couch and watching cool sports on the tube. Nothing could be better. Except if I am playing a game myself. Sometimes, my buddies and I go out to the neighborhood park and shoot some hoops. Sometimes we play one on one for hours on end. The exercise is good and the sweat I build up helps me lose some of those extra pounds. Of course, snacking in front of the TV watching my favorite sport shows does not help either. But, what are you going to do? I am just addicted to watching sports on television and with so many great sports and games to choose from, it is a wonder that I ever get anything done.

Strong Response

A Sport I Like to Watch

Watching sporting events—whether on television or in person—is for me a wonderful experience. I am a huge sports enthusiast, and in my house, I am always tuned into the latest game or sports show. I like being informed and can hardly wait to learn who is winning, losing, or just plainly outshining the competition. I love competition, especially in sports—whether it be college or professional—and I can hardly wait to tune into the latest matchup to see how my favorite and least favorite teams are doing. Yet, of all sports to watch, I have a special fondness for golf. I like to watch professional golfers play for three main reasons: relaxation, excitement, and instruction. Simply, I enjoy watching professional golfers at the top of their game.

I like to watch the game of golf, especially as broadcast on television. Every weekend, you can probably find me nestled in my easy chair, soft drink in one hand, television remote in the other, flipping channels, watching professional golfers "do their thing." As an avid golfer, I have a special fondness for watching others maneuver themselves on some of the world's greatest golf courses. I enjoy watching golfers walk the green, size up their shots, and compete with their opponents. Calmly and precisely, they position themselves to be the best they possibly can be in this most cordial of sports. True, golfers can be and are fiercely competitive, but anger and drive hardly ever spills out onto the course. Instead, what I see from my vantage point at home is a nice leisurely walk, interrupted by long shots and inspired swings, all making for a most enjoyable and relaxing sport to watch from the comfort of my living room.

This is not to say golf is a dull sport. If anything, I find it to be the most exciting of sports. I seldom know what is going to happen. Each weekend, I find myself sitting on the edge of my chair in anticipation of what each golfer will bring to the game. Some begin strong and end weak. Others do the reverse. And still others have strong games from beginning to end. What is most exciting is to watch golfers sink or nearly sink long putts. Standing far off to the side of the green, these professional golfers manage to make putts or near-putts that I can hardly believe are possible. To be sure, I am an amateur golfer with an equally high handicap. I cannot imagine participating in a golfing game where a person competes with such skill and precision. The sheer power and talent makes for an invigorating and engaging sport to watch.

Finally, I watch professional golf for the instruction. As a viewer, I learn how to improve my stance, my swing, and my follow-through simply by watching professional golfers at work. Additionally, television broadcasters supplement their golf programs with lessons about how to improve one's game. Complete with instructional video clips, these brief but informative golfing lessons are just the thing to help me improve my game. Often, I find myself sitting close to my television set, trying to absorb the latest golfing advice from a recognized and established professional. Easy, cheap, and useful, these golfing lessons help me improve my game, keep me interested and involved in the sport, and provide useful information to share with my fellow golfers.

Thus, watching professional golf on television is one of my most pleasurable activities. I enjoy the pleasantness of this peaceful and relaxing sport, and I relish the quiet time that I have in front of my television watching true professionals display their natural talent. Moreover, I learn to improve my own game while reveling in the heated excitement of a close and competitive round. To the untrained eye, golf is simply hitting balls into a faraway hole, but to me, golf is a beautiful walk, highlighted by great highs and lows, each one bringing its own engagement and insight into a game that I have long cherished for the ease and calmness it brings to my life.

The English Language Skills subtest of the FTCE GK Test consists of 40 multiple-choice questions, which you must complete in 40 minutes. Each test question requires that you choose from among four answer choices. You must click on the oval corresponding to your answer choice on the computer screen. You cannot bring written notes or scratch paper into the testing room.

The English Language Skills Review in This Study Guide

The English Language Skills review in this CliffsNotes book is organized around the four language-skill areas tested on the FTCE GK Test:

- Conceptual and Organizational Skills
- Word Choice Skills
- Sentence Structure Skills
- Grammar, Spelling, Capitalization, and Punctuation Skills

Each area has a general review and sample questions. The review sections present language skill concepts with examples and explanations for each area. "Test Yourself" exercises are found throughout the review sections. These sample questions are similar to what you might expect to see on the FTCE GK Test, and give you an opportunity to practice what you just learned. The answers to the "Test Yourself" exercises are found immediately following the set of exercises. When doing the "Test Yourself" exercises, you should cover up the answers. Then check your answers when you've finished the exercises.

Conceptual and Organizational Skills

As listed in the *Competencies and Skills Required for Teacher Certification in Florida, Fifteenth Edition* (available at www.fldoe.org/asp/ftce), the English language competencies/skills you should have mastered for this area are the following:

- Identify logical order in a written passage.
- Identify irrelevant sentences.

Identify Logical Order in a Written Passage

Every written passage should present its information in a logical order. A sentence that is not presented in logical order is a sentence that is out of order or does not relate to its accompanying sentences. Look at this example of a written passage with sentences that are not in logical order:

> Starving, Rover ate quickly from his favorite dish. We were relieved to have Rover home. Yet, no matter where we looked, we could not find our beloved pet. Quickly, we notified our neighbors that Rover was missing. Last week, we discovered our dog, Rover, was missing. Soon, everyone was looking for Rover. Finally, after a long, tiring week, Rover came home, hungry but healthy.

The passage is confusing because the sentences are not presented in a logical order. The way the passage is written is confusing to the reader. You must rearrange the sentences in your mind before the passage begins to make sense.

You can correct the confusion by revising the passage like this:

> Last week, we discovered our dog, Rover, was missing. Quickly, we notified our neighbors. Soon, everyone was looking for Rover. Yet, no matter where we looked, we could not find our beloved pet. Finally, after a long, tiring week, Rover came home, hungry but healthy. Starving, Rover ate quickly from his favorite dish. We were relieved to have Rover home.

Identify Irrelevant Sentences

Every written passage should contain a main idea accompanied by supporting details. All sentences in the passage must relate to the main idea. When a passage contains material that has little or no connection to the main idea (or the connection is not clear), the sentences containing such material are **irrelevant.** Find the irrelevant sentence in this written passage:

> The winter months are the harshest for people living in our uppermost northern states near Canada. There, in places like Maine, Vermont, Minnesota, Michigan, Wisconsin, and North Dakota, winter stays for days on end, making life outside a burden for all who must travel to and from work or run errands. Days are spent shoveling snow, starting cold engines, and just keeping warm and safe. Sometimes, violent storms wreak havoc on roads and homes, causing days of endless cold snaps and lost electricity. Hawaii is pleasant during this time of the year. On such days, northerners learn to bundle up, enjoy what food items they have stored for safekeeping, and just enjoy each other's company. Harsh winters are simply a fact of life for those who dwell near the Canadian border.

This passage is confusing because it contains an irrelevant sentence (*Hawaii is pleasant during this time of the year*). Although the sentence relates to the passage's main idea, it is irrelevant to the passage's logical progression of ideas.

You can correct the confusion by revising the passage like this:

> The winter months are the harshest for people living in our uppermost northern states near Canada. There, in places like Maine, Vermont, Minnesota, Michigan, Wisconsin, and North Dakota, winter stays for days on end, making life outside a burden for all who must travel to and from work or run errands. Days are spent shoveling snow, starting cold engines, and just keeping warm and safe. Sometimes, violent storms wreak havoc on roads and homes, causing days of endless cold snaps and lost electricity. On such days, northerners learn to bundle up, enjoy what food items they have stored for safekeeping, and just enjoy each other's company. Harsh winters are simply a fact of life for those who dwell near the Canadian border.

Test Yourself

Directions: For items 1 and 2, read the entire passage carefully and then answer the questions. (Note: Intentional errors have been included in this passage.)

(1) Florida's citizens face many serious socio-economic problems that may leave the state with fewer resources in the twenty-first century. (2) Each day, individuals from across the globe descend upon Florida's large coastal cities—Miami, Tampa, Jacksonville—seeking work and a place to live. (3) First, Florida is the home to many immigrant populations. (4) They come with the promise of finding a new life in America, having been led to believe in their native lands that America is the land of richness and opportunity. (5) And although some find untold riches, many find only minimum-paying jobs and unaffordable housing. (6) Second, with this constant influx, Florida's eligible school population rises exponentially. (7) As more families arrive, the demand for better and improved entertainment venues—from theme park to restaurants and rodeos—becomes ever more demanding. (8) Moreover, Florida, like elsewhere in the country, faces a growing teacher shortage that dramatically impacts the quality of the state's education program. (9) Finally, the gravest socioeconomic problems facing Florida are its serious environmental problems that will threaten proper growth and development. (10) Burgeoning populations mean a greater drain on fewer natural resources and less suitable land upon which to grow. (11) For example, drying up swampland for irrigation of farmland and proper disposal of litter become a constant concern as Florida's population increases uncontrollably. (12) Thus, unless Florida's citizens and leaders come to terms on how best to deal with these serious socioeconomic problems, Florida will soon find itself in a crisis for which there is no immediate solution.

1. Select the arrangement of sentences 1, 2, and 3 that provides the most logical sequence of ideas and supporting details in the paragraph. If no change is needed, select Choice A.

   A. Florida's citizens face many serious socioeconomic problems that may leave the state with fewer resources in the twenty-first century. Each day, individuals from across the globe descend upon Florida's large coastal cities—Miami, Tampa, Jacksonville—seeking work and a place to live. First, Florida is the home to many immigrant populations.

   B. First, Florida is the home to many immigrant populations. Florida's citizens face many serious socioeconomic problems that may leave the state with fewer resources in the twenty-first century. Each day, individuals from across the globe descend upon Florida's large coastal cities—Miami, Tampa, Jacksonville —seeking work and a place to live.

   C. Each day, individuals from across the globe descend upon Florida's large coastal cities—Miami, Tampa, Jacksonville—seeking work and a place to live. First, Florida is the home to many immigrant populations. Florida's citizens face many serious socioeconomic problems that may leave the state with fewer resources in the twenty-first century.

   D. Florida's citizens face many serious socioeconomic problems that may leave the state with fewer resources in the twenty-first century. First, Florida is the home to many immigrant populations. Each day, individuals from across the globe descend upon Florida's large coastal cities—Miami, Tampa, Jacksonville—seeking work and a place to live.

2. Which numbered sentence is LEAST relevant to the passage?

   A. sentence 7
   B. sentence 8
   C. sentence 9
   D. sentence 10

(1) A zoo is a place where animals—both wild and domesticated—are shown in captivity. (2) In such a special place, animals can be given the kind of care and nurturing that is possible in less protected and more natural preserves. (3) Most zoos show animals of all kinds and types; but in recent years, a few zoos have become more specialized in their approach. (4) Known for its many family-fun animal shows, Sea World is a leading pioneer in marine life research, nurturing and saving many sea animals throughout the world. (5) For example, Sea World, not known formally as a zoo, is an attraction that is open to the public and primarily specializes in taking care of marine life. (6) In Canada, there is African Lion Safari, in which visitors travel in their cars over a 50-acre reserve, where in excess of 1,000 animals of over 100 species roam freely. (7) From the closeness of their vehicles, visitors see wild life up-close and personal. (8) And in Miami, Florida, one can find Parrot Jungle, a home for 1,100 tropical birds, all flying freely within the confines of the exhibit. (9) There, visitors can enjoy a leisurely lunch and listen to tourists complain about Miami's crowded beaches and roads. (10) Each of these specialized venues demonstrates how the concept of zoo has changed dramatically in the twentieth century.

3. Select the arrangement of sentences 4, 5, and 6 that provides the most logical sequence of ideas and supporting details in the paragraph. If no change is needed, select Choice A.

A. Known for its many family-fun animal shows, Sea World is a leading pioneer in marine life research, nurturing and saving many sea animals throughout the world. For example, Sea World, not known formally as a zoo, is an attraction that is open to the public and primarily specializes in taking care of marine life. In Canada, there is African Lion Safari in which visitors travel in their cars over a 50-acre reserve, where in excess of 1,000 animals of over 100 species from freely.

B. For example, Sea World, not known formally as a zoo, is an attraction that is open to the public and primarily specializes in taking care of marine life. Known for its many family-fun animal shows, Sea World is a leading pioneer in marine life research, nurturing and saving many sea animals throughout the world. In Canada, there is African Lion Safari in which visitors travel in their cars over a 50-acre reserve, where in excess of 1,000 animals of over 100 species roam freely.

C. In Canada, there is African Lion Safari in which visitors travel in their cars over a 50-acre reserve, where in excess of 1,000 animals of over 100 species roam freely. For example, Sea World, not known formally as a zoo, is a leading pioneer in marine life research, nurturing and saving many sea animals throughout the world. Known for its many family-fun animal shows, Sea World is a leading pioneer in marine life research, nurturing and saving many sea animals throughout the world.

D. Known for its many family-fun animal shows, Sea World is a leading pioneer in marine life research, nurturing and saving many sea animals throughout the world. In Canada, there is African Lion Safari in which visitors travel in their cars over a 50-acre reserve, where in excess of 1,000 animals of over 100 species roam freely. For example, Sea World, not known formally as a zoo, is an attraction that is open to the public and primarily specializes in taking care of marine life.

4. Which numbered sentence is LEAST relevant to the passage?

A. sentence 1
B. sentence 8
C. sentence 9
D. sentence 10

Answer Explanations for Test Yourself

1. **D.** For this paragraph, Choice **D** shows the arrangement of sentences 1, 2, and 3 that provides the most logical sequence of ideas and supporting details. Choices **A, B,** and **C** reflect an arrangement of sentences that are disconnected in thought and thus, are not logical choices.

2. **A.** In this paragraph, Choice **A** or sentence 7 is the sentence that is least relevant to this passage. The sentence about Florida's lack of entertainment venues does not make sense in a paragraph in which the discussion is centered on Florida's ever-increasing socioeconomic needs.

3. **B.** For this paragraph, Choice **B** shows the arrangement of sentences 4, 5, and 6 that provides the most logical sequence of ideas and supporting details. Choices **A, C,** and **D** reflect an arrangement of sentences that are disconnected in thought and thus, are not logical choices.

4. **C.** In this paragraph, Choice **C** or sentence 9 is the sentence that is least relevant to the passage. The sentence about sitting at Parrot Jungle and eating a leisurely lunch and listening to tourists complain about Miami's crowded beaches and roads does not make sense in a paragraph in which the discussion is centered on innovative venues to preserve wildlife animals.

Word Choice Skills

As listed in the *Competencies and Skills Required for Teacher Certification in Florida, Fifteenth Edition* (see the first section in this chapter for the Web address), the English language competencies/skills you should master for this area are the following:

- Choose the appropriate word or expression in context.
- Recognize commonly confused or misused words or phrases.
- Recognize diction and tone appropriate to a given audience.

Choose the Appropriate Word or Expression in Context

Choosing the appropriate word or expression in context is essential to all good writing. When an inappropriate word or expression is chosen to complete a sentence, then the meaning of the sentence can be obstructed. Look at this example of a sentence with an inappropriate word choice:

Steven has the addiction of eating with his mouth open.

The sentence is poorly written because the word *addiction* is an inappropriate choice for this sentence. The way the sentence is written, it sounds like eating with your mouth open is a severe and debilitating ailment that requires medical and psychological help, a description that clearly is not the intent of the writer.

You can correct this confusion by revising the sentence like this:

Steven has the habit of eating with his mouth open.

Recognize Commonly Confused or Misused Words or Phrases

Often, writers include **commonly confused or misused words or phrases** in their writing. These are words that may sound appropriate because they are used frequently in everyday language and written text; however, the use of an inappropriate word or expression in a sentence can obstruct the meaning of the sentence. Find the commonly confused or misused word in this example:

The mechanic will access the car's apparent engine trouble.

The sentence is poorly written because the word *access* is an inappropriate choice for this sentence. The writer meant to use the more appropriate word *assess*. The word *access* means "the ability to enter or approach"; the word *assess* means "to evaluate a problem or concern."

You can correct the confusion by revising the sentence like this:

The mechanic will assess the car's apparent engine trouble.

Here is a list of some words or phrases that are commonly confused or misused:

accede—to agree with

*The lawyers will **accede** to the judge's request for more time for the defendant to prepare his case.*

concede—to yield, to compromise, or to grant, but not really agree

*I **concede** that I lack the strength to become an Olympic runner, but I still intend to try.*

exceed—to be more than

*My daily intake of vitamins **exceeds** the minimum daily requirement.*

access—the ability to enter or approach

*The small crowd that assembled at the Vatican was given **access** to see His Holiness, the Pope.*

assess—to evaluate a problem or concern

*Before we proceed, we should **assess** the situation more carefully.*

excess—more than enough

*Our monthly grocery bill is far in **excess** of the money we have allotted to spend.*

accept—to take or to receive

*I will **accept** only a handful of people on the varsity tennis team.*

except—to exclude (preposition)

*They did not leave the house **except** to buy groceries, get the mail, and walk the dog.*

except—to leave out (verb)

*Everyone was charged admission to the park, but the children were **excepted.***

except—to object (verb)

*The lawyer **excepted** to the judge's ruling that the witness be allowed to testify.*

adapt—to modify or to change

*Most of my colleagues can **adapt** to the sudden mood changes of our boss.*

adopt—to take on or to assume

*The young couple decided to **adopt** a baby from China.*

adept—to be skillful or to have aptitude

*The star athlete was **adept** at playing many sports, most notably football, hockey, and baseball.*

affect—to influence (verb)

*The cold wind and rain will **affect** your health.*

effect—the outcome or consequence (noun)

*The **effect** of the last hurricane is still felt among the residents of the badly damaged village.*

effect—to cause change or accomplish (verb)

*The unexpected blizzard **effected** a dramatic lack of activity at the ski resort; patrons wanted to ski, but were stuck inside for several days until it became safe to go out on the slopes.*

all ready—to have everyone or everything together and prepared

*The students were **all ready** to take the examination when the teacher arrived.*

already—to have come before or to have happened previously

*The dancers had **already** been practicing their routines when their director entered the room.*

all right—to be acceptable or to be agreeable

*As long as you practice for an hour, going to the movies is **all right** with me.*

(**alright** is not a word; it is always spelled as two words: **all right**.)

all together—to include everybody or everything

*At the end of the campfire, the two competing camp tribes sang the closing songs **all together.***

altogether—to be totally inclusive

*Without a doubt, I was **altogether** confused by his sudden change of mood.*

all ways—to include every possible way imaginable

*To our chagrin, the laziest student was in **all ways** amenable to doing the least amount of schoolwork.*

always—to happen at all times

*His sense of humor was **always** present when he was around a crowd of people.*

a lot—to include a large number

*There were **a lot** of people at tonight's ice-hockey game.*

(**alot** is not a word; it is always spelled as two words: **a lot**.)

among—refers to three or more people or things

*At the end of the day, the grandfather made sure that his hugs and kisses were evenly distributed **among** his four grandchildren.*

between—refers to only two people or things

*I had to decide **between** going to the movies or staying home and watching television; I stayed home.*

amount—refers to large quantities that cannot be counted by hand

*We had a large **amount** of grain stored in a bin to be used during the long winter months.*

number—refers to smaller quantities that can be counted by hand

*I counted the **number** of bags of candy; and there were approximately 36, one for each child present.*

as—refers to a similarity or to the same extent

*The film wasn't nearly **as** bad as you made it out to be.*

like—to resemble something or to be similar to

*That cat is **like** a small tiger.*

both—refers to two things considered together

***Both** of them were being considered for the high school honor award.*

each—refers to only one of two or more things

*The wrestling coach made sure that **each** member of the team wrestled in the competition.*

can—to be physically able to complete a task

*The little boy **can** tie his shoes without his mother's help.*

may—to ask (or be given) permission to complete a task

*"**May** I leave my dessert and go out and play?" the young girl asked her grandmother.*

*"You **may** be seated," said the pastor to the congregation.*

capital—refers to the city; the town wherein the seat of government resides

*This vacation, we are visiting the old and beautiful town of Albany, the **capital** of New York.*

capitol—refers to the building; the building that houses the United States Congress

*All eyes were on the Washington **Capitol** as the nation waited to hear the vote on the impending legislation.*

cease—to end or to bring to a conclusion

*Soon, the army will **cease** its fire and set up camp for the night.*

seize—to take hold of or to capture

*In short order, the detectives will **seize** the unsuspecting thief.*

cite—to summon to court; to quote; to mention in a citation

*The officer **cited** the suspect for breaking and entering.*

*Responsible writers **cite** the sources of their material.*

sight—to glimpse or view with the eyes or mind (or something glimpsed or viewed)

*The balloon rose higher and higher until it disappeared from **sight.***

*Listening to Paul's defense of his actions caused Sheila to lose **sight** of her original complaint.*

site—the place where something is, was, or will be

*Gettysburg National Military Park in southeastern Pennsylvania is the **site** of the Battle of Gettysburg.*

coarse—vulgar or unduly rude

***Coarse** mannerisms are repulsive to most people.*

course—a path

*Looking straight ahead, the captain told the first mate to steer the ship on a **course** heading due north.*

course—prescribed studies

*After looking at the schedule, I have decided to take another geometry **course.***

complement—to complete a part or to bring to perfection

*Your brand new black-and-white checked shirt **complements** your black Bermuda shorts.*

compliment—to praise or to show admiration for

*I paid my sister a **compliment** for the wonderful love and care she gives my new baby boy.*

desert—a dry arid piece of land (noun)

*The army heads to the **desert,** equipped with plenty of water, sunscreen, and dark glasses.*

desert—to abandon or to leave behind (verb)

*When we go to the mall, my mother always **deserts** us and heads right for the latest sales.*

dessert—the final course of a meal

*My favorite **dessert** is a strawberry ice-cream sundae, complete with real whipped cream and a cherry.*

disinterested—to be impartial or without judgment

*The bystander served as a **disinterested** witness to the accident.*

uninterested—to show no interest or fondness for

*Jack and Barbara are **uninterested** in anything Mary and Bill do or say.*

either . . . or—to be used when referring to choices

*"**Either** we go to the Grand Canyon **or** we explore the Rocky Mountains this summer," my father said emphatically. "We cannot do both."*

neither . . . nor—to be used when referring to two unacceptable or unlikely choices

***Neither** you **nor** I have any real chance of winning the position of Student Council President.*

eligible—to be acceptable or chosen

*Lauren's winning ticket number makes her **eligible** to become the next recipient of an all-expense paid vacation to Hawaii.*

ineligible—to be unacceptable or not chosen

*Since she was under twelve, Marie was **ineligible** to ride on the high-speed roller coaster by herself.*

illegible—to be difficult or nearly impossible to read or understand

*The doctor's handwriting was **illegible,** making it difficult for the pharmacist to read the prescription.*

emigrate—to leave one's native country for a new country

*Most of America's Jewish people **emigrated** from Eastern Europe prior to the start of World War II.*

immigrate—to enter and live in a new country

*In June, I will **immigrate** to South Africa to live with my aunt and uncle.*

elicit—to call forth or draw out

*My shocking red hair always **elicits** the strangest looks.*

illicit—to be not sanctioned by custom or law; to be unlawful

Underage drinking is illicit behavior.

fewer—refers to people and things that can be counted by hand; used for plural nouns

*There are **fewer** people on hand for the store's grand opening than were anticipated.*

less—refers to people and things that are usually considered in mass numbers; used for singular nouns

*I have **less** gas than I imagined.*

formally—to be considered in an official and dignified manner

*When we went to see the Justice of the Peace, my boyfriend was dressed **formally.***

formerly—refers to an earlier time or position

***Formerly** a member of the United States Congress, my uncle now teaches at Harvard.*

if—introduces a conditional statement

***If** I exercise regularly, I will certainly lose weight.*

whether—refers to introducing a decision or choice

***Whether** you win or lose depends not on how hard you practice, but on how lucky you prove to be.*

weather—refers to the general climate

*When we were in Arizona, the **weather** was hot but dry; there was little humidity.*

imply—to suggest, to hint, or to indicate indirectly

*By asking you about your hair color, I did not mean to **imply** that I thought you dyed it.*

infer—to deduce, to conclude, or to conclude from evidence

*"Are we to **infer** that you simply do not care about your schoolwork?" the desperate mother asked her tenth-grade son when he showed his parents his poor report card.*

incite—to provoke and to urge on

*"The politician's inflammatory language is sure to **incite** the crowd to riot," thought the police officer standing watch.*

insight—the ability to discern the true nature of something

*The news commentator had much **insight** into why the President was so reluctant to tell the nation the truth.*

peak—the highest part of anything

*Climbing to the **peak** of Mount Everest is considered to be a great feat of courage and determination.*

peek—to glance or look quickly, to look furtively from behind or through something

*Toto gave Dorothy, the Scarecrow, the Tin Man, and the Lion more than just a **peek** at the so-called wizard.*

persecute—to torture or to make life horrible for someone

*We should not **persecute** people whose beliefs are different from ours.*

prosecute—to conduct a criminal investigation or to take legal action against someone

*After much deliberation, the district attorney decided to **prosecute** the accused for manslaughter.*

precede—to come before

*We will **precede** the marching bands and floats as we lead the Christmas parade down Main Street.*

proceed—to move on ahead

*After being given the proper verification, we will **proceed** with the experimentation of the new cancer drug.*

supersede—to replace or to take the place of

*It is more than likely that our initial discovery will **supersede** in knowledge and importance all our latest discoveries.*

principal—the head or main leader of an organization; the building supervisor of a school (noun)

*After school, the new **principal** was introduced to the anticipating faculty.*

principal—main or chief (adjective)

The principal reason for the meeting is to elect a new president.

principle—a basic and fundamental truth, value, or belief (noun)

*Conan believes in the **principle** of treating every individual with kindness and respect.*

respectably—acting in a decent and moral manner

*"When attending a formal function, you should dress **respectably**," admonished my socially conscious mother.*

respectfully—marked by a proper manner

*Despite sitting in the cramped and crowded gym bleachers for over an hour, the students listened **respectfully** to the school assembly's guest speaker.*

respectively—refers to the order mentioned or designated

*The first contestant and the second contestant were Jan and Jill, **respectively.***

their—is the possessive form; refers to belonging to a group of people

***Their** plane arrived late because of inclement weather.*

there—is the directional word; refers to a specific place

*I saw my many friends from school walk over **there** to the ice-cream store.*

they're—is the contraction for *they are*

*After the movies, **they're** coming with us to the diner for dinner.*

then—is used to refer to time or consequence

*After holding up the convenience mart, the perpetrator was **then** tried, found guilty, and incarcerated.*

*If this is true, **then** the butler must be the murderer.*

than—is used to compare or contrast things

*He is smarter **than** his younger brother.*

two—is the number 2

*The teacher had only **two** tickets left for the field trip to the ballet.*

to—is the directional word

*I went **to** the grocery store to buy my mother's favorite cookies.*

too—means more than or also

*The young campers wanted to go hiking in the mountains, **too.***

your—is the possessive form; refers to belonging to one person

*"I am sure **your** mother will not want you to sleep in the backyard without a sleeping bag," my best friend's dad said to me just before our sleepover.*

you're—is the contraction for *you are*

*When **you're** ready, we will leave for the train station.*

Recognize Diction and Tone Appropriate to a Given Audience

In any given passage, the words you choose must be appropriate for the audience for which the passage is meant. Would you talk to police officers and attorneys the same way you would to a group of four-year-olds in a preschool? Recognizing diction and tone appropriate to a given audience is essential to good writing. When diction or tone for a given sentence is inappropriate, the intent of the author's meaning can be unclear to the reader. Look at this example of a sentence that is inappropriate in its diction or tone:

As the new student body president, Michael addressed his high school teachers during the faculty meeting by shouting, "Hey, teachers! What's up?"

Clearly, Michael should not have addressed his high school teachers in such a loose and cavalier fashion (*"Hey, teachers! What's up?"*). Michael's teachers are not his friends or relatives.

You can correct this inappropriate diction and tone by revising the sentence like this:

As the new student body president, Michael addressed his high school teachers during the faculty meeting by saying, "Good afternoon, ladies and gentlemen. As the new student body president, I would like to tell you . . . ."

Test Yourself

Directions: For questions 1–3, choose the most appropriate word to complete the sentence.

1. After the football game, the players on the losing team _____ their mistakes and discussed how they could improve their game.

   A. reviewed
   B. reminded
   C. received
   D. relished

2. With seconds left, the frightened family _____ quickly into the shelter, hoping to escape the path of the oncoming storm.

   A. ambled
   B. sauntered
   C. scurried
   D. meandered

3. Filled with trepidation, the little child stepped _____ onto the waiting roller coaster ride.

   A. eagerly
   B. hurriedly
   C. gingerly
   D. willingly

For questions 4–13, choose the option that corrects an error in an underlined portion. If no error exists, choose "No change is necessary."

4. The principle talked to everyone, except the
       A   B   C
   misbehaving boys' parents.

   A. principal
   B. every one
   C. accept
   D. No change is necessary

5. "Either you go to school nor stay home," said
           A B   C
   the child's father.

   A. you're
   B. goes
   C. or
   D. No change is necessary

6. After their school day, the talented young boys
           A
   took an extra coarse in math.
    B   C

   A. they're
   B. have taken
   C. course
   D. No change is necessary

7. Upon finishing their dessert, the two lovers
                          A
   preceded to walk home, enjoying the cool
    B
   weather.
    C

   A. desert
   B. proceeded
   C. whether
   D. No change is necessary

8. Their insights about the upcoming elections
    A   B
   were most appreciated by the graduate
    C
   students in political science.

   A. They're
   B. incites
   C. was
   D. No change is necessary

9. Your brother is more helpful then everyone
    A   B
   all together.
    C

   A. You're
   B. than
   C. altogether
   D. No change is necessary

10. Only thirteen years old, he is ineligible to play
                     A   B   C
    varsity baseball.

    A. are
    B. unelig ible
    C. too
    D. No change is necessary

11. Despite the great weather, we were
                 A
    disinterested in sitting among the team players
      B   C
    and watching the game.

    A. whether
    B. uninterested
    C. between
    D. No change is necessary

12. All afternoon, everyone except Mother
                    A   B
    complemented me on my new dress.
      C

    A. accept
    B. mother
    C. complimented
    D. No change is necessary

13. We'll need to decide among two places to visit.
     A   B   C

    A. Will
    B. between
    C. too
    D. No change is necessary

For question 14, choose the most appropriate option to answer the question.

14. Angelo, president of the student debate team, is speaking to his community's civic club about the need for the debate team to raise money for their trip to participate in the national debate championship.

Choose the most appropriate opening statement.

A. "My friends and fellow citizens, please attend to the following observations as I proceed to enumerate the many substantial reasons that you should choose to sponsor the illustrious debate team's winning journey."
B. "As you are well aware, the high school debate team plays a vital role in helping students understand today's social issues."
C. "Hey, have you noticed? The debate team has no money."
D. "The debate is lots of fun. Would you be willing to give us some money so we can go to the championship game?"

Answer Explanations for Test Yourself

1. **A.** In this sentence, the missing word is *reviewed* (Choice A), meaning "to evaluate or assess," as in "the losing team reviewed their mistakes." Choices **B, C,** and **D** are not logical selections, given the context of this sentence. Choice **B** is the word *reminded,* and you would not write "the losing team reminded their mistakes." Choice **C** is the word *received,* and although you might write "the losing team received their mistakes," it is not the most logical choice. Choice **D** is the word *relished,* meaning "to enjoy." Clearly, a losing team would not relish mistakes.

2. **C.** In this sentence, the missing word is *scurried* (Choice C), meaning "to dash or rush" as in "the frightened family scurried into the shelter." Choices **A, B,** and **D** are not logical selections, given the context of this sentence. Choice **A,** *ambled,* means "to stroll or wander," and you would not write "the frightened family ambled into the shelter." Choice **B,** *sauntered,* means "to amble or walk," and you would not write "the frightened family sauntered into the shelter." Choice **D,** *meandered,* means "to ramble or roam," and you would not write "the frightened family meandered into the shelter." Clearly, a frightened family would scurry in the face of an impending storm.

3. **C.** In this sentence, the missing word is *gingerly* (Choice **C**), meaning "cautiously or tentatively," as in "the little girl stepped gingerly onto the roller coaster." Choices **A, B,** and **D** are not logical selections, given the context of this sentence. Choice **A,** *eagerly,* implies enthusiastically, and you would not write "Filled with trepidation (or fear), the little girl stepped enthusiastically onto the roller coaster." Choice **B,** *hurriedly,* implies quickly, and you would not write "Filled with trepidation, the little girl stepped hurriedly onto the roller coaster." Choice **D,** *willingly,* implies without hesitation, and you would not write "Filled with trepidation, the little girl stepped willingly onto the roller coaster." Clearly, the word *gingerly* is the most logical choice to demonstrate the little girl's fear.

4. **A.** In this sentence, the word *principle* should be replaced with the word *principal* (Choice **A**). The word *principle* means "a standard or a belief," whereas the word *principal* means "a school administrator." In Choice **B,** the word *everyone* is used as a pronoun, and thus is spelled correctly. In Choice **C,** the word *except,* meaning "to leave out," is used correctly.

5. **C.** In this sentence, the word *nor* should be replaced with the word *or* (Choice **C**). *Either . . . or* is used when referring to choices; *Neither . . . nor* is used when referring to negative choices. In Choice **A,** the pronoun *you* is used correctly. In Choice **B,** the correct form of the verb *to go* is used correctly.

6. **C.** In this sentence, the word *coarse* should be replaced with the word *course* (Choice **C**). The word *coarse* is an adjective meaning "rough or abrasive." The word *course,* though, is a noun of which one of its meanings is "a lesson or a class." In Choice **A,** the word *their,* indicating possession, is used correctly. In Choice **B,** the word *took,* the correct verb form of the word *taken,* is used correctly.

7. **B.** In this sentence, the word *preceded* should be replaced with the word *proceeded* (Choice **B**). The word *preceded* means "to come before," whereas the word *proceeded* means "to go ahead." In Choice **A,** the word *dessert,* meaning "a sweet dish served after a meal," is used correctly. In Choice **C,** the word *weather* is used correctly.

8. **D.** In this sentence, no changes are necessary. Choices **A, B,** and **C** are used correctly.

9. **B.** In this sentence, the word *then* should be replaced with the word *than* (Choice **B**). The word *then* refers to time *or* consequences; the word *than* refers to comparing and/or contrasting things. In Choice **A,** the word *your,* the possessive form of *you,* is used correctly. In Choice **C,** the phrase *all together,* meaning "everybody or everything," is used correctly.

10. **D.** In this sentence, no changes are necessary. Choices **A, B,** and **C** are used correctly.

11. **B.** In this sentence, the word *disinterested* should be replaced with *uninterested* (Choice **B**). The word *disinterested* means "impartial"; the word *uninterested* means "not interested." In Choice **A,** the word *weather* is used correctly. In Choice **C,** the word *among,* a word used when referring to more than two people or things, is used correctly.

12. **C.** In this sentence, the word *complemented* should be replaced with the word *complimented* (Choice **C**). The word *complemented* means "a completing or finishing part." The word *compliment* means "an expression of admiration." In Choice **A,** the word *except,* meaning "excluding," is used correctly. In Choice **B,** the word *Mother* is used correctly because the name refers to a specific person in the family.

13. **B.** In this sentence, the word *among* should be replaced with the word *between* (Choice **B**). The word *among* is used when referring to more than two people or things; the word *between* is used when referring to only two people or things. In Choice **A,** the word *We'll,* the contraction of *we will,* is used correctly. In Choice **C,** the word *to,* meaning "in the direction of," is used correctly.

14. **B.** In this question, the most appropriate opening statement is Choice **B.** The high school student speaks in a reasonable voice and tone. Choice **A** reflects a ponderous and obsequious tone of voice. Choice **C** is much too casual for a high school student speaking to a civic club. Choice **D** is not as casual as Choice **C,** but still seems to lack the dignity and respect that a student should demonstrate when speaking to a civic club.

Sentence Structure Skills

As listed in the *Competencies and Skills Required for Teacher Certification in Florida, Fifteenth Edition* (see earlier in this chapter for the Web address), the English language competencies/skills you should be able to do for this area are the following:

- Recognize misplaced modifiers.
- Recognize faulty parallelism.
- Recognize fragments and run-on sentences.

What Are Misplaced Modifiers?

A **modifier** is a word or group of words that conveys information about another word or word group. To avoid confusion, modifiers should be placed close to the word or words they modify. A modifier is a **misplaced modifier** when it is placed in the sentence in such a way that the intent of the writer is unclear to the reader. Look at this example of a misplaced modifier:

The photographer saw several black bears driving through the woods.

This sentence is confusing because the modifier (*driving through the woods*) is not close to the word it modifies (*photographer*). The way the sentence is written, it sounds like the bears are driving through the woods, a situation that clearly is not the intent of the writer.

You can correct the confusion by revising the sentence like this:

Driving through the woods, the photographer saw several black bears.

Here is another example of a misplaced modifier:

I only have one dollar in my wallet.

In this sentence, the word *only* should be placed immediately before the word *one*, which it modifies:

I have only one dollar in my wallet.

What Is Faulty Parallelism?

The ideas in sentences should be **parallel,** meaning they should be expressed in the same way. For instance, you might write, "I like to sunbathe, but I don't like to swim." Your ideas on sunbathing and swimming are expressed using the same type of grammatical construction. **Faulty parallelism** occurs when the ideas in a sentence are not parallel. The result is an awkward construction, the meaning of which is often unclear. Look at this example of faulty parallelism:

Jude's actions were heroic and to be praised.

This sentence sounds awkward because the ideas are not expressed in the same way. The words *heroic* and *to be praised* do not have the same grammatical construction. You can correct the problem by revising the sentence like this:

Jude's actions were heroic and praiseworthy.

Always check for faulty parallelism in the following situations:

- When elements are linked by coordinating conjunctions (*and, but, or, nor,* or *yet*)
  For example, change "interesting and to be remembered" to "interesting and memorable."

- When elements are linked by correlative conjunctions (pairs of connector words such as *both . . . and, not only . . . but also, either . . . or*, and *neither . . . nor*)

  For example, change "both kind and a generous person" to "both kind and generous."
- When making comparisons

  For example, change "Sophie's contribution is more noteworthy than Gregory" to "Sophie's contribution is more noteworthy than Gregory's."

What Are Fragments and Run-On Sentences?

A **clause** is a group of words that contains a subject and a verb. An **independent** or **main clause** can stand alone as a sentence. A **dependent clause** or **subordinate clause** begins with a subordinating conjunction (for example, *because, if, when*) or a relative pronoun (for example, *who, whom, that*) and can *never* stand alone.

A **simple sentence** is an example of an independent clause. It has a subject and a verb and expresses a complete thought. Look at this example:

My favorite subject is history.

A **fragment** is a group of words that looks like a sentence, but does not express a complete thought. A fragment is missing something. Sometimes it is missing a subject. Look at this fragment:

Didn't run fast enough.

This fragment needs a subject. Who or what didn't run fast enough? To make this fragment into a sentence, you can add a subject:

Jamie didn't run fast enough.

Sometimes a fragment is missing a verb. Look at this fragment:

Hundreds of screaming fans.

This fragment needs a verb. What did the hundreds of screaming fans do? To make this fragment into a sentence, you can add a verb:

Hundreds of screaming fans rushed through the gates.

Sometimes a fragment has a subject and a verb, but it still does not express a complete thought. This often occurs when the fragment is a subordinate clause. Look at this fragment:

Because I've always liked reading about real events.

To make this fragment into a sentence, you can add a main clause:

My favorite subject is history because I've always liked reading about real events.

Because I've always like reading about real events, my favorite subject is history.

A **run-on sentence** is two independent clauses joined without a proper punctuation mark or word to separate them. Look at this run-on sentence:

Your first test in geometry is tomorrow you'd better study.

A run-on sentence in which the two sentences are joined (spliced) *only* with a comma is called a **comma splice**. Look at this comma splice:

The test was very hard to finish in the time allotted, it had too many questions on it.

Run-on sentences and comma splices can usually be corrected in one of three ways:

1. Insert a period or a semicolon between the two independent clauses.

    Your first test in geometry is tomorrow. You'd better study.

    The test was very hard to finish in the time allotted; it had too many questions on it.

2. Insert a comma and a connector word (for example, *and, but, or, so*) between the two independent clauses.

    Your first test in geometry is tomorrow, so you'd better study.

3. Make one clause subordinate to the other.

    The test was very hard to finish in the time allotted because it had too many questions on it.

Test Yourself

Directions: For questions 1–2, choose the most appropriate word to complete the sentence.

1. My daughter's homework assignment in English consists of writing her spelling words, memorizing her vocabulary word definitions, and _____ her favorite things to do.

    A. to list
    B. must list
    C. listing

2. Amazingly, my children like to help out at home by both washing clothes and occasionally _____ dinner.

    A. cook
    B. cooking
    C. to cook

3. Choose the sentence in which the modifiers are placed correctly.

    A. Drifting down the river on a raft, the girls spotted a deer feeding her young fawn.
    B. Feeding her young fawn, the girls spotted a deer drifting down the river on a raft.
    C. The girls spotted a deer feeding her young fawn drifting down the river on a raft.

4. Choose the option that is punctuated correctly.

    A. Of course, you should take your allergy medicine, your doctor told you that it would relieve your symptoms.
    B. Of course, you should take your allergy medicine your doctor told you that it would relieve your symptoms.
    C. Of course, you should take your allergy medicine. Your doctor told you that it would relieve your symptoms.
    D. Of course you should take your allergy medicine your doctor told you that it would relieve your symptoms.

Answer Explanations for Test Yourself

1. **C.** In this sentence the missing word is parallel with the words *writing* and *memorizing*, so it needs to have the same grammatical construction. The correct form is *listing* (Choice **C**). Choices **A** and **B** result in faulty parallelism.

2. **B.** In this sentence the missing word is parallel with the word *washing*, so it needs to have the same grammatical construction. The correct form is *cooking* (Choice **B**). Choices **A** and **C** result in faulty parallelism.

3. **A.** The modifiers in sentence A are placed correctly. The participial phrase *drifting down the river on a raft* modifies *girls* and should be close to it. In Choices **B** and **C**, *drifting down the river on a raft* is separated from the noun *girls*, resulting in ambiguity. Additionally, the participial phrase *feeding her young fawn* modifies the noun *deer* and should be close to it. In Choice **B**, the participial phrase *feeding her young fawn* is separated from the noun *deer*, resulting in ambiguity.

4. **C.** All punctuation in sentence C is correct. Choice **A** is incorrect because it is a run-on sentence. It is two complete sentences connected by only a comma. Choices **B** and **D** are also run-on sentences. Each of these sentences is two complete sentences joined without a word to connect them or a proper punctuation mark to separate them. Further, in Choice **D** a comma is needed to set off the introductory element *of course*.

Grammar, Spelling, Capitalization, and Punctuation Skills

As listed in the *Competencies and Skills Required for Teacher Certification in Florida, Fifteenth Edition* (see earlier in this chapter for the Web address), the English language competencies/skills you should be able to recognize and do for this area are the following:

- Subject-verb agreement.
- Standard verb tenses.
- Faulty tense shifts.
- Pronoun-antecedent agreement.
- Faulty pronoun shifts.
- Clear pronoun references.
- Proper pronoun case forms.
- The correct use of adjectives and adverbs.
- Appropriate comparative and superlative degree forms of adjectives and adverbs.
- Standard spelling.
- Standard punctuation.
- Standard capitalization.

What Is Subject-Verb Agreement?

Subject-verb agreement means a singular subject must have a singular verb and a plural subject must have a plural verb. In other words, a subject and its verb must agree *in number*. To make sure the subject and verb agree, you need to be able to identify the subject of the sentence, decide whether it is singular or plural, and then match the verb accordingly. If the subject is singular, the verb will end in –*s* or –*es* (*the dog barks, the bird flies*). If the subject is plural, the verb will *not* have an –*s* or –*es* ending (*the dogs bark, the birds fly*).

Errors in subject-verb agreement may occur when other words in the sentence separate the subject and verb. Look at this example of an error in subject-verb agreement:

> *A chorus of cheers were heard from the crowd.*

The verb must agree with its singular noun subject *chorus*, not the plural word *cheers*. Change *were* to *was* to make the sentence grammatically correct:

> *A chorus of cheers was heard from the crowd.*

To help with recognizing errors in subject-verb agreement, read the sentence without the intervening words. Try this example:

> *The president of the club, as well as the other officers, feel that the membership dues need to be raised.*

The subject of the verb is *president*. Does *The president . . . feel* sound correct to you? Change *feel* to *feels* to make the sentence grammatically correct:

> *The president of the club, as well as the other officers, feels that the membership dues need to be raised.*

It should be noted that if the sentence began with *The president and the other officers of the club . . .* , the verb would be *feel*:

> *The president and the other officers of the club feel that the membership dues need to be raised.*

The reason for using the word *feel* in this example is that *the president and the other officers of the club* is regarded as a plural subject and thus requires a plural verb to complete the sentence.

The contractions *doesn't* and *don't* can also cause errors in subject-verb agreement.

Doesn't is a contraction of *does not*, so it is used when you have a singular subject. *Don't* is a contraction of *do not*, so it is used when you have a plural subject.

> For example, change *He don't like me* to *He doesn't like me.*

Tip: When in doubt, mentally substitute *does not* for *doesn't* and *do not* for *don't* to see which sounds correct.

When two or more subjects are joined by the word *or* or *nor*, the verb agrees with the noun that is closest to the verb. Look at these examples:

> *The woman's children or her husband has the videotape of the event.*
> *Neither the teacher nor the students care that the bell has rung.*

Most indefinite pronouns (for example, *each, everyone, everybody*) take singular verbs. Look at this example:

> *Everybody needs to bring a sack lunch to the picnic.*

The words *there* and *here* are never subjects, so look for the subject to come after the verb.

> For example, change *There is many reasons to be upset* to *There are many reasons to be upset.*

For further clarification, see the section on pronoun-antecedent agreement in this chapter.

What Do You Need to Know About Verb Tenses?

Verbs have different forms called **tenses.** The tense of a verb in a sentence tells you when the action of the verb takes place. The verb tenses you will need to know for the FTCE GK Test are the **simple tenses** and the **perfect tenses.**

The simple tenses are the **present tense** (*I work, he writes*), the **past tense** (*I worked, he wrote*), and the **future tense** (*I will work, he will write*).

The perfect tenses use a form of the helping verb *to have* in their construction. The perfect tenses are the **present perfect** (*I have worked, he has written*), which indicates a past action that is ongoing; the **past perfect** (*I had worked, he had written*), which indicates a past action that occurred before a previous past action; and the **future perfect** (*I will have worked, he will have written*), which indicates a past action that will occur before a future action.

Principal Parts

All six tenses of a verb are formed using its three **principal parts:** present (*work*), past (*worked*), and past participle (*worked*). For **regular verbs,** the past and past participle are formed by adding *–ed*. Some verbs do not form their past and past participle this way. These verbs are called **irregular verbs.** Table 2.1 lists the principal parts of 27 frequently used irregular verbs that you should memorize in preparation for the FTCE GK Test.

Table 2.1: Principal Parts of 27 Frequently Used Irregular Verbs								
Present	begin	break	bring	catch	choose	come	do	drink	drive
Past	began	broke	brought	caught	chose	came	did	drank	drove
Past participle	begun	broken	brought	caught	chosen	come	done	drunk	driven
Present	eat	fall	get	give	go	grow	know	lose	ride
Past	ate	fell	got	gave	went	grew	knew	lost	rode
Past participle	eaten	fallen	gotten	given	gone	grown	known	lost	ridden
Present	rise	run	see	sing	speak	swim	take	throw	write
Past	rose	ran	saw	sang	spoke	swam	took	threw	wrote
Past participle	risen	run	seen	sung	spoken	swum	taken	thrown	written

Faulty Tense Shifts

Sometimes a writer will start a sentence with one tense and shift to another tense for no logical reason. This is called a **faulty tense shift.** Look at this example of a faulty tense shift:

My fearless sister walks up to the tiger and quickly took a picture.

This sentence starts off in the present tense, but then shifts to the past tense for no reason. This shifting of tenses is distracting and confusing to the reader. Revise the sentence by using the same tense for both verbs:

My fearless sister walked up to the tiger and quickly took a picture.

What Do You Need to Know About Pronouns?

A **pronoun** stands for or refers to a person, place, or thing whose identity is made clear earlier in the text. The noun to which a pronoun refers is called the pronoun's **antecedent.** Look at the following example:

Dentists are concerned with oral health. They say that flossing is good for your gums.

In this sentence, *They* is a pronoun referring to the antecedent *Dentists.*

Types of Pronouns

The types of pronouns you need to know for the FTCE GK Test are the following:

- Personal
- Demonstrative
- Indefinite
- Relative
- Reflexive
- Intensive
- Interrogative
- Reciprocal

A **personal pronoun** is a specific person or thing and changes its form to indicate person, number, gender, and case. There are three kinds of personal pronouns. They are *subjective*, *objective*, and *possessive*.

A **subjective personal pronoun** indicates the pronoun is acting as the subject of the sentence. Subjective personal pronouns are *I, you, he, she, it, we, you,* and *they*.

An **objective personal pronoun** indicates that the pronoun is acting as the object of a verb, compound verb, preposition, or infinitive phrase. Objective personal pronouns are *me, her, him, it, us, you,* and *them*.

A **possessive personal pronoun** indicates ownership. Possessive personal pronouns are *my, your, mine, yours, his, her, hers, its, our, ours, theirs and whose*.

Tip: Notice that possessive pronouns do *not* contain apostrophes.

A **demonstrative pronoun** points to and identifies a noun or a pronoun. Demonstrative pronouns are *this, these, that,* and *those*.

An **interrogative pronoun** is a pronoun used to ask a question. The interrogative pronouns are *who, whom, which, what,* and the compounds formed with the suffix *ever*. They are *whoever, whomever, whichever,* and *whatever*.

An **indefinite pronoun** refers to an identifiable but not specified person or thing. The most common indefinite pronouns are *all, another, any, anybody, anyone, anything, each, everybody, everything, few, many, nobody, none, one, several, some, somebody,* and *someone*.

A **relative pronoun** links one phrase or clause to another phrase or clause. The relative pronouns are *who, whom, that,* and *which,* and their respective compounds are *whoever, whomever,* and *whichever*.

A **reflexive pronoun** refers to the subject of the clause of the sentence. The reflexive pronouns are *myself, yourself, himself, herself, itself, ourselves, yourselves,* and *themselves*.

An **intensive pronoun** is a word used to refer to its *antecedent* or the word that comes before the pronoun.

For example:

> *The governor himself said he would sign the bill into law.* (*Himself* is an intensive pronoun that refers to the governor.)

Note: Intensive pronouns are identical in form to reflexive pronouns. Do not use these pronouns in place of the ordinary pronouns *I, me, she, her,* and so on. They are to be used for two purposes only: (1) to refer to the subject, and (2) to emphasize. For example, change *Richard, Rose, and myself are going* to *Richard, Rose, and I are going*.

A **reciprocal pronoun** expresses a mutual feeling or relationship between the individuals indicated in the plural subject. Reciprocal pronouns are *each other* and *one another*.

Pronoun-Antecedent Agreement

A pronoun must agree with its antecedent, the noun it replaces. Therefore, if the antecedent is singular, the pronoun must be singular; if the antecedent is plural, the pronoun must be plural; if the antecedent is feminine, the pronoun must be a feminine pronoun; and so on.

Errors in pronoun-antecedent agreement make it difficult for the reader to understand what the writer means. Look at this example:

> *A woman who works hard to achieve success may find they are not accepted as equals in certain situations.*

The pronoun *they* does not agree with its singular antecedent, *woman*. Change *they are* to *she is* to make the sentence grammatically correct. Also change *equals* to *an equal*:

> *A woman who works hard to achieve success may find she is not accepted as an equal in certain situations.*

Most indefinite pronoun antecedents (for example, *each, everyone, everybody*) take singular pronouns. Look at this example:

> *Each of the girls needs to obtain her parents' permission to go on the trip.*

The pronoun *her* agrees with its singular antecedent, *each*.

For further clarification on pronoun-antecedent agreement, see the section on subject-verb agreement in this chapter.

Pronoun Reference

When a writer uses a pronoun, it should be clear to the reader what the antecedent for the pronoun is. When it is unclear, the reader may find the sentence ambiguous. Look at this example:

> *My mother removed the roses from the two vases and threw them in the trash.*

What did the mother throw in the trash? The *roses* or the *vases*? The pronoun *they* does not have a clear reference. You can revise the sentence like this:

> *My mother removed the roses from the two vases and threw the flowers in the trash.*

Pronoun Shifts

The **person** form tells you whether the pronoun is the speaker (**first person**—*I talk; we talk*), the person spoken to (**second person**—*you talk*), or the person spoken about (**third person**—*he, she, it talks; they talk*).

Pronouns should have the same person as their antecedents in a sentence. When a writer fails to do this, the resulting faulty construction is called a **pronoun shift.** Look at this example of a pronoun shift:

> *If one studies hard for the test, you will make a good grade.*

The sentence goes from third person (*one*) to the second person (*you*). You can revise the sentence like this:

> *If you study hard for the test, you will make a good grade.*

Pronoun Case

Case shows the function of a pronoun in a sentence. The form the pronoun takes tells you whether the pronoun is a subject (**subjective case**—*I, you, he, she, it, we, they, who, whoever*), an object (**objective case**—*me, you, him, her, it, us, them, whom, whomever*), or shows ownership (**possessive case**—*my, mine, her, hers, his, its, our, ours, your, yours, their, theirs, whose*).

Use the subjective case when the pronoun is the subject of a verb or has an antecedent that is the subject of a verb. Look at these examples:

> *My spouse and I often travel abroad.*

The pronoun *I* is in the subjective case because it is part of the subject of the verb *travel*.

> *The coach gave tickets to whoever arrived first.*

The relative pronoun *whoever* is in the subjective case because it is the subject of the verb *arrived*.

Use the objective case when the pronoun is the object of a verb or a verbal (a verb form used as a noun, adjective, or adverb), the object of a preposition, or the subject of an infinitive. Look at these examples:

> *Ask whomever you want.*

The relative pronoun *whomever* is in the objective case because it is the object of the verb *want*.

> *I hope there will be no secrets between you and me.*

The pronoun *me* is in the objective case because it is the object of the preposition *between*.

> *I could not believe that the committee invited her to serve as master of ceremonies at the banquet.*

The pronoun *her* is in the objective case because it is the subject of the infinitive *to serve*.

Use the possessive case when the pronoun shows ownership or if it precedes a gerund (the *–ing* form of a verb used as noun). Look at these examples:

> *Her jewelry is exquisite.*

The pronoun *her* is in the possessive case because it shows ownership of the noun *jewelry*.

> *His interrupting every few minutes is becoming annoying.*

The pronoun *his* is in the possessive case because it precedes the gerund *interrupting*.

What Do You Need to Know About Adjectives and Adverbs?

Adjectives and adverbs are modifiers that describe things or actions in a sentence. **Adjectives** modify nouns or pronouns. **Adverbs** modify verbs, adjectives, or other adverbs.

Correct Usage

To decide whether a word used as a modifier is an adjective or an adverb, ask yourself what word does the modifier describe? If it describes a noun or pronoun, it is an adjective. If it describes a verb, adjective, or other adverb, it is an adverb. Look at these examples:

> *The <u>rotten</u> fruit smells <u>bad</u>.*

In this sentence the word *rotten* describes the noun *fruit,* so *rotten* is an adjective. The word *bad* following the verb *smells* also tells you something about the noun *fruit*—that it has a bad odor. Therefore, the word *bad* is an adjective describing the noun *fruit*.

> *The racer drove <u>slowly</u> as he passed the accident on the track.*

In this sentence the word *slowly* following the verb *drove* tells how the racer drove, so *slowly* is an adverb describing the verb *drove*.

On the FTCE GK Test, you will need to recognize incorrect use of adjectives or adverbs. Be wary when the verb in the sentence is based on one of your senses (*feel, taste, smell, look, sound*) or is a form of the verb *to be*. Usually, adjectives should follow such verbs. Here is an example of incorrect construction:

> *I feel <u>badly</u> that I missed your graduation from college.*

The modifier after the verb *feel* describes the pronoun *I*, so it should be an adjective, not an adverb. Replace *badly* with *bad* to make the sentence grammatically correct:

I feel bad that I missed your graduation from college.

Here is another example:

He ran <u>quick</u> and turned off the alarm.

The modifier *quick* describes the verb *ran*, so it should be an adverb, not an adjective. Replace *quick* with *quickly* to make the sentence grammatically correct:

He ran quickly and turned off the alarm.

Appropriate Comparative and Superlative Degree Forms

When you compare two things, you either add *–er* to the modifier or precede the modifier with the word *more* or *less.* The resulting grammatical construction is the *comparative* form of the adjective or adverb. When you compare more than two things, you either add *–est* to the modifier or precede the modifier with the word *most* or *least.* The resulting grammatical construction is the *superlative* form of the adjective or adverb.

Use *–er* to form the comparative and *–est* to form the superlative of most one-syllable adjectives and adverbs. For most two-syllable adjectives and adverbs, you can use *–er* and *–est, more* and *most,* or *less* and *least.* With all adjectives and adverbs of three or more syllables, use *more* and *most* or *less* and *least.* Look at these examples:

The boy on the left is taller than the boy on the right, but the boy in the middle is the tallest of all three.

The lab assistant poured the liquid more (or less) carefully the second time than he did the first time.

Tip: You'll often find the word *than* used with an adjective or adverb to form the comparative. *The cheetah ran faster than the antelope. Peggy's book bag is larger than Alicia's.*

If an adverb ends in *–ly,* change the *–y* to *–i* when using the *–er* or *–est* ending. Look at this example:

Sam is lucky, but Kendra is luckier than he.

When making a comparison, do not include the person or thing being compared. Look at this example:

That movie is more entertaining than any other movie currently in theaters.

The word *other* is needed to make the sentence logical. The sentence, *That movie is more entertaining than any movie currently in theaters* says that the movie is more entertaining than itself!

Some common adjectives and adverbs have irregular forms (*good/well, better, the best; bad/badly, worse, the worst*). Look at these examples:

Kim submitted a good essay, but Juan's was better because it was more interesting. When your essay is due, you should try to write the best one of all.

My favorite driver drove badly in the race last week. This week he drove worse than before. Frankly, I think he drove the worst of all the drivers in the race.

You should avoid redundant constructions like *more better, most easiest,* and so on:

*The room temperature is better (not **more better**) after you lowered the thermostat.*

*That was the easiest (not **most easiest**) exam I have ever taken.*

Tip: For some adjectives and adverbs, such as *unique, universal,* and *perfect,* it is illogical to form comparative and superlative forms. These words are absolute in their meaning, so constructions like *more unique* or *most unique,* for example, should be avoided.

What Do You Need to Know About Spelling, Punctuation, and Capitalization?

Standard English has many rules for spelling, punctuation, and capitalization. This CliffsNotes guide describes the basic rules that should prove most helpful on the FTCE GK Test.

Spelling

Memorize the following guidelines for correct spelling:

- When you know a word contains *ie* or *ei*, recall the following rhyme:

  I before *e,* except after *c,*

  Or when sounding like "*ay*" as in *neighbor* and *weigh*.

  Look at these examples:

I before e	Comes after c	Sounds like "ay"
believe	receive	eight

Exceptions: heifer, height, seize, surfeit, weird

- When a word ends in silent *–e*, drop the *–e* before you add an ending that begins with a vowel. Keep the final *–e* if the ending begins with a consonant or to prevent mispronunciation. Look at these examples:

Ending begins with a vowel	Ending begins with a consonant	Mispronunciation may occur
care + –ing = caring	care + –ful = careful	notice + –able = noticeable

Exceptions: Sometimes the final *–e* is dropped when it comes after another vowel, as in *truly* (*true* + *–ly*) and *argument* (*argue* + *–ment*).

- When a word ends in *–y* preceded by a consonant, change *–y* to *–i* before you add an ending. Keep the *–y* if it is preceded by a vowel, the ending is *–ing*, or the word is a proper name. Look at these examples:

–y preceded by a consonant	–y preceded by a vowel	Ending is –ing	Proper noun
happy + –ly = happily	day + –s = days	study + –ing = studying	Murphy + –s = Murphys

- In one-syllable words that have a consonant-vowel-consonant (CVC) pattern, double a final consonant that is preceded by a single vowel when you add a suffix beginning with a vowel (for example, *–ed*, *–ing*). For multisyllabic words ending in *–CVC*, where the stress is on the CVC syllable after the suffix is added, double the final consonant when you add a suffix beginning with a vowel. Note: This rule does not apply to words ending in *–v*, *–w*, *–x*, or *–y*, because these consonants should never be doubled when adding suffixes. Look at these examples:

One-syllable CVC word	Multisyllabic word ending in –CVC, where stress is on CVC syllable	Word ending in –v, –w, –x, or –y
pat + –ed = patted	begin + –ing = beginning	tow + –ing = towing

- When you add a prefix (for example, *mis–*, *dis–*), do not add to or drop a letter from the original word. For instance, *mis– + spell = misspell*.
- When you are deciding whether a word should end in *–ible* or *–able*, a general rule is that if the root is not a complete word, the ending is *–ible;* otherwise, the ending is *–able*. Here are examples:

  terrible, dependable, permissible, acceptable

If the root is a complete word ending in –e, drop the final –e and add –able. For instance, *love + –able = lovable.*
Exceptions: *contemptible, digestible, flexible, inevitable, irritable, changeable, responsible*

- When you form the plural of a singular noun, you add –s or –es. If the noun ends in –s, –sh, –ch, or –x, or if the noun ends in –o preceded by a consonant, add –es; otherwise, just add –s. These rules apply to proper names as well, and please, do not insert apostrophes anywhere. Note: If the singular noun ends in –y, follow the rules given earlier for adding suffixes to nouns ending in –y. Look at these examples:

  girl, girls; face, faces; video, videos; kiss, kisses; church, churches; box, boxes; tomato, tomatoes; Hutto; Huttoes

- Use –sede to spell *supersede*. Use –ceed to spell *exceed, proceed,* and *succeed*. For all other words, the "seed" sound is spelled –cede. For example, *intercede, precede,* and *concede*.

- When a word has a homophone (word that sounds like it, but is spelled differently), check how the word is used in the sentence. Look at this example of a spelling error caused by homophone confusion:

  The students displayed there projects at the science fair.

  In this sentence the word preceding the noun *project* should be a possessive pronoun referring to the antecedent *students*. Change *there* to *their* to make the sentence grammatically correct:

  The students displayed their projects at the science fair.

- Avoid faulty pronunciation that can lead to misspelling. For instance, *mathematics* has an *e* that you might omit in the spelling if you say, "math mat ics" instead of "math e mat ics."

- Some nouns have irregular plurals. Look at these examples:

  child, children; woman/man, women/men; person, people; goose, geese; tooth, teeth; mouse, mice; deer, deer; sheep, sheep; knife, knives; life, lives; half, halves; criterion, criteria; analysis, analyses; crisis, crises; focus, foci; die, dice

Punctuation

You use end punctuation to show when a sentence ends. Depending on the type of sentence, end punctuation might be a period, a question mark, or an exclamation point:

- Use a period at the end of a statement. Example: *I love to read.*
- Use a question mark at the end of a question. Example: *Is this your book?*
- Use an exclamation point after an emphatic statement. Example: *That is an exciting idea!*

You use commas to indicate pauses and to prevent confusion:

- Use commas to separate three or more words or phrases in a series. Example: *I will need scissors, paper, and glue.*
- Use a comma to separate a date from its year. Example: *He was born on August 7, 1976.*
- Use a comma to separate a date and year from the rest of the sentence. Example: *Our family reunion on July 4, 2005, was a memorable one.*
- Use a comma to separate a city and its state from the rest of the sentence. Example: *We were living in Austin, Texas, before we moved to Florida.*
- Use a comma to set off most introductory elements. Example: *Fortunately, I was allowed to use a calculator when I took the mathematics portion of the test.*
- Use a comma to separate two main clauses joined by a connector word (*and, or, but, so, for, nor, yet*). Example: *I broke my watch, so I couldn't tell what time it was.*
- Use a comma to set off an introductory subordinate clause. Example: *When I'm working on a project, I find it hard to stop to eat.*

- Use a comma to set off an introductory participial phrase. Example: *Driving through the park, I saw several squirrels gathering nuts.*

- Use commas to separate nonrestrictive elements from the rest of the sentence. Nonrestrictive elements are elements that are not essential to the meaning of the sentence. Example: *My neighbor, who is a mathematics professor, often chats with me in the front yard.*

- Use a comma to set off a direct quotation. Example: *"I wish you wouldn't do that," she pleaded.*

Semicolons are used in two main ways:

- Use a semicolon between two independent clauses when no connector word is used. Example: *I broke my watch; I couldn't tell what time it was.*

- Use a semicolon between two independent clauses linked by a transitional word or phrase. Example: *I broke my watch; therefore, I couldn't tell what time it was.*

- Use semicolons to separate three or more items in a series that already contains commas. Example: *We have lived in Chicago, Illinois; Austin, Texas; and Tampa, Florida.*

Colons are used in three main ways:

- Use a colon to alert the reader to pay attention to something that follows. Example: *The number 13 has only two factors: 1 and 13.*

- Use a colon to punctuate time. Example: *We will leave at 12:15 p.m.*

- Use a colon in the salutation of a business letter. Example: *Dear Committee Members:*

Tip: Do not use a colon between a verb and its object, a preposition and its object, or directly after a form of the verb *to be*. Do not use a colon after *such as* or directly after *include, includes,* or *including*.

Apostrophes are used in three main ways:

- Use an apostrophe to stand in for a missing letter or letters in a contraction. Example: *You shouldn't worry.*

- Use an apostrophe to show possession. Add *–'s* to singular nouns or indefinite pronouns and to plural nouns that do not end in *–s*. Add *–'s* to singular nouns ending in *–s*. Add only an apostrophe to plural nouns ending in *–s*. Look at these examples:

Singular noun or indefinite pronoun	Plural noun not ending in –s	Plural noun ending in –s
the car's motor, everyone's name, James's father	the children's mother	the dogs' collars

- Use *–'s* to form the plural of words, letters, and numbers used as words. Example: *How many s's are in that word?*

Quotation marks are used to show the exact words of a speaker and to set off certain titles (for example, song titles). Place commas and periods within quotation marks. Place other punctuation within the quotation marks only when the punctuation is part of the quotation. Look at these examples:

Commas and periods go inside	Other punctuation not part of the quotation goes outside	Punctuation that's part of the quotation goes inside
"I dislike washing my car," she complained.	I am excited about singing "The Star-Spangled Banner"!	"Stop that!" the teacher demanded.

Capitalization

Capitalization tells the reader when a sentence begins and when specific persons, places, or things are being named:

- Capitalize the first word of a sentence. Example: *This sentence begins with a capital letter.*
- Capitalize proper nouns. Example: *I live in Florida.*
- Capitalize adjectives derived from proper nouns. Example: *My English teacher has a good sense of humor.*
- Capitalize titles when they precede a proper name. Example: *The memo came from Dean Jacobson.*

In modern writing, the trend is toward *less* capitalization. Therefore, as a general rule, do not capitalize the following words (unless a specific convention given in the previous capitalization guidelines requires it):

- Common names or adjectives used in place of proper nouns or adjectives
- Compass directions: north, south, east, west, southeast, and so on that do not refer to specific geographic locations
- The names of the seasons: spring, summer, fall/autumn, winter
- Titles (president, major, dean) that do not directly precede a proper name
  Exception: The title of President of the United States is capitalized.
- Relationships (mom, dad, aunt, uncle, cousin) preceded by a possessive and not used as part of a proper name

Test Yourself

Directions: For questions 1–3, select the answer choice that corrects an error in the underlined portion. If there is no error, choose D indicating "No change is necessary."

---

1. The <u>Dean</u> of the College of Education
      A

   <u>occasionally</u> likes to visit the <u>professors'</u>
      B   C

   classes.

   A. dean
   B. ocassionally
   C. professor's
   D. No change is necessary.

2. When the guest of honor <u>arrived, everyone</u> in
                          A

   the room <u>cheered</u> <u>loud</u> and with gusto.
          B   C

   A. arrived everyone
   B. cheared
   C. loudly
   D. No change is necessary.

3. As the curtain <u>closes</u>, the audience rose and
                 A

   gave the performance a standing ovation.

   A. is closing
   B. closed
   C. is closed
   D. No change is necessary.

4. Choose the option that is punctuated correctly.

   A. The bridesmaids' dresses for the bride's three sisters were the boldest blue color that I have ever seen.
   B. The bridesmaid's dresses for the bride's three sisters were the boldest blue color that I have ever seen.
   C. The bridesmaids' dresses, for the bride's three sisters' were the boldest blue color that I have ever seen.
   D. The bridesmaids' dresses for the brides three sisters were the boldest blue color, that I have ever seen.

Answer Explanations for Test Yourself

1. **A.** The title *dean* at A should not be capitalized. Titles are capitalized when they precede proper names, but as a rule are not capitalized when used alone. The word *occasionally* at B is spelled correctly. The possessive word *professors'* is punctuated correctly. Add only an apostrophe to plural nouns ending in –*s*.

2. **C.** The word at C tells how everyone cheered, so it is an adverb. Change *loud* at C to *loudly* to make the sentence grammatically correct. A comma is needed at A to separate the introductory subordinate clause from the rest of the sentence. The word *cheered* at B is spelled correctly.

3. **B.** The tense of the verb in Choice **B** relates logically to the verb in the main clause. The verb tenses in Choices **A** and **C** do not. These choices result in a faulty tense shift in the sentence.

4. **A.** All punctuation in Choice **A** is correct. In Choice **B**, the word *bridesmaid's* needs to be *bridesmaids'*. To form the possessive of a plural noun ending in –*s*, add an apostrophe after the –*s*. In Choice **C**, the word *sisters'* should not have an apostrophe because no ownership is indicated for this word in the sentence. Also, in Choice **C**, no comma is needed after the word *dresses*. In Choice **D**, the word *brides* needs to be *bride's* because ownership is indicated for this word in the sentence. Also, in Choice **D**, no comma is needed after the word *color*.

Review for the GK Mathematics Subtest

The mathematics subtest of the FTCE GK Test consists of 45 multiple-choice questions, which you must complete in 100 minutes. Each test question requires that you choose from among four answer choices. You must click on the oval corresponding to your answer choice on the computer screen. The test center provides a 4-function calculator and a mathematics reference sheet for you to use during the test. You cannot bring written notes or scratch paper into the testing room.

The Math Review in This Study Guide

The mathematics review in this CliffsTestPrep Book is organized around the five mathematics areas tested on the FTCE GK Test:

1. Operations and Numeration
2. Measurement
3. Geometry
4. Algebraic Reasoning
5. Probability and Data Analysis

Each area has a general review and sample questions. The review sections present math concepts with examples and explanations for each area. "Test Yourself" exercises are found throughout the review sections. These exercises give you an opportunity to practice what you just learned. The answers to the "Test Yourself" exercises are found immediately following the set of exercises. When doing the "Test Yourself" exercises, you should cover up the answers. Then check your answers when you've finished the exercises. The sample questions are multiple-choice questions that are similar to what you might expect to see on the FTCE GK Test. The answer explanations for the sample questions are provided immediately after the questions. A mathematics reference sheet is included on the next two pages.

Mathematics Reference Sheet

Area

Triangle

$A = \frac{1}{2}bh$

Rectangle

$A = lw$

Trapezoid

$A = \frac{1}{2}h(b_1 + b_2)$

Parallelogram

$A = bh$

Circle

$A = \pi r^2$
$C = \pi d = 2\pi r$

Key	
b = base	d = diameter
h = height	r = radius
l = length	A = area
w = width	C = circumference
$S.A.$ = surface area	V = volume
	B = area of base

Use $\pi = 3.14$ or $\frac{22}{7}$

Surface Area

1. Surface area of a prism or pyramid = the sum of the areas of all faces of the figure.

2. Surface area of a cylinder = the sum of the areas of the two bases + the area of its rectangular wrap.

$S.A. = 2(\pi r^2) + (2\pi r)h$

3. Surface area of a sphere: $S.A. = 4\pi r^2$

Volume

1. Volume of a prism or cylinder equals (Area of the Base) times (height): $V = Bh$
2. Volume of a pyramid or cone equals $\frac{1}{3}$ times (Area of the Base) times (height): $V = \frac{1}{3}Bh$
3. Volume of a sphere: $V = \frac{4}{3}\pi r^3$

Mathematics Reference Sheet, continued

Pythagorean Theorem:

$a^2 + b^2 = c^2$

Simple Interest Formula:

$I = prt$

I = simple interest, p = principal, r = rate, t = time

Distance Formula:

$d = rt$

d = distance, r = rate, t = time

Given a line containing points (x_1, y_1) and (x_2, y_2),

- Slope of line $= \dfrac{y_2 - y_1}{x_2 - x_1}$
- Distance between two points $= \sqrt{(x_2 - x_1)^2 + (y_2 - y_1)^2}$
- Midpoint between two points $= \left(\dfrac{x_1 + x_2}{2}, \dfrac{y_1 + y_2}{2}\right)$

Conversions	
1 yard = 3 feet = 36 inches	1 cup = 8 fluid ounces
1 mile = 1,760 yards = 5,280 feet	1 pint = 2 cups
1 acre = 43,560 square feet	1 quart = 2 pints
1 hour = 60 minutes	1 gallon = 4 quarts
1 minute = 60 seconds	1 pound = 16 ounces
	1 ton = 2,000 pounds
1 liter = 1000 milliliters = 1000 cubic centimeters	
1 meter = 100 centimeters = 1000 millimeters	
1 kilometer = 1000 meters	
1 gram = 1000 milligrams	
1 kilogram = 1000 grams	

Note: Metric numbers with four digits are written without a comma (e.g., 2543 grams).
For metric numbers with more than four digits, a space is used instead of a comma (e.g., 24 300 liters).

Numeration and Operations

According to the *Competencies and Skills Required for Teacher Certification in Florida, Fifteenth Edition* (available at www.fldoe.org/asp/ftce/ftcecomp.asp#Fifteenth), the competencies/skills you should be able to do for this area of mathematics are the following:

- Compare and order real numbers (that is, fractions, decimals, integers, percents, irrational numbers, and numbers expressed in exponential or scientific notation).
- Select and use appropriate operations to solve real-world problems involving rational numbers (that is, whole numbers, integers, fractions, decimals, and percents).
- Solve problems involving number theory concepts including primes, composites, factors, and multiples.
- Simplify expressions using the order of operations.

What Are Operations?

Addition, subtraction, multiplication, and **division** are the four basic arithmetic operations. Each of the operations has special symbolism and terminology associated with it. Make it a point to learn this symbolism and terminology, so that you can better understand mathematical "talk." Table 3.1 shows the terminology and symbolism you need to know.

Table 3.1: Terminology and Symbolism for the Four Basic Arithmetic Operations			
Operation	*Symbols(s) Used*	*Name of Parts*	*Example*
Addition	+ (plus sign)	addend + addend = sum	$4 + 9 = 13$
Subtraction	− (minus sign)	sum − addend = difference	$13 - 4 = 9$
Multiplication	× (times sign)	factor × factor = product	$10 \times 5 = 50$
	· (raised dot)	factor · factor = product	$10 \cdot 5 = 50$
	( )( ) parentheses	(factor)(factor) = product	$(10)(5) = 50$
Division	÷ (division sign)	dividend ÷ divisor = quotient	$50 \div 10 = 5$
	$\overline{)}$ (long division symbol)	$\text{divisor}\overline{)\text{dividend}}^{\text{quotient}}$	$10\overline{)50}^{\,5}$
	/ (fraction bar or slash)	$\dfrac{\text{dividend}}{\text{divisor}} = \text{quotient}$	$\dfrac{50}{10} = 5$
		dividend/divisor = quotient	$50/10 = 5$

As you can see from the examples in Table 3.1, addition and subtraction "undo" each other. Mathematicians express this relationship by saying that addition and subtraction are **inverses** of each other. Similarly, multiplication and division are **inverses** of each other; they "undo" each other, *as long as division by 0 is not involved.*

You must be *very* careful when division involves zero. Zero can be a dividend; that is, you can divide a nonzero number into zero—the quotient will be zero. However, 0 *cannot* be a divisor, which means that you *cannot* divide by 0. The quotient of any number divided by zero has no meaning; that is, **division by zero is undefined—you can't do it!** Table 3.2 provides a summary of division involving zero.

Table 3.2: Division Involving Zero		
Rule	**Meaning**	**Example**
You <u>cannot</u> divide by zero.	any number $\div$ 0 = can't do it!	$6 \div 0$ = can't do it! $0 \div 0$ = can't do it!
	$\dfrac{\text{any number}}{0}$ = can't do it!	$\dfrac{25}{0}$ = can't do it! $\dfrac{0}{0}$ = can't do it!
	$0\overline{)\text{any number}}$ = can't do it!	$0\overline{)14}$ = can't do it! $0\overline{)0}$ = can't do it!
You <u>can</u> divide zero by a nonzero number. The quotient is <u>always</u> zero.	$0 \div$ any nonzero number = 0	$0 \div 8 = 0$
	$\dfrac{0}{\text{any nonzero number}} = 0$	$\dfrac{0}{15} = 0$
	any nonzero number $\overline{)0}$	$3\overline{)0}$

Test Yourself

1. The parts of an addition problem are _____ + _____ = _____ .

2. The answer to a subtraction problem is the _____ .

3. The numbers that are multiplied together in a multiplication problem are _____ .

4. The answer to a multiplication problem is the _____ .

5. Zero _____ (can, cannot) be a divisor in a division problem.

6. $30 \div 0 = $ _____ .

7. $0 \div 30 = $ _____ .

8. $\dfrac{0}{17} = $ _____ .

9. $\dfrac{17}{0} = $ _____ .

10. $\dfrac{0}{0} = $ _____ .

Answers

1. addend, addend, sum
2. difference
3. factors
4. product
5. cannot
6. can't do it!
7. 0
8. 0
9. can't do it!
10. can't do it!

What Are Counting Numbers?

The **counting numbers** (also called the **natural numbers**) are 1, 2, 3, and so on. Counting numbers that are greater than 1 are either *prime* or *composite*. A **prime number** is a whole number greater than 1 that has exactly two distinct factors: itself and 1. Thus, the primes are 2, 3, 5, 7, 11, 13, and so on.

The counting numbers greater than 1 that are *not* prime are the **composite numbers.** They are 4, 6, 8, 9, 10, 12, and so on.

The counting number 1 is neither prime nor composite.

Besides classifying a counting number as prime or composite, a counting number can be classified as either *even* or *odd*. Counting numbers that divide evenly by 2 are **even.** The **even counting numbers** are 2, 4, 6, 8, and so on.

Counting numbers that do *not* divide evenly by 2 are **odd.** The **odd counting numbers** are 1, 3, 5, 7, 9, and so on.

The **Fundamental Theorem of Arithmetic** states that every counting number ≥ 2 is either a prime or can be factored into a product of primes in one and only one way, except for the order in which the factors appear. To find the prime factors of a number, you can use a **factor "tree."** Here is an example of using a factor tree to find the prime factors of the number 36.

The numbers at the bottom of each branch of the tree are the prime factors of 36—you cannot factor them any further. So the prime factors of 36 are 2 and 3. You can write 36 as the product of its prime factors like this: $36 = 2 \cdot 2 \cdot 3 \cdot 3$.

Divisibility rules can help with factoring numbers. A counting number is **divisible by** another counting number if, after dividing by that number, the remainder is zero. You write $a|b$ to mean a divides b evenly or, equivalently, b "is divisible by" a. For example $3|36$ means 36 is divisible by 3. Therefore, 3 is a factor of 36. Table 3.3 shows some common divisibility rules that you will find helpful.

Table 3.3 Some Common Divisibility Rules		
Divisibility by	**Rule**	**Example**
2	A number is divisible by 2 if and only if the last digit of the number is even.	2|2,347,854 since 4 (the last digit) is even.
3	A number is divisible by 3 if and only if the sum of its digits is divisible by 3.	3|151,515 since 3 divides 1 + 5 + 1 + 5 + 1 + 5 = 18 (the sum of the digits).
4	A number is divisible by 4 if and only if the last 2 digits form a number that is divisible by 4.	4|47,816 since 4 divides 16 (the number formed by the last two digits).
5	A number is divisible by 5 if and only if the last digit of the number is 0 or 5.	5|42,115 since the last digit is 5.
6	A number is divisible by 6 if and only if it is divisible by both 2 and 3.	6|18,122,124 since 2|18,122,124 (the last digit is even) and 3|18,122,124 (21, the sum of the digits, is divisible by 3).
7	To test for divisibility by 7, double the last digit and subtract the product from the number formed by the remaining digits. If the result is a number divisible by 7, the original number is also divisible by 7.	7|875 since 87-10 = 77, which is divisible by 7.
8	A number is divisible by 8 if and only if the last 3 digits form a number that is divisible by 8.	8|55,864 since 8 divides 864 (the number formed by the last three digits).
9	A number is divisible by 9 if and only if the sum of its digits is divisible by 9.	9|151,515 since 9 divides 1 + 5 + 1 + 5 + 1 + 5 = 18 (the sum of the digits).
10	A number is divisible by 10 if and only if the last digit of the number is 0.	10|66,660 since the last digit is 0.

The **greatest common factor** of two or more counting numbers is the greatest number that will divide evenly into each of the counting numbers. It can be obtained by listing the factors of each number, and then selecting the greatest factor that appears on both lists. The greatest common factor of two counting numbers m and n is denoted **GCF (m, n)**. For example, the greatest common factor of 24 and 36 is denoted GCF (24, 36). To find GCF (24, 36), first, list the factors of each of these numbers. The factors of 24 are 1, 2, 3, 4, 6, 8, 12, and 24; the factors of 36 are 1, 2, 3, 4, 6, 9, 12, 18, and 36. Next, select the greatest common factor that appears on both lists, namely, 12; therefore, GCF (24, 36) is 12.

The **least common multiple** of a set of counting numbers is the least product that is a multiple of each of the counting numbers. It can be obtained by factoring each counting number and building a product consisting of each factor the *most* number of times it appears as a factor in any *one* of the counting numbers in the set. The least common multiple of two counting numbers m and n is denoted **LCM (m,n)**. For example, $24 = 2 \cdot 2 \cdot 2 \cdot 3$ and $36 = 2 \cdot 2 \cdot 3 \cdot 3$, so LCM (24, 36) = $\underset{\text{3 factors of 2}}{2 \cdot 2 \cdot 2} \cdot \underset{\text{2 factors of 3}}{3 \cdot 3} = 72$.

Tip: The least common multiple of a set of numbers is the least number that is divisible by each of the numbers in the set.

Test Yourself

1. A prime number has exactly _____ distinct factors.

2. The number 1 is prime. True or False?

3. The number 2 is prime. True or False?

4. The number 15 is composite. True or False?

5. The number zero is even. True or False?

6. The number 414 is divisible by 4. True or False?

7. The number 414 is divisible by 3. True or False?

8. The prime factorization of 96 = _____.

9. GCF (18, 24) = _____ .

10. LCM (18, 24) = _____.

Answers

1. two

2. False. The counting number 1 is neither prime nor composite.

3. True, because it has only two factors: 2 and 1.

4. True, because it has more than two factors: 15, 5, 3, and 1.

5. True, because $\frac{0}{2} = 0$, meaning that 0 is divisible by 2.

6. False, because 14 (the number formed by the last 2 digits of 414) is not divisible by 4.

7. True, because 3 divides 4 + 1 + 4 = 9 (the sum of the digits of the number 414).

8. The prime factorization of 96 = $2 \cdot 2 \cdot 2 \cdot 2 \cdot 2 \cdot 3$.

9. GCF (18, 24) = 6

10. LCM (18, 24) = 72

What Are Rational Numbers?

The **rational numbers** are the numbers that you are familiar with from school and from your everyday experiences with numbers. The rational numbers include the whole numbers, integers, positive and negative fractions, decimals, and percents.

The **whole numbers** are the counting numbers and zero: 0, 1, 2, 3, . . .

The three dots to the right of the number 3 mean that you are to keep going in the same manner.

The **integers** are the numbers . . . –3, –2, –1, 0, 1, 2, 3, . . .

Integers are either **positive** (1, 2, 3, . . .), **negative** (. . . –3, –2, –1), or **zero.** Negative numbers have a small horizontal line (–) on the left of the number. Notice that you do not have to write the + sign on positive numbers (although it's not wrong to do so). If no sign is written with a number, then you know that it is a positive number. The number zero is neither positive nor negative.

Integers that are divisible by 2 are **even integers.** The **even integers** are . . . , –8, –6, –4, –2, 0, 2, 4, 6, 8, . . .

Notice that zero is an even integer because 0 divided by 2 is 0 (no remainder).

Integers that are *not* divisible by 2 are **odd integers.** The **odd integers** are . . . , –7, –5, –3, –1, 1, 3, 5, 7, . . .

The **rational numbers** are all the numbers that can be written as ratios of two integers, where zero is *not* the denominator of the ratio. In other words, the rational numbers include all the numbers that can be written as positive or negative fractions. Here are examples:

$\frac{3}{4}$ is a rational number: It is the ratio of two integers.

$\frac{-2}{5}$ is a rational number: It is the ratio of two integers. This rational number can be written as $-\frac{2}{5}$.

$\frac{9}{2}$ is a rational number: It is the ratio of two integers.

All the counting numbers, whole numbers, and integers are rational numbers because you can write each as a ratio whose denominator is 1. For instance,

$$\dots, -3 = \frac{-3}{1}, -2 = \frac{-2}{1}, -1 = \frac{-1}{1}, 0 = \frac{0}{1}, 1 = \frac{1}{1}, 2 = \frac{2}{1}, 3 = \frac{3}{1}, \dots$$

Rational numbers can be expressed as **fractions, decimals,** or **percents.**

Test Yourself

1. A rational number is the ratio of two _____, where zero is *not* the _____ of the ratio.

2. Which of the numbers in the following set are rational numbers? $\frac{2}{3}, 0, \frac{-1}{1}, 100, -\frac{4}{5}$

3. Is $\frac{0}{4}$ a rational number?

4. Is $\frac{12}{0}$ a rational number?

5. Which of the following sets of numbers are rational numbers? whole numbers, integers, positive and negative fractions, decimals, and percents.

Answers

1. integers, denominator

2. All of them

3. Yes, $\frac{0}{4} = 0$, which is a rational number.

4. No, $\frac{12}{0}$ has no meaning because you can't divide by zero.

5. All of them

What Are Fractions?

Fractions are used to express parts of a whole, for example, $\frac{3}{4}$ is a fraction. The **denominator,** the number below the **fraction bar (division line),** tells you the number of equal parts into which the whole has been divided. The **numerator,** the number above the **fraction bar,** tells how many equal parts you have.

The whole can be a single quantity or entity or the whole can be a set of objects or quantities. Here is an example when the whole is a single entity, a circle.

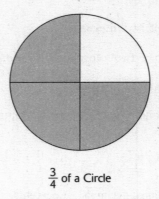

$\frac{3}{4}$ of a Circle

Here is an example when the whole is a set of 8 smiley faces.

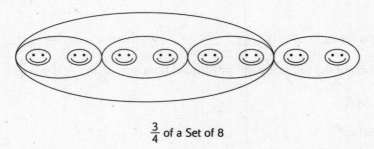

$\frac{3}{4}$ of a Set of 8

When you work with a fraction, you need to make sure you know what the whole for the fraction is. This isn't always easy because in some problems the whole shifts from one quantity to another quantity. Here is an example:

> What is $\frac{3}{4}$ of $\frac{1}{2}$?

To illustrate this problem, you must first show $\frac{1}{2}$ of a whole. Let's use Rectangle A for the whole.

Rectangle A

$\frac{1}{2}$ of Rectangle A

Next, you must find $\frac{3}{4}$ of this $\frac{1}{2}$. This means you must treat the $\frac{1}{2}$ of Rectangle A as a whole and divide it into 4 equal parts. Three of these 4 equal parts is $\frac{3}{4}$ of $\frac{1}{2}$.

Rectangle A

$\frac{3}{4}$ of $\frac{1}{2}$ of Rectangle A

Finally, you shift back to Rectangle A as the whole, to determine that the part shaded is $\frac{3}{8}$ of Rectangle A.

Rectangle A

$\frac{3}{8}$ of Rectangle A

Thus, $\frac{3}{4}$ of $\frac{1}{2} = \frac{3}{8}$.

Equivalent fractions are fractions that have the same value. For example, $\frac{1}{2}$ and $\frac{4}{8}$ are equivalent fractions. You can illustrate the equivalency as shown in the following.

$\frac{1}{2}$ of a Whole

$\frac{4}{8}$ of a Whole

The shaded portion is the same size in the two figures, which shows that $\frac{4}{8} = \frac{1}{2}$.

If the numerator and denominator of a fraction can be divided by the same number, you can **simplify** the fraction to an equivalent fraction in **lowest terms** by doing the division, as in $\frac{4}{8} = \frac{4 \div 4}{8 \div 4} = \frac{1}{2}$. The number you divide by is the greatest common factor (GCF) of the numerator and denominator. In this case, GCF (4, 8) = 4. It is the largest number that will divide evenly into both the numerator and denominator.

Other times when you are working with fractions, you may need to write a fraction as an equivalent fraction with a larger denominator. You can accomplish this by multiplying the numerator and denominator by the same whole number (greater than 1). For example, $\frac{3}{4} = \frac{3 \times 25}{4 \times 25} = \frac{75}{100}$.

It is important that you recognize that even though it takes two numerical components—a numerator and a denominator—to make a fraction, the fraction itself is just one number. Specifically, it is a rational number. For instance, $\frac{3}{4}$ is the rational number that lies between 0 and 1 on a number line as shown here.

Fractions like $\frac{1}{2}$, $\frac{3}{8}$, and $\frac{75}{100}$, in which the numerator is smaller than the denominator, are **proper fractions.** Fractions like $\frac{7}{4}$, $\frac{29}{8}$, and $\frac{6}{6}$, in which the numerator is greater than or equal to the denominator, are **improper fractions.** Any improper fraction has a value greater than or equal to one. A **mixed number** is the sum of a whole number and a fraction, written together like these examples: $1\frac{3}{4}$, $2\frac{1}{3}$, and $3\frac{5}{8}$. Although a mixed number is a sum, you don't put a plus sign in it; but you do say the word "and" in between the whole number and the fraction when you read it. For instance, $2\frac{1}{3}$ is read as "Two and one-third."

You can change an improper fraction to a mixed number or a whole number by dividing the numerator by the denominator and writing the remainder like this: $\frac{\text{remainder}}{\text{denominator}}$. For example, $\frac{7}{4} = 4\overline{)7}^{1R3} = 1\frac{3}{4}$.

You can change a mixed number to an improper fraction by multiplying the whole number part by the denominator of the fractional part, adding the numerator of the fractional part to the resulting product, and then placing the resulting sum over the denominator of the fractional part. For example, $2\frac{1}{3} = \frac{2 \times 3 + 1}{3} = \frac{6+1}{3} = \frac{7}{3}$.

What Are Decimals?

Decimals are rational numbers that are written using a **base-10 place-value system.** The value of a decimal number is based on the placement of the decimal point in the number as shown below.

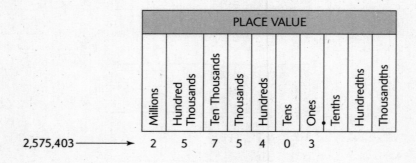

To interpret the value of a decimal number, look at each digit and determine the value it represents according to its place in the number. For example, the value of the number 2,575,403 is

2 millions + 5 hundred thousands + 7 ten thousands + 5 thousands + 4 hundreds + 0 tens + 3 ones

or

2,000,000 + 500,000 + 70,000 + 5,000 + 400 + 0 + 3.

Each digit has a **face value** and a **place value.** For example, in the number 2,575,403, starting at the decimal point (which is understood to be at the far right of a whole number) and counting left, the 4th digit and the 6th digit both have the same face value, namely 5. However, they represent different amounts because their place values are different. The 5 that is the 4th digit from the decimal point represents 5,000, while the 5 that is the 6th digit from the decimal point represents 500,000. Place value makes a big difference!

Tip: If no decimal point is shown in a number, the decimal point is understood to be to the immediate right of the rightmost digit.

To write numbers that are less than 1, you must recognize that numbers to the right of the decimal point represent fractions whose denominators are powers of 10: 10, 100, 1,000, and so on. Here are examples.

PLACE VALUE										
Millions	Hundred Thousands	Ten Thousands	Thousands	Hundreds	Tens	Ones	Tenths	Hundredths	Thousandths

0.7 ⟶ 0 7

0.07 ⟶ 0 0 7

0.007 ⟶ 0 0 0 7

The value of 0.7 is 7 tenths or $\frac{7}{10}$.

The value of 0.07 is 7 hundredths or $\frac{7}{100}$.

The value of 0.007 is 7 thousandths or $\frac{7}{1000}$.

Tip: Notice that the place values after the decimal point start with tenths.

In a decimal number, the number of digits to the right of the decimal point up to and including the final digit is the number of decimal places in the number. For instance, 0.7 has one decimal place, 0.07 has two decimal places, and 0.007 has three decimal places. Other examples are 35.62, which has two decimal places, and 4.250, which has three decimal places.

You can obtain the decimal representation of a fractional number by dividing the numerator by the denominator.

Tip: To remember that the denominator is the divisor, notice that both of these words begin with the letter d. A visual way to remember is to think of the fraction as a cowhand (numerator) riding a horse (denominator): $\frac{\text{cowhand (numerator)}}{\text{horse (denominator)}}$. **The horse stays outside when the cowhand goes into the bunkhouse, represented by the long division symbol ($\overline{)}$): denominator (horse)$\overline{)\text{numerator (cowhand)}}$.**

Here are examples.

$$\frac{1}{2} = 0.5 \text{ because } \frac{1}{2} = 2\overline{)1.0}^{\,0.5} \;;\; \frac{3}{5} = 0.6 \text{ because } \frac{3}{5} = 5\overline{)3.0}^{\,0.6} \;;\; \text{and } \frac{7}{4} = 1.75 \text{ because } \frac{7}{4} = 4\overline{)7.00}^{\,1.75}$$

In these cases, the decimal **terminates** (eventually has a zero remainder). For some rational numbers, the decimal keeps going, but in a block of one or more digits that repeats over and over again. These decimals are **repeating.**

Here is an example of a repeating decimal.

$$\frac{2}{3} = 3\overline{)2.000...}^{\,0.666...}$$

No matter how long you continue to add zeroes and divide, the 6s in the quotient continue without end. Put a bar over the repeating digit (or digits when more than one digit repeats) to indicate the repetition. Thus, $\frac{2}{3} = 0.\bar{6}$. All terminating and repeating decimals are rational numbers.

How Do You Round a Number?

To **round a number** to a specified place value, find the digit in the place value to which you want to round and look at the digit to the immediate right of it. If that digit is *less than* 5, do not change the digit in the specified place value but change all digits to the right of the specified place value digit to zero. If the digit to the immediate right of the specified place value digit is *greater than* or equal to 5, add one to the digit in the specified place value and change all digits to the right of the specified place value digit to zero. Here are examples.

253,410 rounded to the nearest thousand is 253,000.

0.8729 rounded to the nearest thousandth is 0.8730 = 0.873.

3.452171 rounded to the nearest tenth is 3.50000 = 3.5.

Note: When decimals repeat, they are usually rounded to a specified degree of accuracy; for example, 0.666. . . is 0.67 when rounded to two decimal places.

What Are Percents?

You also can write rational numbers as **percents.** Percent means "per hundred." The percent sign is a short way of writing $\frac{1}{100}$ or 0.01. When you see a percent sign, you can substitute $\frac{1}{100}$ or 0.01 for the percent sign.

A percent is a way of writing a fraction as an equivalent fraction in which the denominator is 100. Thus, $25\% = 25 \cdot \frac{1}{100} = \frac{25}{100}$. You can think of percents as special ways to write ordinary decimals or fractions. For instance, 100% is just a special way to write the number 1, because $100\% = 100 \cdot \frac{1}{100} = \frac{100}{100} = 1$. If you have 100% of something, you have all of it. Here are examples.

100% of a Circle

100% of a Set of 8

100% of a Rectangle

A percent that is less than 100% is less than 1. When you have less than 100% of something, you have less than the whole thing. Here are examples.

75% of a Circle

75% of a Set of 8

50% of a Rectangle

A percent that is greater than 100% is greater than 1. When you have more than 100% of something, you have more than the whole thing. Here are examples.

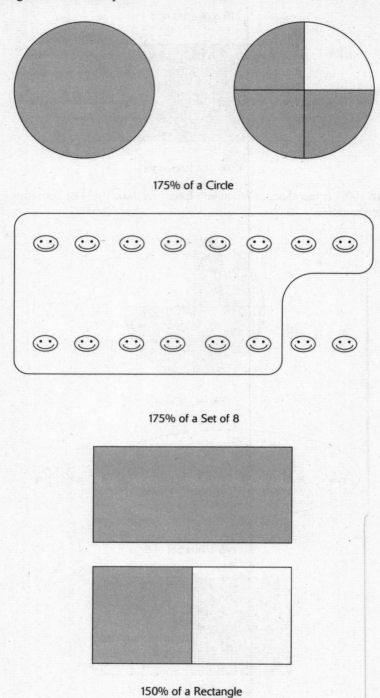

175% of a Circle

175% of a Set of 8

150% of a Rectangle

Any percent can be written as an equivalent fraction by writing the number in front of the percent sign as the numerator of a fraction in which the denominator is 100. The resulting fraction may then be simplified to lowest terms, if possible. Here are examples.

$$5\% = \frac{5}{100} = \frac{5 \div 5}{100 \div 5} = \frac{1}{20}$$

$$25\% = \frac{25}{100} = \frac{25 \div 25}{100 \div 25} = \frac{1}{4}$$

$$50\% = \frac{50}{100} = \frac{50 \div 50}{100 \div 50} = \frac{1}{2}$$

$$125\% = \frac{125}{100} = \frac{125 \div 25}{100 \div 25} = \frac{5}{4} = 1\frac{1}{4}$$

When percents contain decimal fractions, multiply the numerator and denominator by 10, 100, or 1,000, and so on, to remove the decimal in the numerator and then simplify the resulting fraction, if possible. Here are examples.

$$12.5\% = \frac{12.5}{100} = \frac{12.5 \times 10}{100 \times 10} = \frac{125}{1000} = \frac{125 \div 125}{1000 \div 125} = \frac{1}{8}$$

$$0.25\% = \frac{0.25}{100} = \frac{0.25 \times 100}{100 \times 100} = \frac{25}{10000} = \frac{25 \div 25}{10000 \div 25} = \frac{1}{400}$$

If a percent contains a simple common fraction, multiply the fraction by $\frac{1}{100}$ and then simplify, if possible. Here is an example.

$$\frac{1}{4}\% = \frac{1}{4} \times \frac{1}{100} = \frac{1}{400}$$

When percents contain mixed fractions, change the mixed fraction to an improper fraction, use $\frac{1}{100}$ for the percent sign, and then multiply and simplify, if possible. Here are examples.

$$12\frac{1}{2}\% = \frac{25}{2}\% = \frac{25}{2} \times \frac{1}{100} = \frac{25}{200} = \frac{25 \div 25}{200 \div 25} = \frac{1}{8}$$

$$33\frac{1}{3}\% = \frac{100}{3}\% = \frac{100}{3} \times \frac{1}{100} = \frac{\overset{1}{\cancel{100}}}{3} \times \frac{1}{\underset{1}{\cancel{100}}} = \frac{1}{3}$$

A percent can be written as an equivalent decimal number by changing it to an equivalent fraction in which the denominator is 100, and then dividing by 100. For example, $75\% = \frac{75}{100} = 100\overline{)75.00}^{\,0.75}$. A shortcut for this process is to move the decimal point two places to the left (which is the same as dividing by 100) and drop the percent sign. Here are examples.

$$25\% = 0.25$$
$$32\% = 0.32$$
$$45.5\% = 0.455$$
$$8\% = 0.08$$
$$200\% = 2.00 = 2$$

To write a decimal number in percent form, move the decimal point two places to the right and attach the percent sign (%) at the end. Why does this make sense? Recall that the percent sign is a short way to write $\frac{1}{100}$, which means 1 divided by 100. When you move the decimal place in your number two places to the right, you are multiplying by 100. Since the percent sign has division by 100 built into it, when you put the percent sign at the end of the number, you undo the multiplication by 100 that you did earlier. Thus, the value of the number does not change. Here are examples.

$$0.45 = 45\%$$
$$0.01 = 1\%$$
$$0.125 = 12.5\%$$
$$2 = 2.00 = 200\%$$
$$0.0025 = 0.25\%$$

Tip: Notice that the % sign is equivalent to two decimal places. When your number "gives up" two decimal places, you replace the two decimal places with a % sign.

To write a fraction in percent form, first convert the fraction to a decimal number by performing the indicated division and then change the resulting decimal number to a percent. When the quotient is a repeating decimal number, carry the division to two places, and then write the remainder as a fraction like this: $\frac{\text{remainder}}{\text{divisor}}$. Here are examples.

$$\frac{1}{4} = 4\overline{)1.00}^{\,0.25} = 0.25 = 25\%$$

$$\frac{3}{5} = 5\overline{)3.00}^{\,0.60} = 0.60 = 60\%$$

$$\frac{5}{8} = 8\overline{)5.000}^{\,0.125} = 0.125 = 12.5\%$$

$$\frac{1}{3} = 3\overline{)1.00}^{\,0.33R1} = 0.33\frac{1}{3} = 33\frac{1}{3}\%$$

Before you take the FTCE GK Test, you should memorize the following list of common percents with their fraction and decimal equivalents. Make a set of flashcards to carry with you, and drill on these when you have spare time.

$$100\% = 1.00 = 1,\ 75\% = 0.75 = \frac{3}{4},\ 50\% = 0.50 = 0.5 = \frac{1}{2},\ 25\% = 0.25 = \frac{1}{4}$$

$$90\% = 0.90 = 0.9 = \frac{9}{10},\ 80\% = 0.80 = 0.8 = \frac{4}{5},\ 70\% = 0.70 = 0.7 = \frac{7}{10},\ 60\% = 0.60 = 0.6 = \frac{3}{5}$$

$$40\% = 0.40 = 0.4 = \frac{2}{5},\ 30\% = 0.30 = 0.3 = \frac{3}{10},\ 20\% = 0.20 = 0.2 = \frac{1}{5},\ 10\% = 0.10 = 0.1 = \frac{1}{10}$$

$$87\frac{1}{2}\% = 0.875 = \frac{7}{8},\ 62\frac{1}{2}\% = 0.625 = \frac{5}{8},\ 37\frac{1}{2}\% = 0.375 = \frac{3}{8},\ 12\frac{1}{2}\% = 0.125 = \frac{1}{8}$$

$$66\frac{2}{3}\% = 0.66\frac{2}{3} = \frac{2}{3},\ 33\frac{1}{3}\% = 0.33\frac{1}{3} = \frac{1}{3}$$

$$5\% = 0.05 = \frac{1}{20},\ 4\% = 0.04 = \frac{1}{25},\ 1\% = 0.01 = \frac{1}{100}$$

Test Yourself

1. In the fraction $\frac{3}{10}$, the whole is divided into _____ equal parts. How many equal parts do you have?

2. Which of the following fractions, $\frac{30}{100}, \frac{6}{10}, \frac{12}{20}$, are equivalent to $\frac{3}{5}$?

3. What is the greatest common factor of 16 and 24? Simplify the fraction $\frac{16}{24}$ to lowest terms by dividing the numerator and denominator by the GCF (16, 24).

4. Which of the following fractions, $\frac{20}{17}, 1\frac{3}{5}, \frac{12}{24}, \frac{4}{4}$, are improper fractions?

5. Change $\frac{8}{5}$ to a mixed fraction.

6. In the number 564.27, the 6 represents what value?

7. Write the fraction $\frac{4}{5}$ as a percent and as a decimal.

8. Write 0.34 as a percent.

9. Write 73.5% as a decimal number.

10. Which of the following are rational numbers?

    $\frac{3}{8}$, 0, 9.3, $\frac{-7}{0}$, 225%, -5, 100, $-\frac{20}{17}$, $\frac{9}{0}$, -0.4, $0.\bar{3}$, 100%, $1\frac{3}{5}$, $\frac{12}{24}$, $\frac{4}{4}$, 0.85

Answers

1. 10, 3

2. $\frac{6}{10}$, because $\frac{3}{5} = \frac{3 \times 2}{5 \times 2} = \frac{6}{10}$; and $\frac{12}{20}$, because $\frac{3}{5} = \frac{3 \times 4}{5 \times 4} = \frac{12}{20}$.

3. The greatest common factor of 16 and 24 is the greatest number that will divide into both 16 and 24 evenly. The factors of 16 are 1, 2, 4, 8, and 16. The factors of 24 are 1, 2, 3, 4, 6, 8, 12, and 24. Looking at the two lists of factors, you can see that 8 is the greatest factor that appears in both lists. Thus, GCF (16, 24) = 8;
   $\frac{16}{24} = \frac{16 \div 8}{24 \div 8} = \frac{2}{3}$.

4. $\frac{20}{17}$ and $\frac{4}{4}$

5. $\frac{8}{5} = 5\overline{)8}^{1R3} = 1\frac{3}{5}$

6. 6 tens or 60

7. $\frac{4}{5} = 5\overline{)4.00}^{0.80} = 0.80 = 80\%$

8. $0.34 = 34\%$

9. $73.5\% = 0.735$

10. All of them, except $\frac{-7}{0}$ and $\frac{9}{0}$ (which have no meaning because you can't divide by zero).

What Are Irrational Numbers?

Irrational numbers are numbers that cannot be written as the ratio of two integers. They have nonterminating, nonrepeating decimal representations. An example of an irrational number is the positive number that multiplies by itself to give 2. This number is the principal square root of 2. Usually, the square root symbol $\left(\sqrt{}\right)$ is used to show a principal square root. Thus, the principal square root of 2 is written like this: $\sqrt{2}$. Every number, except zero, has two square roots: a positive square root (designated the *principal* square root) and a negative square root. The other square root of 2 is $-\sqrt{2}$. It also is an irrational number. Note: Zero has only one square root, namely, zero (which is a rational number).

You cannot express $\sqrt{2}$ as the ratio of two integers, nor can you express it precisely in decimal form. No matter how many decimal places you use, you can only approximate $\sqrt{2}$. If you use the calculator to take the square root of the number 2, the display will show a decimal approximation of $\sqrt{2}$. An approximation of $\sqrt{2}$ to nine decimal places is 1.414213562. You can check to see whether this is $\sqrt{2}$ by multiplying it by itself to see whether you get 2.

$$1.414213562 \cdot 1.414213562 = 1.999999999$$

The number 1.999999999 is very close to 2, but it is not equal to 2. For most purposes, you can use 1.41 as an approximation for $\sqrt{2}$.

Even though an exact value for $\sqrt{2}$ cannot be determined, $\sqrt{2}$ is a number that occurs frequently in the real world. For instance, architects, carpenters, and other builders encounter $\sqrt{2}$ when they measure the length of the diagonal of a square that has sides with lengths of one unit as shown here.

The diagonal of such a square measures $\sqrt{2}$ units.

There are infinitely many other square roots that are irrational. Here are examples.

$$\sqrt{3}, \ \sqrt{10}, \ -\sqrt{24}, \ \sqrt{41}, \ \sqrt{89}$$

On the FTCE GK Test, you might have to estimate the value of an irrational square root by finding a pair of consecutive whole numbers that the square root lies between. Here is an example.

Estimate $\sqrt{41}$.

To do this problem, you need to find two consecutive integers such that the square of the first integer is less than 41 and the square of the second integer is greater than 41. Since $6 \times 6 = 36$, which is less than 41, and $7 \times 7 = 49$, which is greater than 41, the approximate value of $\sqrt{41}$ is between 6 and 7.

Another important irrational number is the number represented by the symbol π (pi). The number π also occurs frequently in the real world. For instance, π is the number you get when you divide the circumference of a circle by its diameter. The number π cannot be expressed as the ratio of two integers, nor can it be written as a terminating or repeating decimal. Here is an approximation of π to nine decimal places: 3.141592654.

Tip: There is no pattern to the digits of π. For the FTCE GK Test, use the rational number 3.14 as an approximation for the irrational number π in problems involving π.

Are All Square Roots Irrational?

Not all square roots are irrational. For example, the principal square root of 25, denoted $\sqrt{25}$, is not irrational because $\sqrt{25} = 5$, which is a rational number. When you want to find the principal square root of a number, try to find a nonnegative number that multiplies by itself to give the number. Since you will not be allowed to use a calculator with a square root key on the FTCE GK Test, you should memorize the following 20 principal square roots.

$$\sqrt{1} = 1, \sqrt{4} = 2, \sqrt{9} = 3, \sqrt{16} = 4, \sqrt{25} = 5, \sqrt{36} = 6, \sqrt{49} = 7, \sqrt{64} = 8, \sqrt{81} = 9, \sqrt{100} = 10,$$

$$\sqrt{121} = 11, \sqrt{144} = 12, \sqrt{169} = 13, \sqrt{196} = 14, \sqrt{225} = 15, \sqrt{256} = 16, \sqrt{289} = 17, \sqrt{400} = 20, \sqrt{625} = 25$$

Make yourself a set of flashcards or make matching cards for a game of "Memory." For the Memory game, turn all the cards face down. Turn up two cards at a time. If they match (for instance $\sqrt{144}$ and 12 are a match), remove the two cards; otherwise, turn them face down again. Repeat until you have matched all the cards.

Keep in mind, however, that every positive number has <u>two</u> square roots. The two square roots are equal in absolute value, but opposite in sign. For instance, the two square roots of 25 are 5 and –5, with 5 being the principal square root.

What Are the Real Numbers?

The real numbers are the numbers that describe the world in which we live. They are made up of all the rational numbers plus all the irrational numbers. You can show the real numbers on a number line. Every point on the real number line corresponds to a real number and every real number corresponds to a point on the real number line. Positive numbers are located to the right of zero, and negative numbers are to the left of zero. Here are examples.

Test Yourself

1. A real number is any _____ or _____ number.

2. Which of the following numbers are rational? –15, 0, $\sqrt{36}$, –3.45, 130%, $\sqrt{12}$, $\frac{6}{10}$, $-\frac{1}{20}$, 0.0005, π, 3.14

3. Which of the following numbers are irrational? –25, 0, $\sqrt{36}$, –125.4, 50%, $\sqrt{6}$, $-\frac{1}{200}$, 0.0005, π, 3.14, $0.\overline{3}$

4. Which of the following numbers are real numbers? –16, 0, $\sqrt{37}$, –13.25, 30%, $\sqrt{49}$, $\frac{3}{5}$, $-\frac{12}{24}$, 0.03, π

5. A decimal number that terminates is a _____ (rational, irrational) number.

6. A decimal number that repeats is a _____ (rational, irrational) number.

7. Nonterminating and nonrepeating decimal numbers are _____ (rational, irrational).

8. Estimate the value of $\sqrt{37}$.

9. The number $\sqrt{400}$ is _____ (rational, irrational).

10. Is $\frac{1}{0}$ a real number?

Answers

1. rational, irrational
2. All except $\sqrt{12}$ and π
3. $\sqrt{6}$ and π
4. All of them
5. rational
6. rational
7. irrational
8. between 6 and 7
9. rational, because $\sqrt{400} = 20$.
10. No, $\frac{1}{0}$ has no meaning because you can't divide by zero.

What Is Exponential Notation?

You can use **exponential notation** to write a compact version of a product in which the same number is repeated as a factor. The compact version for a product such as $10 \cdot 10 \cdot 10$ is 10^3. The ^{3}, which is written as a small number to the upper right, is the **exponent.** If the exponent is a whole number, it tells how many times 10, the **base,** is used as a factor. The resulting **exponential expression** is a **power** of the base. For instance, 10^3 is "10 to the third power." Here are other examples of exponential notation using **whole number exponents.**

$3 \times 3 \times 3 \times 3 = 3^4$, "3 to the fourth power"

$(2)\,(2)\,(2)\,(2)\,(2) = 2^5$, "2 to the fifth power"

$15 \cdot 15 = 15^2$, "15 to the second power," but more commonly—"15 squared"

$6 \cdot 6 \cdot 6 = 6^3$, "6 to the third power," but more commonly—"6 cubed"

$2 \cdot 2 \cdot 2 \cdot 5 \cdot 5 \cdot = 2^3 \cdot 5^2$, "2 cubed times 5 squared"

You **evaluate** exponential expressions that use whole number exponents by performing the indicated multiplication. Here are examples.

$3^4 = 3 \times 3 \times 3 \times 3 = 81$, "the fourth power of 3"

$2^5 = (2)\,(2)\,(2)\,(2)\,(2) = 32$, "the fifth power of 2"

$2^3 \cdot 5^2 = 2 \cdot 2 \cdot 2 \cdot 5 \cdot 5 = 8 \cdot 25 = 200$

Negative exponents are used to show reciprocals. Here are examples.

$$2^{-3} = \frac{1}{2^3}$$

$$10^{-4} = \frac{1}{10^4}$$

You evaluate exponential expressions that use negative (integer) exponents by writing the reciprocal, performing the indicated multiplication, and converting to a decimal (if desired). Here are examples.

$$2^{-3} = \frac{1}{2^3} = \frac{1}{8} = 0.125$$

$$10^{-4} = \frac{1}{10^4} = \frac{1}{10000} = 0.0001$$

Caution: Do not make the mistake of putting a negative sign in front of your answer. The negative part of the exponent means for you to write a reciprocal; it does not mean that you should make your answer negative.

You also can use **zero as an exponent.** When zero is the exponent on a *nonzero* number, the value of the exponential expression is 1. Here are examples.

$$3^0 = 1$$

$$\left(\frac{3}{4}\right)^0 = 1$$

$$(5.12)^0 = 1$$

What Is Scientific Notation?

Scientific notation is a way to write real numbers in a shortened form. When the numbers are very large or very small, scientific notation helps keep track of the decimal places and makes performing computations with these numbers easier.

A number written in scientific notation is written as a product of two factors. The first factor is a number that is greater than or equal to 1, but less than 10. The second factor is a power of 10. The idea is to make a product that will equal the given number. Any decimal number can be written in scientific notation. Here are examples of numbers written in scientific notation.

- Written in scientific notation, $34,000 = 3.4 \times 10^4$
- Written in scientific notation, $6.5 = 6.5 \times 10^0$
- Written in scientific notation, $1,235,000 = 1.235 \times 10^6$
- Written in scientific notation, $0.00047 = 4.7 \times 10^{-4}$
- Written in scientific notation, $0.00000001662 = 1.662 \times 10^{-8}$

Follow these steps to write a number in scientific notation:

1. Move the decimal point to the immediate right of the first *nonzero* digit of the number.
2. Indicate multiplication by the proper power of 10. The exponent for the power of 10 is the number of places you moved the decimal point in Step 1.

   If you moved the decimal point to the left, make the exponent positive. For example,

   $$34,000 = 3.\underset{\substack{\text{4 places} \\ \text{left}}}{\underline{4000}} \cdot 10^? = 3.4 \cdot 10^4$$

   If you moved the decimal point to the right, make the exponent negative. For example,

   $$0.00047 = 0\underset{\substack{\text{4 places} \\ \text{right}}}{\underline{.0004}}.7 \cdot 10^? = 4.7 \cdot 10^{-4}$$

As long as you make sure your first factor is greater than or equal to 1 and less than 10, you can always check to see whether you did it right by multiplying out your answer to see whether you get your original number back. Look at these examples.

$$3.4 \cdot 10^4 = 3.4 \cdot 10 \cdot 10 \cdot 10 \cdot 10 = 34,000 \checkmark$$

$$4.7 \cdot 10^{-4} = 4.7 \cdot \frac{1}{10^4} = 4.7 \cdot \frac{1}{10 \cdot 10 \cdot 10 \cdot 10} = 4.7 \cdot \frac{1}{10000} = \frac{4.7}{10000} = 0.00047 \checkmark$$

Test Yourself

1. In the exponential expression 4^3, _____ is the base and _____ is the exponent.

2. Write 144 as a product of its prime factors using exponential notation.

3. Evaluate 4^3.

4. Evaluate 5^{-4}.

5. Evaluate $\left(\dfrac{4}{5}\right)^0$.

6. Write 456,000,000 in scientific notation.

7. Write 0.000000975 in scientific notation.

8. Write $2.68 \cdot 10^9$ in standard form.

9. Write $1.572 \cdot 10^{-3}$ in standard form.

10. Exponential expressions such as 10^{-2}, 10^{-8}, 10^3, and 10^7 are _____ of 10.

Answers

1. 4, 3

2. $144 = 2 \cdot 2 \cdot 2 \cdot 2 \cdot 3 \cdot 3 = 2^4 \cdot 3^2$

3. $4^3 = 4 \cdot 4 \cdot 4 = 64$

4. $5^{-4} = \dfrac{1}{5^4} = \dfrac{1}{5 \cdot 5 \cdot 5 \cdot 5} = \dfrac{1}{625} = 0.0016$

5. $\left(\dfrac{4}{5}\right)^0 = 1$

6. $456,000,000 = 4.\underbrace{56000000}_{\substack{8\ \text{places} \\ \text{left}}} \cdot 10^7 = 4.56 \cdot 10^8$

7. $0.000000975 = 0\underbrace{0000009}_{\substack{7\ \text{places} \\ \text{right}}}.75 \cdot 10^7 = 9.75 \cdot 10^{-7}$

8. $2.68 \cdot 10^9 = 2.68 \cdot 10 \cdot 10 \cdot 10 \cdot 10 \cdot 10 \cdot 10 \cdot 10 \cdot 10 \cdot 10 = 2.68 \cdot 1,000,000,000 = 2,680,000,000$

9. $1.572 \cdot 10^{-3} = 1.572 \cdot \dfrac{1}{10^3} = 1.572 \cdot \dfrac{1}{10 \cdot 10 \cdot 10} = 1.572 \cdot \dfrac{1}{1000} = \dfrac{1.572}{1000} = 0.001572$

10. powers

How Do You Compare and Order Real Numbers?

For the FTCE GK Test you will need to know how to compare two or more real numbers to determine which is greater and which is less. For these questions, you will need to understand inequality symbols. Table 3.4 summarizes commonly used inequality symbols.

Table 3.4: Common Inequality Symbols

Inequality Symbol	Read As	Example
<	"is less than"	$0.5 < 1$
>	"is greater than"	$7.2 > 3.1$
≤	"is less than or equal to"	$9 \le 9$
≥	"is greater than or equal to"	$3\frac{4}{5} \ge 2$
≠	"is not equal to"	$0 \ne -10$

A number line is helpful when you want to compare real numbers. On a number line, positive numbers are located to the right of zero and negative numbers are to the left of zero.

When comparing two real numbers, think of their relative location on the number line. The number that is farther to the right is the greater number. For example, $-7 < -2$ because as you can see on the number line below, -2 lies to the right of -7 on the number line.

When you compare decimal numbers, compare the digits in each place value from left to right. If the decimal numbers do not have the same number of decimal places, annex or delete zeros after the last digit to the right of the decimal point to make the number of decimal places the same. Remember, annexing or deleting zeroes after the last digit to the right of the decimal point does not change the value of a decimal number.

For example, $2.5 = 2.50 = 2.500 = 2.5000$ and so on. Thus, $2.28 < 2.5$ because $2.28 < 2.50$.

When comparing fractions that have the same denominator, compare the numerators. For example, $\frac{7}{8} > \frac{5}{8}$ because $7 > 5$.

If the denominators of the fractions are not the same, write the fractions as equivalent fractions using a common denominator. For example, $\frac{3}{4} < \frac{7}{8}$ because $\frac{6}{8} < \frac{7}{8}$.

To compare a mixture of decimals and fractions, use the calculator to change the fractions to decimals. Round them off if they repeat. When you are instructed to order a list of numbers, you put them in order from **least to greatest** or from **greatest to least,** depending on how the question is stated. Here is an example.

Order the numbers $\frac{7}{8}$, 0.35, 4.8, and $\frac{2}{3}$ from least to greatest.

Before proceeding, write $\frac{7}{8}$ as a decimal by performing the division on the calculator like this: $7 \div 8 = 0.875$. Similarly, write $\frac{2}{3}$ as 0.667 (rounding to 3 places). Write 0.35 as 0.350 and 4.8 as 4.800. Next, compare the transformed numbers and put them in order as follows: 0.350, 0.667, 0.875, 4.800. Lastly, substitute the original numbers for their stand-ins to obtain the final answer: 0.35, $\frac{2}{3}$, $\frac{7}{8}$, 4.8.

Here are some tips on handling other situations that may occur in problems that involve comparing and ordering real numbers.

- If negative numbers are involved, they will be less than all the positive numbers and 0.
- If percents are involved, change the percents to decimals.
- If the problem contains exponential expressions, evaluate them before making comparisons.
- If you have square roots that are rational numbers, find the square roots before making comparisons.
- If you have irrational square roots, estimate the square roots before comparing them to other numbers.

> For example, order the following list of numbers from least to greatest.
>
> $\sqrt{37}$, 3^2, 4.39, -4, $\dfrac{9}{2}$

You do not have to proceed in the order the numbers are listed. Clearly, -4 is less than all the other numbers. Evaluate 3^2 to obtain 9. Write $\dfrac{9}{2}$ as 4.50. In order from least to greatest, these four numbers are -4, 4.39, 4.50, 9. Estimate $\sqrt{37}$ to be between 6 and 7, which puts it between 4.5 and 9 in the list. Thus, your final answer is -4, 4.39, $\dfrac{9}{2}$, $\sqrt{37}$, 3^2.

What Is Absolute Value?

The **absolute value** of a real number is its distance from zero on the number line. The absolute value is indicated by two vertical bars $\big(|\ \ |\big)$, one on either side of the number. For example, as shown below $|-6| = |6| = 6$ because each is 6 units from zero on the number line.

Here are additional examples:

$$|-17| = 17, \left|\frac{2}{3}\right| = \frac{2}{3}, |0| = 0, |-2.5| = 2.5, |245| = 245$$

Because distance always has a *nonnegative* (*positive* or *zero*) value, absolute value is always nonnegative. Furthermore, the absolute value of any *nonzero* number is positive. That is, |nonzero number| > 0.

If a negative sign immediately precedes an absolute value expression, always *first* determine the absolute value before applying the negative sign. Here are examples.

$$-|-17| = -17, -\left|\frac{2}{3}\right| = -\frac{2}{3}, -|-2.5| = -2.5, -|245| = -245$$

Tip: Don't try to "cancel out" the two negative signs when you have expressions like $-|-17|$. The absolute value bars keep you from doing that.

Test Yourself

For 1–13 insert <, >, or = in the blank to make a true statement.

1. -100 ____ -2

2. -25 ____ 0

3. -3.25 ____ -3.5

4. $3\frac{3}{4}$ ____ 3.34

5. $\frac{7}{15}$ ____ $\frac{4}{15}$

6. $\frac{1}{3}$ ____ 0.35

7. $\sqrt{37}$ ____ 5.4

8. 0.625 ____ $\frac{5}{8}$

9. 100% ____ 99

10. 3 ____ 200%

11. $|-64|$ ____ $|64|$

12. $-\left|-\frac{9}{10}\right|$ ____ $-\left|\frac{9}{10}\right|$

13. $|-5|$ ____ 0

14. Order the following list of numbers from least to greatest.
$-25, 0, \sqrt{36}, 50\%, \sqrt{6}$

15. Order the following list of numbers from least to greatest.
$3.256, \frac{3}{5}, -\frac{6}{7}, 3.9, 2^2$

Answers

1. <

2. <

3. >

4. >

5. >

6. <

7. >

8. =

9. <

10. >

11. =

12. <

13. >

14. $-25, 0, 50\%, \sqrt{6}, \sqrt{36}$

15. $-\dfrac{6}{7}, \dfrac{3}{5}, 3.256, 3.9, 2^2$

How Do You Add and Subtract Fractions and Decimals?

Even though you are allowed to use a calculator on the FTCE GK Test, you still need to know and understand how to add and subtract fractions and decimals. Understanding the process will make it less likely that you will make an error when performing a calculation and will also help you evaluate the reasonableness of the result of your computation.

Adding and Subtracting Fractions

Table 3.5 summarizes the rules for addition and subtraction with fractions.

Table 3.5: Rules for Addition and Subtraction of Fractions		
Operation	**Rule**	**Example**
Addition	1. To add two fractions that have the same denominator:	$\dfrac{5}{8} + \dfrac{1}{8} =$
	Add the numerators of the fractions to find the numerator of the answer, which is placed over the common denominator.	$\dfrac{5+1}{8} = \dfrac{6}{8}$
	Simplify to lowest terms, if possible.	$= \dfrac{6 \div 2}{8 \div 2} = \dfrac{3}{4}$
	2. To add two fractions that have different denominators:	$\dfrac{1}{4} + \dfrac{2}{3} =$
	Find a common denominator. The best choice for a common denominator is the least common multiple (LCM) of the denominators.	LCM (3, 4) = 12
	Write each fraction as an equivalent fraction having the common denominator as a denominator.	$\dfrac{1}{4} = \dfrac{1 \times 3}{4 \times 3} = \dfrac{3}{12}$ $\dfrac{2}{3} = \dfrac{2 \times 4}{3 \times 4} = \dfrac{8}{12}$
	Add the numerators of the transformed fractions to find the numerator of the answer, which is placed over the common denominator.	$\dfrac{1}{4} + \dfrac{2}{3} = \dfrac{3}{12} + \dfrac{8}{12} = \dfrac{3+8}{12} = \dfrac{11}{12}$
	Simplify to lowest terms, if possible.	Not needed in this problem.
Subtraction	1. To subtract two fractions that have the same denominator:	$\dfrac{5}{8} - \dfrac{1}{8} =$
	Subtract the numerators of the fractions to find the numerator of the answer, which is placed over the common denominator.	$\dfrac{5-1}{8} = \dfrac{4}{8}$
	Simplify to lowest terms, if needed.	$= \dfrac{4 \div 4}{8 \div 4} = \dfrac{1}{2}$
	2. To subtract two fractions that have different denominators:	$\dfrac{3}{4} - \dfrac{2}{3} =$
	Find a common denominator.	LCM (4, 3) = 12
	Write each fraction as an equivalent fraction having the common denominator as a denominator.	$\dfrac{3}{4} = \dfrac{3 \times 3}{4 \times 3} = \dfrac{9}{12}$ $\dfrac{2}{3} = \dfrac{2 \times 4}{3 \times 4} = \dfrac{8}{12}$
	Subtract the numerators of the transformed fractions to find the numerator of the answer, which is placed over the common denominator.	$\dfrac{3}{4} - \dfrac{2}{3} = \dfrac{9}{12} - \dfrac{8}{12} = \dfrac{9-8}{12} = \dfrac{1}{12}$
	Simplify to lowest terms, if possible.	Not needed in this problem.

Adding and Subtracting Decimals

Since you are allowed to use a calculator on the FTCE GK Test, you should do your decimal computations with the calculator when you take the test. Just to refresh your memory, Table 3.6 summarizes rules for addition and subtraction with decimals.

Table 3.6: Rules for Addition and Subtraction of Decimals		
Operation	**Rule**	**Example**
Addition	To add decimals: Line up the decimal points vertically. *Tip:* Fill in empty decimal places with zeroes to avoid adding incorrectly. Add as you would with whole numbers. Place the decimal point in the answer directly under the decimal points in the problem.	65.3 + 0.34 + 7.008 = 65.300 0.340 + 7.008 72.648
Subtraction	To subtract decimals: Line up the decimal points vertically, filling in empty decimal places with zeroes when needed. Subtract as you would with whole numbers. Place the decimal point in the answer directly under the decimal points in the problem.	9.4 − 3.65 = 9.40 − 3.65 5.75

Test Yourself

1. Find the greatest common factor of 16 and 20.

2. Find the sum: $\frac{3}{10} + \frac{1}{2} =$

3. Find the difference: $\frac{1}{2} - \frac{3}{10} =$

4. Find the sum: 0.125 + 7.2 + 320 + 4.23 =

5. Find the difference: 75.2 − 35.046 =

Answers

1. The largest number that will divide evenly into both 16 and 20 is 4, so GCF (16, 20) = 4.

2. $\frac{3}{10} + \frac{1}{2} = \frac{3}{10} + \frac{5}{10} = \frac{3+5}{10} = \frac{8}{10} = \frac{8 \div 2}{10 \div 2} = \frac{4}{5}$

3. $\frac{1}{2} - \frac{3}{10} = \frac{5}{10} - \frac{3}{10} = \frac{5-3}{10} = \frac{2}{10} = \frac{2 \div 2}{10 \div 2} = \frac{1}{5}$

4. 331.555

5. 40.154

How Do You Multiply and Divide Fractions and Decimals?

As with adding and subtracting, if you know and understand how to multiply and divide fractions and decimals, you will be less likely to make an error when doing these calculations, and you will be better able to evaluate the reasonableness of the results of your computations.

Multiplying and Dividing Fractions

Table 3.7 summarizes the rules for multiplication and division with fractions.

Table 3.7: Rules for Multiplication and Division of Fractions

Operation	Rule	Example
Multiplication	1. To multiply two proper fractions, two improper fractions, or a proper fraction and an improper fraction:	$\frac{1}{3} \times \frac{3}{4} =$
	Multiply the numerators to obtain the numerator of the product and multiply the denominators to find the denominator of the product.	$\frac{1 \times 3}{3 \times 4} = \frac{3}{12}$
	Simplify to lowest terms, if possible.	$= \frac{3 \div 3}{12 \div 3} = \frac{1}{4}$
	2. To multiply a fraction times a whole number:	$\frac{3}{4} \times 12 =$
	Write the whole number as an equivalent fraction with denominator 1, and then follow Multiplication Rule 1.	$\frac{3}{4} \times \frac{12}{1} = \frac{3 \times 12}{4 \times 1} = \frac{36}{4} = \frac{36 \div 4}{4 \div 4} = \frac{9}{1} = 9$
	3. To multiply fractions when mixed numbers are involved:	$2\frac{3}{4} \times 1\frac{1}{3} =$
	Change the mixed numbers to improper fractions and then follow Multiplication Rule 1.	$\frac{11}{4} \times \frac{4}{3} = \frac{11 \times 4}{4 \times 3} = \frac{44}{12}$
		$\frac{44 \div 4}{12 \div 4} = \frac{11}{3}$ or $3\frac{2}{3}$
Division	1. To divide two proper fractions, two improper fractions, or a proper fraction and an improper fraction:	$\frac{4}{3} \div \frac{1}{2} =$
	Multiply the first fraction by the reciprocal of the second fraction using Multiplication Rule 1.	$\frac{4}{3} \times \frac{2}{1} = \frac{8}{3}$ or $2\frac{2}{3}$
	2. To divide a fraction by a whole number:	$\frac{4}{5} \div 3 =$
	Write the whole number as an equivalent fraction with denominator 1, and then follow Division Rule 1.	$\frac{4}{5} \div \frac{3}{1} = \frac{4}{5} \times \frac{1}{3} = \frac{4 \times 1}{5 \times 3} = \frac{4}{15}$
	3. To divide fractions when mixed numbers are involved:	$2\frac{1}{3} \div 1\frac{1}{2} =$
	Change the mixed numbers to improper fractions, and then follow Division Rule 1.	$\frac{7}{3} \div \frac{3}{2} = \frac{7}{3} \times \frac{2}{3} = \frac{7 \times 2}{3 \times 3} = \frac{14}{9}$ or $1\frac{5}{9}$

Tip: Here is a mnemonic to help you remember division of fractions: "Keep, change, flip" meaning "<u>Keep</u> the first fraction, <u>change</u> division to multiplication, and then <u>flip</u> the second fraction to its reciprocal."

The process of multiplying or dividing fractions can be simplified by dividing out common factors, if any, before any multiplication is performed. For example, $\frac{1}{3} \times \frac{3}{4} = \frac{1}{1\cancel{3}} \times \frac{\cancel{3}^1}{4} = \frac{1}{4}$. Also, remember you do *not* have to find a common denominator when multiplying or dividing fractions.

Multiplying and Dividing Decimals

As mentioned before, you should do your decimal computations with the calculator when you take the FTCE GK Test. Just for review, Table 3.8 summarizes the rules for multiplication and division with decimals.

Table 3.8: Rules for Multiplication and Division of Decimals

Operation	Rule	Example
Multiplication	To multiply decimals:	$55.7 \times 0.25 =$
	Multiply the numbers as whole numbers.	55.7 (1 place)
	Place the decimal point in the proper place in the product. The number of decimal places in the product is the sum of the number of decimal places in the numbers being multiplied. If there are not enough places, insert one or more zeroes as needed to the left of the leftmost nonzero digit.	$\times\, 0.25$ (+ 2 places) 13.925 (3 places)
Division	To divide two decimals:	$2.04 \div 0.002 =$
	Rewrite the problem as an equivalent fractional problem with a whole number divisor. Do this by multiplying the numerator and denominator by the power of 10 that makes the divisor/denominator a whole number.	$\dfrac{2.04}{0.002} = \dfrac{2.04 \times 1000}{0.002 \times 1000} = \dfrac{2040}{2}$
	Divide as with whole numbers. Place the decimal point in the quotient directly above the decimal point in the dividend.	$\dfrac{1020}{2)\overline{2040}}$; thus, $2.04 \div 0.002 = 1020$

Don't be concerned about having to do computations on the FTCE GK Test. Since you are allowed to use a calculator, you should be able to do the calculations with little or no difficulty. Most of the required computations on the test will be simple calculations, some of which you could probably do mentally.

Test Yourself

1. Find the product: $\frac{3}{10} \times \frac{1}{2} =$

2. Find the product: $1\frac{1}{2} \times \frac{2}{5} =$

3. Find the quotient: $\frac{3}{10} \div \frac{1}{2} =$

4. Find the product: $(0.0125)(7.2) =$

5. Find the quotient: $345.75 \div 0.0005 =$

Answers

1. $\frac{3}{10} \times \frac{1}{2} = \frac{3 \times 1}{10 \times 2} = \frac{3}{20}$

2. $1\frac{1}{2} \times \frac{2}{5} = \frac{3}{2} \times \frac{2}{5} = \frac{3}{{}_1 2} \times \frac{2^1}{5} = \frac{3 \times 1}{1 \times 5} = \frac{3}{5}$

3. $\frac{3}{10} \div \frac{1}{2} = \frac{3}{10} \times \frac{2}{1} = \frac{3}{{}_5 10} \times \frac{2^1}{1} = \frac{3 \times 1}{5 \times 1} = \frac{3}{5}$

4. 0.09

5. 691,500

How Do You Add and Subtract Signed Numbers?

The real numbers are often called **signed numbers** because they may be positive (+), negative (–), or zero (no sign). On the FTCE GK Test you will need to know how to perform addition, subtraction, multiplication, and division with signed numbers.

Addition of Signed Numbers

When you add two signed numbers, you must note whether the two numbers have the same sign (both positive or both negative) or have different signs (one positive and one negative). How you do the addition depends on which of these situations is the case. This type of addition is **algebraic addition.** Table 3.9 summarizes the rules for algebraic addition of two signed numbers.

Table 3.9: Rules for Algebraic Addition of Two Signed Numbers		
If the signs are:	**The rule is:**	**Examples**
1. the same—both positive or both negative	Add the absolute values and attach the common sign to the sum.	$4 + 6 = 10$ $-4 + -6 = -10$
2. different—one positive and one negative	Subtract the lesser absolute value from the greater absolute value, and indicate that the result has the same sign as the number with the greater absolute value; if both numbers have the same absolute value, the sum is zero.	$-4 + 6 = 2$ $4 + -6 = -2$ $5 + -5 = 0$

As you can see, algebraic addition is different from arithmetic addition; particularly, since you don't always "add" to get the sum. In fact, if the signs are different, you subtract to find the sum. How does this make sense? What you must keep in mind is that the numbers you worked with in arithmetic were amounts only—they had no signs. Real numbers have an amount *and* a sign. The sign adds a direction to the number. Every real number has an amount and a direction. The number +5 is 5 units in the positive direction. The number –5 is 5 units in the negative direction.

When you add signed numbers, you have to take into account both the amount and the direction of the number. You can model addition on the number line to help you understand the process. Here are examples.

$2 + 5 = ?$

Start at 0 and go 2 units in the positive direction. Then from that point go 5 additional units in the positive direction. You end up at +7. The model shows that $2 + 5 = 7$.

$-2 + -5 = ?$

Start at 0 and go 2 units in the negative direction. Then from that point go 5 additional units in the negative direction. You end up at –7. The model shows that $-2 + -5 = -7$.

$2 + -5 = ?$

Start at 0 and go 2 units in the positive direction. Then from that point go 5 units in the negative direction. You end up at –3. The model shows that $2 + -5 = -3$.

$-2 + 5 = ?$

Start at 0 and go 2 units in the negative direction. Then from that point go 5 units in the positive direction. You end up at +3. The model shows that $-2 + 5 = 3$.

If you have three or more signed numbers to add together, you may find it convenient to, first, add up all the positive numbers; second, add up all the negative numbers; and then add the resulting two answers. Here is an example.

$14 + -35 + 6 + -25 =$

Add the positives together: $14 + 6 = 20$
Add the negatives together: $-35 + -25 = -60$
Add the two results: $20 + -60 = -40$

When two numbers have the same absolute value, but different signs, they are **opposites** of each other. The number zero is its own opposite. The algebraic sum of two numbers that are opposites is zero. For example, $-5 + 5 = 0$.

Subtraction of Signed Numbers

You may be happily surprised to learn that you do not have to memorize a set of new rules for subtraction of signed numbers! The reason is that subtraction of signed numbers is accomplished by changing the subtraction problem in a special way to an algebraic addition problem, so that the rules in Table 3.9 will apply. Here's how you do it (see Table 3.10).

Table 3.10: Algebraic Subtraction of Signed Numbers		
Operation	**Rule**	**Example**
Subtraction	To subtract two signed numbers:	$-10 - 4 =$
	(1) Keep the first number. (2) Change the minus (–) sign to a plus sign (+).	$-10 +$
	(3) Change the sign of the second number.	$-10 + -4 =$ (Change 4 to –4)
	(4) Perform algebraic addition according to the rules of Table 3.9.	$-10 + -4 = -14$

Think of the minus sign as "+ opposite of." Incorrectly interpreting subtraction is a common mistake. Here are examples of correctly rewriting subtraction problems.

$$9 - 16 = 9 + -16 \ (9 + \text{opposite of } 16)$$
$$24 - 15 = 24 + -15 \ (24 + \text{opposite of } 15)$$
$$-8 - 20 = -8 + -20 \ (-8 + \text{opposite of } 20)$$
$$3 - -6 = 3 + 6 \ (3 + \text{opposite of } -6)$$
$$-18 - -4 = -18 + 4 \ (-18 + \text{opposite of } -4)$$

Here are examples of algebraic subtraction.

$$9 - 16 = 9 + -16 = -7$$
$$24 - 15 = 24 + -15 = 9$$
$$-8 - 20 = -8 + -20 = -28$$
$$3 - -6 = 3 + 6 = 9$$
$$-18 - -4 = -18 + 4 = -14$$

Tip: Here is a mnemonic to help you remember subtraction of signed numbers: "Keep, change, change" meaning "<u>Keep</u> the first number, <u>change</u> subtraction to addition, and then <u>change</u> the second number to its opposite."

Multiplication and Division of Signed Numbers

Algebraic multiplication and division of signed numbers share the same pattern. Table 3.11 summarizes the rules for multiplication or division of two signed numbers.

Table 3.11: Rules for Algebraic Multiplication or Division of Two Signed Numbers		
If the signs are:	*The rule is:*	*Examples*
1. the same—both positive or both negative	Multiply or divide the absolute values as indicated, and label the product as positive (no sign is necessary).	$2 \cdot 5 = 10$ $-2 \cdot -5 = 10$ $\dfrac{12}{4} = 3$ $\dfrac{-12}{-4} = 3$
2. different—one positive and one negative	Multiply or divide the absolute values as indicated, and label the product as negative.	$-2 \cdot 5 = -10$ $2 \cdot -5 = -10$ $\dfrac{-12}{4} = -3$ $\dfrac{12}{-4} = -3$

Notice that, unlike algebraic addition, for algebraic multiplication/division when the signs are the same, it doesn't matter what the common sign is, the product/quotient is positive no matter what.

Similarly, unlike algebraic addition, for algebraic multiplication/division when the signs are different, it doesn't matter which number has the greater absolute value—the product/quotient is negative no matter what.

The rules for algebraic addition, subtraction, multiplication, and division apply to all real numbers. Here are examples.

$$-\frac{5}{8} + -\frac{1}{8} = -\frac{6}{8} = -\frac{3}{4}$$

$$\frac{2}{3} - \frac{3}{4} = \frac{8}{12} - \frac{9}{12} = \frac{8}{12} + \underset{\substack{\uparrow \\ \text{Apply to} \\ \text{Numerator}}}{-} \frac{9}{12} = \frac{8 + -9}{12} = \frac{-1}{12} = -\frac{1}{12}$$

$$24.5 + 134.28 = 158.78$$

$$-18.5 + 7.25 = -11.25$$

$$\frac{3}{4} \cdot -12 = \frac{3}{\cancel{4}_1} \cdot -\frac{\cancel{12}^3}{1} = -\frac{9}{1} = -9$$

$$\left(-2\frac{3}{4}\right)\left(-1\frac{1}{3}\right) = -\frac{11}{\cancel{4}_1} \cdot -\frac{\cancel{4}^1}{3} = \frac{11}{3} \text{ or } 3\frac{2}{3}$$

$$(-0.75)(400) = -300$$

$$(-125.43)(-0.005) = 0.62715$$

The two rules for multiplication tell you how to multiply two numbers, but often you will want to find the product of more than two numbers. To do this, multiply in pairs. You can keep track of the appropriate sign as you proceed, or you can use the following:

When *zero* is one of the factors, the product is *always* zero; otherwise, products involving an *even* number of *negative* factors are *positive,* whereas, those involving an *odd* number of *negative* factors are *negative.*

Here are examples.

$$\underbrace{(-10)(2)(0)(-5)}_{\text{zero is a factor}} = 0$$

$$\underbrace{(-10)(2)(3)(-5)(-1)(-2)}_{\text{even number of negative factors}} = 600$$

$$\underbrace{(-10)(2)(3)(-5)(-1)}_{\text{odd number of negative factors}} = -300$$

Test Yourself

1. The sum of two positive numbers is always _____ (positive, negative).

2. The sum of two negative numbers is always _____ (positive, negative).

3. The sum of a positive number and a negative number can be either positive or negative, depending on which of the two numbers has the _____(lesser, greater) absolute value.

4. The product of two positive numbers is always _____ (positive, negative).

5. The product of two negative numbers is always _____ (positive, negative).

6. The product of a positive number and a negative number is always _____ (positive, negative).

7. $-5 + 20 = $ _____ .

8. $2.45 + -8 =$ _____ .

9. $-\frac{2}{5} + -\frac{4}{5} =$ _____ .

10. $45 - -15 = 45 +$ _____ $=$ _____ .

11. $-\frac{1}{2} - -\frac{1}{2} = -\frac{1}{2} +$ _____ $=$ _____ .

12. $-304.75 - 20.015 = -304.75 +$ _____ $=$ _____ .

13. $\frac{1}{2} \cdot -\frac{2}{5} =$ _____ .

14. $-\frac{3}{10} \div 2 =$ _____ .

15. $(-0.0125)(-7.2) =$ _____ .

Answers

1. positive

2. negative

3. greater

4. positive

5. positive

6. negative

7. 15

8. -5.55

9. $-\frac{2}{5} + -\frac{4}{5} = \frac{-2 + -4}{5} = \frac{-6}{5} = -\frac{6}{5}$ or $-1\frac{1}{5}$

10. 15, 60

11. $\frac{1}{2}$, 0

12. -20.015, -324.765

13. $\frac{1}{2} \cdot -\frac{2}{5} = \frac{1}{\cancel{2}_1} \cdot -\frac{\cancel{2}^1}{5} = -\frac{1}{5}$

14. $-\frac{3}{10} \div 2 = -\frac{3}{10} \cdot \frac{1}{2} = -\frac{3}{20}$

15. 0.09

In What Order Do You Do the Operations?

When more than one operation is involved in a numerical expression, you must follow the **order of operations** to **simplify** the expression:

1. Do computations inside **Parentheses.** If there is more than one operation inside the parentheses, follow the order of operations given here as you do the computations inside the parentheses.

2. Evaluate any terms with **Exponents.**

3. **Multiply** and **Divide** in the order in which they occur from left to right.

4. **Add** and **Subtract** in the order in which they occur from left to right.

Here is a sentence to help you remember the order of operations: **Please Excuse My Dear Aunt Sally**—abbreviated as **PE(MD)(AS).** The first letter of each word gives the order of operations:

1. **P**arentheses
2. **E**xponents
3. **M**ultiply and **D**ivide from left to right, whichever comes first.
4. **A**dd and **S**ubtract from left to right, whichever comes first.

Note that multiplication does not always have to be done before division, or addition before subtraction. You multiply and divide in the order from left to right they occur in the problem. Similarly, you add and subtract in the order they occur in the problem. That's why there are parentheses around **MD** and **AS** in **PE (MD)(AS).**

Here are examples of using the order of operations to simplify numerical expressions.

Simplify: $90 - 5 \cdot 3^2 + 42 \div (5 + 2)$

$$
\begin{aligned}
90 - 5 \cdot 3^2 + 42 \div (5 + 2) &= 90 - 5 \cdot 3^2 + 42 \div (7) \\
&= 90 - 5 \cdot 9 + 42 \div 7 \\
&= 90 - 45 + 6 \\
&= 51
\end{aligned}
$$

First, do computations inside parentheses.
Next, evaluate exponents.
Then, multiply and divide from left to right.
Finally, add and subtract from left to right.

When simplified, the numerical expression $90 - 5 \cdot 3^2 + 42 \div (5 + 2) = 51$

Simplify: $-50 + 40 \div 2^3 - 5(4 + 6)$

$$
\begin{aligned}
-50 + 40 \div 2^3 - 5(4 + 6) &= -50 + 40 \div 2^3 - 5(10) \\
&= -50 + 40 \div 8 - 5(10) \\
&= -50 + 5 - 50 \\
&= -95
\end{aligned}
$$

First, do computations inside parentheses.
Next, evaluate exponents.
Then, multiply and divide from left to right.
Finally, add and subtract from left to right.

When simplified, the numerical expression $-50 + 40 \div 2^3 - 5(4 + 6) = -95$

Simplify: $8 - 4 \div (7 - 5) - (7 + 3) \div 2$.

$$
\begin{aligned}
8 - 4 \div (7 - 5) - (7 + 3) \div 2 &= 8 - 4 \div (2) - (10) \div 2 \\
&= 8 - 4 \div 2 - 10 \div 2 \\
&= 8 - 2 - 5 \\
&= 1
\end{aligned}
$$

First, do computations inside parentheses.
Next, evaluate exponents—none, so skip this step.
Then, divide from left to right.
Finally, subtract from left to right.

When simplified, the numerical expression : $8 - 4 \div (7 - 5) - (7 + 3) \div 2 = 1$.

Caution: Don't count on the calculator from the testing center to follow the order of operations. Most 4-function calculators are not programmed to follow the order of operations. They usually perform operations in the order they are keyed into the calculator. If you start at the left and key in the problem from left to right and then press the equal sign, most likely the answer displayed will not be the correct answer. Instead, key in the computations according to the order of operations, starting with the computations inside parentheses and ending with addition and subtraction from left to right. As shown in the examples, rewrite the problem as you work through the computations to avoid making careless errors.

Test Yourself

1. When simplifying numerical expressions, follow the _____ _____ _____ (three words).

2. Simplify: $(3 + 2)(14 + 4) \div 9 - 2^4 \cdot 10 + 148$

3. Simplify: $24 \div 6 - 2 \cdot 10 + 34$

4. Simplify: $-2(3 - 8) + 9^2 \div 3$

5. Simplify: $20 + 5 \cdot 7 - 4$

Answers

1. order of operations

2. $(3 + 2)(14 + 4) \div 9 - 2^4 \cdot 10 + 148$

    $= (5)(18) \div 9 - 2^4 \cdot 10 + 148$

    $= (5)(18) \div 9 - 16 \cdot 10 + 148$

    $= 90 \div 9 - 160 + 148$

    $= 10 - 160 + 148$

    $= -2$

3. $24 \div 6 - 2 \cdot 10 + 34$

    $= 4 - 20 + 34$

    $= 18$

4. $-2(3 - 8) + 9^2 \div 3$

    $= -2(-5) + 9^2 \div 3$

    $= -2(-5) + 81 \div 3$

    $= 10 + 27$

    $= 37$

5. $20 + 5 \cdot 7 - 4$

    $= 20 + 35 - 4$

    $= 51$

How Do You Solve Real-World Problems Involving Rational Numbers?

On the FTCE GK Test, you will have real-world problems in the form of word problems involving rational numbers to solve. Use the following steps when solving word problems.

1. **Understand the problem.**

    Read the problem and identify what you need to find. Look for a sentence that has words like *find, determine, what is, how many, how far,* and *how much.* Often (but not always) this is the last sentence in the problem.

    Organize the information you are given. Ask yourself, "What information is given in the problem that will help me answer the question? Is there a formula I need that is not provided? Are any facts missing? Is there information given that I don't need? Are measurement units involved and, if so, what units should my answer have? Can I draw a picture to help me better understand the problem? Would it help to make a chart or table?

2. Make a plan.

Decide how you can use the information you are given to solve the problem. Ask yourself, "What math concepts apply to this situation?" Decide which operation or operations to use. Table 3.12 has some guidelines to help you decide.

Table 3.12 Guidelines for Selecting Operations	
When You Need to:	*Use:*
Find a sum. Find a total. Combine quantities. Increase a quantity.	Addition
Find a difference. Take away. Find how many or how much is left. Find out how many more or how many less. Decrease a quantity.	Subtraction
Find a product. Put equal quantities together to find a total. Determine how much or how many is a portion of a whole. Find the cost of a given number of units when you know the unit price. Find a percent of a quantity. Determine how many different ways something can occur. Determine how many different combinations are possible.	Multiplication
Find a quotient. Find a ratio or fractional part. Determine how many equal parts are in a whole. Determine the size of equal parts of a whole. Separate an amount into groups of equal size. Find the probability of a simple event.	Division

After you have decided on what operation or operations to use, roughly outline how you will proceed. If measurement units are involved, make sure they work out to give the proper units. This is a powerful tool that is used extensively in the sciences.

3. Carry out your plan.

Solve the problem, using the information and the operation or operations you decided upon.

Double-check to make sure you copied all information accurately. Check the order of the numbers if subtraction or division is involved. Check the signs if you are using positive and negative numbers.

Key the numbers into the calculator carefully. Look at the display after every entry to make sure you entered what you intended to enter. Be especially careful when decimals or fractions are involved.

4. Look back.

Ask yourself:

Did I answer the question? Check whether you answered the question asked.

Does my answer make sense? Note: Explanations will vary in response to this question. Sample explanations are given in this chapter.

Is the answer stated in the correct units? Make sure the units are the proper units for the answer.

Here is an example of using the problem-solving steps.

> Problem: A motor home rents for $250 per week plus $0.20 per mile. Find the rental cost for a 3-week trip of 600 miles for a family of 4.

1. **Understand the problem.**

   What do you need to find?

   The rental cost for a 3-week trip of 600 miles.

   What information are you given?

   cost per week: $250

   cost per mile: $0.20

   number of weeks: 3

   number of miles: 600

   Is there information given that you don't need?

   number of family members: 4

2. **Make a plan.**

   The total rental cost includes the cost for 3 weeks of rental and the cost for mileage. Solving the problem will involve three steps: Find the cost for the 3 weeks of rental, find the cost for mileage, and then find the total rental cost.

3. **Carry out the plan.**

   Step 1. Find the cost for 3 weeks of rental. You know the cost per week is $250. Multiply to get the cost for 3 weeks.

   $$\frac{3\text{ wk}}{1} \cdot \frac{\$250}{\text{wk}} = \frac{3 \text{ \cancel{wk}}}{1} \cdot \frac{\$250}{\cancel{\text{wk}}} = \$750 \qquad \text{Notice that weeks divide out, leaving \$ as the units.}$$

   Step 2. Find the cost for mileage. You know the cost per mile is $0.20. Multiply to get the cost for 600 miles.

   $$\frac{600\text{ mi}}{1} \cdot \frac{\$0.20}{\text{mi}} = \frac{600 \text{ \cancel{mi}}}{1} \cdot \frac{\$0.20}{\cancel{\text{mi}}} = \$120 \qquad \text{Notice that miles divide out, leaving \$ as the units.}$$

   Step 3. Find the total rental cost for the motor home. Add the results from steps 1 and 2 to find the total.

   cost for 3 weeks of rental + cost for mileage = $750 + $120 = $870.

   The total rental cost for the motor home is $870.

4. **Look back.**

   Did I answer the question? Yes, I found the total rental cost for the motor home. ✓

   Does my answer make sense? Yes, the answer seems like a reasonable cost. ✓

   Is the answer stated in the correct units? Yes, the units are dollars, which is correct. ✓

Ratios and Proportions

A ratio is the comparison of two quantities. In a paint mixture that uses 2 parts white paint to 5 parts blue paint, the ratio of white paint to blue paint is two to five. You can express this ratio in three different forms: 2 to 5, 2:5, or $\frac{2}{5}$. The numbers 2 and 5 are the **terms** of the ratio. A ratio is a pure number—it does not have any units. When you find the ratio of two quantities, you must make sure they have the same units so that when you write the ratio, the units will divide out. For example, the ratio of 2 pints to 5 quarts is *not* $\frac{2}{5}$ because these quantities are not expressed in the same units. Since 2 pints = 1 quart, the relationship is 1 quart to 5 quarts, which gives a ratio of $\frac{1}{5}$. If the two quantities cannot be converted to like units, then you must keep the units and write the quotient as a **rate**. For instance, $\frac{140\text{ miles}}{2\text{ hours}} = 70$ mph is a rate of speed.

A **proportion** is a mathematical statement that two ratios are equal. The **terms** of the proportion are the four numbers that make up the two ratios. For example, take the proportion $\frac{3}{4} = \frac{9}{12}$. This proportion has terms 3, 4, 9, and 12. In a proportion, cross products are equal. **Cross products** are the product of the numerator of the first ratio times the denominator of the second ratio and the product of the denominator of the first ratio times the numerator of the second ratio.

Here is an example showing the equal cross products for the proportion.

$$\frac{3}{4} \times \frac{9}{12}$$

$$3 \cdot 12 = 4 \cdot 9$$
$$36 = 36$$

When you are given a proportion that has a missing term, you can use cross products to find the missing term. Look at this example.

Find the value of x that makes the following proportion true.

$$\frac{x}{40} = \frac{3}{4}$$

$x \cdot 4 = 40 \cdot 3$ Find the cross products.
$x \cdot 4 = 120$

You can see from the cross products that x is the number that multiplies times 4 to give 120. Logical reasoning should tell you that

$$x = \frac{120}{4}$$

$$x = 30$$

Note: In the "Algebraic Reasoning" section of this chapter, you will learn to solve the equation $x \cdot 4 = 120$ by dividing both sides of the equation by 4, which also gives $x = 30$.

You can shorten the preceding process for solving a proportion by doing the following: Find a cross product that you can calculate and then divide by the numerical term in the proportion that you did not use. Since you are allowed to use a calculator on the FTCE GK Test, this is the quickest and most reliable way to solve a proportion on the test. Here's how it would work for the previous example.

Find the value of x that makes the following proportion true.

$$\frac{x}{40} = \frac{3}{4}$$

$40 \cdot 3$ Find a cross product you can calculate. You don't know the value of x, so the only cross
$x = \frac{40 \cdot 3}{4}$ product you can calculate is 40 times 3.

     Divide by 4, the numerical term you didn't use.

$x = \frac{120}{4}$

$x = 30$

Here's how you key the computations into the calculator: $40 \times 3 \div 4 =$. The display will show 30, the correct answer. *Note:* This keying is one of the few instances you can count on the calculator to give you a correct answer.

Word problems involving proportional relationships are one type of word problem you will encounter on the FTCE GK Test. These are problems that deal with ratios, map scales, and scale factors. Here is an example.

> Problem: On a map, the distance between two cities is 10.5 inches. If 0.5 inch represents 20 miles, how far, in miles, is it between the two cities (to the nearest mile)?

1. **Understand the problem.**

   What do you need to find?

   the actual distance in miles between the two cities

   What information are you given?

   distance between the cities on the map is 10.5 inches

   scale for map: 0.5 inch represents 20 miles

   Is there information given that you don't need?

   No

2. **Make a plan.**

   This problem is a proportion problem involving a map scale. To solve the problem, determine the ratios being compared, being sure to compare corresponding quantities in the same order; write a proportion using the two ratios; and then use cross products to solve the proportion.

3. **Carry out the plan.**

   Step 1. Determine the ratios being compared.

   Let d be the actual distance in miles between the two cities. The first sentence gives the first ratio: $\dfrac{d\,(\text{in miles})}{10.5 \text{ in.}}$. The second sentence gives the second ratio: $\dfrac{20 \text{ miles}}{0.5 \text{ in.}}$. (Notice, you put miles in the numerator in the second ratio because you have miles in the numerator in the first ratio.)

   Step 2. Write a proportion using the two ratios.

   $$\frac{d\,(\text{in miles})}{10.5 \text{ in.}} = \frac{20 \text{ miles}}{0.5 \text{ in.}}$$

   Step 3. Use cross products to solve the proportion (omitting the units for convenience).

   $$\frac{d}{10.5} = \frac{20}{0.5}$$

   $10.5 \cdot 20$ Find a cross product you can calculate. You don't know the value d, so the only cross product you can calculate is 10.5 times 20.

   $d = \dfrac{10.5 \cdot 20}{0.5}$ Divide by 0.5, the numerical term you didn't use.

   $d = \dfrac{210}{0.5}$

   $d = 420$ miles

   Here's how you key the computations into the calculator: $10.5 \times 20 \div 0.5 =$. The display will show 420, the correct answer.

   The actual distance in miles between the two cities is 420 miles.

4. **Look back.**

   Did I answer the question? Yes, I found the actual distance in miles between the two cities. ✓

   Does my answer make sense? Yes, if 0.5 inch corresponds to 20 miles, then 1 inch corresponds to 40 miles, so 10.5 inches should represent at least 400 miles. ✓

   Is the answer stated in the correct units? Yes, the units are miles, which is correct. ✓

Percent Problems

Percent problems can be solved in several ways. Most of the percent problems on the FTCE GK Test can be solved using a "percent proportion" that has the following form:

$$\frac{r}{100} = \frac{\text{part}}{\text{whole}}$$

r = the number in front of the % sign

part = the quantity that is near the word "is"

whole = the quantity that immediately follows the word "of"

Tip: Think *is* over *of*" to help you get $\dfrac{\text{part ("is")}}{\text{whole ("of")}}$ correct.

The relationship between the three elements r, **part**, and **whole** can be explained in a percent statement like this:

The part is r% of the whole.

The secret to solving percent problems is being able to identify the three elements correctly. Start with r and the whole because they are usually easier to find. The part will be the other amount in the problem. The value of two of the elements will be given in the problem, and you will be solving for the third element. After you identify the three elements, plug the two you know into the percent proportion and solve for the one that you don't know.

Here is an example of what to do when the part is missing.

What is 20% of 560?

Identify the elements.

$r = 20$

part = ? = x

whole = 560

Plug into the percent proportion.

$$\frac{r}{100} = \frac{\text{part}}{\text{whole}}$$
$$\frac{20}{100} = \frac{x}{560}$$

Solve the proportion.

$20 \cdot 560$ Find a cross product you can calculate. You don't know the value of x, so the only cross product you can calculate is 20 times 560.

$x = \dfrac{20 \cdot 560}{100} = 112$ Divide by 100, the numerical term you didn't use.

$x = 112$

Here's how you key the computations into the calculator: $20 \times 560 \div 100 =$. The display will show 112, the correct answer.

Here is an example of what to do when the whole is missing.

---

30 is 25% of what amount?

Identify the elements.

$$r = 25$$
$$\text{part} = 30$$
$$\text{whole} = ? = x$$

Plug into the percent proportion.

$$\frac{r}{100} = \frac{\text{part}}{\text{whole}}$$

$$\frac{25}{100} = \frac{30}{x}$$

Solve the proportion.

$100 \cdot 30$ — Find a cross product you can calculate. You don't know the value of x, so the only cross product you can calculate is 100 times 30.

$x = \dfrac{100 \cdot 30}{25} = 120$ — Divide by 25, the numerical term you didn't use.

$x = 120$

Here's how you key the computations into the calculator: $100 \times 30 \div 25 =$. The display will show 120, the correct answer.

Here is an example when r is missing.

---

400 is what percent of 500?

Identify the elements.

$$r = ?$$
$$\text{part} = 400$$
$$\text{whole} = 500$$

Plug into the percent proportion.

$$\frac{r}{100} = \frac{\text{part}}{\text{whole}}$$

$$\frac{r}{100} = \frac{400}{500}$$

Solve the proportion.

$100 \cdot 400$ — Find a cross product you can calculate. You don't know the value of r, so the only cross product you can calculate is 100 times 400.

$r = \dfrac{100 \cdot 400}{500} = 80$ — Divide by 500, the numerical term you didn't use.

$r = 80$

$r\% = 80\%$

Notice that since r is the number in front of the percent sign in the percent statement, you have to put a % sign after your calculated value of r to answer the question.

Just so you know, there are other ways to work percent problems. For instance, to answer "What is 20% of 560?", change 20% to a fraction or a decimal fraction and then multiply 560 by the converted number.

$$20\% \text{ of } 560 = 0.20 \cdot 560 = 112 \qquad \text{or} \qquad 20\% \text{ of } 560 = \frac{1}{5} \cdot \frac{560}{1} = \frac{1}{\cancel{5}_1} \cdot \frac{\overset{112}{\cancel{560}}}{1} = 112$$

You get the same answer as was obtained earlier. The proportion method is emphasized in this study guide because when you are allowed to use a calculator, it is a reliable and efficient way to solve percent problems.

Word Problems Involving Percents

You can expect to encounter word problems involving percents on the FTCE GK Test. These are problems that deal with finding percentages, percents, and wholes in various every day situations. Here is an example.

> Problem: A stereo system that regularly sells for $650 is marked 20% off for a one-day sale. What is the amount saved if the stereo is purchased at the sale price?

1. **Understand the problem.**

   What do you need to find?

   the amount saved at the sale price

   What information are you given?

   regular price: $650

   amount saved: 20% off regular price

   Is there information given that you don't need?

   that it's a one-day sale

2. **Make a plan.**

   To find the amount saved, you will need to answer the question: What is 20% of $650? To solve the problem: Identify the elements of the percent problem, plug the values into the percent proportion, and then solve the proportion.

3. **Carry out the plan.**

   Step 1. Identify the elements.

   $r = 20$

   part = ?= x

   whole = $650

   Step 2. Plug into the percent proportion (omitting the units for convenience).

   $$\frac{r}{100} = \frac{\text{part}}{\text{whole}}$$

   $$\frac{20}{100} = \frac{x}{650}$$

   Step 3. Solve the proportion.

   $20 \cdot 650$ Find a cross product you can calculate. You don't know the value of x, so the only cross product you can calculate is 20 times 650.

   $x = \dfrac{20 \cdot 650}{100} = 130$ Divide by 100, the numerical term you didn't use.

   $x = \$130$

Here's how you key the computations into the calculator: $20 \times 650 \div 100 =$. The display will show 130, the correct answer.

The amount saved is $130.

4. Look back.

Did I answer the question? Yes, I found the amount saved. ✓

Does my answer make sense? Yes, 20% is $\frac{1}{5}$. For a \$500 item, the savings would be \$100. For a \$650 item, the savings would be a little over \$100. ✓

Is the answer stated in the correct units? Yes, the units are dollars, which is correct. ✓

Test Yourself

1. The four problem-solving steps are _____, _____, _____, and _____.

2. A _____ is the comparison of two quantities. It is a pure number. It does not have any _____.

3. A _____ is a statement that two _____ are equal.

4. If 12 ounces of salt are mixed with 5 ounces of ground pepper, what is the ratio of salt to pepper?

5. What are the terms of the proportion $\frac{x}{50} = \frac{7}{25}$?

6. In a proportion, the _____(two words) are equal.

7. Solve the proportion $\frac{x}{50} = \frac{7}{25}$ for x.

8. What is 40% of \$1,200?

9. In a paint mixture that uses 2 parts white paint to 5 parts blue paint, how many quarts of white paint are needed to mix with 20 quarts of blue paint?

10. At an art exhibit at a local gallery, 15 of the 25 paintings displayed were purchased by a well-known art connoisseur. What percent of the paintings were purchased by the art connoisseur?

Answers

1. Understand the problem, make a plan, carry out the plan, look back.

2. ratio, units

3. proportion, ratios

4. 12 to 5

5. x, 50, 7, 25

6. cross products

7. $\frac{x}{50} = \frac{7}{25}$

$50 \cdot 7$ Find a cross product you can calculate. You don't know the value of x, so the only cross product you can calculate is 50 times 7.

$x = \frac{50 \cdot 7}{25} = 14$ Divide by 25, the numerical term you didn't use.

$x = 14$

8. What is 40% of $1,200?

   Identify the elements.

   $$r = 40$$

   $$\text{part} = ? = x$$

   $$\text{whole} = \$1200$$

   Plug into the percent proportion.

   $$\frac{r}{100} = \frac{\text{part}}{\text{whole}}$$

   $$\frac{40}{100} = \frac{x}{\$1200}$$

   Solve the proportion (omitting the units for convenience).

   $40 \cdot 1200$ Find a cross product you can calculate. You don't know the value of x, so the only cross product you can calculate is 40 times 1200.

   $x = \dfrac{40 \cdot 1200}{100} = 480$ Divide by 100, the numerical term you didn't use.

   40% of $1,200 is $480.

9. This problem is a proportion problem involving ratios in a mixture. To solve the problem, determine the ratios being compared, being sure to compare corresponding quantities in the same order; write a proportion using the two ratios; and then use cross products to solve the proportion.

   Step 1. Determine the ratios being compared.

   The first sentence gives the first ratio: $\dfrac{2 \text{ parts white paint}}{5 \text{ parts blue paint}}$. The second sentence gives the second ratio:

   $$\text{ratio} = \frac{x \text{ (quarts) white paint}}{20 \text{ quarts blue paint}}.$$

   Step 2. Write a proportion using the two ratios.

   $$\frac{2 \text{ parts white paint}}{5 \text{ parts blue paint}} = \frac{x \text{ (quarts) white paint}}{20 \text{ quarts blue paint}}$$

   Step 3. Use cross products to solve the proportion (omitting the units for convenience).

   $$\frac{2}{5} = \frac{x}{20}$$

   $2 \cdot 20$ Find a cross product you can calculate. You don't know the value of x, so the only cross product you can calculate is 2 times 20.

   $x = \dfrac{2 \cdot 20}{5} = 8$ Divide by 5, the numerical term you didn't use.

   The number of quarts of white paint needed is 8 quarts.

   Did I answer the question? Yes, I found the number of quarts of white paint needed. ✓

   Does my answer make sense? Yes, the paint is mixed in a ratio of 2 parts white paint to 5 parts blue paint, so you need 2 quarts of white paint for every 5 quarts of blue paint. Thus, 8 quarts of white paint for 20 quarts of blue paint makes sense. ✓

   Is the answer stated in the correct units? Yes, the units are quarts, which is correct. ✓

10. To find the percent purchased, you will need to answer the question: 15 is r% of 25? To solve the problem: Identify the elements of the percent problem, plug the values into the percent proportion, and solve the proportion.

Step 1. Identify the elements.

$$r = ?$$

$$\text{part} = 15$$

$$\text{whole} = 25$$

Step 2. Plug into the percent proportion (omitting the units for convenience).

$$\frac{r}{100} = \frac{\text{part}}{\text{whole}}$$

$$\frac{r}{100} = \frac{15}{25}$$

Step 3. Solve the proportion.

$100 \cdot 15$ Find a cross product you can calculate. You don't know the value of r, so the only cross product you can calculate is 100 times 15.

$r = \dfrac{100 \cdot 15}{25}$ Divide by 25, the numerical term you didn't use.

$r = 60$

$r\% = 60\%$

The percent of the paintings purchased by the art connoisseur is 60%.

Did I answer the question? Yes, I found the percent of the paintings purchased by the art connoisseur. ✓

Does my answer make sense? Yes, since $\dfrac{15}{25}$ is a little over one-half (50%), 60% is a reasonable answer. ✓

Is the answer stated in the correct units? The answer is a percent, so it should not have any units. ✓

Sample Questions

Directions: Read each question and select the best answer choice.

1. Find the greatest common factor of 18 and 30.

   A. 2
   B. 3
   C. 6
   D. 90

2. Express the product $5 \cdot 5 \cdot 7 \cdot 7 \cdot 7$ in exponential notation.

   A. $2^5 \cdot 3^7$
   B. 57^5
   C. $5^2 \cdot 7^3$
   D. $5^3 \cdot 7^2$

3. Which of the following should be performed first to simplify this expression?

   $-8 + 45 \cdot 18 \div 3^2$

   A. $-8 + 45$
   B. $45 \cdot 18$
   C. $18 \div 3^2$
   D. 3^2

4. If 25% of a monthly salary of $2,800 is budgeted for food, how much money is budgeted for food?

   A. $70
   B. $210
   C. $700
   D. $2,100

Answer Explanations for Sample Questions

1. **C.** The greatest common factor of 18 and 30 is the largest number that will divide into both 18 and 30 evenly. The factors of 18 are 1, 2, 3, 6, 9, and 18. The factors of 30 are 1, 2, 3, 5, 6, 10, 15, and 30. Looking at the two lists of factors, you can see that 6 is the largest factor that is common to both lists, so it is the largest number that will divide into both 18 and 30 evenly. Thus, GCF (18, 30) = 6.

2. **C.** Expressed in exponential notation, the product $5 \cdot 5 \cdot 7 \cdot 7 \cdot 7 = 5^2 \cdot 7^3$, which indicates 2 factors of 5 and 3 factors of 7. The other answer choices do not indicate 2 factors of 5 and 3 factors of 7.

3. **D.** To simplify the expression $-8 + 45 \cdot 18 \div 3^2$, follow "<u>P</u>lease <u>E</u>xcuse <u>M</u>y <u>D</u>ear <u>A</u>unt <u>S</u>ally." The order of operations requires that any operations in parentheses be performed first. There are no parentheses in this expression, so the next step is to simplify any exponents. Since 3^2 is in exponential form, it should be performed first. It would be incorrect to perform $-8 + 45$ first (Choice **A**) because addition and subtraction, from left to right, are performed last when there are no parentheses indicating to do otherwise. It would be incorrect to perform $45 \cdot 18$ (Choice **B**) or $18 \div 3$ (Choice **C**) first because multiplication and division, from left to right, are performed after exponentiation, unless there are parentheses indicating to do otherwise.

4. **C.** To find the amount budgeted for food, you will need to answer the question: what is 25% of 2800?

   Method 1: To solve the problem, identify the elements of the percent problem, plug the values into the percent proportion, and solve the proportion.

Step 1. Identify the elements.

$$r = 25$$

$$\text{part} = ? = x$$

$$\text{whole} = \$2800$$

Step 2. Plug into the percent proportion.

$$\frac{r}{100} = \frac{\text{part}}{\text{whole}}$$

$$\frac{r}{100} = \frac{x}{\$2800}$$

Step 3. Solve the proportion (omitting the units for convenience).

$25 \cdot 2800$ Find a cross product you can calculate. You don't know the value of x, so the only cross product you can calculate is 25 times 2800.

$x = \dfrac{25 \cdot 2800}{100} = 700$ Divide by 100, the numerical term you didn't use.

$$x = \$700$$

The amount budgeted for food is $700, Choice **C**.

Did I answer the question? Yes, I found the amount budgeted for food. ✓

Does my answer make sense? Yes, 25% is one-fourth, so $700 is a reasonable answer. ✓

Is the answer stated in the correct units? Yes, the units are dollars, which is correct. ✓

Method 2: Change 25% to a decimal fraction or common fraction and multiply:

$$25\% \text{ of } \$2800 = 0.25 \cdot \$2800 = \$700.00$$

$$\text{Or } 25\% \text{ of } \$2800 = \frac{1}{4} \cdot \frac{\$2800}{1} = \frac{1}{\cancel{4}_1} \cdot \frac{\cancel{\$2800}^{700}}{1} = \$700.00$$

Choice **A** results if you make a decimal point error. Choice **B** results if you solve the problem incorrectly by finding 75% of $2,800 and you make a decimal point error. Choice **D** results if you solve the problem incorrectly by finding 75% of $2,800.

Measurement

According to the *Competencies and Skills Required for Teacher Certification in Florida, Fifteenth Edition* (see the first section of this chapter for the Web address), the competencies/skills you should be able to do for this area of mathematics are the following:

- Convert units of measure of length, weight, mass, volume, and time.
- Estimate measurements.
- Solve real-world problems involving unit rate.
- Read a measuring instrument (for example, ruler, graduated cylinder, thermometer, gauge) to a specified degree of accuracy.
- Solve real-world problems involving scaled drawings such as maps and models.
- Solve real-world problems involving perimeter, area, and volume.

How Do You Convert from One Measurement Unit to Another?

On the FTCE GK Test, you will have to demonstrate your knowledge of measurement using the U.S. customary system and the metric system. Your Mathematics Reference Sheet contains the conversion facts, as reproduced here, that you will need to know for the test.

Conversions	
1 yard = 3 feet = 36 inches	1 cup = 8 fluid ounces
1 mile = 1,760 yards = 5,280 feet	1 pint = 2 cups
1 acre = 43,560 square feet	1 quart = 2 pints
1 hour = 60 minutes	1 gallon = 4 quarts
1 minute = 60 seconds	1 pound = 16 ounces
	1 ton = 2,000 pounds
1 liter = 1000 milliliters = 1000 cubic centimeters	
1 meter = 100 centimeters = 1000 millimeters	
1 kilometer = 1000 meters	
1 gram = 1000 milligrams	
1 kilogram = 1000 grams	

You can convert from one measurement unit to another by using an appropriate "conversion fraction." You make conversion fractions by using the conversion facts given in the Mathematics Reference Sheet. For each conversion fact in the table, you can write *two* conversion fractions. For example, for the conversion fact 1 yard = 3 feet, you have $\frac{1 \text{ yd}}{3 \text{ ft}}$ and $\frac{3 \text{ ft}}{1 \text{ yd}}$ as your two conversion fractions. Each of these conversion fractions is equivalent to the number 1 because the numerator and denominator are different names for the same length. Therefore, if you multiply a quantity by either of these fractions, you will not change the value of the quantity.

When you need to change one measurement unit to another unit, multiply by the conversion fraction whose *denominator is the same as the units of the quantity to be converted.* This strategy is called **unit analysis.** When you do the multiplication, the units you started out with will "divide out," and you will be left with the new units. If this doesn't happen, then you used the wrong conversion fraction, so do it over again with the other conversion fraction.

It is a good idea to assess your final answer to see whether it makes sense. When you are converting from *a larger unit to a smaller unit,* you should expect that it will take *more* of the smaller units to equal the same amount.

When you are converting from *a smaller unit to a larger unit,* you should expect that it will take *less* of the larger units to equal the same amount.

Here is an example of converting from a larger unit to a smaller unit:

> Convert 5 yards to feet.

The conversion fractions are $\frac{1 \text{ yd}}{3 \text{ ft}}$ and $\frac{3 \text{ ft}}{1 \text{ yd}}$. Write 5 yards as a fraction with denominator 1 and let unit analysis tell you whether to multiply by $\frac{1 \text{ yd}}{3 \text{ ft}}$ or $\frac{3 \text{ ft}}{1 \text{ yd}}$. Multiply by $\frac{3 \text{ ft}}{1 \text{ yd}}$ because the denominator has the same units as the quantity to be converted:

$$\frac{5 \text{ yd}}{1} \cdot \frac{3 \text{ ft}}{1 \text{ yd}} = \frac{5 \text{ yd}}{1} \cdot \frac{3 \text{ ft}}{1 \text{ yd}} = 15 \text{ ft}$$ The yards (yd) units divide out, leaving feet (ft) as the units for the answer.

Does this answer make sense? Feet are smaller than yards, so it should take more of them to equal the same length as 5 yards.

Here is an example of converting from a smaller unit to a larger unit:

> Convert 250 centimeters to meters.

The conversion fractions are $\frac{1 \text{ m}}{100 \text{ cm}}$ and $\frac{100 \text{ cm}}{1 \text{ m}}$. Write 250 centimeters as a fraction with denominator 1 and let unit analysis tell you whether to multiply by $\frac{1 \text{ m}}{100 \text{ cm}}$ or $\frac{100 \text{ cm}}{1 \text{ m}}$. Multiply 250 centimeters by $\frac{1 \text{ m}}{100 \text{ cm}}$ because the denominator has the same units as the quantity to be converted:

$$\frac{250 \text{ cm}}{1} \cdot \frac{1 \text{ m}}{100 \text{ cm}} = \frac{250 \text{ cm}}{1} \cdot \frac{1 \text{ m}}{100 \text{ cm}} = \frac{250 \text{ m}}{100} = 2.5 \text{ m}$$ The centimeters (cm) units divide out, leaving meters (m) as the units for the answer. Notice that since 100 is in the denominator, you divide 250 by 100 to obtain the 2.5 in the answer.

Does this answer make sense? Meters are larger than centimeters, so it should take fewer of them to equal the same distance as 250 centimeters.

Another way to work this problem is to use "**K**ing **H**enry **D**oesn't **U**sually **D**rink **C**hocolate **M**ilk," which is a mnemonic for remembering the following metric prefixes:

> kilo-, hecto-, deca-, unit measurement (no prefix), deci-, centi-, milli-
> (1000)(100)   (10)   (.1)   (.01)   (.001)

Because the metric system is a decimal-based system, the prefixes are based on powers of 10. You can convert from one unit to another by either multiplying or dividing by a power of 10. If you move from left to right on the list, then you multiply by the power of 10 that corresponds to the number of times you moved. If you move from right to left on the list, then you divide by the power of 10 that corresponds to the number of times you moved.

In this problem, the unit measurement is meters. You are going from centimeters to meters. Since to go from centi- to your unit measurement (meters) you move left two times on the list above, you will divide by $10^2 = 100$ to convert centimeters to meters. Thus,

$$250 \text{ cm} = 250 \div 10^2 \text{ (2 moves left)} = 250 \div 100 = 2.5 \text{ m}$$

For some conversions, you may need to make a "chain" of conversion fractions to obtain your desired units. Here is an example:

> Convert 3 gallons to cups.

The conversion table does not have a fact that shows the equivalency between gallons and cups. You have 1 pint = 2 cups, 1 quart = 2 pints, and 1 gallon = 4 quarts. These facts yield 3 conversion fraction pairs, respectively: $\frac{1\ pt}{2\ c}$ and $\frac{2\ c}{1\ pt}$, $\frac{1\ qt}{2\ pt}$ and $\frac{2\ pt}{1\ qt}$, and $\frac{1\ gal}{4\ qt}$ and $\frac{4\ qt}{1\ gal}$. Start with your quantity to be converted and keep multiplying by conversion fractions until you obtain your desired units.

$$\frac{3\ gal}{1} \cdot \frac{4\ qt}{1\ gal} \cdot \frac{2\ pt}{1\ qt} \cdot \frac{2\ c}{1\ pt} = \frac{3\ \cancel{gal}}{1} \cdot \frac{4\ \cancel{qt}}{1\ \cancel{gal}} \cdot \frac{2\ \cancel{pt}}{1\ \cancel{qt}} \cdot \frac{2\ c}{1\ \cancel{pt}} = 48\ c$$

Does this answer make sense? Cups are smaller than gallons, so it should take more of them to equal the same amount as 3 gallons.

For the FTCE GK Test, you will not have to convert between the customary system and the metric system. You will convert only within a given system. If you are not very familiar with the metric system, here are some "rough" equivalencies of the more common units for your general knowledge.

Equivalencies Chart	
Meter	about 3 inches longer than a yard
Centimeter	about the width of a large paper clip
Millimeter	about the thickness of a dime
Kilometer	about 5 city blocks or a little farther than half a mile
Liter	a little more than a quart
Milliliter	takes about five of them to make a teaspoon
Gram	about the weight of a small paper clip
Milligram	about the weight of a grain of salt
Kilogram	the weight of a liter of water or a little more than 2 pounds

How Do You Solve Problems Involving Unit Rates?

A **unit rate** is an amount per unit. It is a rated measure such as miles per hour, cost per item, cost per unit, words per page, and so on. Unit rates are used in many real-life situations.

Here is an example of using unit rates for comparison shopping.

Which is a better buy? 3 $10\frac{3}{4}$ oz cans of soup for $2.00 or 4 $10\frac{3}{4}$ oz cans for $3.50?

The unit price for 3 cans for $2.00 $= \frac{\$2.00}{3\ cans} = \$0.67$ per can (rounded to the nearest cent).

The unit price for 4 cans for $3.50 $= \frac{\$3.50}{4\ cans} = \$0.88$ per can (rounded to the nearest cent).

Assuming there's no difference in quality, the better buy is 3 cans for $2.00.

Here is an example of using unit rates to compare the speeds of two vehicles.

Car A traveled 156 miles in 2.4 hours. Car B traveled 245 miles in 3.5 hours. Which car averaged the faster speed?

The average speed (unit rate) for car A is $\frac{156\ miles}{2.4\ hours} = 65$ miles per hour (mph).

The average speed (unit rate) for car B is $\frac{245 \text{ miles}}{3.5 \text{ hours}} = 70$ miles per hour (mph).

Car B had a faster average speed.

You can use unit rates to find the total miles, total cost, total words, and so on by multiplying by the unit rate.

Here are examples.

> A train travels 3 hours at a rate of 55 miles per hour. How many miles did the train travel?

From the Mathematics Reference Sheet, you have $d = rt$; that is, distance = rate · time. To find the total miles traveled, multiply 55 mph (the unit rate) times 3 hours:

$$d = rt = \frac{55 \text{ mi}}{\text{h}} \cdot 3 \text{ h} = \frac{55 \text{ mi}}{\cancel{\text{h}}} \cdot 3 \cancel{\text{h}} = 165 \text{ miles}$$

The hours (h) units divide out, leaving miles (mi) as the units for the answer.

> If it costs $220 to rent a motor home for one week, how much will it cost to rent the motor home for 2 weeks?

To find the total cost, multiply 2 weeks by $220 per week (the unit rate).

$$\text{total cost} = 2 \text{ wk} \cdot \frac{\$220}{\text{wk}} = 2 \cancel{\text{wk}} \cdot \frac{\$220}{\cancel{\text{wk}}} = \$440$$

The weeks (wk) units divide out, leaving dollars ($) as the units for the answer.

How Do You Read Measurement Instruments?

On the FTCE GK Test, you will have to read a measurement instrument to the nearest specified unit. The gauge or scale of the measuring instrument will have markings that divide the gauge or scale into equal intervals. Usually, not every mark is labeled with a number. For example, on a standard customary ruler, inches will be labeled, but not the markings in between, as shown in the following.

To read a measuring instrument, it is most important that you determine what each mark on the measuring instrument represents. To do this, find the two consecutive labeled points immediately below and above the reading on the scale. Find the difference between the two points. Count the number of markings it takes to get from the lower point to the higher point. Divide the difference between the two points by the number of marks you counted. After you determine what each mark represents, take the reading. Here is an example.

> What is the temperature to the nearest degree?

The thermometer is reading between 20° and 40°. The difference between these two points is 40° − 20° = 20°. It takes ten marks to go from 20° up to 40°. Divide the difference between the two points by 10: 20° ÷ 10 = 2°. Therefore, each mark on the thermometer represents 2°. The thermometer is reading five marks above 20°. Since each mark represents 2°, the thermometer is reading 10° above 20°, which is 30°C.

How Do You Solve Problems Involving Scaled Drawings or Models?

The scale for a drawing or model is a ratio that compares the measurement on the drawing (or model) to the actual measurement in real life. For example, if a drawing has a scale of 1 cm = 10 meters, for every centimeter measured on the drawing, the actual length is 10 meters. To solve problems involving scaled drawings or models, set up a proportion and solve the problem. Here is an example.

On a map, the distance between two cities is 18 inches. If 0.75 inch represents 20 miles, how far, in miles, is it between the two cities (to the nearest mile)?

This problem is a proportion problem involving a map scale. To solve the problem, determine the ratios being compared, being sure to compare corresponding quantities in the same order; write a proportion using the two ratios; and then use cross products to solve the proportion.

Step 1. Determine the ratios being compared.

Let d be the actual distance in miles between the two cities. The first sentence gives the first ratio: $\frac{d \text{ (in miles)}}{18 \text{ in.}}$. The second sentence gives the second ratio: $\frac{20 \text{ miles}}{0.75 \text{ in.}}$. (Notice, you put miles in the numerator in the second ratio because you have miles in the numerator in the first ratio.)

Step 2. Write a proportion using the two ratios.

$$\frac{d \text{ (in miles)}}{18 \text{ in.}} = \frac{20 \text{ miles}}{0.75 \text{ in.}}$$

Step 3. Use cross products to solve the proportion (omitting the units for convenience).

$\frac{d}{18} = \frac{20}{0.75}$

$18 \cdot 20$ Find a cross product you can calculate. You don't know the value of d, so the only cross product you can calculate is 18 times 20.

$d = \frac{18 \cdot 20}{0.75} = 480$ Divide by 0.75, the numerical term you didn't use.

$d = 480$ miles

The actual distance in miles between the two cities is 480 miles.

Did I answer the question? Yes, I found the actual distance in miles between the two cities. ✓

Does my answer make sense? Yes, since 0.75 inch represents 20 miles, a rough estimate of the answer is 20 inches times 20 miles per inch, which is 400 miles. Thus, 480 miles is a reasonable answer. ✓

Is the answer stated in the correct units? Yes, the units are miles, which is correct. ✓

Test Yourself

1. The conversion fractions for the conversion fact 1 yard = 36 inches are _____ and _____ .

2. To change 2.5 yards to inches multiply by _____ .

3. To change 720 inches to yards multiply by _____ .

4. 720 inches = _____ yards.

5. 4.35 kilometers = _____ meters.

6. 2 hours = _____ seconds.

7. Which is a better buy for an item? 5 for $4.25 or 6 for $5.00?

8. A motor home rents for a weekly rate plus $0.25 per mile. What is the total cost for mileage for a trip of 500 miles?

9. The scale for a model airplane is 1:10. If the actual airplane has a wingspan of 42 feet, what is the wingspan of the model airplane?

10. What is the temperature to the nearest degree?

Answers

1. $\dfrac{1 \text{ yd}}{36 \text{ in.}} \quad \dfrac{36 \text{ in.}}{1 \text{ yd}}$

2. $\dfrac{36 \text{ in.}}{1 \text{ yd}}$

3. $\dfrac{1 \text{ yd}}{36 \text{ in.}}$

4. $\dfrac{720 \text{ in.}}{1} \cdot \dfrac{1 \text{ yd}}{36 \text{ in.}} = \dfrac{720 \text{ in.}}{1} \cdot \dfrac{1 \text{ yd}}{36 \text{ in.}} = 20 \text{ yards}$

5. **Method 1:** $\dfrac{4.35 \text{ km}}{1} \cdot \dfrac{1000 \text{ m}}{1 \text{ km}} = \dfrac{4.35 \text{ k\!\!\!/m}}{1} \cdot \dfrac{1000 \text{ m}}{1 \text{ k\!\!\!/m}} = 4350$ meters

   Method 2: $4.35 \text{ km} = 4.35 \cdot 10^3$ (3 moves right) $= 4.35 \cdot 1000 = 4350$ meters

6. $\dfrac{2 \text{ h}}{1} \cdot \dfrac{60 \text{ min}}{1 \text{ h}} \cdot \dfrac{60 \text{ s}}{1 \text{ min}} = \dfrac{2 \text{ h\!\!\!/}}{1} \cdot \dfrac{60 \text{ m\!\!\!/in}}{1 \text{ h\!\!\!/}} \cdot \dfrac{60 \text{ s}}{1 \text{ m\!\!\!/in}} = 7200$ seconds

7. The unit price for 5 items for \$4.25 is $\dfrac{\$4.25}{5 \text{ items}} = \$0.85$ per item.

   The unit price for 6 items for \$5.00 is $\dfrac{\$5.00}{6 \text{ items}} = \$0.83$ per item (rounded to the nearest cent).

   The better buy is 6 items for \$5.00.

   Did I answer the question? Yes, I found the better buy. ✓

   Does my answer make sense? Yes. ✓

   Is the answer stated in the correct units? No units are required. ✓

8. To find the total cost for mileage, multiply 500 miles by \$0.25 per mile (the unit rate).

   $500 \text{ mi} \cdot \dfrac{\$0.25}{1 \text{ mi}} = 500 \text{ m\!\!\!/i} \cdot \dfrac{\$0.25}{1 \text{ m\!\!\!/i}} = \$125$ The miles (mi) units divide out, leaving dollars (\$) as the units for the answer.

   The total cost for mileage is \$125.

   Did I answer the question? Yes, I found the total cost for the mileage. ✓

   Does my answer make sense? Yes, \$0.25 is one-fourth of a dollar. A 400 mile trip would cost \$100, so \$125 for a 500 mile trip is a reasonable answer. ✓

   Is the answer stated in the correct units? Yes, the units are dollars, which is correct. ✓

9. This problem is a proportion problem involving a scale model. To solve the problem, determine the ratios being compared, being sure to compare corresponding quantities in the same order; write a proportion using the two ratios; and then use cross products to solve the proportion.

   Step 1. Determine the ratios being compared.

   The scale of the model as 1:10. This means: $\dfrac{\text{wingspan of model}}{\text{wingspan of actual plane}} = \dfrac{1}{10}$.

   Step 2. Let w = the wingspan of the model. Write a proportion using the two ratios.

   $$\dfrac{w \, (\text{in feet})}{42 \text{ ft}} = \dfrac{1}{10}$$

   Step 3. Use cross products to solve the proportion (omitting the units for convenience).

   $$\dfrac{w}{42} = \dfrac{1}{10}$$

   $42 \cdot 1$ Find a cross product you can calculate. You don't know the value of w, so the only cross product you can calculate is 42 times 1.

   $w = \dfrac{42 \cdot 1}{10} = 4.2$ Divide by 10, the numerical term you didn't use.

   $w = 4.2 \text{ ft}$

   The wingspan of the model is 4.2 feet.

   Did I answer the question? Yes, I found the wingspan of the model. ✓

   Does my answer make sense? Yes, the model is smaller than the actual plane, so the wingspan of the model should be less than the wingspan of the actual plane. ✓

   Is the answer stated in the correct units? Yes, the units are feet, which is correct. ✓

10.

The thermometer is reading between 70° and 80°. The difference between these two points is 80° − 70° = 10°. It takes five marks to go from 70° up to 80°. Divide the difference between the two points by 5: 10° ÷ 5 = 2°. Therefore, each mark on the thermometer represents 2°. The thermometer is reading two marks above 70°. Since each mark represents 2°, the thermometer is reading 4° above 70°, which is 74°F.

How Do You Find Perimeter and Circumference?

The perimeter of a figure is the distance around it. You measure perimeter in units of length, such as inches, feet, yards, miles, kilometers, meters, centimeters, and millimeters. To find the perimeter of a closed figure that is made up of line segments, add up the lengths of the line segments. Here is an example.

Find the perimeter of the figure shown.

To find the perimeter, add the lengths of the four sides:

$$\text{Perimeter} = 6 \text{ cm} + 3 \text{ cm} + 7 \text{ cm} + 4 \text{ cm} = 20 \text{ cm}$$

Sometimes, the lengths for every side are not labeled. This occurs when the figure is a special geometric shape. On the FTCE GK Test, the four figures that you most likely will encounter when this happens are a rectangle, square, or an equilateral or an isosceles triangle. The Mathematics Reference Sheet does not give formulas for the perimeters of these figures. If you are finding the perimeter of such a figure, you can simply add up the lengths of the sides—so you really don't need a formula as such. In the discussion that follows, formulas are given because they often simplify the process of finding the perimeter, but more important, the formulas are very useful when you are given a perimeter and asked to determine one or more dimensions of these special geometric shapes.

Tip: When you work problems involving geometric figures, sketch a diagram if no diagram is given.

A **rectangle** is a closed, four-sided plane figure that has four right angles. It has two dimensions: **length** and **width.** Both pairs of opposite sides are congruent (the same size).

Length

Rectangle

The formula for the perimeter of a rectangle is $P = 2l + 2w$, where l is the length and w is the width.

Here is an example of finding the perimeter of a rectangle.

How many feet of fencing are needed to enclose a rectangular garden that is 25 feet by 35 feet?

Sketch a diagram and label it.

$l = 35\text{ft}$

Plug into the formula:

$$P = 2l + 2w = 2(35 \text{ ft}) + 2(25 \text{ ft}) = 70 \text{ ft} + 50 \text{ ft} = 120 \text{ ft}$$

Thus, 120 feet of fencing is needed.

A **square** is a rectangle that has four congruent **sides.** Its two dimensions, length and width, are equal.

Side

The formula for the perimeter of a square is $P = 4s$, where s is the length of one of its congruent sides.

Here is an example of finding the perimeter of a square.

What is the perimeter of a square that is 3.5 meters on a side?

Sketch a diagram and label it:

3.5 m

Plug into the formula:

$$P = 4s = 4(3.5 \text{ m}) = 14 \text{ m}$$

A **triangle** is a closed, three-sided plane figure.

Triangle

An **equilateral triangle** has three congruent sides.

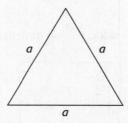

Equilateral Triangle

An **isosceles triangle** has at least two congruent sides.

Isosceles Triangle

Note: See "What is Congruence" in this chapter for an explanation of what "congruent" means.

The formula for the perimeter of a triangle is $P = a + b + c$, where a, b, and c are the lengths of the sides of the triangle.

Here is an example of finding the perimeter of an equilateral triangle.

What is the perimeter of an equilateral triangle that is 20 cm on a side?

Sketch a diagram and label it:

Plug into the formula:

$$P = a + b + c = 20 \text{ cm} + 20 \text{ cm} + 20 \text{ cm} = 60 \text{ cm}$$

Here is an example of finding the perimeter of an isosceles triangle.

> Find the perimeter of an isosceles triangle with congruent sides of 10 feet and a third side of 6 feet.

Sketch a diagram and label it:

Plug into the formula:

$$P = a + b + c = 10 \text{ ft} + 10 \text{ ft} + 6 \text{ ft} = 26 \text{ ft}$$

On the FTCE GK Test, you may have to find the distance around a **circle**. A **circle** is a closed plane figure for which all points are the same distance from a point within, called the **center**. A **radius** of a circle is a line segment joining the center of the circle to any point on the circle. A **diameter** is a line segment through the center of the circle with endpoints on the circle. The diameter of a circle is twice the radius. Conversely, the radius of a circle is half the diameter.

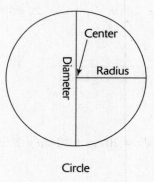

Circle

The **circumference** of a circle is the distance around the circle. In other words, the circumference of a circle is its perimeter. The formula for the circumference of a circle is given on the Mathematics Reference Sheet as $C = \pi d = 2\pi r$, where d and r are the diameter and radius of the circle, respectively. The Mathematics Reference Sheet states that you are to use 3.14 or $\frac{22}{7}$ for the number π. Since you are allowed to use a calculator, you should use 3.14 for π for ease of calculation.

Here is an example of finding the circumference of a circle.

Find the circumference of the circle in the diagram. Use $\pi = 3.14$.

20 in.
radius

From the diagram, you can see that the radius of the circle is 20 in. Plug into the formula:

$$C = 2\pi r = 2\pi(20 \text{ in.}) = 2 \cdot 3.14 \cdot 20 \text{ in.} = 125.6 \text{ in.}$$

How Do You Find Area?

The **area** of a plane figure is the amount of surface enclosed by the boundary of the figure. You measure area in square units, such as square inches (in.^{2}), square feet (ft^2), square miles (mi^2), square meters (m^2), square kilometers (km^2), square centimeters (cm^2), and square millimeters (mm^2). The area is always described in terms of square units, regardless of the shape of the figure.

The boundary measurements of a figure are measured in two dimensions (that is, length and width, base and height). The units for the boundary measurements are linear units (for example, inches, feet, miles, meters, and so on). You obtain the square units needed to describe area when you multiply the unit by itself. For example, (1 in.)(1 in.) = 1 in.^{2} = 1 square inch.

Finding the Area of a Rectangle

Here is an example of finding the area of a rectangle.

The formula for the area of a rectangle is $A = lw$, where l is the length and w is the width.

What is the area of a rectangle that is 4 cm by 3 cm?

Sketch a diagram and label it.

$w = 3$ cm

$l = 4$ cm

Plug into the formula:

$$A = lw = (4 \text{ cm})(3 \text{ cm}) = 12 \text{ cm}^2$$

You can verify that the formula works by dividing the rectangle into 1-cm squares and counting how many square centimeters are inside the boundary.

☐ = 1 cm²

Multiplying 4 cm by 3 cm gives you the same number of square centimeters as counting the squares inside the rectangle. The rectangle has an area of 12 cm².

Finding the Area of a Square

The formula for the area of a square is:

$$A = s^2, \text{ where } s \text{ is the length of a side.}$$

This formula is not given on the Mathematics Reference Sheet. To find the area of a square, you can use the formula for the area of a rectangle, $A = lw$. You will get the same answer either way.

Here is an example of finding the area of a square.

Find the area of the square in the diagram.

$s = 6$ m

From the diagram, you can see that s, the length of a side of the square, is 6 m. Since all sides are congruent, the width is also 6 m. Plug into either formula:

$$A = lw = (6 \text{ cm})(6 \text{ cm}) = 36 \text{ cm}^2 \text{ or } A = s^2 = (6 \text{ cm})^2 = 36 \text{ cm}^2$$

Finding the Area of a Triangle

To find the area of a triangle, you must know the measure of the triangle's **base** and **height.** The base can be any of the three sides of the triangle. The height for the base is a line drawn from the opposite vertex that meets that base at a right angle. A **vertex** of a triangle is the point where two sides meet.

The formula for the area of a triangle is $A = \frac{1}{2}bh$, where b is the length of a base of the triangle, and h is the height for that base. When you are finding the area of a triangle, you can pick any convenient side of the triangle to serve as the base in the formula.

Here is an example of finding the area of a triangle.

Find the area of the triangle in the diagram.

10 cm

25 cm

From the diagram, you can see that b = 25 cm and h = 10 cm. Plug into the formula:

$$A = \frac{1}{2}bh = \frac{1}{2}(25 \text{ cm})(10 \text{ cm}) = \frac{(25 \text{ cm})(10 \text{ cm})}{2} = 125 \text{ cm}^2$$

Here is how to key in the calculation: $25 \times 10 \div 2 =$. The display will show 125, the correct value.

Finding the Area of a Circle

The formula for the area of a circle is $A = \pi r^2$, where r is the radius of the circle.

Here is an example of finding the area of a circle.

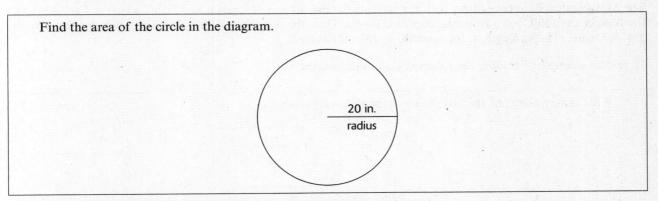

Find the area of the circle in the diagram.

20 in.
radius

From the diagram, you can see that the radius is 20 in. Plug into the formula:

$$A = \pi r^2 = \pi (20 \text{ in.})^2 = 3.14 \cdot 400 \text{ in.}^2 = 1256 \text{ in.}^2$$

Notice, that you must perform the exponentiation before multiplying by 3.14. Don't forget to follow **PE(MD) (AS)** when performing calculations. You cannot rely on the calculator to do the operations in the correct order.

How Do You Find Surface Area?

When you have a solid figure such as a rectangular prism (a box), a cylinder, or a pyramid, you can find the area of every face (surface) and add the areas together. The sum is the **surface area** of the solid figure.

Here is an example of finding the surface area of a rectangular box.

What is the surface area of the box shown below?

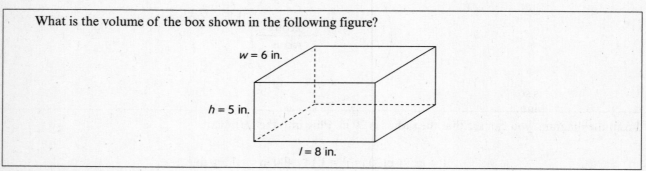

$w = 6$ in.

$h = 5$ in.

$l = 8$ in.

The box is composed of six **faces,** all of which are rectangles. Use the length and height to find the areas of the front and back faces. Use the length and width to find the areas of the top and bottom faces. Use the width and height to find the areas of the two side faces.

Surface Area $= 2(8$ in.$)(5$ in.$) + 2(8$in.$)(6$ in.$) + 2(6$ in.$)(5$ in.$) = 80$ in.$^2 + 96$ in.$^2 + 60$ in.$^2 = 236$ in.^{2}

How Do You Find Volume?

The **volume** of a solid figure is the amount of space inside the solid. Solid figures have three dimensions (for example, length, width, and height of a box). When you use the dimensions of a solid to find its volume, the units for the volume are cubic units, such as cubic inches (in.^{3}), cubic feet (ft^3), cubic miles (mi^3), cubic meters (m^3), cubic kilometers (km^3), cubic centimeters (cm^3), and cubic millimeters (mm^3).

The Mathematics Reference Sheet gives the formula for the volume of a prism as $V = Bh$, where $B =$ the Area of the Base of the solid. For a rectangular prism, $B = lw$. Thus, the formula for the volume of a rectangular prism is $V = lwh$, where l is the **length,** w is the **width,** and h is the **height.**

Here is an example of finding the volume of a rectangular prism.

What is the volume of the box shown in the following figure?

$w = 6$ in.

$h = 5$ in.

$l = 8$ in.

Plug into the formula:

$$V = Bh = lwh = (8 \text{ in.})(6 \text{ in.})(5 \text{ in.}) = 240 \text{ in.}^3$$

Notice that the units for the volume of the box are in.^{3} = cubic inches. Cubic units are obtained when a unit is used as a factor in a product three times, as in the following: (in.)(in.)(in.) = in.^{3}

How Do You Solve Real-World Problems Involving Perimeter, Area, and Volume?

When you have real-world problems in the form of word problems involving perimeter, area, or volume on the FTCE GK Test, you should always make a sketch to help you understand the problem. Otherwise, you solve these problems the same way you solve other word problems on the test. Here is an example.

> A homeowner wants to paint the walls in a large playroom that is 20 feet by 14 feet with an 8-foot-high ceiling. One gallon of paint will cover 350 square feet. The paint is sold in gallon containers only. How many gallons of paint will the homeowner need to buy?

Make a sketch to illustrate the problem.

Two steps are needed to solve the problem. First, find the surface area of the walls to be painted. Second, find the number of gallons needed to cover the walls by using the unit rate: 350 square feet per gallon.

Step 1. Find the surface area of the walls to be painted. Use the length and the height to find the areas of the two longer walls. Use the width and the height to find the area of the other two walls.

Surface area to painted = 2(20 ft)(8 ft) + 2(14 ft)(8 ft) = 320 ft^2 + 224 ft^2 = 544 ft^2

Step 2. Find the number of gallons of paint needed.

$$\text{one gallon of paint per 350 square feet} = \frac{350 \text{ ft}^2}{1 \text{ gal}}$$

$$\text{number of gallons needed } 544 \text{ ft}^2 \div \frac{350 \text{ ft}^2}{1 \text{ gal}} = \frac{544 \text{ ft}^2}{1} \cdot \frac{1 \text{ gal}}{350 \text{ ft}^2} = \frac{544 \text{ ft}^2}{1} \cdot \frac{1 \text{ gal}}{350 \text{ ft}^2} = \frac{544 \text{ gal}}{350}$$

$$\approx 1.55 \text{ gal}$$

Because the paint is sold in gallon containers only, the homeowner will need to buy 2 gallons of paint to have enough paint to paint the walls.

Did I answer the question? Yes, I found the number of gallons of paint needed. ✓

Does my answer make sense? Yes, two gallons to paint a room seems reasonable. ✓

Is the answer stated in the correct units? Yes, the units are gallons, which is correct. ✓

Test Yourself

1. The perimeter of a figure is the _____ around it.

2. Perimeter is measured in units of _____.

3. To find the perimeter of a closed figure whose sides are line segments, add up the _____ of the _____.

4. The formula for the circumference of a circle is _____ or _____ .

5. The area of a plane figure is the amount of _____ enclosed by the boundary of the figure.

6. Area is measured in _____ units.

7. The formula for the area of a rectangle is _____ .

8. The formula for the area of a circle is _____ .

9. The formula for the volume of a rectangular prism is _____ .

10. How many square yards of carpet are needed to carpet a room that measures 15 feet by 18 feet?

Answers

1. distance

2. length

3. lengths, sides

4. πd, $2\pi r$

5. surface

6. square

7. $A = lw$

8. $A = \pi r^2$

9. $V = Bh$ or $V = lwh$

10. Sketch a diagram.

15 ft

18 ft

Analyze the problem. Square yards are units of area, so you will need to find the area of the carpet in square yards. To find how many square yards of carpet are needed, two steps are needed. First, convert the dimensions of the room from feet to yards. Next, find the area of the rectangular room in square yards.

Step 1. Convert the dimensions of the floor to yards.

The conversion fractions are $\frac{1 \text{ yd}}{3 \text{ ft}}$ and $\frac{3 \text{ ft}}{1 \text{ yd}}$. Write your measurement as a fraction with denominator 1 and let unit analysis tell you whether to multiply by $\frac{1 \text{ yd}}{3 \text{ ft}}$ or $\frac{3 \text{ ft}}{1 \text{ yd}}$. Since you want the feet to divide out, multiply by $\frac{1 \text{ yd}}{3 \text{ ft}}$.

$$\frac{18 \text{ ft}}{1} \cdot \frac{1 \text{ yd}}{3 \text{ ft}} = \frac{18 \cancel{\text{ft}}}{1} \cdot \frac{1 \text{ yd}}{3 \cancel{\text{ft}}} = \frac{\overset{6}{\cancel{18}} \cancel{\text{ft}}}{1} \cdot \frac{1 \text{ yd}}{\underset{1}{\cancel{3}} \cancel{\text{ft}}} = 6 \text{ yd}$$

$$\frac{15 \text{ ft}}{1} \cdot \frac{1 \text{ yd}}{3 \text{ ft}} = \frac{15 \cancel{\text{ft}}}{1} \cdot \frac{1 \text{ yd}}{3 \cancel{\text{ft}}} = \frac{\overset{5}{\cancel{15}} \cancel{\text{ft}}}{1} \cdot \frac{1 \text{ yd}}{\underset{1}{\cancel{3}} \cancel{\text{ft}}} = 5 \text{ yd}$$

Step 2. Find the area of the carpet:

The Mathematics Reference Sheet shows the formula for the area of a rectangle is $A = lw$.

$A = lw = (6 \text{ yd})(5 \text{ yd}) = 30 \text{ yd}^2$

At least 30 yd^2 of carpet are needed to carpet the room.

Did I answer the question? Yes, I found how many square yards of carpet are needed. ✓

Does my answer make sense? Yes, it is consistent with my knowledge of the real world. ✓

Is the answer stated in the correct units? Yes, the units are square yards, which is correct. ✓

Sample Questions

Directions: Read each question and select the best answer choice.

1. A runner ran a cross country race of 14 500 meters. How many kilometers did the runner run in the race?

    A. 1.45 kilometers
    B. 14.5 kilometers
    C. 145 kilometers
    D. 14500000 kilometers

2. What is the temperature to the nearest degree?

    A. 80°
    B. 81°
    C. 82°
    D. 85°

3. What is the perimeter of a rectangle that measures 6 yards by 5 yards?

    A. 11 yd
    B. 22 yd
    C. 30 yd
    D. 60 yd

4. How many cubic feet of cement are in a rectangular cement slab that is 3 inches thick and measures 10 feet long and 5 feet wide?

    A. 12.5 ft^3
    B. 15.25 ft^3
    C. 40 ft^3
    D. 150 ft^3

Answer Explanations for Sample Questions

1. **B.**

   Method 1: The conversion fractions are $\dfrac{1\ km}{1000\ m}$ and $\dfrac{1000\ m}{1\ km}$. Write your measurement as a fraction with denominator 1 and let unit analysis tell you whether to multiply by $\dfrac{1\ km}{1000\ m}$ or $\dfrac{1000\ m}{1\ km}$. Since you want the meters to divide out, multiply by $\dfrac{1\ km}{1000\ m}$.

   $$\frac{14\ 500\ m}{1} \cdot \frac{1\ km}{1000\ m} = \frac{14\ 500\ \cancel{m}}{1} \cdot \frac{1\ km}{1000\ \cancel{m}} = \frac{14\ 500\ km}{1000} = 14.5\ \text{kilometers}$$

   The runner ran 14.5 kilometers in the race, Choice **B**.

   Method 2: 14 500 m = 14 500 ÷ 10^3 (3 moves left) = 14 500 ÷ 1000 = 14.5 kilometers, Choice **B**.

   The other choices occur if you make a mistake in placing the decimal point in your answer.

2. **C.**

   The thermometer is reading between 80° and 90°. The difference between these two points is 90° − 80° = 10°. It takes five marks to go from 80° up to 90°. Divide the difference between the two points by 5: 10° ÷ 5 = 2°. Therefore, each mark on the thermometer represents 2°. The thermometer is reading one mark above 80°. Since each mark represents 2°, the thermometer is reading 2° above 80°, which is 82°F (Choice **C**). Choice **A** results if you determine incorrectly that the reading is at 80°. Choice **B** results if you determine incorrectly that each mark represents 1°. Choice **D** results if you determine incorrectly that each mark represents 5°.

3. B. First, sketch a diagram to illustrate the problem:

Plug into the formula.

$$P = 2l + 2w = 2(6 \text{ yd}) + 2(5 \text{ yd}) = 12 \text{ yd} + 10 \text{ yd} = 22 \text{ yd, Choice } \mathbf{B}.$$

Choice **A** results if you fail to multiply each dimension by 2. Choice **C** results if you incorrectly confuse perimeter with area. Choice **D** results if you use an incorrect formula.

4. A. First, sketch a diagram to illustrate the problem:

Analyze the problem. Cubic feet are units of volume. The amount of cement in the slab is equal to the volume of the slab, which is a rectangular prism. To find the volume of the slab in units of cubic feet, two steps are needed. First, convert 3 inches to feet. Next, find the volume of the cement in cubic feet.

Step 1. Convert 3 inches to feet.

The conversion fractions are $\frac{1 \text{ ft}}{12 \text{ in.}}$ and $\frac{12 \text{ in.}}{1 \text{ ft}}$. Write 3 inches as a fraction with denominator 1 and let unit analysis tell you whether to multiply by $\frac{1 \text{ ft}}{12 \text{ in.}}$ or $\frac{12 \text{ in.}}{1 \text{ ft}}$. Since you want the inches to divide out, multiply by $\frac{1 \text{ ft}}{12 \text{ in.}}$.

$$\frac{3 \text{ in.}}{1} \cdot \frac{1 \text{ ft}}{12 \text{ in.}} = \frac{3 \text{ in.}}{1} \cdot \frac{1 \text{ ft}}{12 \text{ in.}} = \frac{3^1 \text{ in.}}{1} \cdot \frac{1 \text{ yd}}{12_4 \text{ in.}} = \frac{1}{4} \text{ ft} = 0.25 \text{ ft}$$

Step 2. Find the volume of the cement in cubic feet.

$$V = Bh = lwh = (10 \text{ ft})(5 \text{ ft})(0.25 \text{ ft}) = 12.5 \text{ ft}^3$$

There are 12.5 ft³ of cement in the slab, Choice **A**.

Did I answer the question? Yes, I found how many cubic feet of cement are in the slab. ✓

Does my answer make sense? Yes, it is consistent with my knowledge of the real world. ✓

Is the answer stated in the correct units? Yes, the units are cubic feet, which is correct. ✓

Choices **B** and **C** result if you use an incorrect formula for the volume of a rectangular prism. Choice **D** results if you neglect to convert 3 inches to 0.25 feet.

Geometry

According to the *Competencies and Skills Required for Teacher Certification in Florida, Fifteenth Edition* (see the first section of this chapter for the Web address), the competencies/skills you should be able to do for this area of mathematics are the following:

- Identify and classify geometric shapes and solids according to their properties.
- Identify examples of geometric concepts including perpendicularity, parallelism, tangency, symmetry, and transformations.
- Solve real-world problems involving similar and congruent figures and the Pythagorean theorem.
- Locate and name points on a coordinate graph and use the concepts of slope and distance to solve problems.

What is Congruence?

Congruent (denoted ≅) geometric figures have exactly the same size and same shape. They are superimposable, meaning that they will fit exactly on top of each other. Corresponding parts of congruent figures are congruent.

Here are examples of congruent figures (same size, same shape).

Congruent Figures

Hash marks (as shown in the figure below) can be used to draw attention to corresponding congruent parts.

Congruent Triangles

The figures below are not congruent. They have the same shape, but not the same size.

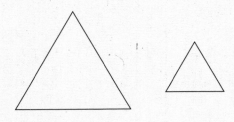

Not Congruent

These figures are not congruent. They are about the same size, but they do not have the same shape. One is a right triangle and the other one is an equilateral triangle.

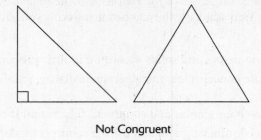

Not Congruent

How Do You Classify Angles?

In geometry, the terms **point**, **line**, and **plane** are undefined. You can think of a point as a location in space. You can think of a line as a set of points that extends infinitely in both directions. You can think of a plane as a set of points that form a flat infinite surface. *Note:* For discussions in this chapter, unless specifically stated otherwise, all plane figures and objects are considered to lie in the same plane.

A **ray** is a line extending from a point. When two rays meet at a common point, they form an **angle.** The point where the rays meet is the **vertex** of the angle.

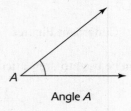

Angle A

You measure angles in degrees. You use the symbol, °, to stand for degrees. You can classify angles by the number of degrees in their measurement.

An **acute angle** measures between 0° and 90°.

Acute Angle

A **right angle** measures exactly 90°.

Right Angle

An **obtuse angle** measures between 90° and 180°.

Obtuse Angle

A **straight angle** measures exactly 180°.

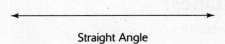

Straight Angle

Two angles whose sum is 90° are **complementary angles.**

Complementary Angles

Two angles whose sum is 180° are **supplementary angles.**

Supplementary Angles

Adjacent angles are two angles that have a common vertex and a common side.

Adjacent Angles

A **bisector of an angle** is a line that passes through the vertex of the angle and divides it into two congruent angles.

Bisector *AB* of Angle *A*

How Do You Classify Lines?

Lines in a plane can be parallel or intersecting.

Intersecting lines cross at a point in the plane.

Intersecting Lines

Parallel lines (in a plane) never meet. The distance between them is always the same.

Pairs of Parallel Lines

A shorthand way to indicate that line *AB* is parallel to line *CD* is to write $AB \parallel CD$.

Perpendicular lines intersect at right angles.

Perpendicular Lines

A shorthand way to indicate that line *AB* is perpendicular to line *CD* is to write $AB \perp CD$.

A **tangent line** to a circle intersects the circle in exactly one point.

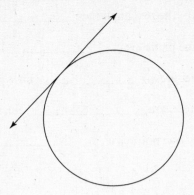

Tangent Line

Following are theorems about lines that are useful to know.

- **Euclid's Parallel Postulate:** Given a line and a point in the same plane but not on the line, there is one and only one line through the given point that is parallel to the given line.
- The shortest distance from a point to a line is the measure of the perpendicular line segment from the point to the line.
- Two distinct lines (in a plane) that are perpendicular to the same line are parallel.
- If a line in a plane is perpendicular to one of two parallel lines, it is perpendicular to the other parallel line.
- Two nonadjacent angles formed by intersecting lines are **vertical angles.** Vertical angles formed by two intersecting lines are congruent as shown in the following figure.

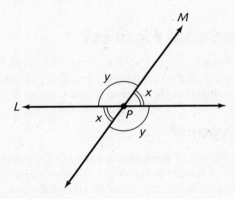

Two Pairs of Congruent Vertical Angles

- A radius drawn to the point of contact of a tangent to a circle is perpendicular to the tangent at that exact point.

Test Yourself

1. A right angle measures exactly _____ .

2. An angle that measures 40° is a(n) _____ angle.

3. An angle that measures 165° is a(n) _____ angle.

4. An angle that measures exactly 180° is a(n) _____ angle.

5. If one of two complementary angles measures 25°, what is the measure of the other angle?

6. If two angles measure 120° and 60°, the two angles are _____ angles.

7. Two lines that cross at a point in the plane are _____ lines.

8. Two lines in a plane that never meet are _____ lines.

9. Two lines that intersect at right angles are _____ lines.

10. A line that meets a circle in exactly one point is a _____ line to the circle.

Answers

1. 90°

2. acute

3. obtuse

4. straight

5. 90° – 25° = 65°

6. supplementary

7. intersecting

8. parallel

9. perpendicular

10. tangent

What Are Two-Dimensional Figures?

Two-dimensional (plane) figures are flat shapes that lie in a plane. The plane figures that are most important for you to know for the FTCE GK Test are polygons including triangles, quadrilaterals, pentagons, hexagons, and octagons and the circle (which was discussed in the Measurement section, earlier in this chapter).

How Do You Classify Polygons?

A **polygon** is a closed plane figure composed of **sides** that are straight line segments. The point at which the two sides of a polygon intersect is a **vertex**. A **regular polygon** has all sides and angles congruent. Polygons are classified by the number of sides they have. Following are examples of regular polygons.

Triangle (3 sides)

Quadrilateral (4 sides)

Pentagon (5 sides)

Hexagon (6 sides)

The sum of the measures of the interior angles of an n-sided polygon equals $(n-2)180°$. Thus, the sum of the measures of the interior angles of a triangle is $(3-2)180° = 1 \cdot 180° = 180°$, of a quadrilateral is $(4-2)180° = 2 \cdot 180° = 360°$, of a pentagon is $(5-2)180° = 3 \cdot 180° = 540°$, and so on.

A line segment that connects two nonconsecutive vertices of a polygon is a **diagonal.** The number of diagonals of an n-sided polygon is given by the formula: $\dfrac{n(n-3)}{2}$. Here are examples of regular polygons with the number of diagonals indicated below the figure.

Triangle	Quadrilateral	Pentagon	Hexagon
0 diagonals	2 diagonals	5 diagonals	9 diagonals

If all the diagonals of a polygon lie within the interior of the polygon, the polygon is **convex;** otherwise, the polygon is **concave.** Here are examples.

Convex Hexagon   Concave Hexagon   Convex Decagon   Concave Decagon

How Do You Classify Triangles?

A **triangle** is a three-sided polygon. The sum of the interior angles of a triangle is 180°. Triangles can be classified in two different ways. You can classify triangles according to their sides as equilateral, isosceles, or scalene.

An **equilateral triangle** has three congruent sides. An **isosceles** triangle has at least two congruent sides. A **scalene** triangle has no congruent sides.

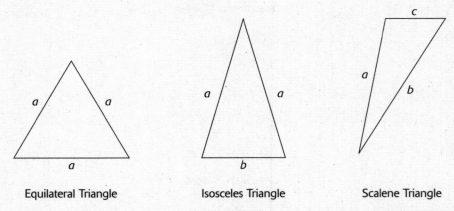

| Equilateral Triangle | Isosceles Triangle | Scalene Triangle |

Another way to classify triangles is according to their interior angles. An **acute** triangle has three acute angles. A **right** triangle has exactly one right angle. An **obtuse** triangle has exactly one obtuse angle.

| Acute Triangle | Right Triangle | Obtuse Triangle |

Congruent triangles are triangles for which corresponding sides and corresponding angles are congruent. In the figure shown, triangle *ABC* is congruent to triangle *DEF,* denoted as $\triangle ABC \cong \triangle DEF$.

Congruent Triangles

You can use the following theorems to prove two triangles are congruent.

- If three sides of one triangle are congruent, correspondingly, to three sides of another triangle, then the two triangles are congruent (**SSS**). Note: To make sure a triangle exists, the sum of the lengths of any two sides must be greater than the length of the third side.
- If two sides and the included angle of one triangle are congruent, correspondingly, to two sides and the included angle of another triangle, then the two triangles are congruent (**SAS**).
- If two angles and the included side of one triangle are congruent, correspondingly, to two angles and the included side of another triangle, then the two triangles are congruent (**ASA**).
- If two angles and the nonincluded side of one triangle are congruent, correspondingly, to two angles and the nonincluded side of another triangle, then the two triangles are congruent (**AAS**).

Tip: Two methods that do NOT work for proving congruence are AAA (three corresponding angles congruent) and SSA (two corresponding sides and the nonincluded angle congruent).

Here are other theorems about triangles that are useful to know.

- **Triangle inequality:** the sum of the measures of any two sides of a triangle must be greater than the measure of the third side.
- If two sides of a triangle are congruent, then the angles opposite those sides are congruent; and, conversely, if two angles of a triangle are congruent, then the sides opposite those angles are congruent.
- The segment between the midpoints of two sides of a triangle is parallel to the third side and half as long.

How Do You Classify Quadrilaterals?

Some quadrilaterals can be classified as either trapezoids or parallelograms.

A **trapezoid** has two definitions, both of which are widely accepted. One definition is that a trapezoid is a quadrilateral that has *exactly* one pair of opposite sides that are parallel. This definition would exclude parallelograms as a special case. The other definition is that a trapezoid is a quadrilateral that has *at least* one pair of parallel sides. This definition would allow any parallelogram to be considered a special kind of trapezoid. This conflicting situation is one of the few times that mathematicians do not agree on the definition of a term. You can expect that answers to problems involving trapezoids on the FTCE GK Test will not hinge on which of these definitions for trapezoid you choose to use during the test. This test prep book uses the following definition for trapezoid:

A **trapezoid** is a quadrilateral that has exactly one pair of parallel sides.

Trapezoid

In a **parallelogram** opposite sides are parallel and congruent.

Parallelogram

137

Some parallelograms have special names because of their special properties.

A **rhombus** is a parallelogram that has four congruent sides.

Rhombus

A **rectangle** is a parallelogram that has four right angles.

Rectangle

A **square** is a parallelogram that has four right angles and four congruent sides.

Square

Following are theorems about quadrilaterals that are useful to know.

- The sum of the angles of a quadrilateral is 360°.
- If the diagonals of a quadrilateral bisect each other, the quadrilateral is a parallelogram.
- If two sides of a quadrilateral are parallel and congruent, the quadrilateral is a parallelogram.
- The lengths of the diagonals of a rectangle, square, or rhombus are equal.
- In a rhombus or square, the diagonals are perpendicular to each other.
- If the diagonals of a quadrilateral are perpendicular bisectors of each other, the quadrilateral is a rhombus.
- If a parallelogram has one right angle, it has four right angles and is a rectangle.

What Is Symmetry?

Symmetry describes the shape of a figure or object. A figure or object is **symmetric** if it can be folded exactly in half and the two parts are congruent. The line along the fold is the **line of symmetry.**

Here are three examples of symmetric shapes. A line of symmetry is shown in each figure.

Symmetric Figures

Some shapes have more than one line of symmetry. For the figures that follow, you can fold along any of the lines of symmetry and the two halves will be congruent.

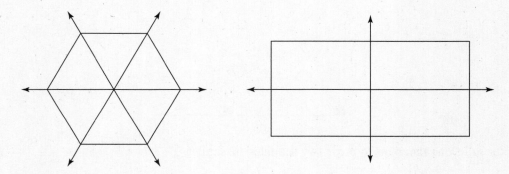

Symmetric Figures with More than One Line of Symmetry

What Is Similarity?

Similar (denoted ≈) geometric figures have the same shape, but not necessarily the same size.

Similar, but <u>not</u> congruent   **Similar** <u>and</u> congruent

Corresponding sides of similar shapes are proportional. That is, the ratios of the lengths of corresponding sides are equal. Here is an example.

In the figure shown, rectangle *A* is similar to rectangle *B*. What is the ratio of the lengths of the sides of rectangle *A* compared to the lengths of the corresponding sides of rectangle *B*?

The ratio of the lengths of corresponding sides is $\dfrac{12 \text{ ft}}{6 \text{ ft}} = \dfrac{12}{6} = \dfrac{2}{1}$ or 2 to 1.

Similar triangles are triangles for which corresponding sides are proportional and corresponding angles are congruent. In the figure shown, triangle *CAB* is similar to triangle *EAD*, denoted as $\triangle CAB \approx \triangle EAD$.

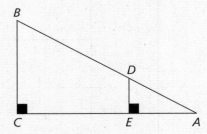

You can use the following theorems to prove two triangles are similar.

- If corresponding angles of two triangles are congruent, the two triangles are similar.
- If corresponding sides of two triangles are proportional, the two triangles are similar.
- If two angles of one triangle are congruent to two corresponding angles of another triangle, then the two triangles are similar.
- If two sides of one triangle are proportional to two corresponding sides of another triangle, and the included angles are congruent, then the two triangles are similar.
- The ratio of the areas of two similar triangles is the square of the ratio of the lengths of any two corresponding sides.

What Are Three-Dimensional Figures?

Three-dimensional figures are solid figures that occupy space. The solid figures you should be able to recognize for the FTCE GK Test are prisms, pyramids, cylinders, cones, and spheres.

A **prism** is a solid with two congruent and parallel bases. The sides of a prism are rectangles. The bases of a prism can have the shape of any polygon. Prisms are named according to the shape of their bases.

Rectangular Prism · Triangular Prism

A **cube** is a special rectangular prism that has six congruent faces, all of which are squares.

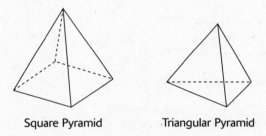

Cube

A **pyramid** is a solid with exactly one base. The sides of a pyramid are triangles. The base can have the shape of any polygon. Pyramids are named according to the shape of their bases.

Square Pyramid · Triangular Pyramid

A **cylinder** has two parallel congruent bases, which are circles. It has one rectangular side that wraps around.

Cylinder

A **cone** is a three-dimensional solid that has one circular base. It has a curved side that wraps around.

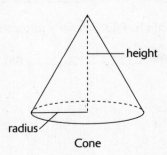

Cone

A **sphere** is a three-dimensional solid that is shaped like a ball. Every point on the sphere is the same distance from a point within, called the **center** of the sphere. The **radius** of the sphere is a line segment from the center of the sphere to any point on the sphere. The **diameter** of the sphere is a line segment joining two points of the sphere and passing through its center. The radius of the sphere is half the diameter. Conversely, the diameter is twice the radius.

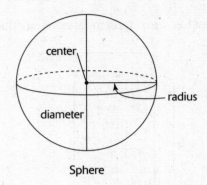

Sphere

Test Yourself

1. A four-sided polygon is a _____ .

2. A pentagon has exactly _____ sides.

3. A hexagon has exactly _____ sides.

4. An octagon has exactly _____ sides.

5. A scalene triangle has _____ congruent sides.

6. The sum of the interior angles of a triangle is _____.

7. An acute triangle has _____ acute angles.

8. A _____ is a quadrilateral that has exactly one pair of parallel sides.

9. In a parallelogram, opposite sides are _____ and _____.

10. Rhombuses, rectangles, and squares are _____.

11. Rectangles and squares have four _____ angles.

12. Rhombuses and squares have four _____ sides.

13. Congruent geometric figures have exactly the same _____ and same _____.

14. A figure is _____ if it can be folded exactly into congruent halves.

15. Similar geometric figures have the same _____, but not necessarily the same _____.

16. In the figure shown, hexagon A is similar to hexagon B. What is the ratio of the lengths of the sides of hexagon A compared to the lengths of corresponding sides of hexagon B?

Hexagon A   Hexagon B

12 ft

6 ft

17. Prisms and cylinders have _____ congruent and parallel bases.

18. _____ and _____ have exactly one base.

19. A _____ is a rectangular prism that has six congruent faces.

20. The points on the three-dimensional solid that is a _____ are the same distance from a point within, called its center.

Answers

1. quadrilateral

2. five

3. six

4. eight

5. no

6. 180°

7. three

8. trapezoid

9. congruent, parallel

10. parallelograms

11. right

12. congruent

13. size, shape

14. symmetric

15. shape, size

16.

Hexagon A

Hexagon B

6 ft

12 ft

The ratio of the lengths of corresponding sides is $\frac{12\ \text{ft}}{6\ \text{ft}} = \frac{12}{6} = \frac{2}{1}$ or 2 to 1.

17. two

18. pyramids, cones

19. cube

20. sphere

How Do You Solve Problems Involving the Pythagorean Relationship?

A **right triangle** is a triangle that has exactly one right angle. The side opposite the right angle is the **hypotenuse** of the triangle. The hypotenuse is *always* the longest side of the right triangle. The other two sides are the **legs** of the triangle. Commonly, the letter c is used to represent the hypotenuse of a right triangle, and the letters a and b to represent the legs.

A special relationship, named after the famous Greek mathematician Pythagoras, exists between the sides of a right triangle. As given on the Mathematics Reference Sheet, this special relationship is the Pythagorean Theorem: $a^2 + b^2 = c^2$; or, equivalently, $c^2 = a^2 + b^2$. Here is an illustration.

The Pythagorean relationship applies only to right triangles. If you know any two sides of a right triangle, you can find the third side by using the formula $c^2 = a^2 + b^2$. Here is an example.

Using the diagram, find the length of the diagonal of a rectangular flower garden that has dimensions of 16 feet by 12 feet.

From the diagram, you can see that the diagonal is the hypotenuse of a right triangle that has legs of 12 ft and 16 ft. Plug into the formula omitting the units:

c = hypotenuse = ?, a = 12, and b = 16

$c^2 = a^2 + b^2 = (12)^2 + (16)^2 = 144^2 + 256^2 = 400$ ft^2

Since $c = 400^2$, to obtain c, you take the square root of 400^2.

Thus, $c = 20$.

Note: Also, from the list of square roots given in "Are All Square Roots Irrational?" (earlier in this chapter), you know that $\sqrt{400} = 20$.

The length of the diagonal of the flower garden is 20 feet.

> *Did I answer the question?* Yes, I found the length of the diagonal of the flower garden. ✓
>
> *Does my answer make sense?* Yes, given that the legs are 12 feet and 16 feet in length, 20 feet for the length of the hypotenuse seems reasonable. ✓
>
> *Is the answer stated in the correct units?* Yes, the units are feet, which is correct. ✓

Tip: If the measures of the three sides of a triangle satisfy the Pythagorean relationship, the triangle is a right triangle. Numbers, such as 3, 4, and 5, that satisfy the Pythagorean relationship are Pythagorean triples. Once you identify a Pythagorean triple, any multiple of the three numbers is also a Pythagorean triple. For example, since 3, 4, and 5 is a Pythagorean triple, then so is 30, 40, and 50.

How Do You Locate and Name Points in a Coordinate System?

In the Numerations and Operations section (earlier in this chapter), you learned that the real numbers can be represented on a number line. If you take two copies of the real number line, one horizontal and one vertical, and position them at right angles so that they intersect at the 0 point on each line, you have a **coordinate system (graph).**

Commonly, the horizontal number line with positive direction to the right is designated the **x-axis,** and the vertical number line with positive direction upward is designated the **y-axis.** The intersection of the two lines is the **origin.** The two intersecting x- and y-axes divide the coordinate grid into four sections, called **quadrants.**

The quadrants are numbered *counterclockwise* using Roman numerals as shown in the following.

With this coordinate system you can match points with an **ordered pair** of numbers, called **coordinates.** An ordered pair of numbers is written in a definite order so that one number is first, and the other is second. The first number is the ***x*-coordinate,** and the second number is the ***y*-coordinate.** You write ordered pairs in parentheses with the two numbers separated by commas. The ordered pair (0, 0) designates the origin.

Look at these examples.

(3, 5) is the ordered pair with *x*-coordinate = 3, and *y*-coordinate = 5

(–2, 3) is the ordered pair with *x*-coordinate = –2, and *y*-coordinate = 3

An ordered pair gives you directions on how to graph a point on the coordinate grid, starting from the origin (0, 0). The *x*-coordinate tells you how far to go right (for positive numbers) or left (for negative numbers). From that spot, the *y*-coordinate tells you how far you need to go up (for positive numbers) or down (for negative numbers) to mark the location of the point.

Here are examples of how to graph a point.

Graph the ordered pair (3, 5).

Start at (0, 0). Go 3 units right. Then go 5 units up.

Graph the ordered pair (–2, 3).

Start at (0, 0). Go 2 units left. Then go 3 units up.

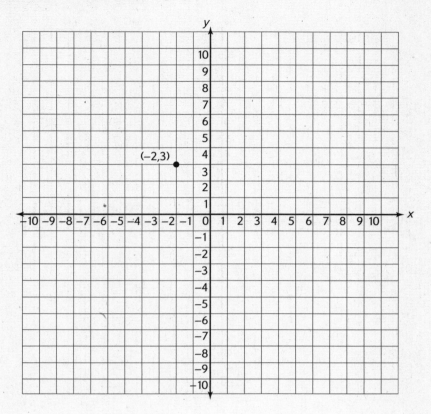

Graph the ordered pair (–4, –5).

Start at (0, 0). Go 4 units left. Then go 5 units down.

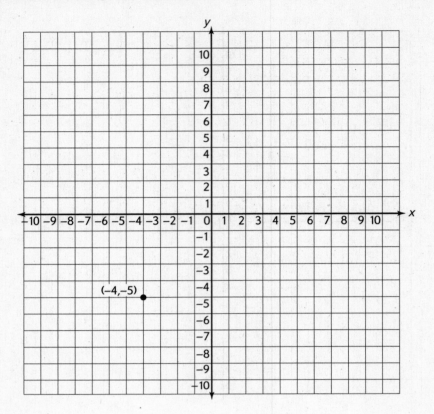

Graph the ordered pair (1, –6).

Start at (0, 0). Go 1 unit right. Then go 6 units down.

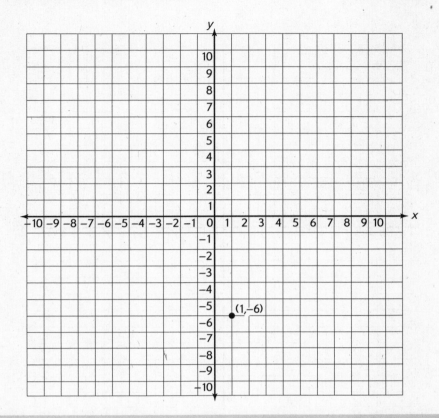

Tip: Note that in Quadrant 1, both the *x*-coordinate and the *y*-coordinate are positive; in Quadrant II, the *x*-coordinate is negative, and the *y*-coordinate is positive; in Quadrant III, both the *x*-coordinate and the *y*-coordinate are negative; and in Quadrant IV, the *x*-coordinate is positive, and the *y*-coordinate is negative.

Points that have zero as one or both of the coordinates lie on the axes. If the *x*-coordinate is zero, the point lies on the *y*-axis. If the *y*-coordinate is zero, the point lies on the *x*-axis. If both coordinates of a point are zero, the point is at the origin. For example, as shown in the following, the point (0, 4) lies on the *y*-axis, and the point (–5, 0) lies on the *x*-axis.

You name a point on a coordinate graph by naming the ordered pair, (*x*, *y*), that specifies the location of the point. The location of every point in the coordinate plane is given by an ordered pair of real numbers. The numbers *x* and *y* are the coordinates of the point. Here is an example.

What ordered pair represents the point *K*?

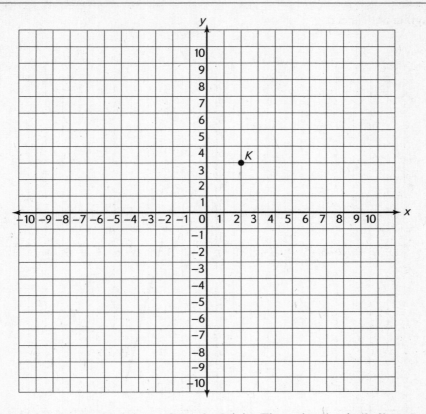

The point *K* is 2 units to the right and 3 units up from the origin. The ordered pair (2, 3) represents the point *K*.

How Do You Find the Slope of the Line Between Two Points?

To find the slope of the line that connects the points (x_1, y_1) and (x_2, y_2) on a coordinate graph, do these steps:

Step 1. Sketch a diagram and label it.

Step 2. Specify (x_1, y_1) and (x_2, y_2). This step is *very* important, so don't skip it. Notice the subscript written to the lower right of each variable. The subscripts are used to emphasize that the coordinates x_1 and y_1 go together and the coordinates x_2 and y_2 go together. Keep this in mind when you do Step 2.

Step 3. Plug into the formula given on the Mathematics Reference Sheet:

$$\text{Slope of line} = \frac{y_2 - y_1}{x_2 - x_1}$$

Tip: Enclose in parentheses any substituted value that is negative to avoid making a sign error.

Here are examples.

> Find the slope of the line that passes through the points (5, –7) and (3, 1).

Step 1. Sketch a diagram and label it.

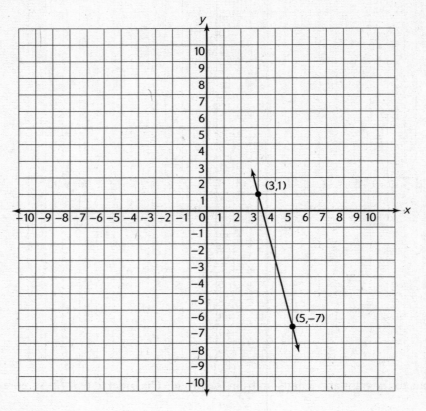

Step 2. Specify (x_1, y_1) and (x_2, y_2).

Let $(x_1, y_1) = (5, -7)$ and $(x_2, y_2) = (3, 1)$. Then $x_1 = 5$, $y_1 = -7$, $x_2 = 3$, and $y_2 = 1$.

Step 3: Plug into the formula.

$$\text{Slope of line} = \frac{y_2 - y_1}{x_2 - x_1} = \frac{1 - (-7)}{3 - 5} = \frac{1 + 7}{3 - 5} = \frac{8}{-2} = -4$$

The line through the points (5, –7) and (3, 1) has slope –4.

Find the slope of the line that connects the points (–4, –5) and (2, 3).

Step 1. Sketch a diagram and label it.

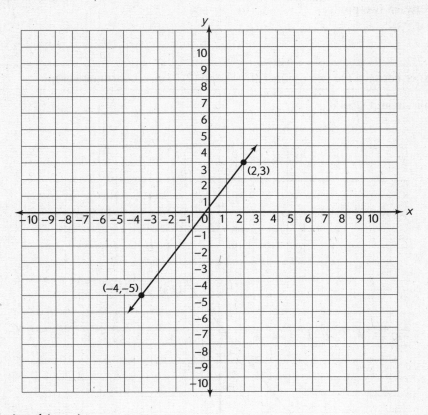

Step 2. Specify (x_1, y_1) and (x_2, y_2).

Let $(x_1, y_1) = (-4, -5)$ and $(x_2, y_2) = (2, 3)$. Then $x_1 = -4$, $y_1 = -5$, $x_2 = 2$, and $y_2 = 3$.

Step 3: Plug into the formula.

Slope of line $= \dfrac{y_2 - y_1}{x_2 - x_1} = \dfrac{3 - (-5)}{2 - (-4)} = \dfrac{3 + 5}{2 + 4} = \dfrac{8}{6} = \dfrac{4}{3}$

The line through the points (–4, –5) and (2, 3) has slope $\dfrac{4}{3}$.

Tip: Lines that slant to the right (that is, slope up from left to right) have positive slope. Lines that slant to the left (that is, slope down from left to right) have negative slope. The slope of a horizontal line is zero. A vertical line has no slope. When you calculate the slope between two points, be sure to note the slant, if any. If your answer has a sign that disagrees with the slant, you made an error.

How Do You Find the Distance between Two Points?

The steps to find the distance between two points on a coordinate graph are basically the same (except you use a different formula) as the steps for finding the slope of the line between the points:

Step 1. Sketch a diagram and label it.

Step 2. Specify (x_1, y_1) and (x_2, y_2).

Step 3. Plug into the formula given on the Mathematics Reference Sheet:

Distance between two points $= \sqrt{(x_2 - x_1)^2 + (y_2 - y_1)^2}$

Here is an example.

> Find the distance between the two points $(-4, -5)$ and $(2, 3)$ on a coordinate graph.

Step 1. Sketch a diagram and label it.

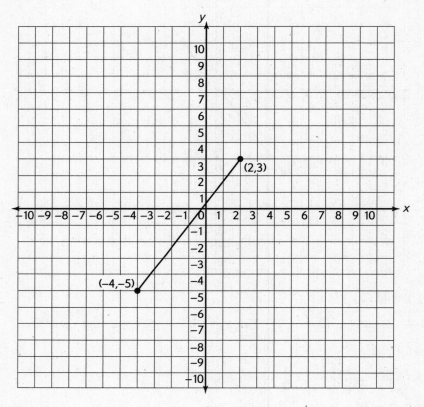

Step 2. Specify (x_1, y_1) and (x_2, y_2).

Let $(x_1, y_1) = (-4, -5)$ and $(x_2, y_2) = (2, 3)$. Then $x_1 = -4$, $y_1 = -5$, $x_2 = 2$, and $y_2 = 3$.

Step 3: Plug into the formula.

Distance between two points $= \sqrt{(x_2 - x_1)^2 + (y_2 - y_1)^2} = \sqrt{(2 - (-4))^2 + (3 - (-5))^2} = \sqrt{(2 + 4)^2 + (3 + 5)^2}$
$= \sqrt{(6)^2 + (8)^2} = \sqrt{36 + 64} = \sqrt{100} = 10$

The distance between the two points $(-4, -5)$ and $(2, 3)$ is 10 units.

How Do You Find the Midpoint between Two Points?

The steps to find the midpoint between two points on a coordinate graph are basically the same (except you use a different formula) as the steps for finding the slope of the line and the distance between the points:

Step 1. Sketch a diagram and label it.

Step 2. Specify (x_1, y_1) and (x_2, y_2).

Step 3. Plug into the formula given on the Mathematics Reference Sheet:

Midpoint between two points $= \left(\dfrac{x_1 + x_2}{2}, \dfrac{y_1 + y_2}{2} \right)$

Tip: Notice that you add, not subtract, the coordinates in the numerator.

Here is an example.

What is the midpoint of the line segment that connects the points (5, –7) and (3, 1) on a coordinate graph?

Step 1. Sketch a diagram and label it.

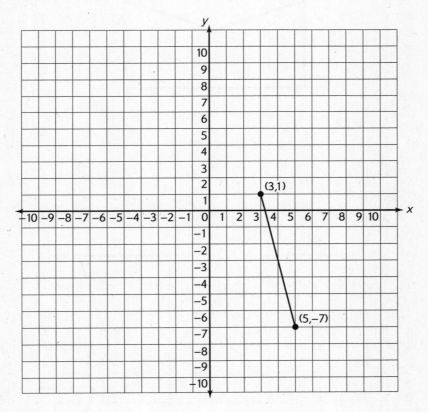

Step 2. Specify (x_1, y_1) and (x_2, y_2).

Let $(x_1, y_1) = (5, -7)$ and $(x_2, y_2) = (3, 1)$. Then $x_1 = 5$, $y_1 = -7$, $x_2 = 3$, and $y_2 = 1$.

Step 3: Plug into the formula.

Midpoint between two points $= \left(\dfrac{x_1 + x_2}{2}, \dfrac{y_1 + y_2}{2} \right) = \left(\dfrac{5+3}{2}, \dfrac{-7+1}{2} \right) = \left(\dfrac{8}{2}, \dfrac{-6}{2} \right) = (4, -3)$

The midpoint of the line segment that connects the points (5, –7) and (3, 1) is the point (4, –3).

What Are Geometric Transformations?

Geometric transformations are ways to change geometric figures without changing their basic properties. The four geometric transformations are translations, reflections, rotations, and dilations.

A **translation** is a sliding movement, horizontally, vertically, or both.

Here is an example of a translation consisting of four units down.

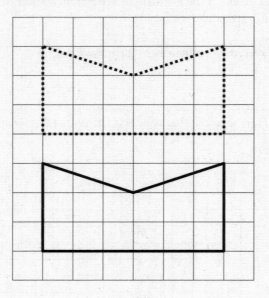

Translation

A **reflection** is a flip across a line.

Here is an example of a reflection.

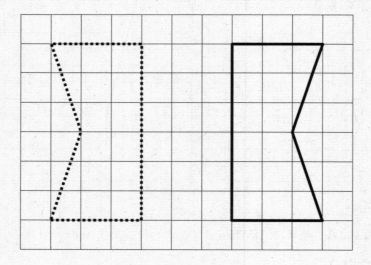

Reflection

A **rotation** is a turn around a point.

Here is an example of a rotation.

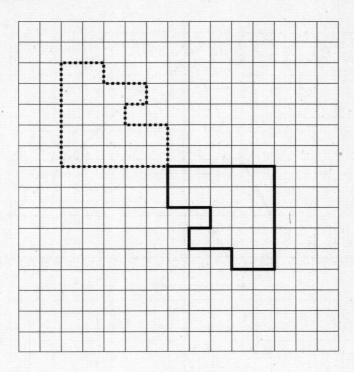

Rotation

A **dilation** is an expanding or shrinking of a geometric shape.

Here is an example of a dilation: Triangle $X'Y'Z'$ is a dilation of triangle XYZ.

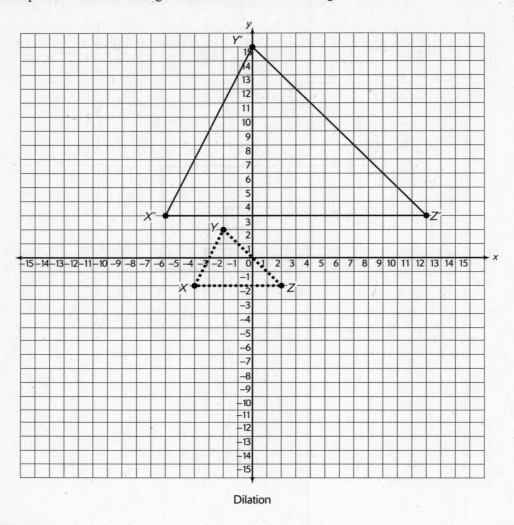

Dilation

Test Yourself

1. In a right triangle, the _____ is the side opposite the right angle.

2. What is the length of the hypotenuse of a right triangle that has legs $a = 3$ units and $b = 4$ units?

3. The point $(0, 0)$ is the _____ of a coordinate graph.

4. The quadrants of a coordinate system are numbered _____ (clockwise, counterclockwise) using Roman numerals.

5. In the ordered pair $(-5, 8)$, -5 is the _____, and 8 is the _____.

6. In Quadrant _____, both coordinates are positive.

7. In Quadrant II, the *x*-coordinate is _____ (positive, negative), and the *y*-coordinate is _____ (positive, negative).

8. In Quadrant IV, the *x*-coordinate is _____ (positive, negative), and the *y*-coordinate is _____ (positive, negative).

9. In Quadrant _____, both coordinates are negative.

10. What ordered pair represents the point *P*?

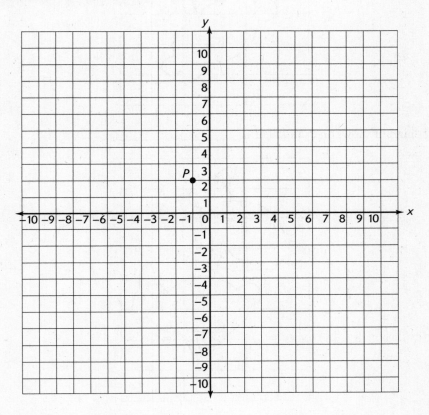

11. What is the slope of the line that passes through the points (–4, 1) and (0, 5)?

12. If a line slants to the left, its slope is _____ (positive, negative).

13. The *x*-coordinate of the midpoint of the line segment between two points is the _____ of the *x*-coordinates of the two points divided by 2, and the *y*-coordinate is the _____ of the *y*-coordinates of the two points divided by 2.

14. The following diagram shows an example of a _____.

15. The following diagram shows an example of a _____.

Answers

1. hypotenuse

2. $c = 5$ units

    Sketch a diagram and label it.

Plug into the formula:

c = hypotenuse = ?, a = 3 units, and b = 4 units

$c^2 = a^2 + b^2$ (3 units)^2 + (4 units)^2 = 9 units^2 + 16 units^2 = 25 units^2

Since c^2 = 25 units^2, to obtain c, you take the square root of 25 units^2.

Thus, c = 5 units.

Note: From the list of square roots given in "Are All Square Roots Irrational?" (earlier in this chapter), you know that $\sqrt{25}$ = 5.

3. origin

4. counterclockwise

5. x-coordinate, y-coordinate

6. I

7. negative, positive

8. positive, negative

9. III

10. The point P is 1 unit to the left and 2 units up from the origin. The ordered pair (–1, 2) represents the point P.

11. slope = 1.

Solution:

Step 1. Sketch a diagram and label it.

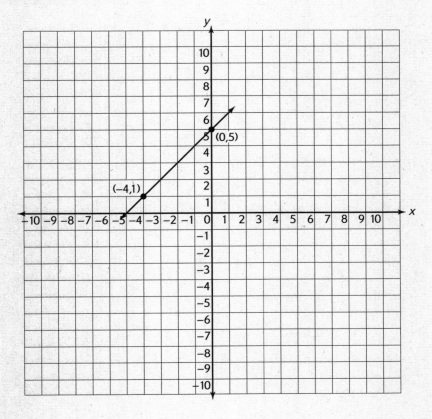

Step 2. Specify (x_1, y_1) and (x_2, y_2).

Let $(x_1, y_1) = (-4, 1)$ and $(x_2, y_2) = (0, 5)$. Then $x_1 = -4$, $y_1 = 1$, $x_2 = 0$, and $y_2 = 5$.

Step 3: Plug into the formula.

Slope of line $= \dfrac{y_2 - y_1}{x_2 - x_1} = \dfrac{5-1}{0-(-4)} = \dfrac{5-1}{0+4} = \dfrac{4}{4} = 1$

The line through the points $(-4, 1)$ and $(0, 5)$ has slope 1.

12. negative

13. sum, sum

14. reflection

15. rotation

Sample Questions

Directions: Read each question and select the best answer choice.

1. Which of the following is the most specific name for the figure below, given that $AB \parallel DC$, but $AB \ncong CD$?

   A. parallelogram
   B. rectangle
   C. rhombus
   D. trapezoid

2. A length of cable is attached to the top of a 12-foot building. The cable is anchored 5 feet from the base of the building. What is the length of the cable?

   A. 7 feet
   B. 13 feet
   C. 17 feet
   D. 169 feet

3. A square is also a:

   A. trapezoid.
   B. pentagon.
   C. parallelogram.
   D. cube.

4. Which of the following shapes contains a correctly drawn line of symmetry?

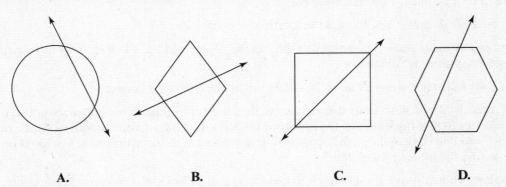

   A.   B.   C.   D.

Answer Explanations for Sample Questions

1. **D.** Examine the diagram. The figure has four sides, so it is a quadrilateral. Note that $AB \parallel DC$ means AB is parallel to DC, and $AB \ncong CD$ means AB and CD are not congruent.

A trapezoid is a quadrilateral that has exactly one pair of opposite sides parallel. The figure shown is a trapezoid. Choices **A, B,** and **C** are incorrect because these figures are parallelograms, which have both pairs of opposite sides parallel and congruent.

2. **B.** First, sketch a diagram to illustrate the problem:

The building and the cable form a right triangle. From the diagram, you can see that the length of the cable is the hypotenuse of the right triangle that has legs of 12 feet and 5 feet. Plug into the formula omitting the units:

c = hypotenuse = ?, $a = 12$, and $b = 5$

$c^2 = a^2 + b^2 = (12)^2 + (5)^2 = 144 + 25 = 169$

Since $c^2 = 169$, to obtain c, you take the square root of 169.

Thus, $c = 13$.

Note: From the list of square roots given in "Are All Square Roots Irrational?" (earlier in this chapter), you know that $\sqrt{169} = 13$.

The length of the cable is 13 feet, Choice **B.**

Did I answer the question? Yes, I found the length of the cable. ✓

Does my answer make sense? Yes, given that the legs are 12 feet and 5 feet in length, 13 feet for the length of the hypotenuse seems reasonable. ✓

Is the answer stated in the correct units? Yes, the units are feet, which is correct. ✓

Choice **A** results if you mistakenly decide to solve the problem by finding the difference between the lengths of the two legs to find the length of the hypotenuse. Choice **C** results if you mistakenly decide to solve the problem by adding the lengths of the two legs to find the length of the hypotenuse. Choice **D** results if you neglect to find the square root of 169.

3. **C.** A square is a parallelogram that has four congruent sides. Choice **A** is incorrect because a trapezoid has exactly one pair of opposite sides parallel, but a square has two pairs of opposite sides parallel. Choice **B** is incorrect because a pentagon has exactly five sides, but a square has exactly four sides. Choice **D** is incorrect because a cube is a three-dimensional figure, but a square is a two-dimensional figure.

4. **C.** Only the figure for Choice **C** has a correctly drawn line of symmetry that cuts the figure into two congruent halves. The lines in the figures for choices **A, B,** and **D** do not cut the figures into two congruent halves.

Algebraic Reasoning

According to the *Competencies and Skills Required for Teacher Certification in Florida, Fifteenth Edition* (see first section of this chapter for Web address), the competencies/skills you should be able to do for this area of mathematics are the following:

- Recognize patterns including arithmetic and geometric sequences.
- Interpret algebraic expressions.
- Solve equations and inequalities.
- Determine whether a number or ordered pair satisfies a system of equations or inequalities.

What Is a Sequence?

A sequence is a list of numbers, called **terms** of the sequence, written in a particular order. On the FTCE GK Test, you will have to identify patterns in sequences. Here are some common sequences you might encounter.

Arithmetic Sequences

In an **arithmetic sequence** the same number (called the **common difference**) is *added* (algebraically) to each term to find the next term in the sequence. Here are examples.

> What is the next term in the sequence 4, 9, 14, 19, 24, . . .?

The number 5 is added to a term to get the term that follows it, so the next term in the sequence is

$$24 + 5 = 29.$$

> What is the next term in the sequence 10, 6, 2, –2, –6, . . .?

The number –4 is added to a term to get the term that follows it, so the next term in the sequence is

$$-6 + -4 = -10.$$

Note: The ellipsis (. . .) indicates that the sequence continues on in the same manner.

In general, an **arithmetic sequence** has the form

$$a_1, a_1 + d, a_1 + 2d, \ldots a_1 + (n-1)d, \ldots$$

where a_1 is the **first term**, d is the **common difference** between terms, and $a_n = a_1 + (n-1)d$ is the **general term**—which you can use to find the nth term of the sequence. Here is an example.

> What is the 50th term in the sequence –2, 2, 6, 10, 14, . . .?

The first term a_1 is –2. The common difference is 4. The general term is $a_n = -2 + (n-1)(4)$. Thus, the 50th term is

$$a_{50} = -2 + (50 - 1)(4) = -2 + (49)(4) = -2 + 196 = 194.$$

Geometric Sequences

In a **geometric sequence** each term in the sequence is *multiplied* by the same number (called the **common ratio**) to find the next term in the sequence. Here are examples.

> What is the next term in the sequence 4, 8, 16, 32, 64, . . .?

Each term is multiplied by 2 to get the term that follows it, so the next term in the sequence is $64 \cdot 2 = 128$.

> What is the next term in the sequence 25, 5, 1, $\frac{1}{5}$, $\frac{1}{25}$, ...?

Each term is multiplied by $\frac{1}{5}$ to get the term that follows it, so the next term in the sequence is $\frac{1}{25} \cdot \frac{1}{5} = \frac{1}{125}$.

In general, a **geometric sequence** has the form

$$a_1, a_1 r, a_1 r^2, \ldots a_1 r^{n-1}, \ldots$$

where a_1 is the **first term**, r is the **common ratio** between terms, and $a_n = a_1 r^{n-1}$ is the **general term**—which you can use to find the nth term of the sequence. Here is an example.

> What is the 9th term in the sequence $-1, -2, -4, -8, -16, \ldots$?

The first term a_1 is -1. The common ratio is 2. The general term is $a_n = (-1)2^{n-1}$. Thus, the 9th term is

$$a_9 = (-1)2^{9-1} = (-1)2^8 = (-1)(256) = -256$$

Of course, you could have worked this problem by continuing to multiply by 2 until you reached the 9th term as shown here.

$$\underset{\substack{1^{st} \quad 2^{nd} \quad 3^{rd} \quad 4^{th} \quad 5^{th} \quad 6^{th} \quad 7^{th} \quad 8^{th} \quad 9^{th}}}{-1, -2, -4, -8, -16, -32, -64, -128, -256}$$

If you use this approach, count the terms to be sure that you have the correct term.

Fibonacci Sequences

A **Fibonacci sequence** begins with two repeating terms; and, thereafter, each term is the sum of the two preceding terms. Here is an example.

$$1, 1, 2, 3, 5, 8, \ldots$$

Additional Patterns

Sequences may also have **repeating patterns.**

Here is an example of a repeating pattern in which the block of numbers 3, 2, 1 repeats.

$$3, 2, 1, 3, 2, 1, 3, 2, 1, \ldots$$

A common pattern for sequences involves using the position number of the term to produce the term. For example, write the numbers 1, 2, 3, 4, 5 under the terms of the sequence 1, 4, 9, 16, 25, . . . as shown here.

$$1, 4, 9, 16, 25, \ldots$$
$$\underset{1 \quad 2 \quad 3 \quad 4 \quad 5}{}$$

You can see that each term is the square of its position number. Symbolically, the nth term is n^2.

How Do You Find Patterns in Sequences?

When a problem requires that you find a pattern in a sequence, you use a systematic plan of attack. First, look for an easily recognizable pattern. For example, the sequence

$$5, 10, 20, 5, 10, 20, \ldots$$

has an easily recognizable repeating pattern of the block of numbers 5, 10, 20.

If you do not see a pattern right away, check for an arithmetic sequence. Do this by subtracting each term from the term that follows it. If the differences are the same, the sequence is arithmetic and you should add the common difference to a term to get the term that follows. Here is an example.

Find the missing term in the following sequence: 10, 12, ___, 16, 18, . . .

Subtract consecutive terms listed from the terms that follow them.

$$12 - 10 = 2$$
$$18 - 16 = 2$$

You get 2 as the difference both times, so the sequence is arithmetic with a common difference of 2. Add 2 (the common difference) to 12 to obtain the missing term: $2 + 12 = 14$.

If the sequence is not arithmetic, check for a geometric sequence. Do this by dividing each term by the term that follows it to see if there is a common ratio. If the quotients are the same, the sequence is geometric and you should multiply a term by the common ratio to get the term that follows. Here is an example.

Find the missing term in the following sequence: 2, ___, 18, 54, 162, . . .

Divide consecutive terms listed by the terms that follow them.

$$54 \div 18 = 3$$
$$162 \div 54 = 3$$

You get 3 as the quotient both times, so the sequence is geometric with a common ratio of 3. Multiply 2 by 3 (the common ratio) to obtain the missing term: $2 \cdot 3 = 6$.

If the sequence is not arithmetic or geometric, then list the position numbers under the terms. Look for a relationship between the term and its position number. Here is an example.

Find the missing term in the following sequence: $1, \frac{1}{2}, \frac{1}{3}, \underline{\quad}, \frac{1}{5}, \ldots$

$$1, \frac{1}{2}, \frac{1}{3}, \underline{\quad}, \frac{1}{5}, \ldots$$
$$\underset{1 \quad 2 \quad 3 \quad 4 \quad 5}{}$$

You can see that the nth term is $\frac{1}{n}$, so the 4th term is $\frac{1}{4}$.

If no pattern has been found, then check for a Fibonacci sequence. With persistence, you should be able to find a pattern that can help you find a missing term of a sequence.

Test Yourself

1. The terms of an arithmetic sequence have a common _____ .

2. The terms of a geometric sequence have a common _____ .

3. A _____ sequence begins with two repeating terms; and, thereafter, each term is the sum of the two preceding terms.

4. Find the missing term in the following sequence: 13, 18, ___, 28, 33, . . .

5. Find the missing term in the following sequence: 5, ___, 20, –40, 80, . . .

Answers

1. difference

2. ratio

3. Fibonacci

4. Check for an arithmetic sequence by subtracting consecutive terms listed from the terms that follow them.

   $18 - 13 = 5$

   $33 - 28 = 5$

   You get 5 as the difference both times, so the sequence is arithmetic with a common difference of 5. Add 5 (the common difference) to 18 to obtain the missing term: $18 + 5 = 23$.

5. Check for an arithmetic sequence by subtracting consecutive terms listed from the terms that follow them.

   $-40 - 20 = -60$

   $80 - (-40) = 80 + 40 = 120$

   No common difference is found. Next, check for a geometric sequence by dividing consecutive terms listed by the terms that follow them.

   $-40 \div 20 = -2$

   $80 \div -40 = -2$

   You get –2 as the quotient both times, so the sequence is geometric with a common ratio of –2. Multiply 5 by –2 (the common ratio) to obtain the missing term: $5 - 2 = -10$.

How Do You Interpret Algebraic Expressions?

For the FTCE GK Test you will need to know how to translate algebraic expressions into words. The language of algebra is symbolic. A variable is a symbol used in algebra to represent some unknown quantity that can take the value of a specific number or, in some cases, a set of numbers. On the FTCE GK Test, letters are used as variables. If there is a number in front of the letter, that number is the **numerical coefficient** of the variable. For instance, in the expression $2x$, 2 is the numerical coefficient of x. If no number is written in front of the variable, it is understood that the numerical coefficient is 1. Writing a variable with a coefficient or writing two or more variables in juxtaposition (side by side) is a way to show multiplication. In other words, $2x$ means 2 times x and abc means a times b times c. No multiplication symbol is necessary.

A **constant** is a quantity whose value remains fixed throughout a discussion. For example, all the real and complex numbers are constants. Each has a fixed, definite value. Thus, when a letter is used to name a constant, the letter has one fixed value. For instance, the Greek letter π stands for the number that equals the ratio of the circumference of a circle to its diameter, which is approximately 3.14159.

A **numerical expression** is any constant or combination of two or more constants joined by operational symbols. For example, 100, 3.5, $\frac{3 \cdot 25}{4 \cdot 5}$, 0.75(2000) + 2500, and $\pi(6)^2$ are numerical expressions.

An **algebraic expression** is any combination of symbols that represents a number. Algebraic expressions consist of one or more variables joined by one or more operational symbols, with or without constants (explicitly) included.

Look at these examples of algebraic expressions.

$2x$	$3(x + 4)$	$\dfrac{3x^4 y^6}{5x^3}$
$5(a + b)$	$\frac{1}{2}mv^2$	$\frac{1}{2}h(b_1 + b_2)$
$p^2 n$	$x + 2y$	$2(\pi r^2) + (2\pi r)h$
$9x^2 - 6x + 1$	abc	$\frac{4}{3}\pi r^3$

You likely recognized the last three expressions in the third column as formulas from the Mathematics Reference Sheet. Formulas are examples of algebraic expressions.

The first step in learning to interpret the language of algebra is to understand how addition, subtraction, multiplication, and division are expressed algebraically. Table 3.13 summarizes the most commonly used algebraic symbolism for the operations. The letter x is used in the table to represent an unknown number.

Table 3.13: Algebraic Symbolism for the Operations			
Operation	**Symbol(s) Used**	**Example**	**Sample Word Phrases**
Addition	+	$x + 10$	x plus 10, the sum of x and 10, x increased by 10, 10 added to x
Subtraction	−	$x - 2$	x minus 2, 2 subtracted from x, the difference between x and 2, 2 less than x, x decreased by 2
Multiplication	juxtaposition or ( )	$2x$ $2(x)$	2 times x, x multiplied by 2, the product of 2 and x, twice x, 2 of x
Division	fraction bar	$\frac{x}{5}$	x divided by 5, the quotient of x and 5, the ratio of x to 5

Besides indicating multiplication, parentheses are used as grouping symbols. Similarly, a fraction bar can be a grouping symbol as well as indicating division. When interpreting an algebraic expression, it is common to use the word "quantity" to indicate that terms are enclosed in a grouping symbol and to avoid ambiguity.

Here are examples.

$3(x + 10)$ is "3 times the quantity $x + 10$."

$\frac{x-2}{5}$ is "the quantity $x - 2$ divided by 5."

$(ab)^2$ is "the quantity ab squared."

When you have more than one operation involved in an algebraic expression, keep in mind that the variables are standing in for numbers, so the indicated calculations must follow the order of operations.

Also, as mentioned earlier, it is important to avoid ambiguity. That is, you want your translation to have only one meaning.

Here is an example of an ambiguous translation.

"the product of 3 and x squared"   Does this mean $(3x)^2$ or $3x^2$?

Here are examples of translating algebraic expressions into words.

> Translate the formula $\frac{4}{3}\pi r^3$ into words.

This expression is a product of three terms: $\frac{4}{3}$, π, and r^3. Notice that the exponent 3 on r applies only to r. A correct translation of the expression is "$\frac{4}{3}$ times π times the quantity r cubed." Another correct translation is "the product of $\frac{4}{3}$, π, and the quantity r cubed."

> Translate the expression $\frac{1}{2}h(b_1 + b_2)$ into words.

This expression is the product of three terms: $\frac{1}{2}$, h, and the quantity $b_1 + b_2$. A correct translation of the expression is "half the product of h times the quantity $b_1 + b_2$." Another correct translation is "$\frac{1}{2}$ times h times the quantity $b_1 + b_2$."

How Do You Simplify Algebraic Expressions?

You simplify algebraic expressions by using the commutative, associative, and distributive properties of the real numbers. These properties are summarized in Table 3.14.

Table 3.14 Properties of the Real Numbers Used in Simplifying		
Property	**Explanation**	**Example**
Commutative Property of Addition	When you add two real numbers, you can change the order of the numbers being added and still obtain the correct sum.	$10 + 25 = 25 + 10$ $35\checkmark = 35\checkmark$
Commutative Property of Multiplication	When you multiply two real numbers, you can change the order of the numbers being multiplied and still obtain the correct product.	$(10)(25) = (25)(10)$ $250\checkmark = 250\checkmark$
Associative Property of Addition	When you add more than two real numbers, you can group the way you add the numbers in different ways and still obtain the correct sum.	$(4 + 6) + 5 = 4 + (6 + 5)$ $10 + 5 = 4 + 11$ $15\checkmark = 15\checkmark$
Associative Property of Multiplication	When you multiply more than two real numbers, you can group the way you multiply the numbers in different ways and still obtain the correct product.	$(4)(6) \cdot 5 = 4 \cdot (6)(5)$ $24 \cdot 5 = 4 \cdot 30$ $120\checkmark = 120\checkmark$
Distributive Property	When a sum of two real numbers is multiplied by a real number, you can add first and then multiply, or you can multiply first and then add the products. Either way, you still obtain the correct result.	$5(10 + 8) = 5 \cdot 10 + 5 \cdot 8$ $5 \cdot 18 = 50 + 40$ $90\checkmark = 90\checkmark$

You may use one or a combination of these properties to simplify algebraic expressions. Here is an example.

> Simplify $5(2x + 3)$.

$5(2x + 3) = 5 \cdot 2x + 5 \cdot 3 =$ Using the distributive property, multiply each term in the parentheses by 5.
$(5 \cdot 2)x + 5 \cdot 3 = 10x + 15$ Using the associative property, regroup $5 \cdot 2x$ as $(5 \cdot 2)x$, then multiply.

Of course, in practice you can do the intermediate steps mentally as shown in this example.

> Simplify $3(x + 4)$

$3(x + 4) = 3x + 12$ Using the distributive property, multiply each term in the parentheses by 3.

Notice that the distributive property means that if you have the sum of two products that have a common factor, you can rewrite the expression as the common factor times the sum of the other two factors. Here is an example.

$6 \cdot 30 + 6 \cdot 70 =$ 6 is a common factor in the two products.

$6(30 + 70) =$ Use the distributive property to rewrite the expression as 6 times the sum of the other two factors.

$6(100) = 600$

This use of the distributive property allows you to combine variable expressions that are the same except for their numerical coefficients into a single term. Variable expressions that are the same except for their numerical coefficients are **like terms.** Here are examples of simplifying like terms.

> Simplify $2x + 3x$.

$2x + 3x = x \cdot 2 + x \cdot 3$ Apply the commutative property of multiplication and observe that the variable x is a common factor in the two products.

$= x(2 + 3)$ Use the distributive property to rewrite the expression as x times the sum of the other two factors.

$= x(5) = 5x$ Apply the commutative property of multiplication.

> Simplify $15y - 8y$.

$15y - 8y = 15y + -8y$ Apply the definition for algebraic subtraction. Then apply the commutative
$= y \cdot 15 + y \cdot -8$ property of multiplication and observe that the variable y is a common factor in the two products.

$= y(15 + -8)$ Use the distributive property to rewrite the expression as y times the sum of the other two factors.

$= y(7) = 7y$ Apply the commutative property of multiplication.

When you understand the mathematical basis for combining like terms, you can abbreviate the process to the following rule:

To add like terms, you add (algebraically) their numerical coefficients and use the result as the numerical coefficient for the common variable. Here are examples.

$20x + 30x = 50x$

$15z - 40z = -25z$ *Hint:* Using the rules for combining signed numbers (see the "Numerations and Operations" section, earlier in this chapter), $15 - 40 = 15 + -40 = -25$.

The addition or subtraction of terms that are *not* like terms can only be indicated. You cannot put them together into a single term. For instance, you would have to leave $2a + 3b$ as it is—you can't make it into a single term.

One further note: When you simplify expressions containing subtraction, as a practical matter, you might find it more convenient not to rewrite subtraction in terms of algebraic addition. You can think of the minus sign as "+ the opposite." For the remainder of this study guide, we will adopt the practice of not rewriting subtraction unless it is necessary to do so to avoid making a sign error in the problem.

Test Yourself

1. An algebraic expression is a combination of symbols that represents a _____ .

2. The numerical coefficient of x is _____ .

3. Translate $2x$ into words.

4. Translate $\frac{m}{3}$ into words.

5. Translate mv^2 into words.

6. Express 10 less than y in symbols.

7. Translate the expression $\frac{1}{2}(x+10)$ into words.

8. Simplify $3(x + 4) + 2x$.

9. Simplify $5 + 2(x - 4)$.

10. Simplify $x + 2$.

Answers

1. number

2. 1

3. "2 times x"

4. "m divided by 3"

5. "m times the quantity v squared"

6. $y - 10$

7. "half the quantity $x + 10$" or "$\frac{1}{2}$ times the quantity $x + 10$"

8. $3(x + 4) + 2x = 3x + 12 + 2x = 3x + 2x + 12 = 5x + 12$

9. $5 + 2(x - 4) = 5 + 2(x + -4) = 5 + 2x + -8 = 2x + 5 + -8 = 2x + -3 = 2x - 3$

10. Leave $x + 2$ as it is. This expression cannot be simplified further.

How Do You Solve Equations?

An **equation** is a statement that two mathematical expressions are equal. An equation may be true or false. For instance, the equation $8 + 5 = 13$ is true, but the equation $0 = 2$ is false. An equation has two sides. Whatever is on the left side of the equal sign is the *left side* of the equation, and whatever is on the right side of the equal sign is the *right side* of the equation.

A variable or variables might hold the place for numbers in an equation. For example, the equation

$$5x + 8 = 2x - 1$$

is an equation that has one variable. To **solve an equation** that has one variable means to find a numerical replacement for the variable that makes the equation true. An equation is true when the left side has the same value as the right side.

To solve an equation, you work backward (so to speak) to find the value of the variable. You "undo" what has been done to the variable until you get an expression like this: variable = number. In other words, the equation is solved when you succeed in getting the variable by itself on one side of the equation only and the coefficient of the variable is an understood 1.

An equation is like balance scales. To keep the equation in balance, whatever you do to one side of the equation you must do to the other side of the equation. The main tools you use in solving equations are

- Adding the same number to both sides.
- Subtracting the same number from both sides.
- Multiplying both sides by the same *nonzero* number.
- Dividing both sides by the same *nonzero* number.

What has been done to the variable determines the operation you choose to do. You do it to both sides to keep the equation balanced. You "undo" an operation by using the inverse of the operation. Addition and subtraction undo each other as do multiplication and division.

With that said, how do you proceed? To solve an equation, follow these five steps.

Step 1.	If parentheses are involved, use the distributive property to remove parentheses.
Step 2.	Combine like terms, if any, on each side of the equation.
Step 3.	If the variable appears on both sides of the equation, add a variable expression to both sides of the equation so that the variable appears on only one side of the equation, and then simplify.
Step 4.	Undo addition or subtraction and then simplify. If a number is added to the variable term, subtract that number from both sides of the equation. If a number is subtracted from the variable term, add that number to both sides of the equation.
Step 5.	Divide both sides of the equation by the coefficient of the variable.

Here are examples of solving an equation.

Solve $5x + 8 = 2x - 1$	
$5x + 8 = 2x - 1$	No parentheses are involved, and there are no like terms to combine, so skip steps 1–2.
$5x + 8 - 2x = 2x - 1 - 2x$	The variable appears on both sides of the equation, so subtract $2x$ from the right side to remove it from that side. To keep the equation balanced, subtract $2x$ from the left side, too.
$3x + 8 = -1$	Then simplify.
$3x + 8 - 8 = -1 - 8$	8 is added to the variable term, so subtract 8 from both sides of the equation.
$3x = -9$	Then simplify.
$\dfrac{3x}{3} = \dfrac{-9}{3}$	You want the coefficient of x to be 1, so divide both sides by 3.
$x = -3$	

You can check your solution by plugging it back into the original equation $5x + 8 = 2x - 1$.

Put in –3 for x on the left side of the equation: $5x + 8 = 5(-3) + 8 = -15 + 8 = -7$. Put in –3 for x on the right side of the equation: $2x - 1 = 2(-3) - 1 = -6 - 1 = -7$. Both sides equal –7, so –3 is the correct solution.

Solve $5(x + 7) = 15$

$5(x + 7) = 15$	
$5x + 35 = 15$	Use the distributive property to remove parentheses.
$5x + 35 - 35 = 15 - 35$	35 is added to the variable term, so subtract 35 from both sides of the equation.
$5x = -20$	Then simplify.
$\dfrac{5x}{5} = \dfrac{-20}{5}$	You want the coefficient of x to be 1, so divide both sides by 5.
$x = -4$	

Check by plugging your solution back into the original equation: $5(x + 7) = 15$

Put in -4 for x on the left side of the equation: $5(x + 7) = 5(-4 + 7) = 5(3) = 15$

The right side of the equation is also 15. Both sides equal 15, so -4 is the correct solution.

Sometimes you can find a replacement for the variable that makes the equation true simply by "guessing and checking." This is a good test-taking strategy for multiple-choice math tests.

Here is an example of using "guessing and checking" to solve an equation.

Solve: $5x + 8 = 2x - 1$

    A. -1
    B. -3
    C. 1
    D. 3

Check the answer choices by plugging the values into the equation, being careful to enclose in parentheses the values that you put in and to follow the order of operations PE(MD)(AS) when you do your calculations.

Check Choice **A:** Put in -1 for x on the left side of the equation: $5x + 8 = 5(-1) + 8 = -5 + 8 = 3$. Put in -1 for x on the right side of the equation: $2x - 1 = 2(-1) - 1 = -2 - 1 = -3$. Choice **A** is incorrect because $3 \neq -3$.

Check Choice **B:** Put in -3 for x on the left side of the equation: $5x + 8 = 5(-3) + 8 = -15 + 8 = -7$. Put in -3 for x on the right side of the equation: $2x - 1 = 2(-3) - 1 = -6 - 1 = -7$. Choice **B** is the correct response because $x = -3$ made the equation true—both sides equal -7.

When you're taking the FTCE GK Test, you would not have to check the other answer choices because the correct answer is **B**. Since the test is timed, it would be best to move on to the next question.

How Do You Solve Inequalities?

An **inequality** is a mathematical statement that contains one of the following inequality symbols: $\neq$, $<$, $>$, $\leq$, or $\geq$. Like equations, inequalities may be true or false. For instance, the inequalities $7 + 5 < 20$ and $\dfrac{-20}{-4} \neq -5$ are true, but the inequality $0 \geq 5$ is false.

Inequalities may contain variables. For example, the inequality $x \leq 6$ is *true* if x is 2 and is *false* if x is 10. In fact, this inequality is true if x is any number that is less than or equal to 6 and is false if x is any number greater than 6. You can show the set of numbers that make the inequality true on a number line. You shade the numbers to the left of 6, and to indicate that the number 6 also belongs in the solution set, you shade in a small circle at the point 6.

For the inequality $x < 6$, you would indicate that the number 6 does not belong in the solution set, by drawing an open circle at the point 6.

You solve inequalities containing $<$, $>$, $\leq$, or $\geq$ the same way you solve equations. However, there is one main difference. When you multiply or divide the inequality by a *negative* number, you must *reverse* the direction of the inequality. To understand why you must do this, consider the following.

You know that $8 > 2$ is a true inequality because 8 is to the right of 2 on the number line as shown in the following figure.

If both sides of the inequality $8 > 2$ are multiplied by a negative number, say -1, the direction of the inequality must be reversed, yielding the inequality $-8 < -2$. This is a true inequality because -2 is to the right of -8 on the number line as shown in the following figure.

If you do not reverse the inequality symbol after multiplying both sides of $8 > 2$ by -1, you obtain $-8 > -2$, which is clearly false.

Here are examples of solving inequalities.

Solve $6x - 5 < 37$

$6x - 5 < 37$

$6x - 5 + 5 < 37 + 5$ 5 is subtracted from the variable term, so add 5 to both sides of the inequality.

$6x < 42$ Then simplify.

$\dfrac{6x}{6} < \dfrac{42}{6}$ You want the coefficient of x to be 1, so divide both sides by 6.

$x < 7$

Solve $-5(x - 2) \leq 15$

$-5(x - 2) \leq 15$

$-5x + 10 \leq 15$ Use the distributive property to remove parentheses.

$-5x + 10 - 10 \leq 15 - 10$ 10 is added to the variable term, so subtract 10 from both sides of the inequality.

$-5x \leq 5$ Then simplify.

$\dfrac{-5x}{-5} \geq \dfrac{5}{-5}$ You want the coefficient of x to be 1, so divide both sides by -5 and reverse the inequality because you divided both sides by a negative number.

$x \geq -1$

Caution: You reverse the direction of the inequality only when you are multiplying or dividing both sides by a negative number. It does not apply if the number is positive or if the operation is addition or subtraction.

How Do You Decide Whether an Ordered Pair Satisfies a System of Equations?

A set of two equations, each with the same two variables, is a **system** when the two equations are considered simultaneously.

Here is an example of a system of two equations with variables x and y.

$$3x + 4y = 2$$
$$4x - y = 9$$

To solve a system of equations in two variables, you must find all ordered pairs of values for the two variables that make *both* equations true simultaneously. An ordered pair that makes an equation true is said to **satisfy** the equation. When an ordered pair makes both equations in a system true, the order pair **satisfies** the system.

To determine whether an ordered pair satisfies a system of two equations, you will need to check whether the ordered pair satisfies both equations in the system. Do this by plugging the x and y values of the ordered pair into the two equations, being careful to enclose in parentheses the values that you put in. Here is an example.

Determine whether the ordered pair $(1, -2)$ satisfies the following system.

$$3x + 4y = 2$$
$$4x - y = 9$$

First, check whether $(1, -2)$ satisfies $3x + 4y = 2$

On the left side of the equation put in 1 for x and -2 for y and simplify: $3x + 4y = 3(1) + 4(-2) = 3 + -8 = -5$. The right side of the equation is 2, since $-5 \neq 2$, $(1, -2)$ does not satisfy $3x + 4y = 2$. Therefore, $(1, -2)$ does *not* satisfy the given system because it fails to satisfy one of the equations in the system.

Determine whether the ordered pair $(2, -1)$ satisfies the following system.

$$3x + 4y = 2$$
$$4x - y = 9$$

First, check whether $(2, -1)$ satisfies $3x + 4y = 2$

On the left side of the equation, put in 2 for x and -1 for y and simplify: $3x + 4y = 3(2) + 4(-1) = 6 + -4 = 2$. The right side of the equation is also 2, so $(2, -1)$ satisfies $3x + 4y = 2$.

Next, check whether $(2, -1)$ satisfies $4x - y = 9$.

On the left side of the equation put in 2 for x and for y and simplify: $4x - y = 4(2) - (-1) = 8 + 1 = 9$. The right side of the equation is also 9, so $(2, -1)$ satisfies $4x - y = 9$.

Therefore, $(2, -1)$ satisfies the given system because it satisfies both equations in the system.

Test Yourself

1. An equation is true when the left side has the _____ value as the right side.

2. When solving an equation, should you "undo" addition or multiplication first?

3. Solve $3x + 50 = 35$.

4. Solve $25 - 3y = 3y + 1$.

5. Solve $6x - 36 = 6(2 - 3x)$.

6. Does $x = -5$ make the inequality $x \geq -9$ true?

7. When you _____ or _____ an inequality by a _____ number, you must reverse the direction of the inequality.

8. Solve $2x + 5 > 21$.

9. Solve $3x - 4(x + 2) \leq -6$.

10. Determine whether the ordered pair (1, 2) satisfies the following system.

$$x + 2y = 5$$
$$4x - y = 2$$

Answers

1. same

2. addition

3. $x = -5$

Solution:

$3x + 50 = 35$	
$3x + 50 - 50 = 35 - 50$	50 is added to the variable term, so subtract 50 from both sides of the equation.
$3x = -15$	Then simplify.
$\dfrac{3x}{3} = \dfrac{-15}{3}$	You want the coefficient of x to be 1, so divide both sides by 3.
$x = -5$	

4. $y = 4$

Solution:

$25 - 3y = 3y + 1$	
$25 - 3y - 3y = 3y + 1 - 3y$	The variable appears on both sides of the equation, so subtract $3y$ from the right side to remove it from that side. To keep the equation balanced, subtract $3y$ from the left side, too.
$25 - 6y = 1$	Then simplify.
$25 - 6y - 25 = 1 - 25$	25 is added to the variable term, so subtract 25 from both sides of the equation.
$-6y = -24$	Then simplify.
$\dfrac{-6y}{-6} = \dfrac{-24}{-6}$	You want the coefficient of y to be 1, so divide both sides by -6.
$y = 4$	

5. $x = 2$

Solution:

$$6x - 36 = 6(2 - 3x)$$

$6x - 36 = 12 - 18x$ Use the distributive property to remove parentheses.

$6x - 36 + 18x = 12 - 18x + 18x$ The variable appears on both sides of the equation, so add $18x$ to the right side to remove it from that side. To keep the equation balanced, add $18x$ to the left side, too.

$24x - 36 = 12$ Then simplify.

$24x - 36 + 36 = 12 + 36$ 36 is subtracted from the variable term, so add 36 to both sides of the equation.

$24x = 48$ Then simplify.

$\dfrac{24x}{24} = \dfrac{48}{24}$ You want the coefficient of x to be 1, so divide both sides by 24.

$x = 2$

6. Yes, −5 is located to the right of −9 on the number line, so $-5 \geq -9$ is true.

7. multiply, divide, negative

8. $x > 8$

Solution:

$$2x + 5 > 21$$

$2x + 5 - 5 > 21 - 5$ 5 is added to the variable term, so subtract 5 from both sides of the inequality.

$2x > 16$ Then simplify.

$\dfrac{2x}{2} > \dfrac{16}{2}$ You want the coefficient of x to be 1, so divide both sides by 2.

$x > 8$

9. $x \geq -2$

$$3x - 4(x + 2) \leq -6$$

$3x - 4x - 8 \leq -6$ Use the distributive property to remove parentheses.

$-x - 8 \leq -6$ Then simplify.

$-x - 8 + 8 \leq -6 + 8$ 8 is subtracted from the variable term, so add 8 to both sides of the inequality.

$-x \leq 2$ Then simplify.

$\dfrac{-x}{-1} \geq \dfrac{2}{-1}$ You want the coefficient of x to be 1, so divide both sides by −1 and reverse the inequality because you divided both sides by a negative number.

$x \geq -2$

10. Yes, (1, 2) satisfies the given system.

Solution:

First, check whether (1, 2) satisfies $x + 2y = 5$.

On the left side of the equation, put in 1 for x and 2 for y and simplify: $x + 2y = (1) + 2(2) = 1 + 4 = 5$. The right side of the equation is also 5, so (1, 2) satisfies $x + 2y = 5$.

Next, check whether (1, 2) satisfies $4x - y = 2$.

On the left side of the equation, put in 1 for x and 2 for y and simplify: $4x - y = 4(1) - (2) = 4 - 2 = 2$. The right side of the equation is also 2, so (1, 2) satisfies $4x - y = 2$.

Therefore, (1, 2) satisfies the given system because it satisfies both equations in the system.

Sample Questions

Directions: Read each question and select the best answer choice.

1. Find the missing number in the following sequence: 3, ___, 12, –24, 48, . . .

   A. –5
   B. 5
   C. –6
   D. 6

2. The formula for the volume of a cone is $\frac{1}{3}\pi r^2 h$ where h is the height of the cone and r is the radius of the base of the cone. Translate the expression into words.

   A. one-third the product of π, the quantity r squared, and h
   B. the quantity one-third π times r times h, all squared
   C. one-third π times one-third r squared times h
   D. one-third the square of the quantity π times r multiplied by h

3. Solve for x in $2(x + 6) = 50$

   A. 19
   B. 22
   C. 31
   D. 38

4. Determine which of the following ordered pairs satisfies the given system.

   $$x - 2y = -7$$
   $$2x + y = -4$$

   A. (2, –3)
   B. (–2, 3)
   C. (–3, 2)
   D. (3, –2)

Answer Explanations for Sample Questions

1. **C.** Check for an arithmetic sequence by subtracting consecutive terms listed from the terms that follow them.

   $$-24 - 12 = -36$$

   $$48 - (-24) = 48 + 24 = 72$$

   No common difference is found. Next, check for a geometric sequence by dividing consecutive terms listed by the terms that follow them.

   $$-24 \div 12 = -2$$

   $$48 \div -24 = -2$$

   You get -2 as the quotient both times, so the sequence is geometric with a common ratio of -2. Multiply 3 by -2 (the common ratio) to obtain the missing term: $3 \cdot -2 = -6$, Choice **C**.

   The other choices result if you multiply $3 \cdot -2$ incorrectly.

2. **A.** This expression is a product of four terms: $\frac{1}{3}$, π, r^2, and h. Notice that the exponent ^{2} on r applies only to r. A correct translation of the expression is "one-third the product of π, the quantity r squared, and h," Choice **A**. Choices **B** and **D** are incorrect because only r, the radius, is squared in the expression. Choice **C** is incorrect because $\frac{1}{3}$ is a factor only once, not twice, in the expression.

3. **A.**

$2(x + 6) = 50$	
$2x + 12 = 50$	Use the distributive property to remove parentheses.
$2x + 12 - 12 = 50 - 12$	12 is added to the variable term, so subtract 12 from both sides of the equation.
$2x = 38$	Then simplify.
$\dfrac{2x}{2} = \dfrac{38}{2}$	You want the coefficient of x to be 1, so divide both sides by 2.
$x = 19$, Choice A	

   Choice **B** results if you fail to use the distributive property correctly. Choice **C** results if you add 12 to both sides instead of subtracting it. Choice **D** results if you fail to divide by 2.

4. **C.** To determine which ordered pair satisfies the system, you will need to find the ordered pair that satisfies *both* equations. Check each ordered pair by plugging the x and y values into the two equations, being careful to enclose in parentheses the values you put in.

   Checking **A:** $x - 2y = (2) - 2(-3) = 2 + 6 = 8 \neq -7$. Choice **A** is incorrect because $(2, -3)$ does not satisfy $x - 2y = -7$.

   Checking **B:** $x - 2y = (-2) - 2(3) = -2 - 6 = -8 \neq -7$. Choice **B** is incorrect because $(-2, 3)$ does not satisfy $x - 2y = -7$.

   Checking **C:** $x - 2y = (-3) - 2(2) = -3 - 4 = -7$ ✓. Since $(-3, 2)$ works in the first equation, try it in the second equation. $2x + y = 2(-3) + (2) = -6 + 2 = -4$ ✓. Choice **C** is the correct response because the ordered pair $(-3, 2)$ satisfies both equations in the system.

   You would not have to continue since Choice **C** is the correct response. However, in case you're interested, Choice **D** is incorrect because $x - 2y = (3) - 2(-2) = 3 + 4 = 7 \neq -7$.

Data Analysis and Probability

According to the *Competencies and Skills Required for Teacher Certification in Florida, Fifteenth Edition* (see the first section in this chapter for the Web address), the competencies/skills you should be able to do for this area of mathematics are the following:

- Analyze and interpret graphical representation of data.
- Recognize how graphical representation of data can lead to inappropriate interpretations.
- Calculate and interpret measures of central tendency and measures of dispersion.
- Calculate probabilities.
- Solve real-world problems involving probability using counting procedures.

How Can You Organize and Present Data?

There are several ways to record, organize, and present data. For the FTCE GK Test, you should be prepared to perform data analysis by reading and interpreting information from **charts** and **tables, pictographs, bar graphs, histograms, circle graphs, line graphs,** and **stem-and-leaf plots.**

Charts and tables are used to put related information into an organized form. Pictographs, bar graphs, and circle graphs display information that is organized into categories. Histograms summarize data by using totals within intervals. Line graphs show trends, usually, over time. Stem-and-leaf plots show organized visual displays of data.

Charts and Tables

Charts and **tables** organize information in columns and rows. Each column or row is labeled to explain the entries. Look at this example.

The table that follows shows the number of snow cone sales for each month during the summer. According to the chart shown, in which month was snow cone sales the highest?

SUMMER SNOW CONE SALES

Month	Number of Snow Cones Sold
June	650
July	800
August	950

Examination of the chart shows that the highest number of sales was 950 snow cones, which occurred in the month of August.

Pictographs

In a **pictograph,** pictures or symbols are used to represent numbers. Each symbol represents a given number of a particular item. The symbol, its meaning, and the quantity it represents should be stated on the graph. To read a pictograph, count the number of symbols in a row and multiply this number by the scale indicated on the graph. Sometimes, a fraction of a symbol is shown. In that case, approximate the fraction and use it accordingly. Look at this example.

The graph that follows shows the results of a survey of 30 cat owners to determine whether they also own a dog. According to the graph, how many cat owners responded "Yes" to the survey question, "Do you own a dog?"

Responses of 30 Cat Owners to the Question "Do You Own a Dog?"

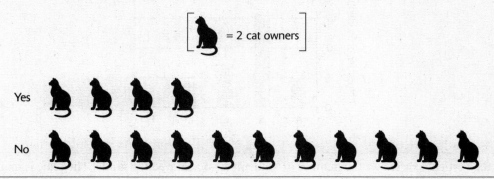

According to the graph, each symbol stands for 2 cat owners. The 4 symbols shown in the graph for "Yes" show that of the 30 cat owners surveyed, the number who also own a dog is 4 · 2 = 8 cat owners.

Bar Graphs

A **bar graph** uses rectangular bars to represent frequencies, percents, or amounts. The bars correspond to different categories that are labeled at the base of the bars. The bars in a bar graph may be arranged vertically or horizontally. The widths of the bars are equal. The length or height of the bar indicates the number, percent, or amount for the category for that particular bar. A scale (usually beginning with 0) marked with equally spaced values will be shown on the graph. To read a bar graph, examine the scale to determine the units and the amount between the marked values. Then determine where the endpoints of the bars fall in relation to the scale. Look at these examples.

The table that follows shows the number of snow cone sales for each month during the summer. According to the chart shown, how many snow cones were sold in July?

Summer Snow Cone Sales

The scale on the horizontal axis shows the number of snow cones sold. The scale is marked in multiples of 200. The bar for July ends at 800, indicating 800 snow cones were sold in July.

The bar graph that follows shows the grade distribution for the first test in a social studies class. According to the graph, how many students made an A on the first test?

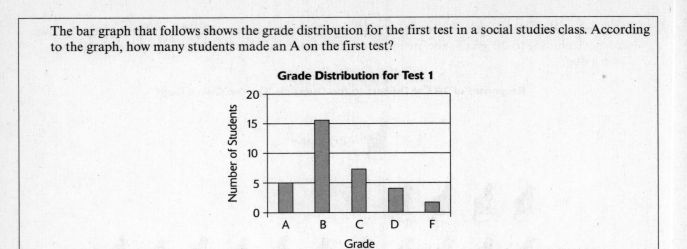

The scale on the vertical axis shows the number of students who achieved the grade. The scale is marked in multiples of 5. The top of the bar for the A category is at 5, indicating 5 students made an A on Test 1.

Bar graphs can show two or more sets of data on the same graph. This allows you to compare how the data sets measure up to each other. Look at this example.

The bar graph shows the grade distribution for the first test for two different social studies classes. According to the graph, which class appears to have had the poorer performance on the test?

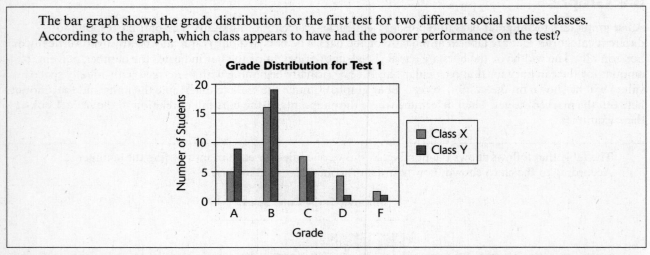

The graph shows that Class X had fewer A's and B's and more C's, D's, and F's than Class Y. Therefore, it appears that Class X had the poorer performance on the test.

Histograms

A **histogram** is a special type of bar graph that summarizes data by using totals within intervals. The intervals are of equal length and cover from the lowest to the highest data value. Unlike the bars in other bar graphs, the bars in a histogram are side-by-side (usually) with no space in between. Look at this example.

The histogram that follows shows the grade distribution for the first test in a social studies class. According to the graph, how many students made above 90 on the first test?

Grade Distribution for Test 1

This symbol means there is a break in the horizontal scale.

The scale on the vertical axis shows the number of students who achieved the grade. The scale is marked in multiples of 2. The top of the bar for the interval 90–99 is halfway between 4 and 6, indicating that 5 students made above 90 on Test 1.

Circle Graphs and Pie Charts

A **circle graph,** or **pie chart,** is a graph in the shape of a circle. Circle graphs are used to display the relationship of each type or class of data within a whole set of data in a visual form. It is also called a "pie" chart because it looks like a pie cut into wedge-shaped slices. The wedges are labeled to show the categories for the graph. Each sector angle represents a specific part of the whole. Commonly, percents are used to show the amount of the graph that corresponds to each category. The total amount in percentage shown on the graph is 100%. The graph is made by dividing the 360 degrees of the circle into portions that correspond to the percentages for each category. Reading a circle graph is a simple matter of reading the percents displayed on the graph for the different categories. Look at this example.

The following circle graph shows how a student plans to budget $2,000 each month. According to the graph, how much money is budgeted for food?

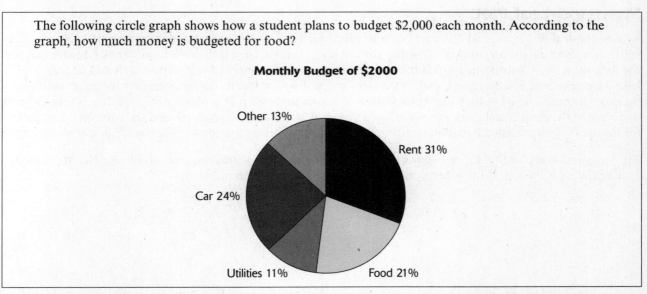

Monthly Budget of $2000

The graph shows that 21% of the budget is designated for food. To find how much money is designated for food, find 21% of $2,000 = $420.

Line Graphs

A **line graph** uses lines or broken lines for representing data. It has both a horizontal and a vertical scale. The data points for the graph are plotted as ordered pairs of numbers, according to the two scales. Line segments are used to connect consecutive points. Sometimes, two or more sets of data are plotted on the same graph. The slant of the line between the points shows whether the data values are increasing, decreasing, or remaining at a constant value. If the line slants upward from left to right, the data values are increasing; if the line slants downward from left to right, the data values are decreasing; and a horizontal line (no slant) means that the data values remain constant. Line graphs are useful for showing change over time. Look at this example.

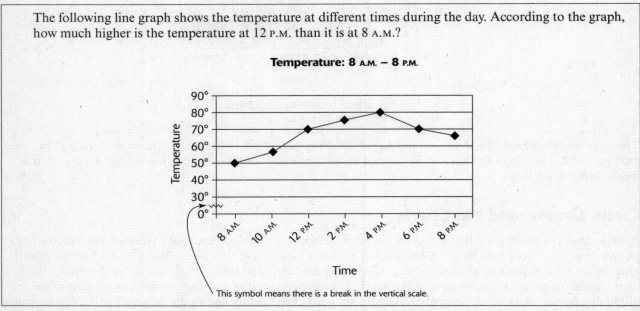

The following line graph shows the temperature at different times during the day. According to the graph, how much higher is the temperature at 12 P.M. than it is at 8 A.M.?

Temperature: 8 A.M. – 8 P.M.

This symbol means there is a break in the vertical scale.

From the graph, you can see that the temperature at 8 A.M. is 50° and the temperature at 12 P.M. is 70°. The difference in temperature at these two times is 70° – 50° = 20°.

Stem-and-Leaf Plots

A **stem-and-leaf plot** is a visual display of data in which each data value is separated into two parts: a stem and a leaf. For a given data value, the leaf is usually the last digit, and the stem is the remaining digits. For example, for the data value 49, 4 is the stem and 9 is the leaf. When you create a stem-and-leaf plot, you should include a **legend** that explains what is represented by the stem and leaf so that the reader can interpret the information in the plot; for example, 4|9 = 49. Note that a feature of a stem-and-leaf plot is that the original data is retained and displayed in the plot. Usually, the stems are listed vertically (from least to greatest), and the corresponding leaves for the data values are listed horizontally (from least to greatest) beside the appropriate stem. Look at this example.

The stem-and-leaf plot that follows shows the ages of 40 people who joined the Over-40 Fitness Health Club in January. What is the age of the oldest person who joined the health club in January?

Ages of 40 People Who Joined the Over-40 Fitness Health Club in January

Stem	Leaf
4	1 2 6 8 9
5	1 1 2 3 3 6 7 7 7 7 7 8 9
6	0 0 3 3 4 4 5 6 8 8 9
7	0 1 2 3 5 7 8
8	0 1
9	0 3

Legend: 4|9 = 49

According to the graph, the age of the oldest person who joined the health club in January is 93.

How Can Presentation of Data Lead to Inappropriate Interpretations?

Drawing valid conclusions from graphical representations of data requires that you have read the graph accurately and analyzed the graphical information correctly. Sometimes a graphical representation will distort the data in some way, leading you to draw an invalid conclusion.

Look at these examples.

Responses of 30 Owners of One Pet to the Question "Do You Own a Cat or a Dog?"

This graph has two major problems. The first problem is that the data are distorted. Visually, it appears that the number of cat owners is greater than the number of dog owners. However, each cat picture represents 2 cats, and each dog picture represents 5 dogs. Thus, the number of dog owners is 15 compared to 10 cat owners, making the number of dog owners greater. The other problem is that the number of pet owners represented in the table is 25, but the number surveyed is 30. The graph should have an additional category for those pet owners surveyed who own neither a cat nor a dog.

Grade Distribution for Test 1

At first glance, the data for this graph look evenly distributed. Upon closer examination, you can see that each of the first two intervals cover a 29-point spread, but the last interval covers only a 19-point spread, making it difficult to draw conclusions from the graph.

When you have to interpret graphical information on the FTCE GK Test, follow these suggestions:

- Make sure that you understand the title of the graph.
- Read the labels on the parts of the graph to understand what is being represented.
- Examine carefully the scale of bar graphs, line graphs, and histograms.
- Make sure you know what each picture in a pictograph represents.
- Look for trends such as increases (rising values), decreases (falling values), and periods of inactivity (constant values, horizontal lines) in line graphs.
- Make sure the numbers add up correctly.
- Be prepared to do some simple arithmetic calculations.
- Use only the information in the graph. Do not answer based on your personal knowledge or opinion.

Test Yourself

1. Pictographs, bar graphs, and circle graphs show information that is organized into _____.

2. In a _____ pictures or symbols are used to represent numbers.

3. The _____ or _____ of a bar graph indicates the number, percent, or amount for its corresponding category.

4. When reading a bar graph, line graph, or histogram, be sure to examine carefully the _____ to determine the amount between the marked values.

5. A histogram summarizes information using totals within _____.

6. The total percentage in a circle graph is _____.

7. _____ graphs are useful for showing change over time.

8. When interpreting information from a graph, do not draw _____ beyond those represented in the graph.

9. What is a problem with the following pictograph?

Number of Butterflies and Lady Bugs Observed in a Month

10. According to the bar graph shown here, in which quarter is the number of points scored by each of the two teams closest?

Answers

1. categories
2. pictograph
3. height, length
4. scale
5. intervals
6. 100%
7. Line
8. conclusions

9.

Number of Butterflies and Lady Bugs Observed in a Month

The graph is misleading, giving the visual impression that the number of butterflies and lady bugs are roughly the same. However, the butterfly picture represents 4 butterflies, but the lady bug picture represents 6 lady bugs. Thus, more lady bugs than butterflies were observed.

10.

The heights of the two bars are closest in the 4th quarter, indicating that the number of points scored by each of the two teams is closest is in that quarter.

What Are Measures of Central Tendency?

A **measure of central tendency** is a numerical value that describes a data set by providing a "central" or "typical" value of the data set. The three most common measures of central tendency are the **mean, median,** and **mode.** Each of these measures represents a different way of describing a typical value of a set of data. Measures of central tendency should have the same units as those of the data values. If no units are specified, as in test scores, then the measure of central tendency will not specify units.

Finding the Mean

The **mean** of a set of numbers is another name for the arithmetic average of the numbers. To calculate the mean: first, sum the numbers; then, divide by how many numbers are in the set. Thus, you have the following formula:

$$\text{mean} = \frac{\text{the sum of the numbers}}{\text{how many numbers in the set}}$$

For example, the mean for the set of five scores 50, 87, 50, 95, 78 is

$$\text{mean} = \frac{50 + 87 + 50 + 95 + 78}{5} = \frac{360}{5} = 72$$

On the FTCE GK Test, you may be given a set of numbers and asked to find the missing number that gives the set a certain average (mean). Here is an example.

> A student's grade is based on the average of five exams. The student has four exam scores of 78, 62, 91, and 79. What is the lowest score needed by the student on the fifth exam to achieve an average of at least 80?

Let x = the score on the fifth exam, then plug into the formula for the mean.

$$80 = \frac{78 + 62 + 91 + 79 + x}{5}$$

$\frac{80}{1} = \frac{310 + x}{5}$	Simplify the numerator on the right. Then write the equation as a proportion.
$(80)(5) = 1(310 + x)$	Cross multiply. *Note:* Enclose quantities in parentheses to avoid errors.
$400 = 310 + x$	Simplify.
$400 - 310 = 310 + x - 310$	Subtract 310 from both sides of the equation.
$90 = x$	Simplify.

The lowest score needed on the fifth exam to achieve an average of 80 for the five exams is 90.

Did I answer the question? Yes, I found the score needed on the fifth exam to achieve an average of 80 for the five exams is 90. ✓

Does my answer make sense? Yes, given that three of the scores are below 80, it seems reasonable that it will take a score of 90 to achieve an average of at least 80. ✓

Is the answer stated in the correct units? No units are required for the answer. ✓

Another way to work the preceding problem is to take advantage of the fact that the FTCE GK Test is a multiple-choice test. You are given the answer to the question—you just have to figure out which one of the four answer choices is the correct one. For a problem like this one, you would plug each answer into the formula for the mean until you found the one that gives you an average of at least 80.

A **weighted mean** is a mean computed by assigning weights to the data values. To find a weighted mean, do the following: First, multiply each data value by its assigned weight, sum the results, and then divide by the sum of the weights. Here is an example.

A student scores 80, 60, and 50 on three exams. Find the weighted mean of the student's three scores, where the score of 80 counts 20%, the score of 60 counts 20%, and the score of 50 counts 60%.

$$\text{weighted mean} = \frac{20\%(80) + 20\%(60) + 60\%(50)}{20\% + 20\% + 60\%} = \frac{16 + 12 + 30}{100\%} = \frac{58}{1} = 58$$

The student's weighted mean score is 58.

Did I answer the question? Yes, I found the weighted mean for the student's three scores is 58. ✓

Does my answer make sense? Yes, since the grade of 50 counts 60 percent, it seems reasonable that the weighted mean is 58. ✓

Is the answer stated in the correct units? No units are required for the answer. ✓

Finding the Median

The **median** is the middle number or the average of the two middle numbers in an ordered set of numbers. Determining the median of a set of numbers is a two-step process.

Step 1: Put the numbers in order from least to greatest (or greatest to least).

Step 2: Find the middle number. If there is no single middle number, average the two middle numbers.

Look at these examples.

> Find the median for the set of scores 50, 87, 50, 95, 78.

Step 1: Put the numbers in order from least to greatest.

$$50, 50, 78, 87, 95$$

Step 2: Find the middle number, which is the median. In this example, which contains an odd number of values, there is a middle number. The median = 78.

> **Caution: When you are asked to find a median, don't make the common mistake of neglecting to put the numbers in order first. In the preceding example, the middle number before the numbers are put in order is 50 (wrong answer).**

> Find the median for the set of numbers 100, 10, 10, 36, 30, 36.

Step 1: Put the numbers in order from least to greatest.

$$10, 10, 30, 36, 36, 100$$

Step 2: Find the middle number. This example contains an even number of values and there is no single middle number. In this case, the median is the average of the two middle numbers, 30 and 36. The median = $\frac{30+36}{2} = \frac{66}{2} = 33$.

Finding the Mode

The **mode** is the number or numbers that occur with the greatest frequency in a set of numbers; there can be one mode, more than one mode, or no mode. If two or more numbers occur with the same frequency that is greater than any of the other frequencies, then each will be a mode. When each number in the data set appears the same number of times, there is no mode.

Look at these examples.

- There is one mode in the data set consisting of the numbers 50, 87, 50, 95, 78. The number 50 occurs with the greatest frequency. Therefore, the mode is 50.
- There are two modes in the data set consisting of the numbers 10, 10, 30, 36, 36, 100. The numbers 10 and 36 both occur with the same frequency that is greater than any of the other frequencies. Therefore, the modes are 10 and 36.
- There is no mode for the data set consisting of the numbers 40, 52, 145, 96, 60. Each number in the data set appears the same number of times.

What Are Important Characteristics of the Measures of Central Tendency?

The mean, median, and mode are ways to describe a central or typical value of a data set. To know which of these measures of central tendency you should use to describe a data set, consider their characteristics.

The **mean** has several important characteristics.

- Although the mean represents a central or typical value of a data set, the mean does not necessarily have the same value as one of the numbers in the set. For instance, the mean of 50, 50, 87, 78, and 95 is 72, yet none of the five numbers in this data set equals 72.
- The actual data values are used in the computation of the mean. If any number is changed, the value of the mean will change. For example, the mean of the data set consisting of 50, 50, 87, 78, and 95 is 72. If the 95 in this set is changed to 100, the mean of the new data set is 73.

- A disadvantage of the mean is that it is influenced by outliers, especially in a small data set. An **outlier** is a data value that is extremely high or extremely low in comparison to most of the other data values. If a data set contains extremely high values that are not balanced by corresponding low values, the mean will be misleadingly high. For example, the mean of the data set consisting of 15, 15, 20, 25, and 25 is 20. If the 20 in this set is changed to 100, the mean of the new data set is 36. The value 36 does not represent the data set consisting of 15, 15, 100, 25, and 25 very well, since four of the data values are less than 30. Similarly, if a data set contains extremely low values that are not balanced by corresponding high values, the mean will be misleadingly low. For example, the mean of the data set consisting of 100, 100, 130, and 150 is 120. If the 150 in this set is changed to 10, the mean of the new data set is 85. The value 85 does not represent the data set consisting of 100, 100, 130, and 10 very well, since three of the data values are greater than or equal to 100.

The **median** is the most useful alternative to the mean as a measure of central tendency.

- Like the mean, the median does not necessarily have the same value as one of the numbers in the set. If the data set contains an odd number of data values, the median will be the middle number; however, for an even number of data values, the median is the arithmetic average of the two middle numbers.

- The median is not influenced by outliers. For instance, the median of the data set consisting of 10, 15, 20, 25, and 30 is 20. If the 30 in this set is changed to 100, the median of the new data set remains 20.

- A disadvantage of the median as an indicator of a central value is that it is based on relative size rather than on the actual numbers in the set. For instance, a student who has test scores of 44, 47, and 98 shows improved performance that would not be reflected if the median of 47, rather than the mean of 63, was reported as the representative grade.

The **mode** is the least commonly used measure of central tendency.

- The mode is the simplest measure of central tendency to calculate.

- If a data set has a mode, the mode (or modes) is one of the data values.

- The mode is the only appropriate measure of central tendency for data that are strictly nonnumeric like data on ice cream flavor preferences (vanilla, chocolate, strawberry, and so on). Although it makes no sense to determine a mean or median ice cream flavor for the data, the ice cream flavor that was named most frequently would be the modal flavor.

- A disadvantage of the mode as an indicator of a central value is that it is based on relative frequency rather than on all the values in the set. For instance, a student who has test scores of 45, 45, and 99 shows improved performance that would not be reflected if the mode of 45, rather than the mean of 63, was reported as the representative grade.

What Are Measures of Dispersion?

A **measure of dispersion** is a value that describes the spread of the data about the central value. Although measures of central tendency are important for describing data sets, their interpretation is enhanced when the spread or dispersion about the central value is known. Two groups of 10 students, both with means of 70 on a 100-point test, may have very different sets of scores. One set of scores may be extremely consistent, with scores like 60, 62, 65, 68, 70, 70, 72, 75, 78, and 80; while the other set of scores may be very erratic, with scores like 40, 40, 50, 55, 60, 80, 85, 90, 100, and 100. The scores in the first set cluster more closely about the mean of 70 than do the scores in the second set. The scores in the second set are more spread out than are the scores in the first set.

For the FTCE GK Test, the two measures of dispersion you will need to know are the **range** and the **standard deviation.** These two measures of dispersion should have the same units as those of the data values. If no units are specified, then the measure of dispersion will not specify units.

The **range** for a data set is the difference between the greatest value and the least value in the data set:

$$range = greatest\ value - least\ value$$

Here are examples of finding the range of a data set.

What is the range for this set of data? 50, 50, 60, 70, 70

$$\text{range} = \text{greatest value} - \text{least value} = 70 - 50 = 20$$

What is the range for this data set? 10, 10, 60, 110, 110

$$\text{range} = \text{greatest value} - \text{least value} = 110 - 10 = 100$$

The range gives some indication of the spread of the values in a data set, but its value is determined by only two of the data values. The extent of the spread of the other numbers is not considered. A measure of dispersion that takes into account all the data values is the standard deviation. The **standard deviation** is a measure of the dispersion of a set of data values about the mean of the data set. When there is no dispersion in a data set, each data value equals the mean, giving a standard deviation of zero. The more the data values vary from the mean, the greater the standard deviation. You will not have to calculate a standard deviation on the FTCE GK Test. Questions about standard deviation will require you to examine two or more data sets and decide which data set has the greatest (or least) standard deviation. Here is an example.

The means of the following two data sets are equal to 50.

Set 1: 30, 40, 50, 60, 70

Set 2: 10, 10, 50, 90, 90

Which data set has the greater standard deviation?

The data values in Set 1 cluster more closely around the mean of 50 than do the data values in Set 2. Therefore, Set 2 has the greater standard deviation.

Test Yourself

1. The mean, median, and mode are measures of _____ (two words).

2. The _____ of a set of numbers is another name for the arithmetic average of the numbers.

3. The median is the middle number or the average of the two middle numbers in an _____ set of numbers.

4. The _____ is the data value or values that occur with the greatest frequency.

5. A disadvantage of the mean is that it is influenced by _____.

6. The median _____ (is, is not) influenced by outliers.

7. The _____ is the only appropriate measure of central tendency for data that are strictly nonnumeric.

8. A measure of dispersion is a value that describes the _____ of the data about the central value.

9. Find the mean, median, mode, and range for the following data set.

   10, 60, 30, 90, 10, 30, 40, 50

10. The standard deviation of a data set is a measure of the spread of the data values about the _____ of the data set.

Answers

1. central tendency

2. mean

3. ordered

4. mode

5. outliers

6. is not

7. mode

8. spread

9. To find the mean, sum the data values and then divide by 8.

$$\text{mean} = \frac{10+60+30+90+10+30+40+50}{8} = \frac{320}{8} = 40$$

To find the median, do the following:

Step 1: Put the numbers in order from least to greatest.

$$10, 10, 30, 30, 40, 50, 60, 90$$

Step 2: Find the middle number. The median is the average of the two middle numbers, 30 and 40.

$$\text{The median} = \frac{30+40}{2} = \frac{70}{2} = 35.$$

To find the mode, find the value (or values) that occurs with the greatest frequency in the data set. The numbers 10 and 30 both occur with the same frequency that is greater than any of the other frequencies. Therefore, the modes are 10 and 30.

To find the range, find the difference between the greatest value and the least value in the data set.

$$\text{range} = \text{greatest value} - \text{least value} = 90 - 10 = 80.$$

10. mean

What Is Probability?

Probability is a measure of the chance that an event will happen. If all outcomes are equally likely, the probability that an event E will occur is determined this way:

$$\text{Probability of event } E = P(E) = \frac{\text{number of outcomes favorable to event } E}{\text{number of total outcomes possible}}$$

On the FTCE GK Test, you will be asked to find simple probabilities. Here is an example.

> A bag contains 5 tiles, numbered 1, 2, 3, 4, and 5. The tiles are all identical in size and shape. If a person picks out a single tile from the bag without looking, what is the probability that the number on the tile will be even?

The possible outcomes are a 1, 2, 3, 4, or 5 on the tile. There are two favorable outcomes for this event: drawing a 2 or a 4. These are the "favorable" outcomes because these are the outcomes you are looking for.

The probability of drawing an even-numbered tile is

$$P(2 \text{ or } 4) = \frac{\text{number of favorable outcomes}}{\text{number of total outcomes possible}} = \frac{2}{5}$$

Probabilities can be expressed as fractions, decimals, or percents. In the preceding example, the probability of drawing an even-numbered tile can be expressed as $\frac{2}{5}$, 0.4, or 40%.

The probability that an event is certain to happen is 1, 1.00, or 100%. The probability of drawing a whole-numbered tile from a bag containing tiles numbered 1, 2, 3, 4, and 5 is 1, since the numbers 1, 2, 3, 4, and 5 are all whole numbers.

If an event cannot occur, then it has a probability of 0. For instance, the probability of drawing a tile with the number 6 on it from a bag containing tiles numbered 1, 2, 3, 4, and 5 is 0, since none of the tiles has a 6 on it.

Thus, the lowest probability you can have is 0, and the highest probability you can have is 1. All other probabilities fall between 0 and 1. You can express this relationship symbolically this way: $0 \le P(E) \le 1$, for any event E. Therefore, if you work a probability problem, and your answer is greater than 1 or your answer is negative, you've made a mistake! Go back and check your work.

> **Tip: In a probability problem, the number of total outcomes possible will always be greater than or equal to the number of outcomes favorable to the event, so check to make sure that the denominator is *larger than or equal to* the numerator when you plug into the formula.**

Keep in mind that the formula for probability in which the outcomes are equally likely will *not* apply to situations in which the events are not equally likely. For instance, the possible outcomes when you spin a spinner that is one-fourth red, one-fourth yellow, and one-half green are R, Y, and G, where "R" means "the spinner lands on red," "Y" means "the spinner lands on yellow," and "G" means "the spinner lands on green." See the figure shown here.

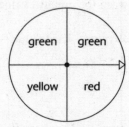

The probabilities for the three different outcomes are the following: $P(\text{R}) = \frac{1}{4}$, $P(\text{Y}) = \frac{1}{4}$, and $P(\text{G}) = \frac{1}{2}$.

The probability of an event B, given that an event A has occurred, is a **conditional probability.** This means that you compute the probability of B by taking into account that A has already occurred. Here is an example.

> Suppose you randomly draw two marbles from a box containing 6 red marbles and 4 blue marbles, all identical except for color. If you draw a red marble on the first draw and do not put it back into the box before you draw the second time, what is the probability you will draw a blue marble on the second draw?

This is a conditional probability problem. After the red marble is drawn and not put back, there are 5 red marbles and 4 blue marbles in the box. Therefore, P(blue on the 2nd draw, *given red drawn on 1st draw and not put back*) $= \frac{4}{9}$.

Note: Not putting back the first item drawn is called drawing "without replacement."

When you want to find the probability that two events A and B occur, you multiply the probability of A times the conditional probability of B (that is, taking into account that the event A has already occurred). Here is an example.

> Suppose a box contains 10 marbles: 3 red marbles, 5 blue marbles, and 2 green marbles, all identical except for color. If you draw two marbles from the box, what is the probability that you will draw two red marbles if your first draw is done without replacement?

This problem involves conditional probability. You use three steps to solve it: First, find P(red on the 1st draw); next, find P(red on the 2nd draw, *given red drawn on 1st draw without replacement*); and then multiply P(red on the 1st draw) times P(red on the 2nd draw, *given red drawn on 1st draw without replacement*).

Step 1. Find P(red on the 1st draw).

P(red on the 1st draw) $= \frac{3}{10}$ because initially you have 3 red marbles in a box of 10 marbles

Step 2. Find P(red on the 2nd draw, *given red drawn on 1st draw without replacement*).

P(red on the 2nd draw, *given red drawn on 1st draw without replacement*) $= \frac{2}{9}$ because after you draw a red marble without replacement, you have 2 red marbles in a box of 9 marbles

Step 3. Multiply P(red on the 1st draw) times P(red on the 2nd draw, *given red drawn on 1st draw without replacement*).

P(red on the 1st draw and red on the 2nd draw) $= \frac{3}{10} \cdot \frac{2}{9} = \frac{\cancel{3}^{1}}{\cancel{10}_{5}} \cdot \frac{\cancel{2}^{1}}{\cancel{9}_{3}} = \frac{1}{15}$.

Of course, if you are flipping coins or tossing numbered cubes, replacement is not a concern. Each flip of the coin or toss of the numbered cube is independent of the other flips or tosses. Independent events do not affect the probabilities of one another, so you simply multiply the probabilities in these cases. Here is an example.

When flipping a coin three times, the probability of getting three heads is $\frac{1}{2} \cdot \frac{1}{2} \cdot \frac{1}{2} = \frac{1}{8}$ because the probability of getting heads on each flip is $\frac{1}{2}$ (one head out of two possible outcomes).

How Do You Count the Number of Ways to Arrange or Combine Things?

There are different methods to find the number of ways to arrange or combine things. Two ways that are commonly used are to list every possibility in an organized table or in a tree diagram. Another way is to use multiplication to count the total number of possibilities.

Here is an example of using an organized table to count the number of possibilities.

> A woman has a choice of a blue, red, orange, or yellow blouse. She also may select either a brown, white, or black skirt. How many different outfits can she make of 1 blouse and 1 skirt?

You should proceed systematically. In the table that follows, first list a blue blouse color with each of the skirt colors that can be chosen. Next, list a red blouse color with each of the skirt colors that can be chosen. Then, list an orange blouse color with each of the skirt colors that can be chosen. Finally, list a yellow blouse color with each of the skirt colors that can be chosen.

Blouse Color	Skirt Color
blue	brown
blue	white
blue	black
red	brown
red	white
red	black
orange	brown
orange	white
orange	black
yellow	brown
yellow	white
yellow	black

The table shows that the woman can choose 12 possible outfits of 1 blouse and 1 skirt.

Caution: When you use an organized table to count possibilities, be sure to proceed in a systematic manner as illustrated in this example. Otherwise, you may overlook a possibility or count one more than once.

You can also use a tree diagram to find the total number of possible outfits.

There are 12 branches in the tree diagram. This shows that the woman can choose a total of 12 possible outfits of 1 blouse and 1 skirt.

You can also use multiplication to find the total number of possible outfits.

> Total number of possible outfits = (number of ways to select a blouse color) ·
> (number of ways to select a skirt color) = 4 · 3 = 12

When the order in which you make a selection determines different outcomes, the arrangement is a **permutation.** For instance, if a club is selecting a president, vice-president, and secretary from three possible candidates (A, B, and C), the order in which the selections are made makes a difference in the possible outcomes as shown in the following table.

President	Vice-President	Secretary
Candidate A	Candidate B	Candidate C
Candidate A	Candidate C	Candidate B
Candidate B	Candidate A	Candidate C
Candidate B	Candidate C	Candidate A
Candidate C	Candidate A	Candidate B
Candidate C	Candidate B	Candidate A

The table shows that there are six different ways that the selection of a president, vice-president, and secretary from the three candidates can be made.

If the order does not determine different outcomes, the arrangement is a **combination.** For instance, if a club is selecting a committee of three people from 5 members (A, B, C, D, or E), the order in which the selections are made does not determine different outcomes, as shown below.

1st Committee Member	2nd Committee Member	3rd Committee Member
Member A	Member B	Member C
Member A	Member B	Member D
Member A	Member B	Member E
Member A	Member C	Member D
Member A	Member C	Member E
Member A	Member D	Member E
Member B	Member C	Member D
Member B	Member C	Member E
Member B	Member D	Member E
Member C	Member D	Member E

The table shows there are a total of 10 different possible committees.

How Do You Solve Real-World Problems Involving Counting and Probability?

To solve real-world word problems involving counting and probability, use the problem-solving process that you learned in the "Numerations and Operations" section (earlier in this chapter).

Here is an example of solving a probability problem.

A bag contains 15 marbles: 7 green, 5 red, and 3 yellow marbles, all identical except for color. If a person draws a single marble from the bag without looking, what is the probability that it will be a red marble?

This is a straightforward probability problem. To solve the problem, find the number of total outcomes possible, find the number of favorable outcomes, and then plug into the probability formula.

There are 15 total possible outcomes. There are 5 favorable outcomes. The probability of drawing a red marble is

$$P(\text{red}) = \frac{\text{number of favorable outcomes}}{\text{number of total outcomes possible}} = \frac{\text{number of red marbles}}{\text{total number of marbles}} = \frac{5}{15} = \frac{1}{3}$$

Did I answer the question? Yes, I found the probability of drawing a red marble from the bag. ✓

Does my answer make sense? Yes, it is consistent with my knowledge of probability. ✓

Is the answer stated in the correct units? No units are required for the answer. ✓

Here is an example of solving a counting problem.

> A man has a choice of a white shirt or a blue shirt. He also may select a striped blue tie, a paisley blue tie, or a solid red tie. How many different outfits can he make of 1 shirt and 1 tie?

This is a counting problem. To solve the problem, multiply the number of ways the man can select a shirt by the number of ways the man can select a tie.

Total number of possible outfits = (number of ways to select a shirt) · (number of ways to select a tie) = 2 · 3 = 6

Did I answer the question? Yes, I found the number of possible outfits. ✓

Does my answer make sense? Yes, it is consistent with my knowledge of probability. ✓

Is the answer stated in the correct units? No units are required for the answer. ✓

Test Yourself

1. _____ is a measure of the chance that an event will happen.

2. The probability that an event is certain to happen is _____.

3. The probability that an event cannot occur is _____.

4. When a coin is flipped, the probability that heads will show on the upface is _____.

5. A die has six faces, numbered 1 through 6. On one toss of the die, the probability that the upface will show the number 5 is _____.

6. Suppose Denzel has a bag of 10 colored tiles: 5 blue, 3 red, and 2 yellow tiles, all identical except for color. If Denzel randomly draws a yellow tile from the bag without replacement, what is the probability that, on a second random draw, he will draw a blue tile?

7. If you flip a coin five times, what is the probability you will get five heads in a row?

8. The faces of a cube are numbered 5, 10, 15, 20, 30, and 40. If you toss the cube two times, what is the probability that the number 40 will show on the upface both times?

9. Sammy is wrapping a gift. She can choose from six different kinds of wrapping paper, and she can select from four different colors of ribbon. If she selects one kind of wrapping paper and one color of ribbon, how many different ways can Sammy wrap the gift?

10. How many 2-character codes using a lowercase letter followed by a digit (0–9) are possible?

Answers

1. Probability

2. 1

3. 0

4. $\frac{1}{2}$

5. $\frac{1}{6}$

6. This is a conditional probability problem. After the yellow tile is drawn and not put back, there are 9 tiles in the bag: 5 blue tiles, 3 red tiles, and 1 yellow tile. Therefore, P(blue on the 2nd draw, *given yellow drawn on 1st draw without replacement*) $= \frac{5}{9}$.

7. This is an independent events probability problem. For each flip of the coin, the probability of heads on the upface is $\frac{1}{2}$, so the probability of five heads in a row is $\frac{1}{2} \cdot \frac{1}{2} \cdot \frac{1}{2} \cdot \frac{1}{2} \cdot \frac{1}{2} = \frac{1}{32}$.

8. This is an independent events probability problem. For each toss of the cube, the probability of 40 on the upface is $\frac{1}{6}$, so the probability that 40 will show on the upface on both tosses is $\frac{1}{6} \cdot \frac{1}{6} = \frac{1}{36}$.

9. This is a counting problem. To solve the problem, multiply the number of ways Sammy can select a wrapping paper by the number of ways she can select a ribbon color.

$$\text{Total number of ways to wrap the gift} = (\text{number of ways to select a wrapping paper}) \cdot$$
$$(\text{number of ways to select a ribbon color}) = 6 \cdot 4 = 24$$

10. This is a counting problem. To solve the problem, multiply the number of ways to select a lowercase letter times the number of ways to select a digit.

$$\text{Total number of 2-character codes} = (\text{number of ways to select a lowercase letter}) \cdot$$
$$(\text{number of ways to select a digit}) = 26 \cdot 10 = 260$$

Sample Questions

Directions: Read each question and select the best answer choice.

1. The graph that follows represents the monthly average temperature in the city of Townville for 6 months of the year. How much higher is the average temperature in May than in January?

Average Monthly Temperatures

A. 2°
B. 20°
C. 40°
D. 80°

2. Given here are students' scores on a social studies test. What is the median of the set of scores?

Student	Score
A	95
B	42
C	55
D	87
E	68
F	72
G	66
H	87

A. 70
B. 71
C. 77.5
D. 87

3. You have a bag containing 25 colored tiles: 10 blue, 7 red, 5 green, and 3 yellow tiles, all identical except for color. If a person picks out a single tile from the bag without looking, what is the probability that it will be a red or green tile?

A. $\dfrac{2}{5}$

B. $\dfrac{7}{25}$

C. $\dfrac{12}{25}$

D. $\dfrac{3}{25}$

4. A boy is making a sandwich for lunch. He has a choice of two kinds of bread (white and whole wheat) and three sandwich fillings (peanut butter, tuna salad, and pimiento cheese). How many different sandwiches can he make if he chooses one type of bread and one kind of sandwich filling?

A. 5

B. 6

C. 8

D. 9

Answer Explanations for Sample Questions

1. **C.**

Average Monthly Temperatures

The bar for January goes up to 40°, and the bar for May goes up to 80°. The difference is 80° − 40° = 40°. Choice **A** results if you mistakenly decide that there is 1° between marks on the graph. Choice **B** results if you mistakenly decide that there are 10° between marks on the graph. Choice **D** results if you fail to subtract, and use the temperature in May as your answer.

2. **A.** To find the median, do the following:

Step 1: Put the numbers in order from least to greatest.

$$42, 55, 66, 68, 72, 87, 87, 95$$

Step 2: Find the middle number. The median is the average of the two middle numbers, 68 and 72.

$$\text{The median} = \frac{68 + 72}{2} = \frac{140}{2} = 70$$

Choice **B** results if you fail to order the scores and mistakenly decide to average 55 and 87 to find the median. Choice **C** results if you fail to order the scores and mistakenly decide to average 68 and 87 to find the median. Choice **D** is the mode, not the median.

3. **C.** This is a straightforward probability problem. To solve the problem, find the number of total outcomes possible, find the number of favorable outcomes, and then plug into the probability formula.

There are 25 total possible outcomes. There are 12 favorable outcomes (7 red and 5 green tiles). The probability of drawing a red or green tile is

$$P(\text{red or green}) = \frac{\text{number of favorable outcomes}}{\text{number of total outcomes possible}} = \frac{12}{25}$$

Did I answer the question? Yes, I found the probability of drawing a red or green tile from the bag. ✓

Does my answer make sense? Yes, it is consistent with my knowledge of probability. ✓

Is the answer stated in the correct units? No units are required for the answer. ✓

Choice **A** is the probability of drawing a blue tile. Choice **B** is the probability of drawing a red tile. Choice **D** is the probability of drawing a yellow tile.

4. B. This problem is a counting problem. To solve the problem, multiply the number of ways the boy can select a bread by the number of ways he can select a sandwich filling.

$$\text{Total number of possible sandwiches} = (\text{number of ways to select a bread}) \cdot$$
$$(\text{number of ways to select a sandwich filling}) = 2 \cdot 3 = 6$$

Did I answer the question? Yes, I found the number of possible sandwiches. ✓

Does my answer make sense? Yes, it is a reasonable answer. ✓

Is the answer stated in the correct units? No units are required for the answer. ✓

Choice **A** results if you add, instead of multiply, in the problem. Choices **C** and **D** result if you count or compute incorrectly.

Review for the GK Reading Subtest

The Reading subtest of the FTCE GK Test consists of 40 multiple-choice questions, which you must complete in 40 minutes. Each test question consists of a reading comprehension passage followed by multiple-choice questions. Each question requires that you choose from among four answer choices. You must click on the oval corresponding to your answer choice on the computer screen. You cannot bring written notes or scratch paper into the testing room.

The Reading Review in This Study Guide

The Reading review in this book is organized around the two reading areas tested on the FTCE GK Test:

1. Literal Comprehension Skills
2. Inferential Comprehension Skills

The review sections present reading concepts with examples and explanations for each area. Each area, furthermore, contains a general review and sample questions. The sample questions are multiple-choice questions similar to what you might expect to see on the FTCE General Knowledge Test. The answer explanations for the sample questions are provided immediately after the questions. At the conclusion of this chapter are "Test Yourself" exercises, which give you an opportunity to practice what you just learned. When doing the "Test Yourself" exercises, you should cover up the answers. Then check your answers when you've finished the exercises.

Literal Comprehension Skills

As listed in the *Competencies and Skills Required for Teacher Certification in Florida, Fifteenth Edition* (available at www.fldoe.org/asp/ftce/ftcecomp.asp#Fifteenth), there are three main Reading Literal Comprehension competencies/skills in which you should be proficient. They are as follows:

- Recognizing main ideas
- Identifying supporting details
- Determining the meaning of words or phrases in context

Recognize Main Ideas

Recognizing the main idea(s) in a reading passage is essential to mastering reading comprehension questions. The key to recognizing main ideas is to identify the *topic sentence* of a reading passage. In the topic sentence, the author states the main idea of the paragraph, and it is the sentence upon which all other sentences in the paragraph are dependent. You can identify the topic sentence as the one sentence that explains the paragraph without any further explanation. Look at this example reading passage and see whether you can identify the main idea:

> Staring at my plate, I realized I was now fully awake and ready to face the day. I was groomed and dressed, sitting at my kitchen table while contemplating my next move. I realized, however, that I could not do anything without eating a good breakfast. By midday, my stomach would be growling, and I would be in a lousy mood if I did not have my daily regimen of orange juice and toast—and hot cereal. I definitely preferred hot cereal. For without hot cereal, I would certainly feel grumpy. Yes, for me, breakfast is the most important meal of my day.

The main idea of this passage is clearly stated in the last sentence (*Yes, for me, breakfast is the most important meal of my day*). All of the accompanying sentences support this main idea.

Generally, the topic sentence of a paragraph is its first or last sentence. Sometimes, its location may be embedded in the paragraph; but in every instance, the topic sentence of a well-written paragraph can be recognized as the essential or main idea of the passage.

Identify Supporting Details

Identifying the supporting details in a reading passage is important in learning to master reading comprehension questions. The supporting details are the examples that support and clarify the topic sentence or main idea of a written passage. When you analyze a reading passage, the supporting details underscore the writer's main idea by providing clarification of its meaning or evidence to corroborate it. Look at this example of a reading passage and identify the supporting details:

> The cyclone had set the house down very gently—for a cyclone—in the midst of a country of marvelous beauty. There were lovely patches of greensward all about, with stately trees bearing rich and luscious fruits. Banks of gorgeous flowers were on every hand, and birds with rare and brilliant plumage sang and fluttered in the trees and bushes. A little way off was a small brook, rushing and sparkling along between green banks, and murmuring in a voice very grateful to a little girl who had lived so long on the dry, gray prairies. –*The Wonderful Wizard of Oz,* L. Frank Baum

The supporting details of this passage describe the marvelous beauty of the country surrounding the house. These explicit sentences demonstrate how essential supporting details are to the development of a main idea. They provide substance to you writing by making vivid the thesis or main point of your paper.

All writing—whether serious or humorous, objective or personal—depends on support to be effective. The types of support authors use in their writing depends on the answers to the following three questions:

- What is the writing goal?
- Who is the intended audience?
- What is the nature of the piece of writing?

You need to be aware that authors rely on more than one kind of supportive detail to help their readers understand the main idea of a reading passage. These are

- **Personal observations:** descriptive remarks and observations about a person, place, or thing
- **Facts:** objective information collected by research or analysis
- **Testimony:** statements, quotations, accounts, observations, and assertions from experts or eyewitnesses
- **Statistics:** hard evidence or facts expressed numerically
- **Examples:** specific illustrations that clarify the thesis statement

Finally, you can reasonably expect that when writing supporting details, authors adhere to the following guidelines:

- Select details that reinforce the thesis statement or main idea.
- Use sources that are reliable, credible, and verifiable.
- Organize supporting details logically and coherently.
- Avoid introducing extraneous or irrelevant information.

Determine the Meaning of Words or Phrases in Context

Determining the meaning of words or phrases in context is essential to mastering skills in reading comprehension. When you know how to interpret the meaning of a word or phrase in context, then you possess the ability to discern logical arguments and conclusions in your reading. Often, readers misinterpret or skip over key words or phrases in their reading and thus fail to comprehend the meaning of a passage. This can be corrected by learning to read any given reading passage with a sharp and discerning eye.

Look at these example passages and identify the key words or key phrases.

Example 1:

The study of intellectual growth cannot be separated from that of physical growth. During the same years that children are developing physically, their mental concepts and skills are taking form. Research studies have indicated a positive correlation between physical maturity and intellectual ability; although, of course, caution should be exercised in making sweeping generalizations from these findings.

Note that the key phrase in this paragraph is "caution should be exercised." This phrase means that before any assumptions are made between physical maturity and intellectual ability, the reader should realize that the mentioned research studies might not have taken into account all relevant factors.

Example 2:

The importance of effective motivation is of primary concern in curricular planning. Motivation involves a two-pronged responsibility, which rests both with the teacher and the student. The student must want to learn, and the teacher must provide motivating experiences. School teachers must be constantly sensitive to the various facets of motivation as they contemplate, plan, and revise their curricular offerings. They must be concerned with short-term and long-term motivation, intrinsic and extrinsic motivation, natural and contrived motivation, students' levels of aspiration, and the ultimate goal of self-motivation.

Note that the key phrase in this paragraph is "School teachers must be constantly sensitive to the various facets of motivation." This phrase means that motivation is not determined by one absolute cause, but by a series of causes that directly relate to the developmental needs of the students who are being motivated.

Example 3:

Teachers must be emotionally prepared for children who dislike them and for those whom they have difficulty tolerating. Teachers, like all other human beings, naturally tend to react negatively to anyone who makes life more difficult for them. Responding with loving kindness toward a sixteen-year-old who continually makes irritating remarks in class can be a challenge. A teacher might easily develop a persistent dislike for such a youngster. But the teaching situation is not an ordinary circumstance, and the teacher is not justified in reacting as other, less understanding, people might react in a normal social situation. Teachers have the special responsibility of helping young people grow up in ways best suited to their own growth needs. Dislike is a strong impediment to providing such help. Nevertheless, the students who need the most help are almost always those who are the most trying.

The key phrase is "the teacher is not justified in reacting as other, less understanding, people might react." This phrase is the key to understanding this passage and its implications for what it means to be a professional educator. To the best of their ability, teachers should not look at disruptive students as making trouble for the teacher, but as individuals who, by their misbehavior, make trouble for themselves.

Inferential Comprehension Skills

Determining the meaning from information that is either explicit or implied is an essential reading comprehension skill. Careful and perceptive readers must be able to find coherent meaning and be able to draw conclusions about the text they are reading. Simply getting the facts in reading is not enough; you must think about what those facts mean to you.

To accomplish this goal, readers must be able to use two sets of skills. They are

- Literal reading comprehension skills
- Inferential reading comprehension skills

Literal comprehension skills refer to the reader's ability to identify and/or recall information that is explicitly stated in a text. Specifically, the reader should be able to determine and define

- Sequence of events
- Main ideas
- Directly stated facts
- Supporting details, including words, phrases, or sentences
- Directly stated opinions

The word "literal" means "the exact words" or "the most obvious meaning of a term or expression." When writers refer to the literal meaning of a word or a passage, they are referring to the explicitly stated facts without embellishment or exaggeration.

Inferential comprehension skills refer to the reader's ability to use information explicitly stated in a passage to determine what is *not* stated. Using these skills, the reader should be able to make predictions and draw conclusions about

- Relationships in a reading passage, like cause and effect, sequence and time, comparisons and contrasts, and classifications and generalizations
- Events and sequences that could follow logically
- Symbols, patterns, and images that would give heightened meaning to the text
- Implicit themes or main ideas embedded in the text
- Unstated reasons for actions and beliefs as implied in the text

Inferring is the process of creating a *personal meaning* from the reading passage. Inferring is the blending of the reader's prior knowledge with what he or she is reading in the text. When readers infer, they create meaning that is not stated explicitly in the passage that they are reading.

Look at these examples and identify possible meanings of the words in this context.

> *Sue blew out the candles and got presents.*
>
> Is it Sue's birthday? anniversary? graduation? Birthday seems most likely, as one does not usually blow out candles for one's graduation. If it were a wedding anniversary, it would likely be Sue and Mike blowing out the candles, not Sue by herself.

> *Maria practices her clarinet for three hours a day.*
>
> Is Maria a great clarinetist? Does she practice because she "must" or because she "wants to?" We don't know the answer to these questions. All we know is that Maria is faithfully committed to practicing.

> *When I woke up, there were branches and leaves all over the yard.*
>
> Is it the result of a storm? yard work? vandalism? A storm seems most likely. Yard work, even done during one's sleep time, shouldn't result in a chaotic mess. Vandalism is a possibility, but ranks second to a storm.

These examples show that the meaning of words or phrases can only be determined when the reader understands the greater context in which the words and phrases appear. Without context, words can mean almost anything.

These two sets of reading comprehension skills—literal and inferential—are used in all reading activities. To become proficient in reading comprehension, you should familiarize yourself with these two distinct skills. They will play a considerable role in helping you to determine the meaning of reading passages on the FTCE GK Test.

As listed in the *Competencies and Skills Required for Teacher Certification in Florida, Fifteenth Edition* (see the Web address mentioned earlier in the chapter), there are eight Reading Inferential Comprehension competencies/skills in which you should be proficient. They are as follows:

- Determining the purpose
- Identifying overall organizational pattern
- Distinguishing between fact and opinion
- Recognizing bias
- Recognizing tone
- Determining relationships between sentences
- Analyzing the validity of arguments
- Drawing logical inferences and conclusions

More specifically, skilled inferential readers are able to

- Recognize the meaning of pronouns in a given reading passage
- Determine the definition of unknown words from the given context
- Discern intonation of a character's or narrator's words
- Understand relationships among characters in a given text
- Recognize author's bias in a given passage
- Offer conclusions from facts presented in a specific passage

Determine the Purpose

Determining the purpose of a reading passage is essential to understanding the meaning in context. Authors write for many reasons, and knowing their reasons for writing can help you considerably in determining meaning and purpose in their writing. Some passages explicitly state the author's purpose. Other passages leave you to guess or interpret the purpose. As a good reader, you should always try to determine the purpose of a passage, because doing so enables you to evaluate the passage in terms of whether the author got his or her point across effectively.

Essentially, there are four common purposes for writing. They are

- Self-expression
- Exposition
- Entertainment
- Persuasion

Often these purposes overlap. For instance, you might want to persuade someone to take an action and decide that the best way to accomplish this goal is to write an essay that is persuasive, yet entertaining.

In any event, each writing purpose has its own style. **Self-expressive writing** is free-flowing in its choice of words and ideas and is often the province of journals and diaries. **Expository writing** is designed to inform or convey beliefs and opinions to an outside audience. Generally, this writing is more structured and stylized in content and tone. **Entertaining writing** is meant to amuse or arouse interest in the reader so that they find enjoyment in the writer's words. Communicating the writer's interest and enthusiasm for his or her subject is one such method to generate interest. Finally, **persuasive writing** is meant to convince the reader to adopt the writer's point-of-view. The effectiveness of persuasive writing is dependent on the clarity of the author's argument, the strength of the author's supporting details, and the attitude of the audience that the author is trying to convince.

When readers know the meaning of a passage in context, they are more equipped to discern the details of the passage. Knowledge of purpose implies an understanding of the overall design of a reading passage and an implicit comprehension of what the passage means in a larger context. Thus, knowing the purpose in a given reading passage is key to mastering reading comprehension skills. Look at this example of a reading passage and try to determine the purpose of the passage.

> All day long, wind howled at unheard-of speeds. Houses shook, cars swayed, and water overflowed. The storm, directly off the Atlantic Ocean, was raging with all that violent wind and rain could possibly bring. Still, the tiny hamlet, nestled between large cliffs and set off behind a protective tanker, had seen worse in its long and torturous history of enduring violent hurricanes. The angry gods of thunder and wind would not disturb the town's sturdy inhabitants. They had seen much before and were confident they would see more in the future.
>
> 1. The purpose of this passage is to
>
>   **A.** describe a violent storm.
>   **B.** explain small town life.
>   **C.** demonstrate resilience.
>   **D.** illustrate ocean currents.

The correct answer is Choice **C,** *demonstrate resilience.* Clearly, the author's purpose or intent is to describe the strength and courage with which the citizens of this small ocean town resist its violent storms. By drawing a vivid picture of the storm, the author is showing us how even such raging weather cannot destroy this town's historical precedent for enduring even the most treacherous weather. Choice **A** is not the correct choice because although the passage does describe a violent storm, the author's purpose is to use the storm as an example or illustration of the reading passage's larger purpose. Choice **B** is not the correct choice because although the passage does refer to this town as being small in size, the author's purpose is not to explain life in a small town. Finally, Choice **D** is not the correct choice because the passage makes no mention of ocean currents.

Identify Overall Organizational Patterns

When reading a given passage, it is always best to recognize or identify its overall organizational pattern. Knowledge of the organizational pattern of a reading passage increases comprehension and enhances fluency skills. Readers who can discern the general structure of a passage tend to have a better grasp of the passage's meaning and the purpose for the choices made in the selection. Seeing a larger pattern clearly helps in improving inferential reading comprehension skills and permits a larger understanding of the author's intent and design in structuring the reading passage.

The organizational pattern of a reading passage may be arranged in a number of ways—but most notably, it will be either direct or indirect. A passage written in a **direct organizational pattern** is written in a literal, "straightforward" style. The author writes about a person, an object, or an event by simply listing the important facts that the reader needs to know about the subject in question. A passage written in an **indirect organizational pattern** is written in a figurative "creative" style. The two styles distinguish themselves by the author's intent and the technique employed to illustrate the intention.

The most common **direct organizational** patterns are as follows:

- **Time-ordered sequence of events:** In this pattern, the events are presented in the order in which they occurred or in a specifically planned order in which they must develop. In either arrangement, the order is important, and changing it would change the meaning of the passage. Signal words/phrases often used to indicate chronological sequence are

    first, second, third

    before, after

    when

    later

    until

    at last

    next

■ **Simple listing of events, ideas, and activities:** In this pattern, the items or topics are listed in a series of supporting facts or details. These supporting elements are of equal value, and the order in which they occur in the passage is of no significant importance. Also, changing the order of the topics presented does not alter the meaning of the paragraph. Signal words/phrases often used for simple listing are

> in addition
>
> another
>
> for example
>
> also
>
> several
>
> a number of

■ **Definition followed by examples of the definition:** In this pattern, the concept is initially defined and then followed by an explanation with examples or simple restatements of the original concept. This pattern is a familiar organizational technique of most textbook passages. Signal words/phrases often used for defining by example are

> is defined as
>
> is described as
>
> is called
>
> term or concept
>
> refers to
>
> means

■ **Division or classification of ideas from general to specific:** In this pattern, the organization of ideas is presented from a general concept to a specific detail. The passage discusses a concept or idea and then divides the discussion into its component parts. Signal words/phrases often used for division or classification are

> whole
>
> part
>
> it follows
>
> category
>
> component
>
> in conclusion

■ **Cause and effect:** In this pattern, one topic or idea is shown as having produced another topic or idea. An event or effect has occurred because of a particular situation or cause. Simply, the cause stimulates the effect or the outcome of the event. Signal words/phrases often used for cause and effect are

> hence
>
> because
>
> made
>
> for this reason
>
> consequently
>
> on that account

■ **Compare and contrast:** In this pattern, topics or ideas are described by their relationship to similar topics or ideas. The author's purpose is to show similarities (comparisons) or differences (contrasts) between or among elements. Signal words/phrases often used for comparing and contrasting relationships are

> similar
>
> like
>
> resembles
>
> different

but

however

bigger than

smaller than

on the other hand

in contrast

parallels

- **Description of place, person, or event:** In this pattern, the topics or ideas that comprise a description are a simple listing of details. In a description, you are writing about what a person, place, or thing is like. No specific order is required. Signal words/phrases often used for describing a person, place, or event are

  is

  like

  resembles

  in

  above

  below

  beside

  near

  north, east, south, west

- **Sequence or process of an event:** In this pattern, the listing of processes or events follows a similar arrangement as the time sequence of events or chronological order. The only difference is that the passage is describing a complex sequence of events, and not single isolated incidents. In the sequence of events, each event is rich in detail and complexity. Signal words/phrases often used for describing a sequence or process of an event are

  first, second, third

  in the beginning

  before

  then

  after

  finally

  at last

  subsequently

  recently

  previously

  afterward

  when

  after

- **Description of spatial or place order:** In this pattern, the topics or ideas are described as they appear in space or place order. Attention is paid to classification or grouping things or ideas into specific categories. Signal words/phrases often used in description of spatial or place order are

  is a kind of

  can be divided into

  is a type of

  falls under

belongs to

is a part of

fits into

is grouped with

is related to

is associated with

is next to, is adjacent to

is across from

- **Stating and defining a choice or opinion:** In this pattern, a preference is indicated for a specific idea, object, or action. Attention is paid to stating an opinion or a choice on an action, idea, or event. Signal words/ phrases often used in the stating and defining of choice or opinion are

  in my opinion

  belief

  idea

  understanding

  I think that

  I consider

  I believe

  it seems to me

  I prefer

  hope

  feel

The most common **indirect organizational** patterns are as follows:

- **Allegorical:** In an allegorical passage, the objects, persons, and actions in a narrative are compared in meanings that lie outside the narrative itself. The true meaning of an allegory lies in its moral, social, religious, or political significance. In an allegory, the characters are often personifications of abstract ideas—like charity, hope, faith, goodness, evil—and thus represent concepts greater than themselves. An allegory is a story with two meanings: its literal or everyday meaning ("This is the story of two people who . . . .") and its symbolic meaning ("This story is really about the true meaning of . . . .").

- **Narrative:** In a narrative passage, an event or incident is recreated for the central purpose of revealing an insight into the actions of the people or events involved. A narrative has a central focus, is highly descriptive in its presentation, is action-oriented, and is usually based on a personal experience.

- **Inferential:** In an inferential passage, a conclusion is drawn based on available information. For an inference to be considered valid, sufficient evidence supporting the claim and/or supposition must be presented. The result is a thorough examination of the topic in discussion that captures the essence of the text and results in a whole new presentation of the topic.

- **Spontaneous:** In a spontaneous passage, the spoken and uncensored free-flowing of ideas and feelings takes precedence. No particular organizational pattern is employed besides the general whimsical nature of the writer's preferences and predilections.

- **Conversational:** In a conversational passage, the narration is written in the vernacular of everyday language, making the passage highly accessible and user-friendly for the reader. Not as free-flowing as the spontaneous pattern, the writing is more tightly controlled and constructed, allowing the reader to learn only what the writer intends, and not what the writer deliberately censors. The object of conversational writing is accessibility, not objectivity.

Look at these examples for identifying overall organizational patterns.

The day was long. The workers arrived at the factory by 7:30 A.M. Upon arrival, they changed into their work clothes and headed directly to the factory's main floor, where they all went to their respective positions and got to work. Each person had an assigned task; and with few interruptions, the workers proceeded to do their jobs until noon. Then, at 12 and 1 P.M., in two previously assigned shifts, they broke and went to lunch, with the second group waiting for all the members of the first group to return before going to lunch themselves. After lunch, the factory was again humming with the sound of workers diligently doing their jobs until around 5 P.M. Then, the whistle blew throughout the factory, and the workers immediately quit their tasks, gathered their belongings, and headed home to rest and prepare for another day.

1. The overall organizational pattern of this passage is

   A. chronological.
   B. inferential.
   C. allegorical.
   D. cause and effect.

The correct answer is **A,** *chronological.* Clearly, the author is providing a timeline description of the exact events in a typical day at this factory. The author chronicles the sequence of events experienced by the workers and no more. Choice **B,** *inferential,* is not correct because the author is not making inferences about the workers' day. Choice **C,** *allegorical,* is not correct because the author has not written a story about life in the factory that is representative of a larger meaning. Choice **D,** *cause and effect,* is not correct because the author is not describing the causes of outcomes.

Thermodynamics is a field of interest studied by a wide array of scientists. They include, among many, physicists, chemists, and engineers. For physicists and chemists, thermodynamics is of interest because they are primarily concerned with basic physical laws, properties of chemical substances, and changes in physical and chemical properties that are caused by the interaction of different kinds of energy. Engineers, however, are interested in these elements as well as in the application of thermodynamic principles to the design and construction of machines. For example, they would apply these principles to mechanisms that convert energy from one form or substance into another. And in the field of engineering, specific thermodynamic conversions are the domain of particular engineers. Electrical engineers are primarily interested in the conversion of mechanical energy into electrical energy, whereas mechanical engineers devote their time to the design of systems that will most efficiently convert thermal or heat energy into mechanical energy.

2. The overall organizational pattern of this passage is

   A. chronological.
   B. definitional.
   C. conversational.
   D. allegorical.

The correct answer is **B,** *definitional.* The author constructs this passage by defining terms and distinctions as they appear. Choice **A,** *chronological,* is not the correct choice because the author does not provide a timeline of events. Choice **C,** *conversational,* is not the correct choice because the author is not writing in the vernacular of everyday language. Choice **D,** *allegorical,* is not the correct choice because the author is not telling a story that is representative of a larger meaning.

After I arrived at college, I realized there were many similarities between my high school and my new school. First, both schools—my high school and my college—were small in size and number. I attended a small high school with fewer than 1,100 total students, and my college has only about 1,600 students. Second, both were situated in primarily rural communities. My high school was surrounded by farmland that was devoted to growing corn and wheat. My college was situated in a rural homestead that was devoted to raising cattle and hogs. Third, my high school and my college were filled with generations of students whose parents attended the very same institutions. Thus, both student bodies felt a deep and intimate connection to their school, their teachers, and each other.

3. The overall organizational pattern of this passage is

   A. allegorical.
   B. narrative.
   C. compare and contrast.
   D. cause and effect.

The correct answer is **C**, *compare and contrast*. The author constructs this passage by comparing two distinct entities: high school and college. Choice **A**, *allegorical*, is not the correct choice because the author is not telling a story that is representative of a larger meaning. Choice **B**, *narrative*, is not the correct choice because the author is not retelling an incident or an event that has occurred. Choice **D**, *cause and effect*, is not correct because the author does not demonstrate that one incident causes another to occur.

In recent years, modern cities and their surrounding suburbs have grown exponentially in size. There are many reasons for this sudden and significant growth. First, as cities become ever more the place for commerce and business, they simply attract more people. People from both rural and urban areas find themselves attracted to urban life because this is where the jobs and opportunities are. Second, as individuals settle into the cities and surrounding suburbs, they, in turn, attract other individuals who are seeking the advantages of urban living. Thus, old and young alike gravitate to urban dwellings seeking affordable housing, strong schools, sophisticated health care, and convenient shopping. Third, as cities and suburbs grow, places of leisure, entertainment, and culture begin to grow as well. Sports stadiums, theaters, and museums soon dot the landscape of these newly defined urban domains. For many people, these facilities and conveniences make life in the city and its surrounding communities much more appealing than life on the farm; and thus, they draw people away from rural communities.

4. The overall organizational pattern of this passage is

   A. narrative.
   B. cause and effect.
   C. compare and contrast.
   D. allegorical.

The correct answer is **B**, *cause and effect*. The author constructs this passage by showing how a series of events, relating to commerce in cities and their surrounding suburbs, resulted in other events occurring. Choice **A**, *narrative*, is not the correct choice because the author is not retelling an incident or an event that has occurred. Choice **C**, *compare and contrast*, is not the correct choice because the author is not primarily showing the similarities and differences between living in an urban and rural setting. Choice **D**, *allegorical*, is not the correct choice because the author is not telling a story that is representative of a larger meaning.

My hometown is noted for several man-made features. First, it has the largest ice-cream store in America. Serving every flavor imaginable, my hometown ice-cream store occupies an old high school gymnasium. In this large converted building, all that is served is ice cream and assorted desserts. People come from miles around just to sample the delicious treats and to watch how ice cream is actually made. Also, parties and functions are regularly held in this wonderful old building, making it a very special place for all who enjoy its old-fashioned decorations and traditional furnishings. Second, my town boasts as the home of one of the largest wooden windmills ever constructed. Built originally to celebrate the Dutch who settled in my hometown, this windmill now serves as a tourist attraction throughout the year. Especially during the summer, visitors come to my town just to marvel at the size of the windmill, nearly six stories high, and to walk the winding stairs leading to the top. Finally, my hometown has a genuine castle. Built in the late 1800s when a wealthy landowner came to the town to settle and live, this castle resembles something from King Arthur's court. Complete with moat, turret, and drawbridge, this fully staffed and furnished castle serves as both a meeting place and tourist attraction for conventioneers and visitors from far and wide. To be sure, these three man-made landmarks make my hometown a very special place.

5. The overall organizational pattern of this passage is

    A. descriptive.
    B. conversational.
    C. compare and contrast.
    D. cause and effect.

The correct answer is **A,** *descriptive.* The author constructs this passage by simply listing the characteristics that make his hometown special. Choice **B,** *conversational*, is not the correct choice because the author does not present a dialogue or discussion as the heart of the narrative. Choice **C,** *compare and contrast*, is not the correct choice because the author is not comparing and/or contrasting two different sides or issues. Choice **D,** *cause and effect*, is not the correct choice because the author is not showing how a series of events has resulted in another series of events.

Distinguish Between Fact and Opinion

In any given passage, the reader must be able to distinguish between fact and opinion. A fact is verifiable. Its truth can be determined by researching the evidence. An opinion is a judgment based on facts. It is an honest attempt to draw a reasonable conclusion from factual evidence.

Look at these examples and determine whether the sentences express a fact or an opinion.

    A. World War II ended in 1945.
    B. The Vietnam War was an unjust war.
    C. Horror movies are the best entertainment.
    D. Lauren served baked Alaska for dessert.
    E. The wind was moving at 20 miles per hour.
    F. Cold weather is enjoyable.

The answers are

    A. Fact. World War II did end in 1945. This is a verifiable fact.

    B. Opinion. This sentence is a statement of opinion. As in any war, there are those who believe the war is a just cause, and there are others who believe the cause, and therefore the war, is unjust. If someone were to say, "The Vietnam War was an unjust war," that person would be stating an opinion, as the justification for the Vietnam War is highly debatable. Please note that if the sentence read, "Some say the Vietnam War was an unjust war," this would be a statement of fact because, in the opinion of some, it was an unjust war and thus this is a true statement of their beliefs.

C. Opinion. This sentence is a statement of opinion. When someone says what their favorite "anything" is, they are stating their preference or opinion. In this example, "Horror movies are the best entertainment," the writer is announcing his or her predilection for a particular movie genre. Like any other statement of preference, this is a pronouncement of bias and not fact. Again, if the sentence read, "Some say that horror movies are the best entertainment," this would be a statement of fact, as it is true that for some people, horror movies are their favorite movie genre.

D. Fact. This sentence is a statement of fact. Lauren did serve baked Alaska for dessert. This is a true and observable incident.

E. Fact. This sentence is a statement of fact. The wind was moving at 20 miles per hour. The evidence for this event can be documented.

F. Opinion. This sentence is a statement of opinion. A description of one's feelings about the weather is an example of a personal predilection. Some enjoy hot weather, others cold, and still others enjoy whatever the weather brings them. Again, if the sentence read, "Many say cold weather is enjoyable," this would be a statement of fact because in the opinion of some, cold weather is considered enjoyable.

Recognize Bias

Recognizing bias in a given reading passage is a critical task in reading comprehension. Bias is a slanted or prejudiced attitude that presents opinion as factual information. The conclusions drawn are based on preconceived beliefs or prejudices and not on the evidence discovered. Recognizing bias protects the reader from accepting the personal opinions of others as truths.

Look at these examples and determine whether they are biased or not biased.

A. The Civil War was a war invented by Northerners to make quick money.
B. The Apollo space mission broke new ground in space travel.
C. Our ballet followed the choral presentation.
D. After lunch, the President spoke about his new proposal.
E. Music videos are designed to corrupt today's youth.

The answers are

A. Biased. This statement, though presented as fact, is expressing the author's point-of-view.

B. Not biased. This statement is a self-evident truth. The Apollo space mission did break new ground in space travel.

C. Not biased. This is a statement of literal fact.

D. Not biased. This is a statement of literal fact.

E. Biased. This statement is presented as fact when it is clearly the author's opinion.

Recognize Tone

In any given passage, the author's tone is the "voice" or attitude that the author adopts toward the subject of the passage. Recognizing tone is directly related to understanding the author's purpose for writing the passage.

A helpful technique for determining an author's tone is to imagine the sound of the author's voice as if the author were reading the passage aloud. Often, helpful adjectives—*optimistic, pessimistic, cheerful, cynical, instructive, ominous,* and *informative*—are apt descriptions used to describe the tone of a given passage.

> Which of the preceding adjectives best describes the tone of each of the following?
>
> **A.** Attention, ladies and gentlemen! Global warming is destroying our planet—and we are doomed!
> **B.** The beginning of the Civil Rights movement was sparked by the refusal of Rosa Parks to move to the back of a city bus. She quietly told the bus driver that she was not going to move to the rear of the bus where African-Americans, or Negroes as they were called then, were designated to sit.
> **C.** I like lollipops! In fact, lollipops make me smile as soon as I plop one in my mouth.
> **D.** When the skies turn gray, I caution you to be on the alert for an impending thunderstorm.
> **E.** Although Jack was disappointed in his math score, he felt better about his overall understanding of algebra.

The answers are

A. Pessimistic. The author is clearly presenting a strong and dire point-of-view.

B. Informative. The author is describing the results of a factual event.

C. Cheerful. The author is communicating feelings.

D. Ominous. The author is sounding a warning.

E. Optimistic. The author is presenting the positive outlook of a central figure.

Determine Relationships between Sentences

Recognizing relationships between words, phrases, and sentences is a vital reading comprehension skill. This skill requires the reader to go beyond the ideas expressed in a passage and make certain inferences and conclusions about them. Knowing whether sentences are related in context and tone is critical to understanding a reading passage.

Relationships among words, phrases, and sentences can either be **implicit** or **explicit. Implicit** indicates that the reader understands the *intuitive* meaning of the given passage. The meaning of the passage is implied and not directly stated. **Explicit** indicates that the meaning of the passage is stated directly.

Transitional words and phrases serve to identify the relationship between one sentence and the next and act as links between paragraphs. Understanding the selection of the transitional word that links two sentences or paragraphs is critical to perceiving the author's meaning of the text.

For example, take the statements "John is incredibly smart. He does not do well in school."

The explicit meaning of those statements can be simply stated: John *is* incredibly smart and he *does not* do well in school.

The implicit relationship is that smart people should do well in school; and, unfortunately, John does not.

Yet, notice that the use of transitional words directly affects the meaning of these two sentences:

John is incredibly smart, but *he does not do well in school.*

John is incredibly smart, *but* he does not do well in school.

This implies that John is very smart, but as a matter of fact, he does not do well in school.

John is incredibly smart *and* he does not do well in school.

This implies that John is very smart, and unfortunately, he does not do well in school.

John is incredibly smart, *yet* he does not do well in school.

This implies that although John is very smart, he surprisingly does not do well in school.

In each instance, the distinction is subtle and, of course, open to interpretation by the reader.

Here is a list of transitional words that are effective in indicating the relationships of meanings between parts of sentences, between sentences, and between paragraphs:

- To repeat an idea just started: *in other words, to repeat, that is, again*
- To illustrate an idea: *for example, for instance, in particular, in this manner*
- To announce a contrast or change in direction: *yet, however, still, nevertheless, in contrast, instead of*
- To restate an idea: *to be exact, to be specific, to be precise*
- To mark a new idea: *also, too, besides, furthermore*
- To connect two or more ideas: *and, but, or, nor, because*
- To show cause and effect: *as a result, for this reason, consequently, accordingly*
- To bring to a conclusion: *in short, in brief, to conclude, on the whole*

A related concept is the understanding of the causality and logical sequence of sentence ideas. Causality implies an understanding of the relationship between or among sentence ideas, and that each idea is generated from the idea that preceded it. A logical sequence of sentence ideas occurs when the concepts expressed in the sentence flow together in a coherent fashion.

Here are examples that demonstrate logical causality:

Professor Wilson is a man. All men are mortal. Therefore, Professor Wilson is mortal.

Julia is a trained athlete. Athletes enjoy being physically fit. Therefore, Julia is a trained athlete who enjoys being physically fit.

In this next example, determine if logical causality exists in the relationships between the sentences:

Alonzo and Hallie loved the roller coaster. The day began with high excitement. Alonzo and Hallie had planned the perfect outing. On their coaster ride, however, Hallie fell ill. She got a headache and threw up. Sadly, she spent the rest of the day relaxing and nursing a bad stomach. Undaunted, they headed to the roller coaster and waited patiently on a very long line for their ride to begin. They decided to take a trip to the local amusement park. When they arrived, they noticed lots of people heading toward the roller coaster.

Clearly, the sentences in this paragraph are not presented in the correct order. The logical order is as follows:

The day began with high excitement. Alonzo and Hallie had planned the perfect outing. They decided to take a trip to the local amusement park. Alonzo and Hallie loved the roller coaster. When they arrived, they noticed lots of people heading toward the roller coaster. Undaunted, they headed to the roller coaster and waited patiently on a very long line for their ride to begin. On their coaster ride, however, Hallie fell ill. She got a headache and threw up. Sadly, she spent the rest of the day relaxing and nursing a bad stomach.

The new order makes logical sense and shows the direct relationship between sentences.

Analyze the Validity of Arguments

Persuasive writing involves the use of argument to motivate the reader to adopt a certain viewpoint, opinion, or attitude. It is up to the reader to decide whether the arguments are valid or invalid. Thus, analyzing the validity of arguments presented in a reading comprehension passage is essential to understanding the passage's meaning. And all writers must inform their readers by writing passages in a logical, coherent progression of ideas in order to be recognized as a valid source of information.

Generally speaking, there are two basic kinds of arguments or reasoning—**inductive** and **deductive.**

Inductive arguments move from the specific points to general ideas, whereas deductive arguments are considered to be the reverse; they begin with general ideas and move to specific points. Inductive arguments are usually based on experience and observation, and deductive arguments are based on widely accepted principles or known truths.

Here are examples of each.

> **Inductive reasoning:** A math student notices that every time she measures the interior angles of a triangle, the sum of the measures of the angles is either 180 degrees or very close to 180 degrees. She concludes that the measures of the interior angles of any triangle sum to 180 degrees.

> **Deductive reasoning:** The measures of the interior angles of any triangle sum to 180 degrees. This figure is a triangle. Therefore, the sum of the measures of its interior angles is 180 degrees.

Knowing the difference between these two types of reasoning—inductive and deductive—is essential to analyzing the validity of arguments. When you use inductive reasoning, your previous observations support the argument in question. When you use deductive reasoning, you apply known truths or generalizations to an issue to arrive at a logical conclusion, which, of course, is the focus of the argument in question.

Because inductive arguments are based on observations and examples, you can never be absolutely certain of the validity of their conclusions. You should, therefore, evaluate an inductive argument in terms of its reasonableness: Does the conclusion make sense, and is it supported by sound assertions?

Deductive arguments use known assertions or premises to logically arrive at their conclusions. You evaluate a deductive argument based on the reasonableness of its assertions and the soundness of the logic used. If the assertions are true and the logic is sound, the conclusion of the argument is valid.

Directions: For the following examples, ask yourself which is used: inductive or deductive reasoning. Then, more important, ask yourself "Does the argument make sense? Are the assertions reasonable? Do they support the conclusions?"

---

1. All high school marching bands play exceptionally well. Kendra plays exceptionally well. Kendra is in a high school marching band.

2. My friend, Angelo, will win his tennis match because he has won all the county and state tournaments in his division.

3. No sane person would jump off a cliff. Stephano is a sane person. Stephano will not jump off the cliff.

4. Michael is very wealthy. Since Michael is very wealthy, we know that he must be the child of someone famous, as you have to be the child of someone famous to be wealthy.

5. Most animals nurture their young. All dogs are animals. Most dogs nurture their young.

Answers

1. Deductive. The correct choice is *deductive reasoning* because the statement begins with a general statement and then proceeds to a specific point. Still, the argument makes no sense. Just because Kendra plays well does not mean she is in a high school marching band.

2. Inductive. The correct choice is *inductive reasoning* because the statement relies on specific details to arrive at a general statement. Still, the conclusion is debatable because even though Angelo is a championship player, there is no guarantee that he will win his next tennis match. Please note, though, that the inclusion of the word "probably" would change the meaning of the text and make the argument more acceptable.

3. Deductive. The correct choice is *deductive reasoning* because the statement begins with a general statement and then proceeds to a specific point. The argument makes sense because the assertions are reasonable and the logic is sound.

4. Deductive. The correct choice is *deductive reasoning* because the argument draws a conclusion about a specific case (Michael) from a general assertion (you have to be the child of someone famous to be wealthy). The argument, however, is faulty because the conclusion is drawn from a questionable assertion; obviously, a person can be or can become wealthy without being the child of someone famous.

5. Deductive. The correct choice is *deductive reasoning* because the statement begins with a general statement and then proceeds to a specific point. Even with the use of the qualifying word "most," the conclusion does not necessarily follow. Be careful of accepting an argument as valid just because you agree with the conclusion.

Following are examples of persuasive writing that try to convince the reader to adopt the author's point-of-view. See if you can discern how the writers are presenting their arguments and the validity of their work.

Example 1:

Today in the United States we face considerable unfinished business in public education, for the complexities of modern society have left their impact on current educational issues. Populations are increasing rapidly. The world is shrinking steadily as a result of the rapid progress made in transportation and communication. Many differing ethnic groups—some unable to speak English, some bilingual, or even multilingual—are appearing in our elementary school classrooms. Children are moving frequently, many of them changing schools five or six times in fewer than four years. They lack the security of firmly established roots. Space travel, rockets, jets, movies, radio, television, and the Internet vie for the interests of children, creating for them images of an exciting world, but also a confusing one. Broken homes and juvenile delinquency are not uncommon, and the child of today, the same as the adult of today, can scarcely be expected to remain unaware of the tensions and upheavals in the modern world. Already, they both sense that if the promise of the future is immense, so is the danger.

In this passage, the author lists example after example to prove the point that today's world is filled with inherent contradictions—great pleasures and great pains—that can make life both pleasurable and confusing for young people. The author is using **inductive reasoning** to make the argument.

Example 2:

For the colonists who arrived in New England, a singleness of religious purpose was a determining influence in the development of their early educational programs. They believed in a close unity between the church and state. To them it was the responsibility of the government to "govern," to support their Calvinistic theology, and to foster the intellectual growth of their children. This was made clear as early as 1642 when the governmental leaders in Massachusetts were empowered to require parents to educate their children. Although this law did not require the establishment of schools, it did require compulsory instruction for youth. It even set up minimum essentials: the reading of English, knowledge of capital laws, the catechism, and apprenticeship in a trade. Thus, the early educational developments in New England clearly reflected the values and beliefs of its early colonists and were instrumental in the design and creation of today's public school system.

In this passage, the author cites known assertions to arrive at a logical conclusion. The author is using **deductive reasoning** to make the argument.

Both deductive and inductive reasoning are central to understanding persuasive writing and essential to analyzing the validity of arguments as they appear in reading passages.

Draw Logical Inferences and Conclusions

An essential skill for understanding a reading passage is the ability to draw logical inferences and conclusions.

Techniques to help the reader draw inferences and conclusions regarding a reading passage are

- Focus on the passage's purpose—Is it well-stated? Clearly implied? Justifiable?
- Focus on the passage's key questions—Are they answered? Are the answers objectively stated?

- Focus on the passage's evidence—Is it relevant? Unbiased? Informative?
- Focus on the passage's concepts—Are they clear? Relevant? Justifiable?
- Focus on the passage's assumptions—Are they valid? Reasonable?
- Focus on the passage's conclusions—Are they sound? Logical? Justifiable?
- Focus on the passage's point-of-view—Is it direct? Indirect? Does it consider alternatives?
- Focus on the passage's implications—Do you understand the consequences?

Look at the following example for drawing logical inferences and conclusions in a reading passage.

The leaders of the progressive education movement emphasize the importance of individualized education, the need for a child-centered school, the necessity for a direct relation of learning experiences to the interests and current needs of each child, and the relationship of the child to the cultural and social environment. Commentaries of leading educational thinkers—from the early twentieth-century works of John Dewey to the contemporary writings of Nel Noddings—demonstrate passionate advocacy for educational reform that involves understanding the developmental needs of the whole child. Unfortunately, in recent years, the progressive movement has become popularly identified with the concept that teaching and learning require a "laissez-faire" approach and should be dependent on the interests and desires of solely the students.

1. In analyzing this passage, the reader is most likely to draw the conclusion that the progressive education movement

   A. has been highly successful.
   B. has been marginalized.
   C. is a recent phenomena.
   D. is universally accepted.

The correct answer is **B**. Although the thought is not finished, the reader can infer from the concluding sentence that the progressive education movement has come under attack by those who advocate a more standardized approach to public education. One can infer that the paragraphs to follow will elaborate on why the progressive education movement has been marginalized. Choice **A** is incorrect because the passage does not state or infer that the progressive education movement has been highly successful; it has simply been advocated by leading educational thinkers. Choice **C** is incorrect because the passage indicates that John Dewey, a leading educational thinker of the early twentieth century, advocated for progressive education. Choice **D** is incorrect because, as the last sentence of the passage implies, progressive education has its detractors.

Test Yourself

Directions: Read the following passage and answer questions 1–6.

(1)   Predicting weather patterns is a difficult job, at best. Meteorology is a demanding science; and it requires patience, fortitude, and know-how to make careful and accurate forecasts. Most of the time, weather forecasters can be trusted, and their predictions allow others to plan their lives accordingly. Modern forecasting involves technology, science, and advanced math to accurately predict the weather. Relying on time-tested instruments and mathematical models, meteorologists are able to predict weather patterns reasonably, rapidly, and accurately.

(2)   The first step in weather forecasting is to get information about the weather. Weather data is collected from the atmosphere by launching balloons twice a day all around the world. These weather balloons gather basic information about the climate conditions around the globe; they record data such as temperature, pressure, humidity, and wind speed. Another successful tool for weather forecasters is satellite technology. Satellites permit meteorologists to see what the earth and its clouds appear like from space. With such knowledge, scientists can see how the Earth's atmosphere is behaving. Finally, using sophisticated computers, weather forecasters are able to discern what ordinary people might logically miss. They can predict oncoming storms, ominous weather patterns, and unpredictable hurricanes. They know enough—both intuitively and mathematically—to <u>discern</u> when there is a movement afoot that might predict danger ahead. Thus, their scientific knowledge has implications far beyond simply predicting the weather.

(3)   Meteorologists are also <u>instrumental</u> in assisting local and state communities to prepare for future weather patterns. In fact, the biggest employer of meteorologists is government agencies. They help these agencies predict weather patterns, climatic changes, and environmental problems. Furthermore, sure knowledge of impending storms—in the near future or years to come—helps responsible government agencies and organizations prepare their citizens for possible dangerous and threatening conditions. Such notification is imperative as emergency and contingency procedures must often be set in place long before a real danger might eventually occur.

(4)   Finally, meteorologists help people live their lives. So much of our daily existence depends upon what we do in the outside world. Our work and play is contingent upon our knowledge of what our day "weather-wise" will be like. That situation is one reason that clear, easy-to-understand, and accurate weather forecasts are so much appreciated by the general public. Accuracy and promptness are the hallmarks of good meteorologists; and, fortunately, many meteorologists now have sophisticated tools to make predicting the weather easier. Using satellite data, climate theory, and computer models of the world's atmosphere, meteorologists can more effectively interpret the results of these models to make national, regional, and local area forecasts. Their good work informs not only the general public, but also those public, private, and governmental agencies that need accurate weather information for both economic and safety reasons. Indeed, our entire world economy is dependent upon such accuracy.

1. Which sentence best states the main idea of this passage?

   A.   Weather forecasting is a fairly routine and mundane task.

   B.   Weather forecasting is limited in scope and design.

   C.   Weather forecasting has far-reaching significance.

   D.   Weather forecasting is primitive in design and content.

2. According to the passage, what is one way that weather forecasting has importance beyond predicting the daily weather?

   A.   It informs community leaders about weather conditions.

   B.   It entertains people watching television news.

   C.   It increases understanding of foreign countries.

   D.   It demonstrates the limitations of meteorology.

3. As used in the third paragraph, the word *instrumental* most nearly means

   A. limited.
   B. helpful.
   C. cautious.
   D. skeptical.

4. The tone of this passage can best be described as

   A. anxious.
   B. skeptical.
   C. curious.
   D. informative.

5. Identify the relationship between the following two sentences in the fourth paragraph:

   Our work and play is contingent upon our knowledge of what our day "weather-wise" will be like. That situation is one reason that clear, easy-to-understand, and accurate weather forecasts are so much appreciated by the general public.

   The second sentence

   A. contradicts the first.
   B. restates the first.
   C. supports the first.
   D. distracts from the first.

6. Which word, when substituted for *discern* in the second paragraph, would maintain the same relationship between the two thoughts in the sentence?

   A. perceive
   B. deceive
   C. illustrate
   D. inform

Answer Explanations for Test Yourself

1. **C.** The sentence that best states the main idea of this passage is *weather forecasting has far-reaching significance.*

2. **A.** One way that weather forecasting has importance beyond informing people of the day's atmospheric conditions is to *inform community leaders about weather conditions.*

3. **B.** As used in the third paragraph, the word *instrumental* most nearly means *helpful.*

4. **D.** The tone of this passage can best be described as *informative.*

5. **C.** The relationship between the two sentences from the fourth paragraph is that the second sentence *supports the first.*

6. **A.** The word that best substitutes for the word *discern* in the second paragraph and maintains the same relationship between the two thoughts in the sentence is *perceive.*

TWO FULL-LENGTH PRACTICE TESTS

Chapter 5

General Knowledge Practice Test 1

Answer Sheet

(Remove This Sheet and Use It To Mark Your Answers)

Diagnostic General Knowledge Test: Essay

Write your essay on lined paper.

General Knowledge Test: English Language Skills

1 Ⓐ Ⓑ Ⓒ Ⓓ	11 Ⓐ Ⓑ Ⓒ Ⓓ	21 Ⓐ Ⓑ Ⓒ Ⓓ	31 Ⓐ Ⓑ Ⓒ Ⓓ
2 Ⓐ Ⓑ Ⓒ Ⓓ	12 Ⓐ Ⓑ Ⓒ Ⓓ	22 Ⓐ Ⓑ Ⓒ Ⓓ	32 Ⓐ Ⓑ Ⓒ Ⓓ
3 Ⓐ Ⓑ Ⓒ Ⓓ	13 Ⓐ Ⓑ Ⓒ Ⓓ	23 Ⓐ Ⓑ Ⓒ Ⓓ	33 Ⓐ Ⓑ Ⓒ Ⓓ
4 Ⓐ Ⓑ Ⓒ Ⓓ	14 Ⓐ Ⓑ Ⓒ Ⓓ	24 Ⓐ Ⓑ Ⓒ Ⓓ	34 Ⓐ Ⓑ Ⓒ Ⓓ
5 Ⓐ Ⓑ Ⓒ Ⓓ	15 Ⓐ Ⓑ Ⓒ Ⓓ	25 Ⓐ Ⓑ Ⓒ Ⓓ	35 Ⓐ Ⓑ Ⓒ Ⓓ
6 Ⓐ Ⓑ Ⓒ Ⓓ	16 Ⓐ Ⓑ Ⓒ Ⓓ	26 Ⓐ Ⓑ Ⓒ Ⓓ	36 Ⓐ Ⓑ Ⓒ Ⓓ
7 Ⓐ Ⓑ Ⓒ Ⓓ	17 Ⓐ Ⓑ Ⓒ Ⓓ	27 Ⓐ Ⓑ Ⓒ Ⓓ	37 Ⓐ Ⓑ Ⓒ Ⓓ
8 Ⓐ Ⓑ Ⓒ Ⓓ	18 Ⓐ Ⓑ Ⓒ Ⓓ	28 Ⓐ Ⓑ Ⓒ Ⓓ	38 Ⓐ Ⓑ Ⓒ Ⓓ
9 Ⓐ Ⓑ Ⓒ Ⓓ	19 Ⓐ Ⓑ Ⓒ Ⓓ	29 Ⓐ Ⓑ Ⓒ Ⓓ	39 Ⓐ Ⓑ Ⓒ Ⓓ
10 Ⓐ Ⓑ Ⓒ Ⓓ	20 Ⓐ Ⓑ Ⓒ Ⓓ	30 Ⓐ Ⓑ Ⓒ Ⓓ	40 Ⓐ Ⓑ Ⓒ Ⓓ

General Knowledge Test: Mathematics

1 Ⓐ Ⓑ Ⓒ Ⓓ	11 Ⓐ Ⓑ Ⓒ Ⓓ	21 Ⓐ Ⓑ Ⓒ Ⓓ	31 Ⓐ Ⓑ Ⓒ Ⓓ	41 Ⓐ Ⓑ Ⓒ Ⓓ
2 Ⓐ Ⓑ Ⓒ Ⓓ	12 Ⓐ Ⓑ Ⓒ Ⓓ	22 Ⓐ Ⓑ Ⓒ Ⓓ	32 Ⓐ Ⓑ Ⓒ Ⓓ	42 Ⓐ Ⓑ Ⓒ Ⓓ
3 Ⓐ Ⓑ Ⓒ Ⓓ	13 Ⓐ Ⓑ Ⓒ Ⓓ	23 Ⓐ Ⓑ Ⓒ Ⓓ	33 Ⓐ Ⓑ Ⓒ Ⓓ	43 Ⓐ Ⓑ Ⓒ Ⓓ
4 Ⓐ Ⓑ Ⓒ Ⓓ	14 Ⓐ Ⓑ Ⓒ Ⓓ	24 Ⓐ Ⓑ Ⓒ Ⓓ	34 Ⓐ Ⓑ Ⓒ Ⓓ	44 Ⓐ Ⓑ Ⓒ Ⓓ
5 Ⓐ Ⓑ Ⓒ Ⓓ	15 Ⓐ Ⓑ Ⓒ Ⓓ	25 Ⓐ Ⓑ Ⓒ Ⓓ	35 Ⓐ Ⓑ Ⓒ Ⓓ	45 Ⓐ Ⓑ Ⓒ Ⓓ
6 Ⓐ Ⓑ Ⓒ Ⓓ	16 Ⓐ Ⓑ Ⓒ Ⓓ	26 Ⓐ Ⓑ Ⓒ Ⓓ	36 Ⓐ Ⓑ Ⓒ Ⓓ	
7 Ⓐ Ⓑ Ⓒ Ⓓ	17 Ⓐ Ⓑ Ⓒ Ⓓ	27 Ⓐ Ⓑ Ⓒ Ⓓ	37 Ⓐ Ⓑ Ⓒ Ⓓ	
8 Ⓐ Ⓑ Ⓒ Ⓓ	18 Ⓐ Ⓑ Ⓒ Ⓓ	28 Ⓐ Ⓑ Ⓒ Ⓓ	38 Ⓐ Ⓑ Ⓒ Ⓓ	
9 Ⓐ Ⓑ Ⓒ Ⓓ	19 Ⓐ Ⓑ Ⓒ Ⓓ	29 Ⓐ Ⓑ Ⓒ Ⓓ	39 Ⓐ Ⓑ Ⓒ Ⓓ	
10 Ⓐ Ⓑ Ⓒ Ⓓ	20 Ⓐ Ⓑ Ⓒ Ⓓ	30 Ⓐ Ⓑ Ⓒ Ⓓ	40 Ⓐ Ⓑ Ⓒ Ⓓ	

General Knowledge Test: Reading

1 Ⓐ Ⓑ Ⓒ Ⓓ	11 Ⓐ Ⓑ Ⓒ Ⓓ	21 Ⓐ Ⓑ Ⓒ Ⓓ	31 Ⓐ Ⓑ Ⓒ Ⓓ
2 Ⓐ Ⓑ Ⓒ Ⓓ	12 Ⓐ Ⓑ Ⓒ Ⓓ	22 Ⓐ Ⓑ Ⓒ Ⓓ	32 Ⓐ Ⓑ Ⓒ Ⓓ
3 Ⓐ Ⓑ Ⓒ Ⓓ	13 Ⓐ Ⓑ Ⓒ Ⓓ	23 Ⓐ Ⓑ Ⓒ Ⓓ	33 Ⓐ Ⓑ Ⓒ Ⓓ
4 Ⓐ Ⓑ Ⓒ Ⓓ	14 Ⓐ Ⓑ Ⓒ Ⓓ	24 Ⓐ Ⓑ Ⓒ Ⓓ	34 Ⓐ Ⓑ Ⓒ Ⓓ
5 Ⓐ Ⓑ Ⓒ Ⓓ	15 Ⓐ Ⓑ Ⓒ Ⓓ	25 Ⓐ Ⓑ Ⓒ Ⓓ	35 Ⓐ Ⓑ Ⓒ Ⓓ
6 Ⓐ Ⓑ Ⓒ Ⓓ	16 Ⓐ Ⓑ Ⓒ Ⓓ	26 Ⓐ Ⓑ Ⓒ Ⓓ	36 Ⓐ Ⓑ Ⓒ Ⓓ
7 Ⓐ Ⓑ Ⓒ Ⓓ	17 Ⓐ Ⓑ Ⓒ Ⓓ	27 Ⓐ Ⓑ Ⓒ Ⓓ	37 Ⓐ Ⓑ Ⓒ Ⓓ
8 Ⓐ Ⓑ Ⓒ Ⓓ	18 Ⓐ Ⓑ Ⓒ Ⓓ	28 Ⓐ Ⓑ Ⓒ Ⓓ	38 Ⓐ Ⓑ Ⓒ Ⓓ
9 Ⓐ Ⓑ Ⓒ Ⓓ	19 Ⓐ Ⓑ Ⓒ Ⓓ	29 Ⓐ Ⓑ Ⓒ Ⓓ	39 Ⓐ Ⓑ Ⓒ Ⓓ
10 Ⓐ Ⓑ Ⓒ Ⓓ	20 Ⓐ Ⓑ Ⓒ Ⓓ	30 Ⓐ Ⓑ Ⓒ Ⓓ	40 Ⓐ Ⓑ Ⓒ Ⓓ

CUT HERE

CUT HERE

General Knowledge Practice Test 1: Essay

Time: 50 minutes

Directions: This section of the examination involves a written assignment. You are to prepare a written response for *one of the two topics* presented below. Select one of these two topics and prepare a 300- to 600-word response. Be sure to read both topics very carefully to make sure that you understand the topic for which you are preparing a written response. Use your allotted time to plan, write, review, and edit what you have written for the assignment.

Topic 1

Why I want to become a teacher

Topic 2

A person whom I admire

Be sure to read the two topics again before attempting to write your response. Your answer must be on only one of the topics presented, and it must address the topic completely.

Your essay is graded holistically, meaning only one score is assigned for your writing—taking into consideration both mechanics and organization. *You are not scored on the nature of the content or opinions expressed in your work.* Instead, you are graded on your ability to write complete sentences, to express and support your opinions, and to organize your work.

At least two evaluators review your work and assign it a score. Special attention is paid to the following specific indicators of quality writing:

- Does your writing demonstrate a strong definitive purpose?
- Is there a clear thesis or statement of a main idea?
- Are your ideas organized?
- Do you support your thesis with clear details?
- Are effective transitions present?
- Do you demonstrate an effective use of language?
- Do you avoid inappropriate use of slang, jargon, and clichés?
- Are a variety of sentence patterns present?
- Is there a consistent point-of-view?
- Are the conventions of Standard American English used?

Before you begin, be sure you plan what you want to say. Organize your thoughts and carefully construct your ideas. This should be your original work, written in your own voice.

As you write your piece, you may revise or add information as necessary.

General Knowledge Practice Test 1: English Language Skills

Time: 40 minutes
40 questions

Directions: For questions 1–4, read the entire passage carefully and then answer the questions. Please note that intentional errors have been included in the passages. The passages are designed to measure both identification of logical order in a written passage and the presence of irrelevant sentences.

(1) Horses are one of the most useful animals in the world. (2) For centuries, they provided the fastest and most convenient way to travel on land. (3) Horses were used by early settlers in America as they traveled the east coast, looking for land to call their home, later by pioneers as they traversed the rugged plains and mountains of America's West in stagecoaches and covered wagons, and, of course, by the Pony Express. (4) Horses were used by hunters for securing food and by soldiers in battle. (5) Today, horses are used mostly for recreation. (6) Moreover, the automobile has become America's number one transportation problem. (7) Riding horses is one of America's favorite pastimes. (8) And, certainly, horse racing remains a popular spectator sport. (9) Today, horses are seen performing in circuses, parades, rodeos, and, naturally, horse shows. (10) It is in horse shows, though, that the true worth of horses is determined as wealthy individuals purchase horses for both personal enjoyment and financial gain.

1. Select the arrangement of sentences 3, 4, and 5 that provides the most logical sequence of ideas and supporting details in the paragraph. If no change is needed, select Choice A.

   A. Horses were used by early settlers in America as they traveled the east coast, looking for land to call their home, later by pioneers as they traversed the rugged plains and mountains of America's West in stagecoaches and covered wagons, and, of course, by the Pony Express. Horses were used by hunters for securing food and by soldiers in battle. Today, horses are used mostly for recreation.

   B. Horses were used by hunters for securing food and by soldiers in battle. Horses were used by early settlers in America as they traveled the east coast, looking for land to call their home, later by pioneers as they traversed the rugged plains and mountains of America's West in stagecoaches and covered wagons, and, of course, by the Pony Express. Today, horses are used mostly for recreation.

   C. Today, horses are used mostly for recreation. Horses were used by hunters for securing food and by soldiers in battle. Horses were used by early settlers in America as they traveled the east coast, looking for land to call their home, later by pioneers as they traversed the rugged plains and mountains of America's West in stagecoaches and covered wagons, and, of course, by the Pony Express.

   D. Today, horses are used mostly for recreation. Horses were used by early settlers in America as they traveled the east coast, looking for land to call their home, later by pioneers as they traversed the rugged plains and mountains of America's West in stagecoaches and covered wagons, and, of course, by the Pony Express. Horses were used by hunters for securing food and by soldiers in battle.

2. Which numbered sentence is LEAST relevant to the passage?

- **A.** Sentence 3
- **B.** Sentence 4
- **C.** Sentence 5
- **D.** Sentence 6

The passage reads as follows:

(1) Diamonds are the hardest naturally occurring substance. (2) Diamonds are also one of the world's most valuable natural substances. (3) Since diamonds are the hardest natural material, they are the most lasting of all gemstones. (4) Throughout the world, especially in Europe, America, and Japan, diamonds are widely used for engagement and wedding rings. (5) Some people prefer simple wedding bands without precious stones. (6) Diamonds are also widely used for industrial purposes, such as for cutting, grinding, and boring other materials. (7) About half the world's diamonds are used for such purposes, while an even smaller percentage is used for jewelry. (8) When diamonds are cut by hand, the diamond cutter uses another diamond to do the cutting. (9) Furthermore, diamonds cannot be destroyed in acid, although they can be damaged by intense heat. (10) Diamonds are precious stones, and only those with an expert knowledge of diamonds can truly judge the worth of individual stones.

3. Select the arrangement of sentences 2, 3, and 4 that provides the most logical sequence of ideas and supporting details in the paragraph. If no change is needed, select Choice D.

- **A.** Since diamonds are the hardest natural material, they are the most lasting of all gemstones. Throughout the world, especially in Europe, America, and Japan, diamonds are widely used for engagement and wedding rings. Diamonds are also one of the world's most valuable natural substances.
- **B.** Throughout the world, especially in Europe, America, and Japan, diamonds are widely used for engagement and wedding rings. Since diamonds are the hardest natural material, they are the most lasting of all gemstones. Diamonds are also one of the world's most valuable natural substances.
- **C.** Throughout the world, especially in Europe, America, and Japan, diamonds are widely used for engagement and wedding rings. Diamonds are also one of the world's most valuable natural substances. Since diamonds are the hardest natural material, they are the most lasting of all gemstones.
- **D.** Diamonds are also one of the world's most valuable natural substances. Since diamonds are the hardest natural material, they are the most lasting of all gemstones. Throughout the world, especially in Europe, America, and Japan, diamonds are widely used for engagement and wedding rings.

4. Which numbered sentence is LEAST relevant to the passage?

- **A.** Sentence 3
- **B.** Sentence 4
- **C.** Sentence 5
- **D.** Sentence 6

For questions 5–37, select the answer choice that corrects an error in the underlined portion. If there is no error, choose Choice D, indicating "No change is necessary."

5. The passenger <u>who's</u> purse I found in the
   A
   taxicab <u>came</u> to the headquarters to <u>retrieve</u>
   B   C
   his belongings.

   A. whose
   B. is coming
   C. retreive
   D. No change is necessary.

6. All of the campers <u>at</u> the <u>summer</u> camp, <u>accept</u>
   A   B   C
   Jamie, will be required to take the swimming

   test.

   A. in
   B. Summer
   C. except
   D. No change is necessary.

7. I <u>respectively</u> submitted my <u>formal</u> letter of
   A   B
   resignation to the school's <u>principal</u>.
   C

   A. respectfully
   B. former
   C. principle
   D. No change is necessary.

8. The <u>fourth</u> box of supplies for the party was
   A
   <u>further</u> from my house <u>than</u> I thought.
   B   C

   A. forth
   B. farther
   C. then
   D. No change is necessary.

9. When my <u>aunt</u> came to visit, I <u>could of</u> baked
   A   B
   cookies for <u>dessert</u>.
   C

   A. Aunt
   B. could have
   C. desert
   D. No change is necessary.

10. Juan and Mary went to Tallahassee, the state

    <u>capitol,</u> to <u>receive</u> an award for <u>their</u>
    A   B   C
    outstanding contributions to the local charity.

    A. capital
    B. recieve
    C. they're
    D. No change is necessary.

11. Despite the inclement <u>whether,</u> the musicians
    A
    performed <u>admirably</u> for the <u>congregants</u>.
    B   C

    A. weather
    B. admirable
    C. congregents
    D. No change is necessary.

12. After the team was declared <u>ineligible,</u>
    A
    <u>everyone</u> <u>preceded</u> to walk off the field.
    B   C

    A. ineligable
    B. every one
    C. proceeded
    D. No change is necessary.

13. We had <u>certainly</u> won more <u>board</u> games <u>then</u>
    A   B   C
    other players in the class.

    A. for certain
    B. bored
    C. than
    D. No change is necessary.

14. My son's <u>exceptional</u> mechanical abilities
    A
    <u>compliment</u> his wife's <u>considerable</u> analytical
    B   C
    skills.

    A. acceptional
    B. complement
    C. considerate
    D. No change is necessary.

15. Between you and me, I don't know whether
    $\quad\quad\quad\quad$A$\quad\quad\quad\quad\quad\quad\quad\quad$B
    you should be first or I.
    $\quad\quad\quad\quad\quad\quad\quad$C

    A. I
    B. as to whether
    C. me
    D. No change is necessary.

16. My brothers and sisters may leave after they
    $\quad\quad\quad\quad\quad\quad\quad\quad\quad\quad$A
    find a sight to eat beside the river.
    $\quad\quad$B$\quad\quad\quad\quad$C

    A. can
    B. site
    C. besides
    D. No change is necessary.

17. The archeologists come up with a list that
    $\quad\quad\quad\quad\quad\quad\quad$A$\quad\quad\quad\quad\quad\quad$B
    included tombs, mummies, pyramids, and
    $\quad\quad\quad\quad\quad\quad\quad\quad\quad\quad\quad\quad$C
    other Egyptian artifacts.

    A. came
    B. which
    C. pyramids and
    D. No change is necessary.

18. The restaurants location by the beach made it
    $\quad\quad$A$\quad\quad\quad\quad\quad\quad\quad\quad$B
    a really romantic place for special dates.
    $\quad\quad$C

    A. restaurant's
    B. beech
    C. real
    D. No change is necessary.

19. When the tourists visited the lighthouse they
    $\quad\quad\quad\quad$A$\quad\quad\quad\quad\quad\quad$B
    were amazed that it looked more like a

    skyscraper than a lighthouse.
    $\quad\quad\quad\quad\quad$C

    A. tourists'
    B. lighthouse, they
    C. then
    D. No change is necessary.

20. The teacher felt badly about giving a failing
    $\quad\quad\quad\quad\quad\quad$A
    grade on the English paper to the daughter of
    $\quad\quad\quad\quad\quad\quad$B
    the school superintendent.
    $\quad\quad\quad\quad$C

    A. bad
    B. english
    C. Superintendent
    D. No change is necessary.

21. In 1492 Columbus, the explorer, landed on the
    $\quad\quad\quad\quad\quad$A$\quad\quad\quad$B
    islands of the west Indies.
    $\quad\quad\quad\quad\quad$C

    A. Columbus the
    B. Explorer
    C. West
    D. No change is necessary.

22. When they got inside the cabin, the hunters
    $\quad$A$\quad\quad\quad\quad\quad\quad\quad$B
    builded a huge fire in the fireplace.
    $\quad$C

    A. Whenever
    B. cabin the
    C. built
    D. No change is necessary.

23. I am convinced the reason there is animosity
    $\quad$A
    between you and I is that we are so much alike.
    $\quad\quad\quad$B$\quad\quad\quad$C

    A. was
    B. you and me
    C. because
    D. No change is necessary.

24. My daughter, who is a track star, can run
    $\quad\quad\quad\quad\quad$A
    much faster than them other athletes.
    $\quad\quad$B$\quad\quad\quad\quad$C

    A. whom
    B. more faster
    C. those other athletes
    D. No change is necessary.

25. It <u>don't</u> matter how smart you <u>are because</u> <u>you</u>
       A   B   C

    still have to work hard to be a success in life.

    A. doesn't
    B. are, because
    C. one
    D. No change is necessary.

26. My <u>siblings</u> say they dislike <u>mathmatics,</u> but I
          A   B

    always have enjoyed <u>it myself.</u>
                         C

    A. siblings'
    B. mathematics
    C. it
    D. No change is necessary.

27. During the recent election, <u>there</u> <u>was</u> much
                              A   B

    discussion about whether the media <u>is</u> biased.
                                 C

    A. their
    B. had been
    C. are
    D. No change is necessary.

28. Because the bus trip was going to take several

    hours, the students <u>should have ate</u> before

    they left.

    A. should of ate
    B. should have eaten
    C. should of eaten
    D. No change is necessary.

29. As the day <u>ends</u>, the planet Venus appeared in

    the sky.

    A. had ended
    B. has been ending
    C. ended
    D. No change is necessary.

30. Everyone in my family <u>have enjoyed</u> watching
                            A

    our five new <u>goldfish</u> scurry around the <u>castle</u>
                B   C

    in the fish tank.

    A. has enjoyed
    B. goldfishes
    C. castel
    D. No change is necessary.

31. Each of the boys thanked <u>their</u> parents for the
                              A

    support <u>provided prior</u> to the match <u>between</u>
              B   .C

    the two teams.

    A. his
    B. provided, prior
    C. among
    D. No change is necessary.

32. My students collected <u>books that</u> were still in
                           A

    good condition from various <u>organizations</u>
                                  B

    around town, so I gave <u>them</u> to our local
                           C

    library.

    A. books, that
    B. organizations'
    C. the books
    D. No change is necessary.

33. Cory's favorite subject in <u>middle</u> school was
                            A

    English because he enjoyed studying <u>grammar</u>,
                                   B

    reading books, and <u>to write</u> papers.
                        C

    A. Middle
    B. grammer
    C. writing
    D. No change is necessary.

34. Barbara has become <u>quite</u> annoyed with <u>his</u>
                          A   B

    meddling in her <u>personal</u> business.
                      C

    A. quiet
    B. him
    C. personnel
    D. No change is necessary.

35. One of the forestry <u>professors</u> at the local
    A
    university <u>was</u> investigating the <u>affect</u> of a new
    B   C
    fertilizer on the growth of pine seedlings.

    A. professors'
    B. were
    C. effect
    D. No change is necessary.

36. Michael <u>measured</u> the length, width, and
    A
    <u>heighth</u> of the <u>box to</u> make sure it would fit in
    B   C
    the trunk of his car.

    A. measures
    B. height
    C. box, to
    D. No change is necessary.

37. <u>Bess's</u> <u>friends</u> tell her that she has the
    A   B
    <u>most unusual</u> hairstyle.
        C

    A. Bess'
    B. freinds
    C. unusualest
    D. No change is necessary.

38. **Directions:** Choose the option that is punctuated correctly.

    A. Within a year my new puppy should weigh about 18 pounds, I'm making sure that I feed him a nutritious diet.
    B. Within a year, my new puppy should weigh about 18 pounds I'm making sure that I feed him a nutritious diet.
    C. Within a year my new puppy should weigh about 18 pounds. I'm making sure that I feed him a nutritious diet.
    D. Within a year my new puppy should weigh about 18 pounds I'm making sure that I feed him a nutritious diet.

39. **Directions:** Choose the option that is punctuated correctly.

    A. Preferring to be hand-fed canned tuna, our family's new Siamese cat refuses to eat dry cat food.
    B. Preferring to be hand-fed canned tuna, our familys' new Siamese cat refuses to eat dry cat food.
    C. Preferring to be hand-fed canned tuna. Our family's new Siamese cat refuses to eat dry cat food.
    D. Preferring to be hand-fed canned tuna our family's new Siamese cat refuses to eat dry cat food.

40. **Directions:** Choose the sentence in which the modifiers are placed correctly.

    A. Rushing to finish the surprise dinner on time, Melissa borrowed an egg from a neighbor that was rotten.
    B. Melissa borrowed an egg from a neighbor that was rotten, rushing to finish the surprise dinner on time.
    C. Rushing to finish the surprise dinner on time, Melissa borrowed an egg that was rotten from a neighbor.
    D. Melissa borrowed an egg that was rotten from a neighbor, rushing to finish the surprise dinner on time.

IF YOU FINISH BEFORE TIME IS CALLED, CHECK YOUR WORK ON THIS SECTION ONLY. DO NOT WORK ON ANY OTHER SECTION IN THE TEST.

STOP

General Knowledge Practice Test 2: Mathematics

Time: **100 minutes**
45 questions

Mathematics Reference Sheet

Area

Triangle

$A = \frac{1}{2}bh$

Rectangle

$A = lw$

Key	
b = base	d = diameter
h = height	r = radius
l = length	A = area
w = width	C = circumference
S.A. = surface area	V = volume
	B = area of base
Use $\pi = 3.14$ or $\frac{22}{7}$	

Trapezoid

$A = \frac{1}{2}h(b_1 + b_2)$

Parallelogram

$A = bh$

Circle

$A = \pi r^2 \quad C = \pi d = 2\pi r$

Surface Area

1. Surface area of a prism or pyramid = the sum of the areas of all faces of the figure.
2. Surface area of a cylinder = the sum of the areas of the two bases + the area of its rectangular wrap.

$S.A. = 2(\pi r^2) + (2\pi r)h$

3. Surface area of a sphere: $S.A. = 4\pi r^2$

Volume

1. Volume of a prism or cylinder equals (Area of the Base) times (height): $V = Bh$
2. Volume of a pyramid or cone equals $\frac{1}{3}$ times (Area of the Base) times (height): $V = \frac{1}{3}Bh$
3. Volume of a sphere: $V = \frac{4}{3}\pi r^3$

CUT HERE

Mathematics Reference Sheet, continued

Pythagorean Theorem: $a^2 + b^2 = c^2$

Simple Interest Formula: $I = prt$

I = simple interest, p = principal, r = rate, t = time

Distance Formula: $d = rt$

d = distance, r = rate, t = time

Given a line containing points (x_1, y_1) and (x_2, y_2),

- Slope of line $= \dfrac{y_2 - y_1}{x_2 - x_1}$
- Distance between two points $= \sqrt{(x_2 - x_1)^2 + (y_2 - y_1)^2}$
- Midpoint between two points $= \left(\dfrac{x_1 + x_2}{2}, \dfrac{y_1 + y_2}{2} \right)$

Conversions	
1 yard = 3 feet = 36 inches	1 cup = 8 fluid ounces
1 mile = 1,760 yards = 5,280 feet	1 pint = 2 cups
1 acre = 43,560 square feet	1 quart = 2 pints
1 hour = 60 minutes	1 gallon = 4 quarts
1 minute = 60 seconds	1 pound = 16 ounces
	1 ton = 2,000 pounds
1 liter = 1000 milliliters = 1000 cubic centimeters	
1 meter = 100 centimeters = 1000 millimeters	
1 kilometer = 1000 meters	
1 gram = 1000 milligrams	
1 kilogram = 1000 grams	

Note: Metric numbers with four digits are written without a comma (e.g., 2543 grams).

For metric numbers with more than four digits, a space is used instead of a comma (e.g., 24 300 liters).

CUT HERE

Directions: Read each question and select the best answer choice.

1. At an art exhibit at a local gallery, 5 of the 20 paintings displayed were purchased by a well-known art connoisseur. Which of the following numbers does <u>not</u> represent the part of the total number of paintings that were purchased by the art connoisseur?

   A. $\frac{1}{4}\%$

   B. 0.25

   C. $\frac{5}{20}$

   D. $\frac{25}{100}$

2. How many $\frac{3}{8}$ pound hamburger patties can be made from $4\frac{1}{2}$ pounds of ground beef?

   A. $1\frac{11}{16}$

   B. 12

   C. 8

   D. 6

3. Simplify: $6 + 2^3 \cdot 3 \div 3 + 7$

   A. 3

   B. 8.4

   C. 17

   D. 21

4. Three grandsons and two granddaughters inherit land from a grandparent's estate. The older granddaughter inherits $\frac{1}{3}$ of the land. The four other grandchildren equally share the remaining land. What fraction of the land does the younger granddaughter inherit?

   A. $\frac{1}{6}$

   B. $\frac{1}{4}$

   C. $\frac{1}{2}$

   D. $\frac{2}{3}$

5. The low temperature recorded one morning was –6°F. The high temperature recorded that afternoon was 35°F. How many degrees did the temperature change from the morning low to the afternoon high?

   A. 29°F

   B. 41°F

   C. –41°F

   D. –29°F

6. The distance from Venus to the Sun is approximately 108,200,000 kilometers. Which of the following numbers shows the approximate distance from Venus to the Sun in scientific notation?

   A. 108.2×10^6

   B. 1.082×10^8

   C. 108.2×10^{-6}

   D. 1.082×10^{-8}

7. In right triangle ABC, what is the approximate length of side $\overline{AB}$, the hypotenuse of the right triangle?

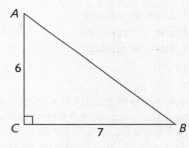

   A. Between 6 and 7

   B. Between 8 and 9

   C. Between 9 and 10

   D. Between 81 and 100

8. A cell phone company charges $29.99 per month for the first 500 minutes of calls and $0.30 a minute for any calls over the 500-minute limit. Last month Demetria made 615 minutes of calls on her cell phone. Excluding tax, what were the total charges for her cell phone calls last month?

   A. $29.99
   B. $34.50
   C. $64.49
   D. $184.50

9. A high school basketball player is 75 inches tall. The basketball hoop is 10 feet above the court. Find the distance in feet between the top of the player's head and the basketball hoop.

   A. 2.5 ft
   B. 3.25 ft
   C. 3.75 ft
   D. 6.25 ft

10. Selma kept track of the exact times she spent playing video games last weekend. On Saturday, she played video games for 1 hour and 44 minutes, and on Sunday she played video games for 2 hours and 32 minutes. What is the total amount of time Selma spent playing video games last weekend?

   A. 3 hours 16 minutes
   B. 4 hours 16 minutes
   C. 4 hours 56 minutes
   D. 4 hours

11. A couple wants to replace their rectangular table that measures 3 feet by 4.5 feet with a circular table that has a diameter of 4 feet. About how much less will the area of the circular table be than the area of the rectangular table? Use $\pi = 3.14$.

   A. 0.94 ft^2
   B. 12.56 ft^2
   C. 26.06 ft^2
   D. 36.74 ft^2

12. A rectangular garden has a perimeter of 50 feet. The width of the garden is 7 feet. What is the area of the garden?

   A. 18 ft^2
   B. 126 ft^2
   C. 50 ft^2
   D. 350 ft^2

13. How many square yards of carpet are needed to cover a rectangular floor that measures 22 feet by 18 feet?

   A. 9 yd^2
   B. 44 yd^2
   C. 396 yd^2
   D. 3,564 yd^2

14. If a crate is packed to capacity with 81 cubes measuring 4 inches on each edge, what is the volume of the crate in cubic inches?

   A. 64 in^3
   B. 81 in^3
   C. 1,296 in^3
   D. 5,184 in^3

15. What is the approximate volume of a cylinder that has a diameter of 8 feet and a height of 1.8 feet? Use $\pi = 3.14$.

   A. 45 ft^3
   B. 90 ft^3
   C. 180 ft^3
   D. 362 ft^3

16. How many cubic feet of cement are in a rectangular cement slab that is 4 inches thick and measures 12.5 feet long and 9 feet wide?

   A. 37.5 ft^3
   B. 75 ft^3
   C. 450 ft^3
   D. 375 ft^3

17. Use the diagram below to answer the question that follows.

A small, open box is made by cutting out 5-inch squares on each corner from a rectangular piece of tag board, measuring 15 inches by 25 inches. The 5-inch squares are discarded, and the box is formed by folding up the sides of the remaining tag board. What is the volume of the box in cubic inches?

  A.   1,125 in³
  B.   1,000 in³
  C.   625 in³
  D.   375 in³

18. A baseball diamond is a square that is 90 feet on a side. What is the approximate distance between bases in a scale model in which 9 feet = 1 inch?

  A.   90 in
  B.   9 in
  C.   810 in
  D.   10 in

19. How many cups of water does a 5-gallon container of water hold?

  A.   20 cups
  B.   40 cups
  C.   60 cups
  D.   80 cups

20. A runner ran a cross-country race of 12,500 meters. How many kilometers did the runner run in the race?

  A.   1.25 kilometers
  B.   12.5 kilometers
  C.   125 kilometers
  D.   12,500,000 kilometers

21. In triangle *ABC*, what type of angle is angle *B*?

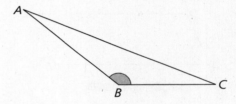

  A.   acute
  B.   obtuse
  C.   right
  D.   straight

22. Which of the following could be the measures of the three interior angles of a triangle?

  A.   30°, 50°, 80°
  B.   100°, 200°, 60°
  C.   120°, 50°, 20°
  D.   40°, 50°, 90°

23. What is the approximate diameter of a circle with a circumference of 48 inches? Use $\pi = 3.14$.

  A.   301.44 in
  B.   150.72 in
  C.   30.57 in
  D.   15.29 in

24. What are the coordinates of a point located 5 units to the right and 6 units down from point *P*?

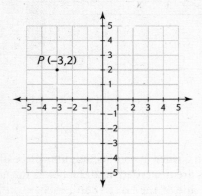

P (−3,2)

A. (2, 8)
B. (2, −4)
C. (−8, 8)
D. (−8, −4)

25. Which of the following is the most specific name for the figure below?

AB∥*DC* and *AD*∥*BC*

A. parallelogram
B. rectangle
C. square
D. trapezoid

26. Which of the following letters has both a horizontal and a vertical line of symmetry?

A. **H**
B. **A**
C. **W**
D. **N**

27. A 10-foot ladder is leaning against the side of a building. The bottom of the ladder is 6 feet from the base of the wall. How high up the side of the building does the ladder reach?

A. 4 ft
B. 8 ft
C. 10 ft
D. 16 ft

28. Use the diagram below to answer the question that follows.

ABCDE and *LMNOP* are regular pentagons. If *AB* = 12 units and *LM* = 6 units, what is the ratio of the perimeter of *ABCDE* to the perimeter of *LMNOP*?

A. 2:1
B. 5:1
C. 6:12
D. 30:60

29. The sizes of the screens of television sets are described by the length of the diagonal across the rectangular screen. The rectangular dimensions of the screen of a portable television set measure 12 inches by 16 inches. What is the size of the television screen?

A. 12 in
B. 16 in
C. 20 in
D. 28 in

30. If 108 of the 120 fans who attended a Little League baseball game on a particular Saturday were parents of the players, what percent of the fans were players' parents at the game on that Saturday?

A. 90%
B. 9%
C. 10%
D. 0.09%

31. What is the midpoint of the line segment connecting points T and U?

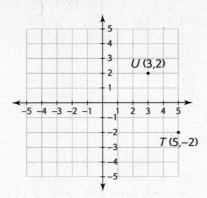

A. (0, 4)
B. (4, 0)
C. (1, –2)
D. (–2, 1)

32. If $x = -5$ and $y = -13$, then $x - y =$ what?

A. 8
B. –8
C. 18
D. –18

33. What is the distance between the two points R and S?

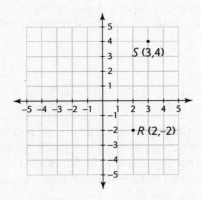

A. $\sqrt{37}$ units
B. $\sqrt{29}$ units
C. 7 units
D. $\sqrt{61}$ units

34. Four less than 5 times a number x is 6. What is the number x?

A. –2
B. $-\frac{2}{5}$
C. $\frac{2}{5}$
D. 2

35. Solve for x:

$$-2x - 5 = 3x + 15$$

A. $x = -20$
B. $x = -4$
C. $x = 2$
D. $x = 4$

36. Determine which of the following ordered pairs satisfies the given system.

$$x + 2y = -1$$
$$3x - 4y = 27$$

A. (5, –3)
B. (–3, –5)
C. (–5, 3)
D. (3, 5)

37. What is the slope of the line that passes through the points T and U?

A. $-\frac{3}{5}$
B. $-\frac{5}{3}$
C. –1
D. $\frac{5}{3}$

38. What is the value of $3x^3 - x^2 + 5$ when $x = 2$?

- **A.** 225
- **B.** 217
- **C.** 33
- **D.** 25

39. Solve for x:

$$4(x - 8) = 24$$

- **A.** −2
- **B.** 4
- **C.** 8
- **D.** 14

40. The graph shows a budget for a monthly salary after taxes.

Monthly Budget

If the monthly salary is $2,800, how much money is budgeted for food?

- **A.** $105
- **B.** $350
- **C.** $700
- **D.** $1,050

41. A spinner for a board game has 4 red sections, 3 yellow sections, 2 blue sections, and 1 green section. The sections are all of equal size. What is the probability of spinning red on the first spin and green on the second spin?

- **A.** $\frac{1}{4}$
- **B.** $\frac{1}{2}$
- **C.** 4
- **D.** $\frac{1}{25}$

42. A student needs an average of at least 80 on four tests to earn a grade of B in algebra. The student has grades of 78, 91, and 75 on the first three tests. What is the *lowest* grade the student can make on the fourth test and still receive a B in the course?

- **A.** 99
- **B.** 82
- **C.** 80
- **D.** 76

43. Mario has participated in eight track meets so far this season. His running times for the 440-meter race have been 73, 63, 68, 64, 69, 61, 66, and 64 seconds. What is Mario's median running time for the eight meets?

- **A.** 64 seconds
- **B.** 65 seconds
- **C.** 66 seconds
- **D.** 66.5 seconds

44. For lunch at the end-of-school picnic, students can choose from four types of sandwiches: ham, turkey, tuna, or peanut butter. They can choose from two drinks: milk or juice. They can select from three types of chips: potato chips, corn chips, or cheese-flavored puffs. How many possible combinations consisting of one sandwich, one drink, and one bag of chips can the students choose from for lunch?

- **A.** 8
- **B.** 9
- **C.** 11
- **D.** 24

45. Yuan has grades of 75, 89, 67, 56, and 92 in her English class and grades of 75, 78, 83, 84, 80, and 77 in her French class. Which of the following is a correct statement about Yuan's grades in the two classes?

- **A.** The grades in the English class have greater variability.
- **B.** The grades in the French class have greater variability.
- **C.** The mean in the English class is higher than the mean in the French class.
- **D.** The means in the two classes are equal.

IF YOU FINISH BEFORE TIME IS CALLED, CHECK YOUR WORK ON THIS SECTION ONLY. DO NOT WORK ON ANY OTHER SECTION IN THE TEST.

General Knowledge Practice Test 1: Reading

Time: **40 minutes**

40 questions

Directions: Please read the following passages carefully. Each passage in this section is followed by questions based on the passage's content. After reading each passage, answer the questions by choosing the best answer from among the four choices given. Be sure to base your answers on what is *implied* or *stated* in the passage.

Passage 1

(1)   Young people, particularly teenagers, love escapist fare. They watch television, go to the movies, or even read books to get away to a world that is often, for many, foreign, or at least, unapproachable. They watch and read about others—maybe their own age, maybe not—fall in and out of love, have wild adventures, travel the globe, or just spend time with their friends. Each journey is marked by a rite of passage, a time-tested travail in which the hero or protagonist must struggle with some conflict—either external or internal—to become a fully realized human being. By challenging the system or overcoming a long-held fear, the hero of a tale embodies the best of what the watcher or reader hopes for in his own life and, thus, symbolizes the hopes and admiration of many.

(2)   To entice young people to become avid readers, teachers and librarians often suggest works that, for some, are difficult to read. Well-intentioned as these informed advocates for young adult readers are, they often neglect a host of stories and novels that are aimed specifically at young adult readers. Too often, young people, particularly high school students, are handed material that is far beyond their knowledge or age range. Yes, Shakespeare, Dickens, and Hawthorne are representative of a class of time-honored, traditionally revered, classical authors; but they are, to be sure, not the only authors that young people should be encouraged to read. Indeed, there are many authors who young people often do not read, but should.

(3)   The burgeoning field of young-adult literature provides a rich panoply of good books from which young people can select to read and enjoy. Hours of escapist fare cloaked in realistic language and stories await eager young readers who find traditional literature too stuffy for their tastes. For younger readers (ages 9–12) there are works by Judy Blume (*Blubber, Are You There God? It's Me, Margaret.*), Paula Danziger (*The Cat Ate My Gymsuit, There's a Bat in Bunk Five*), and E. L. Konigsburg (*From the Mixed up Files of Mrs. Basil E. Frankwiler*). For older readers (ages 13–17), there are S. E. Hinton (*The Outsiders, Rumblefish*) and Robert Cormier (*The Chocolate War, After the First Death*). The books by these authors are but a few of the many books specifically written for young readers. These books appeal to the needs and sensibilities of young people while providing the escape from everyday life that all human beings need when they long for entertainment.

(4)   Thus, the task of lovers of good books—librarians, teachers, and parents, to name a few—is simple. They are duty bound to introduce young people to books that not only provide them a chance to explore new universes but edify them and engage their interest as well. Adults who work with young people in an effort to motivate them to become more than they could possibly imagine should become familiar with the world of young adult fiction so that they can, in turn, recommend good books that are relevant to the lives of the young people with whom they work. Otherwise, too often, these young people will never know the pure joy that reading can bring.

1. Which of the following best describes the focus of this passage?

    A.   appropriate literature for young readers

    B.   young people's choice of entertainment

    C.   why young people should read the classics

    D.   authors that young people should read

2. This passage implies that teenagers

    A.   watch too much television.

    B.   enjoy reading Shakespeare.

    C.   need to escape from their everyday lives.

    D.   prefer going to movies over reading books.

3. In the first paragraph, the word *travail* means

   A. annoyance.

   B. parody.

   C. injustice.

   D. tribulation.

4. What is the main idea of the third paragraph?

   A. All human beings long to escape from their everyday lives.

   B. Many good books written for young readers are available.

   C. Traditional literature is too stuffy for young readers.

   D. There are only a few books written specifically for young readers.

5. According to this passage, Judy Blume is the author of

   A. *The Cat Ate My Gymsuit.*

   B. *Are You There God? It's Me, Margaret.*

   C. *The Outsiders.*

   D. *The Chocolate War.*

6. According to the passage, what is one way in which teenagers can be motivated to read?

   A. Introduce teenagers to classic works of literature.

   B. Substitute watching television for reading.

   C. Provide high-interest, young-adult novels.

   D. Increase attention to nonfiction works.

7. As used in the third paragraph, the phrase "escapist fare cloaked in realistic language" best describes

   A. fiction books.

   B. nonfiction books.

   C. textbooks.

   D. autobiographies.

8. The tone of this passage can best be described as

   A. caustic.

   B. optimistic.

   C. objective.

   D. subjective.

9. Which sentence best states the main idea of this passage?

   A. Young adults should be given literature that speaks to their developmental interests.

   B. Young adults should read literature that inspires good citizenship.

   C. Young adults must read books that underline traditional values.

   D. Young adults must be taught books with universal recognition.

10. Identify the relationship between the following two sentences in the second paragraph.

"To entice young people to become avid readers, teachers and librarians often suggest works that, for some, are difficult to read. Well-intentioned as these informed advocates for young adult readers are, they often neglect a host of stories and novels that are aimed specifically at young adult readers."

The second sentence

   A. expands the first.

   B. contradicts the first.

   C. illustrates the first.

   D. ignores the first.

Passage 2

(1)   Since the dawn of human history, individuals have longed to unlock the eternal mysteries of the universe. They have wanted to know why they are here, for what purpose do they serve, and what, if anything, is in the vast reaches beyond their world. For the first two questions, the reasons for humankind's existence and its noble purpose, people of all races and creeds have turned to religion. There, amidst ancient myths and modern realities, individuals have found great comfort and joy in the teachings and practices of many of the world's most ancient and revered religious traditions. For the other question, though, the mysteries of life beyond our imaginations, individuals have turned to exploration; and there, Americans, in particular, have found some of their greatest challenges.

(2)   We are fortunate to live in an age of intense exploration. Whether Americans are visiting the vast reaches of sea, land, or space, we seem to be always on the move, uncovering new riches and treasures in the vast outer reaches of our world.

Indeed, our space program, marred as it is by tragic setbacks and fatal flaws, still beats a steady drumbeat toward unprecedented human progress and scientific growth. Today, more than ever, we witness what only a few short years ago was considered unimaginable in even the most intimate and secure corners of scientific research and space exploration.

(3) The efforts of our space program have led to the historic walk on the Moon by an American astronaut in July 1969. This giant leap for humankind has spawned an age of travel and exploration into the far reaches of space that has yielded untold benefits and information for our modern industrial universe. While ancient peoples saw a sky filled with mysterious lights and colors, we now know what we are seeing and why. We can recognize planets and stars with startling accuracy, and even more, send individuals hurtling into space with death-defying marksmanship; we can often use the targets that were once mysteries as guideposts for discovery.

To be sure, Americans have seen their share of space tragedy. In January 1986, the space shuttle (4) Challenger—carrying seven astronauts, including America's first teacher to go into space—exploded immediately after takeoff. Then, space shuttle Columbia was lost on re-entry on February 1, 2003. These two space shuttle disasters dramatically curtailed America's exploration into space, but did not dampen the American spirit. Instead, with renewed vigor and intense self-examination, America's space program has set a course for exploration into the far reaches of the universe, to once again answer the eternal question of what lies in the vast reaches of the universe and how we can use the knowledge of what is there to help us know why we are here and to inspire who we will become.

11. Which of the following statements is implied in the first paragraph?

A. Religion is an important part of many people's lives.

B. Religion plays a limited role in most people's lives.

C. Religion is the most important aspect of a person's life.

D. Religion provides answers to all of life's questions.

12. Which of the following is an opinion expressed in this passage?

A. Individuals now fly into space.

B. An American astronaut walked on the Moon.

C. We are fortunate to live in an age of intense exploration.

D. A teacher was on the space shuttle Challenger when it exploded.

13. In the second paragraph, the word *unprecedented* means

A. unparalleled.

B. usual.

C. unremarkable.

D. unexceptional.

14. This passage states that the Challenger disaster occurred in

A. July 1969.

B. January 1986.

C. March 1990.

D. February 2003.

15. According to information given in this passage

A. people seek answers to the reasons for humankind's existence.

B. astronauts brought back rocks from the Moon.

C. the Hubble space telescope provides images of planets and stars.

D. the two shuttle disasters put an end to space exploration.

16. In this narrative, the author speaks of

A. one shuttle disaster.

B. two shuttle disasters.

C. three shuttle disasters.

D. no shuttle disasters.

17. Since the dawn of human history, individuals have been fascinated with exploration because of mankind's

A. natural inquisitiveness about the universe.

B. insatiable desire to rule the world.

C. longing to live in isolation.

D. fervent need to civilize the world.

18. The author would probably agree that

    A. scientific exploration is a risk-free strategy that is filled with unexpected pleasures.

    B. exploring unknown regions of the world is necessary for human development.

    C. only in desperate times do human beings feel the urge to explore.

    D. searching for the unknown is the province of rich entrepreneurs.

19. In the narrative, which of the following statements is NOT implied?

    A. Today, because of America's space program, the unimaginable has become reality.

    B. Our exploration of space has had a positive impact on America.

    C. America is a leader in scientific exploration.

    D. Tragedy has extinguished America's exploratory spirit.

20. Which word or phrase, when substituted for "Instead" in the fourth paragraph, would maintain the same relationship between the last two sentences?

    A. Therefore

    B. In addition

    C. Rather

    D. Obviously

Passage 3

(1)   Maria Montessori is considered a woman who was ahead of her time. She is credited with founding a movement that placed children's needs and desires above all other considerations, which—at that time, in the early twentieth century—was considered radical and revolutionary thought, especially in Europe. Nevertheless, Maria, born of humble but progressive parents, learned to take what she had always intuitively felt about the value and dignity of all human beings—regardless of age, status, and ethnicity—and apply her understandings to the everyday world. In so doing, she changed the face of modern education as we know it.

(2)   Born in Chiaravalle, Italy, in 1870, Maria moved five years later to Rome. There, under the tutelage of her parents, especially her liberal-minded mother, Maria reveled in her own curiosity. Her natural inclination to explore and learn was encouraged; more important, she recognized that she could do and become anything her heart desired. However in Italy, as elsewhere throughout Europe and the United States at that time, the role of women was primarily subservient to that of men. Asserting their independence—whether at home, at work, or at play—was not something that women in the early twentieth century did. Maria's own learning environment, which had no such restrictions, formed the foundation of her later independent, free-spirited, learning environment for children.

(3)   In 1896, Maria Montessori's strong academic record and natural drive to succeed led her to become the first female certified physician in Italy. Graduating at the top of her class, Maria continued her deep and abiding love of the study of psychology, philosophy, and education and gradually began to form the basis of her teaching method known as the "Montessori Method."

(4)   In 1904, she was appointed professor of anthropology at the University of Rome. Now, having authority and position, Maria was able to apply her theories of child development to work in practical settings. Two years later, in 1906, she wasted no time in founding and establishing the first house for children of the industrial working class in one of Rome's worst slum districts. There, in the house known as the Casa dei Bambini, or "Children's House," Maria, at the age of 36, instructed some 60 children in her care on how to do everyday chores. Her philosophy embraced the idea that by doing ordinary work, children would begin to develop a sense of self and pride that would spur their own growth and independence.

(5)   To her delight, the children in her charge prospered. Soon, they were demonstrating self-reliance and maturity to their parents. Left to assert their independence, these young people, who because of position and social class were thought to be useless and unacceptable beyond normal functions, began to demonstrate social usefulness by simply being encouraged. Taking heed to her observations, Maria Montessori began to codify her doctrine of respecting the rights and privileges of young people into a philosophical and practical treatise on how young people learn.

(6)   By treating young people with reverence and respect, Maria revolutionized the teaching profession. Young people were no longer regarded as passive, stoic learners, but active, involved, developing human beings who were quite capable of making sound and independent choices about

their own learning. Advocating age-appropriate learning activities, Maria documented a teaching philosophy that garnered her worldwide attention and lasting influence in educational circles, most notably in the field of early childhood education.

(7)   Nominated three times for the Nobel Peace Prize (1949, 1950, 1951), Maria Montessori continued to work tirelessly, until her death in 1952, training adults in the United States, Europe, and India about her teaching methods for treating young children—indeed, all children—with the respect and dignity they deserve. She was truly ahead of her time.

21. According to this passage Maria Montessori was born in

    A. Germany.
    B. Spain.
    C. India.
    D. Italy.

22. Which of the following statements is implied in the passage?

    A. Maria Montessori's parents were old-fashioned.
    B. In Maria Montessori's time, women were encouraged to pursue careers that traditionally were considered male careers.
    C. Maria Montessori believed that children should be passive learners.
    D. Maria Montessori was well-educated.

23. Which of the following is an opinion about Maria Montessori expressed in this passage?

    A. She revolutionized the teaching profession.
    B. She was the first female certified physician in Italy.
    C. She founded the Casa dei Bambini.
    D. She was nominated three times for the Nobel Peace Prize.

24. This passage states that Maria Montessori

    A. advocated age-appropriate learning activities.
    B. believed that doing everyday chores was demeaning to children.
    C. had the greatest influence in the field of secondary education.
    D. won the Nobel Peace Prize in 1951.

25. According to this passage, Maria Montessori's teaching ideas

    A. were rejected by most educators of her time.
    B. gained attention worldwide during her lifetime.
    C. retired from teaching to practice medicine in her later years.
    D. found practicing medicine to be a difficult and arduous career.

26. According to this passage, the best word to describe Maria Montessori is

    A. passive.
    B. progressive.
    C. cynical.
    D. active.

27. According to this passage, Maria Montessori revolutionized the education profession because

    A. she understood the importance of subject-matter instruction in the development of young people.
    B. she demonstrated the validity of standardized assessment in classroom instruction.
    C. she respected the emotional experiences that young people brought to their learning.
    D. she underscored the power of reading to reinforce rote memorization of material.

28. According to this passage, Maria Montessori's philosophy was

    A. learning by doing ordinary work.
    B. learning by memorization.
    C. learning by objectives.
    D. learning by competition.

29. According to the ideas in this passage, which of the following would best demonstrate active, involved learners who are capable of making independent choices?

    A. A five-year-old practices geometry half-heartedly.
    B. A four-year-old memorizes Shakespeare without choice.
    C. A six-year-old takes a spelling test under extreme duress.
    D. A seven-year-old plays dress-up enthusiastically.

30. As used in the fifth paragraph, the word *self-reliance* means

    A. dependence.

    B. persistence.

    C. autonomy.

    D. caution.

Passage 4

(1)   Around the globe, near the equator, are woodlands lush in vegetation and foliage that enrich our planet with beauty and resources. I am speaking of the world-renowned tropical rain forests, a term purportedly coined by German botanist Andreas F. W. Schimper, who in 1898 ventured into this unexpected, wonderful, and forbidding universe. The breath-taking beauty of the tropical rain forests is indescribable. It is impossible to capture on film or to convey in words what it is like to stand inside the heart of a tropical rain forest. Yet, the rain forests' majesty and richness are sadly in jeopardy as human intervention continues to destroy what nature has designed to exist forever.

(2)   Tropical rain forests have the unique distinction of occupying only 6 to 7 percent of the Earth's surface, but they nourish more than half of the Earth's plant and animal species. In this vast stretch of virtually unexplored territory, literally thousands of species of plant and animal life exist. Home to many varieties of amphibians, reptiles, insects, birds, and mammals, the tropical rain forests are a virtual Noah's ark of all creatures great and small.

(3)   Scientists believe some riches of the rain forests are yet to be discovered. In addition to finding new animal species, they continue to mine the many exotic plants that can yield untold benefits in developing new medicines for individuals with acute and chronic illnesses. In addition, scientists urge world leaders to take every measure possible to preserve the rain forests because of the many and varied plant species they contain that help to regulate the Earth's climate and ensure clean air.

(4)   Thus, when the rain forests are threatened by large industrial companies, desiring to clear land for logging, farming, and mining projects, world citizens object and lobby dignitaries and business leaders to use caution in their desires to expand and grow. Both sides of this issue—those advocating for the use of the rain forests for economic growth and gain and those advocating for the preservation of a natural reserve—are locked in a reasonable and vital discussion about the future use of one of (if not *the*) world's greatest natural resources. This debate, though, is never-ending and always exasperating. Each side—the environmentalists and the industrialists—claim that the other side is violating rules that serve to protect the environment from undue harm. As a result, long legal battles ensue, resulting in few if any reasonable compromises.

(5)   In some instances, though, the debate is almost futile. In 1950, rain forests covered about 8,700,000 square miles of the Earth's surface. Today, in the early twenty-first century, less than half of the original extent of the world's rain forests remains. In an area that once measured in practical terms the equivalent of nearly three-fourths of Africa, today stands vast regions—in places like Madagascar, Sumatra, and the Atlantic coast of Brazil—of arid, dry land.

(6)   Scientists estimate that deforestation—the ridding of the rain forests of valuable trees and foliage—eliminates from the Earth's surface about 7,500 species per year. Even humankind is threatened. Millions of indigenous people, individuals who know little of the outside world of modern conveniences, make their homes in the rain forests. Explorers have discovered and recorded the comings and goings of such groups as the Yanomami of South Africa, the Dayaks of Southeast Asia, and the Pygmies of Central Africa. These people, the last of the earth's primitive tribes, make their living off this lush and forbidding land; and naturally, they have much to tell about using its natural resources for survival.

(7)   Fortunately, a number of governments and conservation organizations are working to preserve the rain forests. Organizations like the World Wildlife Fund and the Nature Conservancy are working with national and international government agencies to conserve rain forests. Their efforts include establishing protected lands, promoting conservation methods, and increasing public awareness. Specific measures include certifying that timber is harvested in a responsible manner and logging is allowed in only designated and protected areas. To be sure, these are small steps; but with perseverance and common sense, the rain forests will continue to survive as one of the Earth's most vital and precious resources.

31. The tone of this passage is best described as

    A. skeptical.
    B. humorous.
    C. sarcastic.
    D. factual.

32. Which of the following is a fact about tropical rain forests that is given in the first paragraph?

    A. Tropical rain forests are found near the equator.
    B. The breath-taking beauty of a tropical rain forest is indescribable.
    C. It is impossible to capture on film or to convey in words what it is like to stand inside the heart of a tropical rain forest.
    D. The rain forests' majesty and richness are sadly in jeopardy.

33. According to the passage, rain forests occupy what percent of the Earth's surface?

    A. less than 2 percent
    B. 6 to 7 percent
    C. 20 to 25 percent
    D. over 50 percent

34. This passage states that

    A. deforestation of rain forests has resulted in the extinction of indigenous people.
    B. government agencies do little to preserve the rain forests.
    C. large industrial companies, desiring to clear land for logging, farming, and mining, threaten the rain forests.
    D. most of the species in the rain forest are insects.

35. In paragraph three, the author uses the word *mine* in the context of

    A. excavating from the Earth's soil.
    B. dissolving with chemicals.
    C. extracting from plants.
    D. supplying with new medicines.

36. Which of the statements about rain forests is neither stated nor implied in this passage?

    A. They provide safe havens for indigenous people.
    B. They provide natural resources for modern medicines.
    C. They provide unique treasures for self-defined explorers.
    D. They provide a rich laboratory for scientific investigation.

37. The primary purpose of this passage is to

    A. introduce rare rain forest plants and species.
    B. inform readers about the plight of the rain forests.
    C. argue the benefits of logging in the rain forests.
    D. underline the importance of scientific exploration.

38. According to this passage, all of the following are true except

    A. in 1950, rain forests covered about 8,700,000 square miles of the Earth's surface.
    B. rain forests nourish more than half of the world's plants and animals.
    C. today, less than half of the world's original rain forests remain.
    D. deforestation is a minor problem in today's rain forest environment.

39. According to this passage, millions of *indigenous* people live in the rain forests. *Indigenous* can best be defined as

A. people who are transitory migrants on the land in which they live.

B. people who own property on the land in which they live.

C. people who are native to the land in which they live.

D. people who work the land on which they live.

40. The author's claim that "the rain forests will continue to survive as one of the Earth's most vital and precious resources" is a/an

A. nonobjectionable, reasoned statement based on scant evidence.

B. contradictory statement based on the passage's prior reasoning.

C. objectionable remark that reveals the author's implicit bias.

D. reasonable statement given the author's previous remarks.

IF YOU FINISH BEFORE TIME IS CALLED, CHECK YOUR WORK ON THIS SECTION ONLY. DO NOT WORK ON ANY OTHER SECTION IN THE TEST.

Answer Key

English Language Skills

1. B	15. D	29. C
2. D	16. B	30. A
3. D	17. A	31. A
4. C	18. A	32. C
5. A	19. B	33. C
6. C	20. A	34. D
7. A	21. C	35. C
8. B	22. C	36. B
9. B	23. B	37. D
10. A	24. C	38. C
11. A	25. A	39. A
12. C	26. B	40. C
13. C	27. C	
14. B	28. B	

Mathematics

1. A	17. D	33. A
2. B	18. D	34. D
3. D	19. D	35. B
4. A	20. B	36. A
5. B	21. B	37. B
6. B	22. D	38. D
7. C	23. D	39. D
8. C	24. B	40. C
9. C	25. A	41. D
10. B	26. A	42. D
11. A	27. B	43. B
12. B	28. A	44. D
13. B	29. C	45. A
14. D	30. A	
15. B	31. B	
16. A	32. A	

Reading

1. A	16. B	31. D
2. C	17. A	32. A
3. D	18. B	33. B
4. B	19. D	34. C
5. B	20. C	35. C
6. C	21. D	36. C
7. A	22. D	37. B
8. D	23. A	38. D
9. A	24. A	39. C
10. A	25. B	40. D
11. A	26. B	
12. C	27. C	
13. A	28. A	
14. B	29. D	
15. A	30. C	

Answer Explanations

Sample Essays

In this section of the examination, you were to prepare a written assignment on one of two topics.

Topic 1

Why I want to become a teacher

Topic 2

A person whom I admire

You were to write a 300- to 600-word response that would be well written, organized, and defined. You also were informed that your writing would be graded holistically, taking into consideration both mechanics and organization.

What follows are examples of a weak and strong response to both prompts.

Topic 1—Why I Want to Become a Teacher

Weak Response

Personally, I want to become a teacher because I like to teach and it seems fun. I enjoy working with young children and more so, the hours seem flexible and manageable. I once wanted to become a doctor, but I realized that the course work was much too difficult, so I decided on teaching instead. My love for young children made me switch and I am glad that I did. I have many good ideas for working with young children and I cannot wait to get started. I also don't know what class or grade I want to teach, but I do know that I don't want to teach the middle grades. I don't believe that I would have the patience or knowledge to work with teenagers. They seem like an real difficult group to work with. Still, I do know that I want to be a teacher and I will try my best to succeed.

Strong Response

Becoming a teacher has been a lifelong dream for me. I can think of no richer occupation for me to pursue than that of working with young children. As I achieve my goal, my life's ambition will become a dream come true. For embedded in my teaching will be the fulfillment of a mission that began as a young child and continued through my school and college years, culminating in my first real teaching position.

When I was a young child, I dreamed of becoming a teacher. I would line up my dolls in my playroom and pretend that I was their teacher. I would do everything that all my real teachers in school would do. I would teach lessons, walk them to recess, sit with them at lunch, and even take them on field trips. I would line my dolls up in my little red wagon—all 14 of them—and pull them along the sidewalk in front of my house. I would pretend we were taking a trip to the zoo or a museum. Like my real teachers in school, I would talk to my dolls, praising them when they did good work and scolding them when they misbehaved.

As I grew older, I became active in school, always nurturing my desire to teach and help others. In middle school, I became a peer counselor, helping other students with their problems and homework. I would work for hours before and after school with sixth and seventh graders who had trouble with their math and science homework since I was particularly good in those subjects. I would also help them solve problems and issues that they had with other students when they just needed someone to listen. In high school, I was active in the Future Teachers of America Organization, helping children in elementary schools with their assignments, and on occasion, teaching lessons for an entire classroom of children. In addition, I spent many hours in high school, volunteering my services in all sorts of organizations—from service clubs to student government—just learning how to become a better "people person."

Finally, during my college years, I started to fulfill my lifelong ambition to become a teacher by majoring in elementary education. Attending the state university, I majored in education and minored in psychology;

so now, when I do obtain a teaching job, I can combine my love for working with children with my desire to understand who they are as human beings. I was most able to put my knowledge to work during my final semester in college when I became a student teacher in a local elementary school. Now, I feel better equipped to become a teacher, for I have both the experience and credentials to succeed.

As stated, I love teaching; and I hope, soon, to get a wonderful teaching position in which I can contribute to the growth and development of young children. I want to return to my childhood days in which I played teacher with my dolls; only this time, I want to work with real children. I have already made an impact with my student peers and during my training years; now I want to make a difference in the real world of teaching.

Topic 2—A Person Whom I Admire

Weak Response

A person that I admire is my uncle. My uncle Ned has been with me since I was little boy and I was able to sit in his lap and listen to his fantastic stories about fishing. His idea of fun has always been to pretend to pull quarters out of my ear. When I was real young, I thought it was magic, but as I got older, I realized that he was just making it up. I really enjoy older people, especially someone I can look up to because you never know what good advice they are going to give you. My uncle and my grandfather always gave me good advice and I have always been eager to follow their smart wisdom. They taught me how to drive and what to study and how to do well in school and with girls. Yes, someone I admire is my uncle because he always helps me when I am in trouble. My uncle is also deaf which is an amazing in and of itself.

Strong Response

Admiration is a strong word that conjures up many meanings and implications. To admire someone is not only to appreciate someone for who they are, but also to hope to emulate them for what they have become. When you admire parents or relatives, you are saying that you both love them and want to be like them. When you admire adults or friends, you are saying that you hope someday to be just like them, and that you hope that they, in turn, will teach you something about how they became who they are. Such is the admiration that I have for my Uncle Ned.

My Uncle Ned is a wonderful human being. He is not rich, famous, or especially talented. He does not play a musical instrument, excel in sports, or have the gift of eloquent speech. In fact, my Uncle Ned is deaf. Born with a congenital birth defect, my uncle can hardly hear (only high-pitched sounds) and speak. He can lip read, and as a result, he has learned to conduct most of his conversations in sign language. He is very adept at signing most anything, and he can move at lightning speed when he is talking with someone who knows sign language as well as he does.

Uncle Ned is truly a remarkable person. Never one to be defeated, he has struggled since his birth to live a normal, everyday life. Attending public schools, he would seek the accommodations that the school would provide—teachers, tutors, special classes—and never once (so I am told) did he ever complain. Uncle Ned just took everything in stride, using his disability as an ability and not a liability. He would compensate for his deafness by working extra hard to make sure his assignments were done exceptionally well and that no one would think he was slacking off because he could not hear and barely could speak. Instead, he made sure, as his sister (my mother) tells me, that his teachers knew that he was really working and that he really cared.

Uncle Ned worked so hard and cared so much about his education that he, too, eventually became a teacher. Only this time, Uncle Ned devoted his teaching years to a special school for children who are just like him, hard of hearing and speaking. After getting his doctorate in education (I told you my uncle is special), he began what has become a nearly 30-year career teaching at Galludet University in Washington, D.C., one of the few institutions in higher education that is devoted solely to working with deaf and hard-of-hearing individuals. And it is there that my uncle has been able to give back to a new generation of students what he received in a public school setting.

Everyone admires somebody—a parent, a teacher, a friend. I have had the privilege of admiring someone who is not only a relative and a friend, but an inspiring role model for countless human beings who are both hearing and nonhearing, and he has truly inspired me above all. I feel very lucky to know my Uncle Ned, who taught me not to try to be someone special, but to live like someone special.

English Language Skills

1. **B.** Choice **B** is the correct response. This arrangement provides the most logical sequence of ideas and supporting details in the paragraph. Choices **A**, **C**, and **D** do not represent a logical arrangement of the possible sentence combinations.

2. **D.** Choice **D** is the correct response. Sentence 6 is the sentence LEAST relevant to this passage. The discussion of the automobile, although important to an overall discussion of transportation, does not belong in a paragraph whose sole discussion is about horses.

3. **D.** Choice **D** is the correct response. This paragraph already reads well. There is no need to rearrange the sentences in a different order.

4. **C.** Choice **C** is the correct response. Sentence 5 is the sentence LEAST relevant to this passage. The discussion of individuals who like engagement and wedding rings without precious stones is interesting but distracting to the paragraph's narrative.

5. **A.** Choice **A** is the correct response. The correct word choice is *whose*. *Who's* is a contraction for the word *who is*. *Whose* is the possessive form of the word *who*. The sentence is in the past tense, so *came* is the correct verb at **B**. The word *retrieve* at **C** is spelled and used correctly.

6. **C.** Choice **C** is the correct response. The correct word choice is *except*. The word *accept* means "to take when offered." The word *except* means "to exclude." The preposition *at* at **A** is used correctly. The word *summer* at **B** does not require capitalization. The seasons of the year do not require capitalization.

7. **A.** Choice **A** is the correct response. The correct word choice is *respectfully*. The word *respectively* means "correspondingly." The word respectfully means "with respect." The word *formal*, meaning "official," is the correct word choice at **B**. The word *principal,* referring to the person who is the building supervisor of the school, at **C** is the correct word choice.

8. **B.** Choice **B** is the correct response. The correct word choice is *farther.* The word *further* is used to describe abstract ideas. The word *farther* is used to describe concrete distance. The other word choices—*fourth* at **A** and *than* at **C**—are spelled and used correctly.

9. **B.** Choice **B** is the correct response. The correct word choice is *could have*. The phrase *could of* is grammatically incorrect. *Could have* is the grammatically acceptable phrase. (*Should of* is also unacceptable.) The other word choices—*aunt* at **A** and *dessert* at **C** — are spelled and used correctly. Only capitalize the word *aunt* when you are naming a specific aunt, like *Aunt Betty*. The word *dessert* means "a treat you eat after a meal." The word *desert* means "a dry, sandy place with little or no plant life."

10. **A.** Choice **A** is the correct response. The correct word choice is *capital*. The word *capitol* refers to a building. The word *capital* refers to a city. The word *receive* at **B** is spelled and used correctly. The word *their* at **C** is properly used as a possessive pronoun.

11. **A.** Choice **A** is the correct response. The correct word choice is *weather*. The word *whether* refers to a choice between two objects. The word *weather* refers to the climate. The word *admirably* at **B** is an adverb modifying the verb *performed* and is used correctly in this sentence. The word *congregants* at **C** is spelled and used correctly.

12. **C.** Choice **C** is the correct response. The correct word choice is *proceeded*. The word *proceeded* means "to venture forth or go ahead." The word *preceded* means "to come before." The other word choices—*ineligible* at **A** and *everyone* at **B**—are spelled and used correctly.

13. **C.** Choice **C** is the correct response. The correct word choice is *than*. The word *than* is used when making a comparison between two objects. The word *then* implies a time frame. The other word choices—*certainly* at **A** and *board* at **B**—are spelled and used correctly in the sentence.

14. **B.** Choice **B** is the correct response. The correct word choice is *complement*. The word *complement* means "to accompany, to match, or to complete something." The word *compliment* means "to laud praise on someone." The other word choices—*exceptional* at **A** and *considerable* at **C**—are spelled and used correctly.

15. **D.** Choice **D** is the correct response. This sentence is correct as written. The word *whether* at **B** refers to a choice between two objects and makes sense in the sentence. The word *me* at **A** is the object of the preposition *Between*, so it should be in the objective case. The word *I* at **C** is the subject of the verb *should be* (which is understood) and thus, should be in the subjective case.

16. **B.** Choice **B** is the correct response. The correct word choice is *site*. The word *site* refers to a place or setting. The word *sight* refers to one's ability to see. The other word choices—*may* at **A** and *beside* at **C**—are spelled and used correctly.

17. **A.** Choice **A** is the correct response. The sentence should be in the past tense, so *came* is the correct verb. The word *that* at **B** is correct because it introduces a restrictive clause. The comma at **C** is correct. Although you may see the omission of the comma before the coordinating conjunction *and,* the final comma in a series of three or more elements is never incorrect.

18. **A.** Choice **A** is the correct response. The word at **A** shows possession. The location belongs to the restaurant, so *restaurants* should be *restaurant's*. The word *beach* at **B** is spelled correctly. The word *really* at **C** is an adverb modifying the adjective *romantic*, so it is correct.

19. **B.** Choice **B** is the correct response. A comma is needed at **B** to separate the introductory subordinate clause from the rest of the sentence. The word *tourists* at **A** does not show possession, so no apostrophe is needed. The word *than* at **C** is correctly used as a conjunction in a comparison. The word *then* is an adverb indicating time.

20. **A.** Choice **A** is the correct response. In this sentence, the word following the verb *felt* at **A** modifies the subject (a noun). The word *badly* is an adverb. It should not be used to modify a noun. The adjective *bad* should be used instead. The word *English* at **B** is a proper noun, so it should be capitalized. The title *superintendent* at **C** should not be capitalized. Titles are capitalized when they precede proper names, but as a rule are not capitalized when used alone.

21. **C.** Choice **C** is the correct response. The *West Indies* is the name of a specific place. The full name must be capitalized. The comma at **A** is needed to set off the nonrestrictive appositive. The word *explorer* at **B** is not a proper noun, so it should not be capitalized.

22. **C.** Choice **C** is the correct response. The past tense of *build* is *built*, not *builded*. The word *When* at **A** is correct and makes sense in the sentence. The comma at **B** is needed to separate the introductory subordinate clause from the rest of the sentence.

23. **B.** Choice **B** is the correct response. The word *between* is a preposition. The object of a preposition should be in the objective case. Change *I* at **B** to *me* to make the sentence grammatically correct. The sentence is in the present tense, so *am* at **A** is the correct verb. The word *that* at **C** is correct. It would be redundant to use *because* at **C** because the word *because* means *for the reason that*.

24. **C.** Choice **C** is the correct response. The underlined portion at **C** is the subject of the verb *can run* (which is understood) and, thus, should be in the subjective case. Change *them other athletes* to *those other athletes* to make the sentence grammatically correct. The pronoun *who* at **A** is correct because it is the subject of the subordinate clause it introduces. The word *faster* at **B** is the correct comparative form of the adverb *fast*.

25. **A.** Choice **A** is the correct response. The singular pronoun *it* is the subject of the verb at **A,** so change *don't* to *doesn't* to make the verb agree with its singular subject. No comma is needed at **B**. The second-person pronoun *you* at **C** is correct. It would be incorrect to switch to the third-person pronoun *one*.

26. **B.** Choice **B** is the correct response. The word at **B** should be spelled *mathematics*. The word *siblings* at **A** does not show possession, so no apostrophe is needed. The reflexive pronoun *myself* at **C** is used correctly to refer to its antecedent *I*.

27. **C.** Choice **C** is the correct response. The plural noun *media* is the subject of the verb at **C,** so change *is* to *are* to make the verb agree with its plural subject. The introductory word *there* at **A** is the correct word choice. The sentence is in the past tense, so *was* is the correct verb at **B.**

28. **B.** Choice **B** is the correct response. The past participle for the verb *to eat* is *eaten*. Note that "should of" in **A** and **C** is an error for "should have."

29. **C.** Choice **C** is the correct response. The tense of the verb in Choice **C** relates logically to the verb in the main clause. The verb tenses in Choices **A** and **B** do not.

30. **A.** Choice **A** is the correct response. The singular pronoun *Everyone* is the subject of the verb at **A,** so change *have enjoyed* to *has enjoyed* to make the verb agree with its singular subject. The plural form of *goldfish* at **B** is written correctly. The word *castle* at **C** is spelled correctly.

31. **A.** Choice **A** is the correct response. The word *Each* is the singular antecedent of the possessive pronoun at **A.** Use *his* instead of the plural pronoun *their* to refer to the singular antecedent *Each*. No comma is needed at **B.** The preposition *between* at **C** is correctly used to indicate a relationship involving two things. The preposition *among* is used when the relationship involves more than two elements.

32. **C.** Choice **C** is the correct response. Does *them* at **C** refer to *students* or *books*? Change *them* to *the books* to avoid ambiguity. No comma is needed at **A.** The word *organizations* at **B** does not show possession, so no apostrophe is needed.

33. **C.** Choice **C** is the correct response. In this sentence the words *studying, reading*, and *to write* are in parallel, but they do not have the same grammatical construction. You can correct this faulty parallelism by changing *to write* at **C** to *writing*. The word *middle* at **A** is not a proper noun, so it should not be capitalized. The word *grammar* at **B** is spelled correctly.

34. **D.** Choice **D** is the correct response. This sentence is correct as written. The word *quite*, meaning "rather," at **A** is spelled correctly and makes sense in the sentence. The possessive pronoun *his* at **B** is correct because *his* modifies the gerund *meddling*. The verb *personal* at **C** is spelled correctly and makes sense in the sentence.

35. **C.** Choice **C** is the correct response. The word at **C** is a noun, so *affect* should be changed to *effect* to make the sentence grammatically correct. The word *professors* at **A** does not show possession, so no apostrophe is needed. The singular verb *was* at **B** agrees with its singular subject *One*.

36. **B.** Choice **B** is the correct response. The word at **B** should be spelled *height*, not *heighth*. The sentence is in the past tense, so *measured* at **A** is the correct verb. No comma is needed at **C.**

37. **D.** Choice **D** is the correct response. This sentence is correct as written. The possessive word *Bess's* is punctuated correctly. The word *friends* at **B** is spelled correctly. At **C** the superlative form of *unusual* is *most unusual*, not *unusualest*.

38. **C.** Choice **C** is the correct response. All punctuation in sentence **C** is correct. Choice **A** is incorrect because it is a run-on sentence. It is two complete sentences connected by only a comma. Choices **B** and **D** are also run-on sentences. Each of these sentences is two complete sentences joined without a word to connect them or a proper punctuation mark to separate them.

39. **A.** Choice **A** is the correct response. All punctuation in Choice **A** is correct. In Choice **B,** the word *familys'* is incorrect. To form the possessive of a noun (either singular or plural) that does not end in *s*, add an apostrophe and *s*. Choice **C** is incorrect because it contains a fragment. (*Preferring to be hand-fed canned tuna.*) A comma is needed in Choice **D** to separate the introductory participial phrase from the rest of the sentence.

40. **C.** Choice **C** is the correct response. The modifiers in Choice **C** are placed correctly. The participial phrase *Rushing to finish the surprise dinner on time* modifies *Melissa,* the noun subject of the main clause of the sentence and should be close to it. In Choices **B** and **D,** *Rushing to finish the surprise dinner on time* is separated from the noun *Melissa,* resulting in ambiguity. The subordinate clause *that was rotten* modifies the noun *egg*, and should be close to it. In Choices **A** and **B,** *that was rotten* seems to modify the noun *neighbor,* which clearly is not the intent of the writer.

Mathematics

1. **A.** Choice **A** is the correct response. The part of the total number of paintings purchased by the art connoisseur is $\frac{5}{20} = \frac{1}{4} = \frac{25}{100} = 0.25$. Choice **A** is the only choice that is <u>not</u> equivalent to $\frac{5}{20}$.

2. **B.** Choice **B** is the correct response. You need to separate $4\frac{1}{2}$ pounds into equal $\frac{3}{8}$ pound patties. You use division to separate a whole into equal parts. You want the units of your answer to be patties. Carry the units along in your computation, so that you can see that the units of the answer work out to be patties.

$$4\frac{1}{2} \text{ pounds} \div \frac{3}{8}\frac{\text{pound}}{\text{patties}} = \frac{9}{2} \text{ pounds} \cdot \frac{8}{3}\frac{\text{patties}}{\text{pound}} = \frac{\cancel{9}^{3}}{\cancel{2}_{1}} \cancel{\text{pounds}} \cdot \frac{\cancel{8}^{4}}{\cancel{3}_{1}}\frac{\text{patties}}{\cancel{\text{pound}}} = \frac{12 \text{ patties}}{1} = 12 \text{ patties}$$

As you can see, the pounds "cancel out" when you multiply.

12 hamburger patties can be made, Choice **B**.

Did I answer the question? Yes, I found how many patties can be made. ✓

Does my answer make sense? Yes. ✓

Is the answer stated in the correct units? Yes, the units are patties, which is correct. ✓

Choice **A** results if you multiply instead of divide. Choices **C** and **D** result if you divide incorrectly.

3. **D.** Choice **D** is the correct response. To simplify the expression $6 + 2^3 \cdot 3 \div 3 + 7$, follow the order of operations using the mnemonic "<u>P</u>lease <u>E</u>xcuse <u>M</u>y <u>D</u>ear <u>A</u>unt <u>S</u>ally":

$6 + 2^3 \cdot 3 \div 3 + 7 = 6 + 8 \cdot 3 \div 3 + 7$ No parentheses are involved; so first, perform exponentiation.

$6 + 24 \div 3 + 7 = 6 + 8 + 7$ Next, multiply and divide from left to right.

$= 21$, Choice **D**   Finally, add from left to right.

Choice **A**, **B**, or **C** results if you fail to follow the order of operations properly.

4. **A.** Choice **A** is the correct response. Two steps are needed to solve the problem. First, subtract the older granddaughter's part from the whole. Then, divide what remains into four equal parts.

Step 1. The older granddaughter inherits $\frac{1}{3}$ of the land. Subtract to find the remaining part of the land.

$$1 - \frac{1}{3} = \frac{2}{3}$$

Step 2. The younger granddaughter and her three brothers equally share the remaining part of the land. Use division to separate $\frac{2}{3}$ into 4 equal parts.

$$\frac{2}{3} \div 4 = \frac{2}{3} \div \frac{4}{1} = \frac{2}{3} \cdot \frac{1}{4} = \frac{\cancel{2}^{1}}{3} \cdot \frac{1}{\cancel{4}_{2}} = \frac{1}{6}$$

The younger granddaughter inherits $\frac{1}{6}$ of the land, Choice **A**.

Did I answer the question? Yes, I found the fraction of the land that the younger granddaughter inherits. ✓

Does my answer make sense? Yes. ✓

Is the answer stated in the correct units? The answer is a fraction, so no units are needed. ✓

Choice **B** results if you fail to subtract the older daughter's part from the whole before dividing. Choice **C** results if you make a computation error in Step 2. Choice **D** results if you fail to do Step 2 after you complete Step 1.

5. **B.** Choice **B** is the correct response. To find the change in temperature, subtract the initial reading (–6°F) from the final reading (35°F):

35°F – (–6°F) = 35°F + 6°F = 41°F. The temperature increased by 41°F, Choice **B.** Choice **A** results if you make the mistake of adding the temperatures algebraically, instead of subtracting them. Choice **C** results if you subtract the final reading from the initial reading. Choice **D** results if you mistakenly add the temperatures algebraically and make a sign error.

6. **B.** Choice **B** is the correct response. A number written in scientific notation is written as a product of two numbers: a number that is greater than or equal to 1, but less than 10, and a power of 10. Eliminate choices **A** and **C** because the first factor is greater than 10.

The number 108,200,000 is greater than 10, so the decimal point must be moved to the left to make the first factor greater than or equal to 1 but less than 10. If the decimal point is moved 8 places to the left, the first factor will be 1.082.

$108{,}200{,}000 = 1.082000000 \times 10^{?} = 1.082 \times 10^{?}$

Since the decimal point was moved to the left 8 places, the exponent for the power of 10 is 8. The exponent needs to be positive 8 so that when you convert back to the original number, the value is the same. The number 108,200,000 is written as 1.082×10^{8} in scientific notation, Choice **B.** You can check your answer by quickly performing the indicated multiplication.

$1.082 \times 10^{8} = 1.082 \times 100{,}000{,}000 = 108{,}200{,}000.$

Choices **A** and **C** result if you fail to make the first factor a number greater than or equal to 1, but less than 10. Choice **D** results if you incorrectly use a negative exponent on the power of 10. Negative exponents are used in scientific notation when you are writing very small numbers that are between 0 and 1. For example, 0.00000007 is 7×10^{-8} in scientific notation.

7. **C.** Choice **C** is the correct response.

Using the Pythagorean Theorem, where $a = 6$, $b = 7$, and $c = \overline{AB}$, the hypotenuse, you have

$c^2 = a^2 + b^2$

$c^2 = 6^2 + 7^2$

$c^2 = 36 + 49$

$c^2 = 85$, which means that $c = \sqrt{85}$, the length of side AB, the hypotenuse of right triangle ABC.

To approximate the value of $\sqrt{85}$, find two consecutive integers such that the square of the first integer is less than 85 and the square of the second integer is greater than 85. Since 9^2 is $81 < 85$ and 10^2 is $100 > 85$, the approximate value of $\sqrt{85}$ is between 9 and 10, Choice **C.**

8. **C.** Choice **C** is the correct response. Three steps are needed to solve the problem: First, find the number of over-limit minutes; next, find the cost of the over-limit minutes; and then, find the total charges by adding the cost of the over-limit minutes to the regular monthly charge.

Step 1. Subtract to find how many minutes of calls are over the 500 limit.

615 minutes − 500 minutes = 115 minutes

Step 2. Find the cost for the over-limit minutes by multiplying by $0.30.

115 minutes × $0.30/minute = $34.50

Step 3. Add the over-limit charges to the monthly charge.

$29.99 + $34.50 = $64.49

Demetria's total charges for her cell phone calls last month are $64.49, Choice **C**.

Did I answer the question? Yes, I found Demetria's total charges for her cell phone last month. ✓

Does my answer make sense? Yes. ✓

Is the answer stated in the correct units? Yes, the units are dollars, which is correct. ✓

Choice **A** does not include the over-limit charges. Choice **B** is the over-limit charges only. Choice **D** is the result of treating the 615 minutes as over-limit charges and not adding in the $29.99.

9. **C.** Choice **C** is the correct response. Two steps are needed to solve the problem: First, find the basketball player's height in feet. Then, find the difference between the basketball player's height and the height of the basketball hoop.

Step 1. Change the basketball player's height to feet.

The Mathematics Reference Sheet shows 3 feet = 36 inches. You can write this fact as $\frac{3 \text{ ft}}{36 \text{ in}}$ and reduce to obtain $\frac{1 \text{ ft}}{12 \text{ in}}$ as one of your conversion fractions and $\frac{12 \text{ in}}{1 \text{ ft}}$ as your other conversion fraction.

Write your measurement as a fraction with denominator 1 and let unit analysis tell you whether to multiply by $\frac{1 \text{ ft}}{12 \text{ in}}$ or $\frac{12 \text{ in}}{1 \text{ ft}}$. Since you want the inches to divide out, multiply by $\frac{1 \text{ ft}}{12 \text{ in}}$.

$$\frac{75 \text{ in}}{1} \cdot \frac{1 \text{ ft}}{12 \text{ in}} = \frac{75 \text{ in}}{1} \cdot \frac{1 \text{ ft}}{12 \text{ in}} = \frac{75 \text{ ft}}{12} = 6.25 \text{ ft}$$

Step 2. Subtract to find the difference between the basketball player's height and the height of the basketball hoop.

10 ft − 6.25 ft = 3.75 ft

The distance in feet between the top of the player's head and the basketball hoop is 3.75 feet, Choice **C**.

Did I answer the question? Yes, I found the distance in feet between the top of the player's head and the basketball hoop. ✓

Does my answer make sense? Yes. ✓

Is the answer stated in the correct units? Yes, the units are feet, which is correct. ✓

Choice **A** results if you use 1 foot = 10 inches, instead of 12 inches. Choice **B** results if you subtract incorrectly. Choice **D** results if you stop at Step 1 and incorrectly use the basketball player's height as your solution to the problem.

10. **B.** Choice **B** is the correct response. By glancing at the answer choices, you can see that to answer the question, you must add up the total number of hours and minutes, and then simplify the results, if needed. Three steps are needed to solve the problem:

Step 1. Add up the total time in hours and minutes.

1 hour, 44 minutes
2 hours, 32 minutes
3 hours, 76 minutes

Step 2. Change 76 minutes to hours and minutes.

The Mathematics Reference Sheet shows 1 hour = 60 minutes, so 76 minutes = 1 hour and 16 minutes.

Step 3. Add the 1 hour and 16 minutes to 3 hours.

3 hours, 76 minutes = 3 hours + 1 hour, 16 minutes = 4 hours, 16 minutes

The total amount of time Selma spent playing video games last weekend is 4 hours, 16 minutes, Choice **B**.

Did I answer the question? Yes, I found the total amount of time Selma spent playing video games last weekend. ✓

Does my answer make sense? Yes. ✓

Is the answer stated in the correct units? Yes, the units are hours and minutes, which is correct. ✓

Choices **A** and **D** result if you add incorrectly in Step 3. Choice **C** occurs if you add incorrectly in Step 1.

11. **A.** Choice **A** is the correct response. First sketch a diagram to illustrate the problem:

Three steps are needed to solve the problem: First, find the area of the rectangular table; next, find the area of the circular table; and then find the difference between the two areas.

Step 1. Find the area of the rectangular table.

The Mathematics Reference Sheet shows the formula for the area of a rectangle is $A = lw$.

$A = lw = 4.5 \text{ ft} \cdot 3 \text{ ft} = 13.5 \text{ ft}^2$

Step 2. Find the area of the circular table.

The Mathematics Reference Sheet shows the formula for the area of a circle is $A = \pi r^2$. You are given that the diameter of the circular table is 4 feet. The radius is half the diameter, or 2 feet.

$A = \pi r^2 = \pi (2 \text{ ft})^2 = 3.14(4 \text{ ft}^2) = 12.56 \text{ ft}^2$

Step 3. Find the difference between the two areas.

$13.5 \text{ ft}^2 - 12.56 \text{ ft}^2 = 0.94 \text{ ft}^2$

The area of the circular table will be 0.94 ft² less than the area of the rectangular table, Choice **A**.

Did I answer the question? Yes, I found how much less the area of the circular table will be than the area of the rectangular table. ✓

Does my answer make sense? Yes. ✓

Is the answer stated in the correct units? Yes, the units are square feet, which is correct. ✓

Choice **B** is the area of the circular table, not the difference in the two areas. Choice **C** is the sum of the two areas, not the difference. Choice **D** results if you use 4 feet for the radius in finding the area of the circular table.

12. B. Choice **B** is the correct response. First, sketch a diagram to illustrate the problem:

$P = 50$ ft

$A = ?$ 7 ft

$l = ?$

Analyze the problem. The garden has a rectangular shape. The Mathematics Reference Sheet shows the formula for the area of a rectangle is $A = lw$. You are given that the width of the garden is 7 feet, but you do not know the length of the garden. You will need to find the length of the garden before you can find its area. Two steps are needed to solve the problem: First, find the length of the garden using the information given about its perimeter. Then, find the area of the garden using the formula $A = lw$.

Step 1. Find the length of the garden.

The formula for the perimeter of a rectangle is $P = 2l + 2w$. The perimeter, P, is 50 feet. The width, w, is 7 feet. Let l equal the length of the rectangle in feet.

$P = 2l + 2w$	
$50 \text{ ft} = 2l + 2(7 \text{ ft})$	Substitute 50 ft for P and 7 ft for w. Solve for l, omitting the units for convenience.
$50 = 2l + 14$	Multiply $2(7) = 14$.
$50 - 14 = 2l + 14 - 14$	Subtract 14 from both sides of the equation.
$36 = 2l$	Simplify
$\dfrac{36}{2} = \dfrac{2l}{2}$	Divide both sides of the equation by 2.
$18 = l$	

The length of the rectangle is 18 feet.

Step 2. Find the area of the rectangular garden.

$A = lw = 18 \text{ ft} \cdot 7 \text{ ft} = 126 \text{ ft}^2$

The area of the garden is 126 ft², Choice **B**.

Did I answer the question? Yes, I found the area of the garden. ✓

Does my answer make sense? Yes. ✓

Is the answer stated in the correct units? Yes, the units are square feet, which is correct. ✓

Choice **A** results if you stop at Step 1 and incorrectly use your solution to the equation as the area of the garden. Choice **C** results if you mistakenly confuse perimeter with area. Choice **D** results if you incorrectly compute the area of the garden by multiplying 50 feet by 7 feet.

13. B. Choice **B** is the correct response. First, sketch a diagram to illustrate the problem:

18 ft

22 ft

Analyze the problem. Square yards are units of area, so you will need to find the area of the carpet in square yards. Two steps are needed to solve the problem: First, convert the dimensions of the floor to yards. Next, find the area of the floor in square yards.

Step 1. Convert the dimensions of the floor to yards.

The Mathematics Reference Sheet shows 1 yard = 3 feet. Therefore, the conversion fractions are $\frac{3 \text{ ft}}{1 \text{ yd}}$ or $\frac{1 \text{ yd}}{3 \text{ ft}}$.

Write each dimension of the floor as a fraction with denominator 1 and let unit analysis tell you whether to multiply by $\frac{3 \text{ ft}}{1 \text{ yd}}$ or $\frac{1 \text{ yd}}{3 \text{ ft}}$. Since you want the feet to divide out, multiply by $\frac{1 \text{ yd}}{3 \text{ ft}}$.

$$\frac{22 \text{ ft}}{1} \cdot \frac{1 \text{ yd}}{3 \text{ ft}} = \frac{22 \cancel{\text{ ft}}}{1} \cdot \frac{1 \text{ yd}}{3 \cancel{\text{ ft}}} = \frac{22 \text{ yd}}{3} = 7\frac{1}{3} \text{ yd}$$

$$\frac{18 \text{ ft}}{1} \cdot \frac{1 \text{ yd}}{3 \text{ ft}} = \frac{\cancel{18}^{6} \cancel{\text{ ft}}}{1} \cdot \frac{1 \text{ yd}}{\cancel{3}_{1} \cancel{\text{ ft}}} = 6 \text{ yd}$$

Step 2. Find the area of the floor.

The Mathematics Reference Sheet shows the formula for the area of a rectangle is $A = lw$.

$$A = lw = \left(7\frac{1}{3} \text{ yd}\right)(6 \text{ yd}) = \left(\frac{22}{3} \text{ yd}\right)\left(\frac{6}{1} \text{ yd}\right) = \left(\frac{22}{\cancel{3}_{1}} \text{ yd}\right)\left(\frac{\cancel{6}^{2}}{1} \text{ yd}\right) = 44 \text{ yd}^2$$

At least 44 yd² of carpet are needed to cover the floor, Choice **B**.

Did I answer the question? Yes, I found how many square yards of carpet are needed to cover the floor. ✓

Does my answer make sense? Yes. ✓

Is the answer stated in the correct units? Yes, the units are square yards, which is correct. ✓

Choices **A** and **D** result if you make a computation error. Choice **C** results if you neglect to convert your dimensions to yards.

14. **D.** Choice **D** is the correct response. First, sketch a diagram to illustrate the problem:

4 in.

Two steps are needed to solve the problem: First, find the volume of one 4-inch cube. Then, find the volume of the crate by multiplying the volume of one 4-inch cube by 81.

Step 1. Find the volume of one 4-inch cube.

The Mathematics Reference Sheet shows the formula for the volume of a prism is $V = Bh$, where B is the area of the base of the prism and h is the height. A cube is a prism in which all edges have the same length. A 4-inch cube has a square base that is 4 inches on a side and the height of the cube is 4 inches. The volume of the 4-inch cube is

$$V_{\text{cube}} = Bh = s \cdot s \cdot h = 4 \text{ in} \cdot 4 \text{ in} \cdot 4 \text{ in} = 64 \text{ in}^3$$

Tip: It might be easier for you to just memorize that the volume of a cube is $V = s^3$, where s is the length of an edge of the cube.

Step 2. Find the volume of the crate.

It takes 81 cubes to fill the crate, so the volume of the crate is

$V_{\text{crate}} = 81 \cdot (\text{volume of one cube}) = 81 \cdot 64 \text{ in}^3 = 5{,}184 \text{ in}^3$, Choice **D**.

Did I answer the question? Yes, I found the volume of the crate. ✓

Does my answer make sense? Yes. ✓

Is the answer stated in the correct units? Yes, the units are cubic inches, which is correct. ✓

Choice **A** results if you stop at Step 1 and mistakenly use the volume of one 4-inch cube as the volume of the crate. Choice **B** results if you mistakenly use the number of cubes in the crate as its volume in cubic inches. Choice **C** results if you make a computation error in Step 2.

15. **B.** Choice **B** is the correct response. First, sketch a diagram to illustrate the problem:

The Mathematics Reference Sheet shows the formula for the volume of a cylinder is $V = Bh$, where B is the area of the base of the cylinder and h is the height. The base of the cylinder is a circle. The Mathematics Reference Sheet shows the area of a circle is πr^2. The diameter of the cylinder is 8 feet. The radius of the circle is half the diameter, or 4 feet. The volume of the cylinder is

$V = Bh = \pi r^2 h = 3.14(4 \text{ ft})^2 \cdot 1.8 \text{ ft} = 90.432 \text{ ft}^3$

The volume of the cube is approximately 90 ft³, Choice **B**.

Choices **A** and **C** result if you use an incorrect formula for the volume of a cylinder. Choice **D** results if you make the error of using 8 feet instead of 4 feet as the radius of the cylinder's base.

16. **A.** Choice **A** is the correct response. First, sketch a diagram to illustrate the problem:

Analyze the problem. Cubic feet are units of volume. The amount of cement in the slab is equal to the volume of the slab, which is a rectangular prism. Two steps are needed to solve the problem: First, convert 4 inches to feet because the question asks for the number of cubic feet of cement. Then, find the volume of the slab in cubic feet.

Step 1. Convert 4 inches to feet.

The Mathematics Reference Sheet shows 3 feet = 36 inches. You can write this fact as $\frac{3 \text{ ft}}{36 \text{ in}}$ and reduce to obtain $\frac{1 \text{ ft}}{12 \text{ in}}$ as one of your conversion fractions and $\frac{12 \text{ in}}{1 \text{ ft}}$ as your other conversion fraction.

Write your measurement as a fraction with denominator 1 and let unit analysis tell you whether to multiply by $\frac{1\text{ ft}}{12\text{ in}}$ or $\frac{12\text{ in}}{1\text{ ft}}$. Since you want the inches to divide out, multiply by $\frac{1\text{ ft}}{12\text{ in}}$.

$$\frac{4\text{ in}}{1}\cdot\frac{1\text{ ft}}{12\text{ in}}=\frac{\overset{1}{\cancel{4}}\text{ in}}{1}\cdot\frac{1\text{ ft}}{\underset{3}{\cancel{12}}\text{ in}}=\frac{1}{3}\text{ ft}$$

Step 2. Find the volume of the slab.

The Mathematics Reference Sheet shows the formula for the volume of a prism is $V = Bh$, where B is the area of the base of the prism and h is the height. The base of the prism is a rectangle. The Mathematics Reference Sheet shows the formula for the area of a rectangle is $A = lw$. The volume of the cement is

$$V = Bh = l\cdot w\cdot h = (12.5\text{ ft})(9\text{ ft})\left(\frac{1}{3}\text{ ft}\right)=(12.5\text{ ft})(\overset{3}{\cancel{9}}\text{ ft})\left(\frac{1}{\underset{1}{\cancel{3}}}\text{ ft}\right)= 37.5\text{ ft}^3$$

Tip: It might be easier for you to just memorize that the volume of a rectangular prism is $V = lwh$, where l is the length, w is the width, and h is the height of the rectangular prism.

There are 37.5 ft³ of cement in the slab, Choice **A**.

Did I answer the question? Yes, I found how many cubic feet of cement are in the slab. ✓

Does my answer make sense? Yes. ✓

Is the answer stated in the correct units? Yes, the units are cubic feet, which is correct. ✓

Choice **B** results if you use an incorrect formula for the volume of a rectangular prism. Choice **C** results if you fail to change 4 inches to $\frac{1}{3}$ feet. Choice **D** results if you place the decimal point incorrectly when computing the volume.

17. D. Choice **D** is the correct response. Sketch and label the dimensions on the diagram:

5-inch squares are cut out on each corner.

Two steps are needed to solve the problem: First, use the diagram to find the dimensions of the box in inches. Next, find the volume of the box in cubic inches.

Step 1. Find the dimensions of the box.

From the preceding diagram, you can see that the length of the box is 25 in –2(5 in) = 25 in – 10 in = 15 in. The width of the box is 15 in – 10 in = 5 in. The height of the box is 5 inches.

Step 2. Find the volume of the box.

The box is a rectangular prism. The Mathematics Reference Sheet shows the formula for the volume of a prism is $V = Bh$, where B is the area of the base of the prism and h is the height. The base of the prism is a rectangle. The Mathematics Reference Sheet shows the formula for the area of a rectangle is $A = lw$. The volume of the box is

$$V = Bh = lw \cdot h = 15 \text{ in} \cdot 5 \text{ in} \cdot 5 \text{ in} = 375 \text{ in}^3$$

Tip: It might be easier for you to just memorize that the volume of a rectangular prism is $V = lwh$, where l is the length, w is the width, and h is the height of the rectangular prism.

The volume of the box is 375 in³, Choice **D**.

Did I answer the question? Yes, I found the volume of the box. ✓

Does my answer make sense? Yes. ✓

Is the answer stated in the correct units? Yes, the units are cubic inches, which is correct. ✓

The other choices result if you determine incorrect measurements for the dimensions of the box.

18. **D.** Choice **D** is the correct response. First, sketch a diagram to illustrate the problem. Of course, you can't draw it exactly to scale, but the sketch will help you "see" the situation:

scale: 9 ft = 1 in.
d
90 ft

Let d = the distance between bases in the scale model. The scale model and the baseball diamond can be represented with two squares. The squares are similar figures, so the measurements of their corresponding sides are proportional. Write a proportion and solve it.

The ratio of the distance between bases in the actual baseball diamond to the distance between bases in the model is $\frac{9 \text{ ft}}{1 \text{ in}}$

$$\frac{\text{distance between bases of actual baseball diamond}}{\text{distance between bases in model}} = \frac{9 \text{ ft}}{1 \text{ in}}$$

Plug in the values from your diagram. Be sure to check that the units match up correctly.

$$\frac{90 \text{ ft}}{d \, (\text{in})} = \frac{9 \text{ ft}}{1 \text{ in}} \qquad \text{Check: Both ratios have feet in the numerator and inches in the denominator.}$$

For convenience, omit the units while you solve the proportion:

$$\frac{90}{d} = \frac{9}{1}$$

Multiply 90 by 1 and then divide by 9:

$$\frac{90 \cdot 1}{9} = 10 \text{ in}$$

The distance between bases in the scale model is 10 inches, Choice **D**.

Did I answer the question? Yes, I found the distance between bases in the scale model. ✓

Does my answer make sense? Yes. ✓

Is the answer stated in the correct units? Yes, the units are inches, which is correct. ✓

Choices **A** and **B** result if you make a computation error when solving the proportion. Choice **C** results if you set up the proportion incorrectly.

19. **D.** Choice **D** is the correct response. Three conversion facts from the Mathematics Reference Sheet are needed to solve the problem:

1 pint = 2 cups, 1 quart = 2 pints, and 1 gallon = 4 quarts. From these three facts, you get six conversion fractions:

$$\frac{1 \text{ pt}}{2 \text{ c}} \text{ and } \frac{2 \text{ c}}{1 \text{ pt}}, \frac{1 \text{ qt}}{2 \text{ pt}} \text{ and } \frac{2 \text{ pt}}{1 \text{ qt}}, \text{ and } \frac{1 \text{ gal}}{4 \text{ qt}} \text{ and } \frac{4 \text{ qt}}{1 \text{ gal}}.$$

Write your measurement as a fraction with denominator 1 and let unit analysis tell you which conversion fractions to multiply by, keeping in mind that you want cups as your final units: $\frac{5 \text{ gal}}{1}$? There are only two conversion fractions that involve gallons: $\frac{1 \text{ gal}}{4 \text{ qt}}$ and $\frac{4 \text{ qt}}{1 \text{ gal}}$. Since you want the gallons to divide out, multiply by $\frac{4 \text{ qt}}{1 \text{ gal}}$.

$$\frac{5 \ \cancel{\text{gal}}}{1} \cdot \frac{4 \text{ qt}}{\cancel{\text{gal}}}$$

This product has quarts as the units. You want to have cups as the units, but there is no conversion fraction that involves quarts and cups, so change quarts to pints by multiplying by $\frac{2 \text{ pt}}{1 \text{ qt}}$:

$$\frac{5 \ \cancel{\text{gal}}}{1} \cdot \frac{4 \ \cancel{\text{qt}}}{\cancel{\text{gal}}} \cdot \frac{2 \text{ pt}}{\cancel{\text{qt}}}$$

Now the product has pints as the units because both gallons and quarts divide out.

To change the pints to cups, multiply by $\frac{2 \text{ c}}{1 \text{ pt}}$:

$$\frac{5 \ \cancel{\text{gal}}}{1} \cdot \frac{4 \ \cancel{\text{qt}}}{\cancel{\text{gal}}} \cdot \frac{2 \ \cancel{\text{pt}}}{\cancel{\text{qt}}} \cdot \frac{2 \text{ c}}{\cancel{\text{pt}}} = 80 \text{ cups}$$

The final answer is in cups because gallons, quarts, and pints divide out when you do the multiplication.

A 5-gallon container of water holds 80 cups of water, Choice **D**. The other answer choices occur if you use incorrect conversion facts or fractions.

Did I answer the question? Yes, I found the number of cups in a 5-gallon container of water. ✓

Does my answer make sense? Yes. ✓

Is the answer stated in the correct units? Yes, the units are cups, which is correct. ✓

20. **B.** Choice **B** is the correct response.

Method 1: Use the conversion fact, 1 kilometer = 1000 meters, from the Mathematics Reference Sheet to obtain two conversion fractions: $\frac{1 \text{ km}}{1000 \text{ m}}$ and $\frac{1000 \text{ m}}{1 \text{ km}}$.

Write your measurement as a fraction with denominator 1 and let unit analysis tell you whether to multiply by $\frac{1 \text{ km}}{1000 \text{ m}}$ or $\frac{1000 \text{ m}}{1 \text{ km}}$. Since you want the meters to divide out, multiply by $\frac{1 \text{ km}}{1000 \text{ m}}$.

$$\frac{12,500 \text{ m}}{1} \cdot \frac{1 \text{ km}}{1000 \text{ m}} = \frac{12,500 \ \cancel{\text{m}}}{1} \cdot \frac{1 \text{ km}}{1000 \ \cancel{\text{m}}} = \frac{12,500 \text{ km}}{1000} = 12.5 \text{ km}$$

Method 2: Use "**K**ing **H**enry **D**oesn't **U**sually **D**rink **C**hocolate **M**ilk," which is a mnemonic for remembering the following metric prefixes:

kilo-, hecto-, deca-, unit measurement, deci-, centi-, milli-

In this problem, the unit measurement is meters. You are going from meters to kilometers. Since to go from meters to kilometers you move left three times on the list above, you will divide by 10 three times to convert meters to kilometers. Of course, dividing by 10 three times is equivalent to dividing by 1000 one time. Therefore,

12,500 m = 12,500 ÷ 1000 (3 moves left) = 12.5 km

The runner ran 12.5 kilometers in the race, Choice **B**.

The other choices occur if you make a mistake in placing the decimal point in your answer.

21. **B.** Choice **B** is the correct response. Mentally construct a box at *B* to represent a right angle.

An obtuse angle measures more than 90° but less than 180°. The angle *B* is greater than 90° but less than 180°. It is obtuse, Choice **B**. An acute angle (**Choice A**) measures more than 0° but less than 90°. A right angle (**Choice C**) measures exactly 90°. A straight angle (**Choice D**) measures exactly 180°.

22. **D.** Choice **D** is the correct response. The sum of the measures of the three interior angles of a triangle always equals 180°. Check the answer choices to find the one that satisfies this requirement.

Checking **A**: 30° + 50° + 80° = 160° ≠ 180°, wrong.

Checking **B**: You should eliminate this choice by sight since 100° + 200° = 300° > 180°.

Checking **C**: 120° + 50° + 20° = 190° ≠ 180°, wrong.

Checking **D**: 40° + 50° + 90° = 180°, correct.

23. **D.** Choice **D** is the correct response. The Mathematics Reference Sheet shows the circumference of a circle is equal to the product of π and the diameter of the circle: $C = \pi d$. To find the diameter, plug in 48 inches for *C* and 3.14 for π and solve for *d*:

$$C = \pi d$$

$$48 \text{ in} = 3.14d$$

$$\frac{48 \text{ in}}{3.14} = \frac{3.14d}{3.14} \qquad \text{Divide both sides of the equation by 3.14.}$$

15.29 in. (approximately) = *d*, Choice **D**.

Choices **A** and **B** result if you solve the equation incorrectly. Choice **C** results if you use an incorrect formula for the circumference of a circle.

24. **B.** Choice **B** is the correct response. The coordinates of point *P* are (−3, 2). The *x*-coordinate of the new point is 5 units to the right of −3. The number 2 is 5 units to the right of −3. The *x*-coordinate of the new point is 2. The *y*-coordinate of point *P* is 2. The *y*-coordinate of the new point is 6 units down from point *P*. The number −4 is 6 units down from 2. The *y*-coordinate of the new point is −4. The coordinates of the new point are (2, −4), Choice **B**. Choice **A** occurs if you calculate the new *y*-coordinate incorrectly. Choice **C** occurs if you calculate both new coordinates incorrectly. Choice **D** occurs if you calculate the *x*-coordinate incorrectly.

25. **A.** Choice **A** is the correct response. Examine the diagram. Note that $\overline{AB} \parallel \overline{DC}$ means $\overline{AB}$ is parallel to $\overline{DC}$, and $\overline{AD} \parallel \overline{BC}$ means $\overline{AD}$ is parallel to $\overline{BC}$.

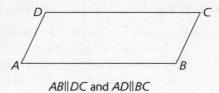

AB‖DC and AD‖BC

A parallelogram is a quadrilateral that has opposite sides parallel. The figure shown is a parallelogram, Choice **A**. Choices **B** and **C** are incorrect because rectangles and squares are parallelograms that have four right interior angles. The figure does not indicate that the angles in the figure are right angles. Choice **D** is incorrect because a trapezoid is a quadrilateral in which only one pair of opposite sides is parallel.

26. **A.** Choice **A** is the correct response. A figure has a horizontal line of symmetry if it can be folded horizontally into two congruent halves. A figure has a vertical line of symmetry if it can be folded vertically into two congruent halves. The letter **H** is the only letter shown that has both a vertical and a horizontal line of symmetry, Choice **A**. Choices **B** and **C** are incorrect because the letters **A** and **W** have vertical lines of symmetry, but not horizontal lines of symmetry. Choice **D** is incorrect because the letter **N** does not have a line of symmetry.

27. **B.** Choice **B** is the correct response. First, sketch a diagram to illustrate the problem:

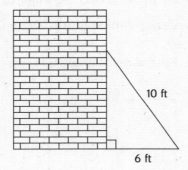

10 ft

6 ft

Analyze the problem. Since the ladder and the wall of the building form a right triangle, use the Pythagorean Theorem to find the length of the missing side. Let b represent the distance from the base of the wall to the top of the ladder. This distance is the length of the missing leg of the right triangle. The length (10 feet) of the ladder is the length of the hypotenuse, c, of the right triangle. The length of the known leg, a, of the triangle is 6 feet. Substitute these values into the Pythagorean Theorem, omitting the units for convenience:

$$a^2 + b^2 = c^2$$

$$6^2 + b^2 = 10^2$$

$$36 + b^2 = 100$$

$$36 + b^2 - 36 = 100 - 36 \qquad \text{Subtract 36 from both sides.}$$

$b^2 = 64$; because $b^2 = 64$, to find b, you must think of a number that multiplies by itself to give 64.

Since $8 \cdot 8 = 64$, $b = 8$ ft

Note: You will find a list of square roots in the section titled "Numeration and Operations" in Chapter 3.

The ladder reaches 8 feet up the wall, Choice **B**.

Did I answer the question? Yes, I found how high up the side of the building the ladder reaches. ✓

Does my answer make sense? Yes. ✓

Is the answer stated in the correct units? Yes, the units are feet, which is correct. ✓

Choice **A** results if you mistakenly decide to solve the problem by finding the difference between the lengths of the hypotenuse and the known leg to find the length of the missing leg. Choice **C** results if you mistakenly use the length of the hypotenuse as the length of the unknown leg. Choice **D** results if you mistakenly decide to solve the problem by adding the lengths of the hypotenuse and known leg to find the length of the missing leg.

28. A. Choice **A** is the correct response.

Since *ABCDE* and *LMNOP* are regular pentagons, they are similar figures. In similar figures, corresponding sides are proportional. The ratio of proportionality of the sides of *ABCDE* to *LMNOP* is $\frac{12 \text{ units}}{6 \text{ units}} = \frac{2}{1}$. In other words, the length of each side of *ABCDE* is twice the length of its corresponding side in *LMNOP*. The scale factor is 2. Therefore, the ratio of the perimeter of *ABCDE* to *LMNOP* $= \frac{5(12 \text{ units})}{5(6 \text{ units})} = \frac{2}{1}$ or 2:1, Choice **A**.

29. C. Choice **C** is the correct response. First, sketch a diagram to illustrate the problem:

The television screen can be modeled by a 16-inch by 12-inch rectangle. The diagonal divides the rectangle into two right triangles, with legs 16 inches and 12 inches in length. The diagonal is opposite the right angle, so it is the hypotenuse of the right triangle. Use the Pythagorean Theorem to find the length of the diagonal. Let *c* represent the diagonal. Substitute 16 for *a* and 12 for *b* into the formula and solve for *c*:

$c^2 = a^2 + b^2$

$c^2 = (16)^2 + (12)^2$

$c^2 = 256 + 144$

$c^2 = 400$

Because $c^2 = 400$, to find *c*, you must think of a number that multiplies by itself to give 400.

Since $20 \cdot 20 = 400$, $c = 20$ in.

Note: You will find a list of square roots in the section titled "Numeration and Operations" in Chapter 3.

The television has a 20-inch screen, Choice **C**.

Did I answer the question? Yes, I found the size of the television screen. ✓

Does my answer make sense? Yes. ✓

Is the answer stated in the correct units? Yes, the units are inches, which is correct. ✓

Choice **A** is the incorrect result of using the width of the television as its size. Choice **B** is the incorrect result of using the length of the television as its size. Choice **D** is the incorrect result of using the sum of the length and width of the television as its size.

30. **A.** Choice **A** is the correct response. To solve the problem, you must answer the question: 108 is r% of 120?

Method 1: To solve the problem, identify the elements of the percent problem, plug the values into the percent proportion, and solve the proportion:

Step 1. Identify the elements.

$$r = ?$$
$$\text{part} = 108$$
$$\text{whole} = 120$$

Step 2. Plug into the percent proportion (omitting the units for convenience).

$$\frac{r}{100} = \frac{108}{120}$$

Step 3. Solve the proportion.

Multiply 108 by 100 (a cross product you can calculate), and then divide by 120 (the numerical term you didn't use):

$$r = \frac{108 \cdot 100}{120} = 90$$

Thus, $r\% = 90\%$

Of the 120 fans at the game, 90% were players' parents, Choice **A**.

Did I answer the question? Yes, I found the percent of the fans who were players' parents. ✓

Does my answer make sense? Yes. ✓

Is the answer stated in the correct units? No units are needed for the answer. ✓

Method 2: Write an equation and solve it:

Let $R = r\%$

$108 = R$ times 120   Hint: The word "of" is "times" when it occurs between two numbers.

$108 = R \cdot 120$

For convenience, you should rewrite the expression on the right of the equation as $120R$:

$108 = 120R$

You are solving for R, so divide both sides of the equation by 120, the coefficient of R:

$$\frac{108}{120} = \frac{120R}{120}$$

$$0.9 = R$$

Change 0.9 to a percent by moving the decimal point two places to the right and adding a percent sign:

$R = 90\%$, Choice **A**.

Choices **B** and **D** result if you make a decimal point mistake. Choice **C** is the percent of fans who were not players' parents.

31. **B.** Choice **B** is the correct response. Sketch the diagram. Draw a line segment connecting the points $T(5, -2)$ and $U(3, 2)$. Mark the midpoint of the line segment.

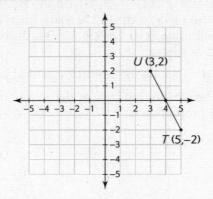

The Mathematics Reference Sheet gives the formula for the midpoint between two points (x_1, y_1) and (x_2, y_2) as $\left(\dfrac{x_1 + x_2}{2}, \dfrac{y_1 + y_2}{2}\right)$. To find the midpoint between $(5, -2)$ and $(3, 2)$, let $x_1 = 5$, $y_1 = -2$, $x_2 = 3$, and $y_2 = 2$. Then plug into the formula:

$$\text{Midpoint} = \left(\frac{x_1 + x_2}{2}, \frac{y_1 + y_2}{2}\right) = \left(\frac{5+3}{2}, \frac{-2+2}{2}\right) = \left(\frac{8}{2}, \frac{0}{2}\right) = (4, 0)$$

The midpoint between the points T and U has coordinates $(4, 0)$, Choice **B**. Choice **A** results if you switch the x and y values. Choices **C** and **D** result if you make an error in computing the coordinates for the midpoint.

32. **A.** Choice **A** is the correct response. Substitute into the expression, being sure to enclose the substituted values in parentheses:

$x - y = (-5) - (-13) = -5 + 13 = 8$, Choice **A**.

Choice **B** occurs if you make a sign error. Choices **C** and **D** result if you deal with the subtraction incorrectly.

33. **A.** Choice **A** is the correct response. Sketch the diagram. Draw a line segment connecting the points $R(2, -2)$ and $S(3, 4)$.

The Mathematics Reference Sheet gives the formula for the distance between two points (x_1, y_1) and (x_2, y_2) as $\sqrt{(x_2 - x_1)^2 + (y_2 - y_1)^2}$. To find the distance between $(2, -2)$ and $(3, 4)$, let $x_1 = 2$, $y_1 = -2$, $x_2 = 3$, and $y_2 = 4$. Then plug into the formula:

$$\text{Distance} = \sqrt{(x_2 - x_1)^2 + (y_2 - y_1)^2} = \sqrt{(2-3)^2 + (-2-4)^2} = \sqrt{(-1)^2 + (-6)^2} = \sqrt{1 + 36} = \sqrt{37}$$

The distance between the points R and S is $\sqrt{37}$ units, Choice **A**.

Choices **B**, **C**, and **D** result if you make a computation error.

34. D. Choice **D** is the correct response. Write an equation and solve it.

The statement 4 less than 5 times x is 6 is written symbolically as $5x - 4 = 6$.

$$5x - 4 = 6$$

$5x - 4 + 4 = 6 + 4$	Add 4 to both sides of the equation.
$5x = 10$	Then simplify.
$\dfrac{5x}{5} = \dfrac{10}{5}$	Divide both sides of the equation by 5.
$x = 2$, Choice **D**.	Then simplify.

Check to see whether your answer makes the statement true. Is 4 less than 5 times 2 equal to 6? Yes, because 4 less than 10 is 6.

Choice **A** occurs if you make a sign error. Choice **B** occurs if you write 4 less than 5 times x as $4 - 5x$. Choice **C** occurs if you translate incorrectly and make a simplification error.

35. B. Choice **B** is the correct response.

$-2x - 5 = 3x + 15$	
$-2x - 5 - 3x = 3x + 15 - 3x$	Subtract $3x$ from both sides of the equation.
$-5x - 5 = 15$	Then simplify.
$-5x - 5 + 5 = 15 + 5$	Add 5 to both sides of the equation.
$-5x = 20$	Then simplify.
$\dfrac{-5x}{-5} = \dfrac{20}{-5}$	Divide both sides of the equation by -5.
$x = -4$, Choice **B**.	Then simplify.

Check your answer by substituting -4 for x into the equation:

$$-2x - 5 = 3x + 15$$
$$-2(-4) - 5 \overset{?}{=} 3(-4) + 15$$
$$8 - 5 \overset{?}{=} -12 + 15$$

$3 = 3$	correct

Choice **A** is incorrect because substituting -20 for x in the equation gives:

$$-2x - 5 = 3x + 15$$
$$-2(-20) - 5 \overset{?}{=} 3(-20) + 15$$
$$40 - 5 \overset{?}{=} -60 + 15$$
$$35 \neq -45$$

Choice **C** is incorrect because substituting 2 for x in the equation gives:

$$-2x - 5 = 3x + 15$$
$$-2(2) - 5 \overset{?}{=} 3(2) + 15$$
$$-4 - 5 \overset{?}{=} 6 + 15$$
$$-9 \neq 21$$

Choice **D** is incorrect because substituting 4 for x in the equation gives:

$$-2x - 5 = 3x + 15$$
$$-2(4) - 5 \overset{?}{=} 3(4) + 15$$
$$-8 - 5 \overset{?}{=} 12 + 15$$
$$-13 \neq 27$$

Another way to work this problem is to check the answer choices rather than solve the equation—a smart test-taking strategy for multiple-choice math tests. Substitute each answer choice into the equation as shown above, and whichever choice makes the equation a true statement is the correct response.

36. **A.** Choice **A** is the correct response. To determine which ordered pair satisfies the system, you will need to find the ordered pair that makes *both* equations true. Check each ordered pair by substituting the x and y values into the two equations, being careful to enclose the substituted values in parentheses.

Checking **A**: $x + 2y = (5) + 2(-3) = 5 + -6 = -1$ ✓. Since $(5,-3)$ works in the first equation, try it in the second equation. $3x - 4y = 3(5) - 4(-3) = 15 + 12 = 27$ ✓. Choice **A** is the correct response because the ordered pair $(5,-3)$ makes both equations true.

It is not necessary to check the other choices since you know that Choice **A** is the correct response.

Choice **B** is incorrect because $x + 2y = (-3) + 2(-5) = -3 + -10 = -13 \neq -1$.

Choice **C** is incorrect because $x + 2y = (-5) + 2(3) = -5 + 6 = 1 \neq -1$.

Choice **D** is incorrect because $x + 2y = (3) + 2(5) = 3 + 10 = 13 \neq -1$.

37. **B.** Choice **B** is the correct response. Sketch the diagram. Draw a line connecting the points $T(4, -3)$ and $U(1, 2)$.

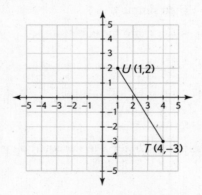

From the diagram, you can see that the line slopes downward from left to right, indicating that the slope is negative; therefore, you can eliminate Choice **D**.

The Mathematics Reference Sheet gives the formula for the slope of the line between two points (x_1, y_1) and (x_2, y_2) as $\frac{y_2 - y_1}{x_2 - x_1}$. To find the slope of the line between $(4, -3)$ and $(1, 2)$, let $x_1 = 4$, $y_1 = -3$, $x_2 = 1$, and $y_2 = 2$. Then plug into the formula (*Hint:* Enclose negative values in parentheses.):

$$\text{Slope} = \frac{y_2 - y_1}{x_2 - x_1} = \frac{2 - (-3)}{1 - 4} = \frac{2 + 3}{-3} = \frac{5}{-3} = -\frac{5}{3}, \text{ Choice } \mathbf{B}.$$

Choice **A** occurs if you make the mistake of putting the difference in the x values in the numerator and the difference in the y values in the denominator. Choice **C** results if you subtract incorrectly. Choice **D** results if you make a sign error.

38. **D.** Choice **D** is the correct response. Rewrite the expression using parentheses for x:

$$3(\ )^3 - (\ )^2 + 5$$

Plug 2 inside the parentheses and evaluate, being sure to follow PE(MD)(AS):

$3(2)^3 - (2)^2 + 5 = 3 \cdot 8 - 4 + 5$	There are no operations to do in parentheses, so first do the exponentiation.

Hint: The term $3(2)^3$ is not 6^3. Also, do not square the $-$ sign in $-(2)^2$. Remember, an exponent applies only to the number immediately to its left.

$= 24 - 4 + 5$	Next, do multiplication and division, from left to right.
$= 25$	Finally, do addition and subtraction, from left to right.

Thus, $3(2)^3 - (2)^2 + 5 = 25$, Choice **D**.

Choice **A** occurs if you incorrectly evaluate by squaring the $-$ sign before $(2)^2$ and multiplying 3 times 2 in $3(2)^3$ before applying the exponent. Choice **B** occurs if you make the mistake of multiplying 3 times 2 in $3(2)^3$ before applying the exponent. Choice **C** occurs if you square the $-$ sign before $(2)^2$.

39. **D.** Choice **D** is the correct response.

$4(x - 8) = 24$	
$4x - 32 = 24$	Use the distributive property to remove parentheses. Be sure to multiply the 8 by 4, too.
$4x - 32 + 32 = 24 + 32$	Add 32 to both sides of the equation.
$4x = 56$	Then simplify.
$\dfrac{4x}{4} = \dfrac{56}{4}$	Divide both sides of the equation by 4.
$x = 14$, Choice **D**.	Then simplify.

Choice **A** results if you subtract 32 from both sides of $4x - 32 = 24$, instead of adding 32. Choice **B** results if you fail to remove the parentheses correctly and you make a subtraction error. Choice **C** results if you obtain $4x - 8$ when removing the parentheses in $4(x - 8)$, instead of $4x - 32$.

40. **C.** Choice **C** is the correct response.

From the pie chart, you can see that 25% of the monthly salary is budgeted for food. To answer the question, you must find 25% of $2,800.

Method 1: Identify the elements of the percent problem, plug the values into the percent proportion, and solve the proportion:

Step 1. Identify the elements.

$r = 25$

part = ?

whole = $2800

Step 2. Plug into the percent proportion (omitting the units for convenience)

$$\frac{25}{100} = \frac{x}{2800}$$

Step 3. Solve the proportion.

Multiply 25 times 2800 (a cross product you can calculate), and then divide by 100 (the numerical term you didn't use):

$$x = \frac{25 \cdot 2800}{100} = 700$$

The amount budgeted for food is $700, Choice **C**.

Did I answer the question? Yes, I found the amount budgeted for food. ✓

Does my answer make sense? Yes. ✓

Is the answer stated in the correct units? Yes, the units are dollars, which is correct. ✓

Method 2: Change 25% to a decimal fraction or common fraction and multiply:

25% of $2800 = 0.25 × $2800 = $700.00; or

25% of $2500 = $\frac{1}{4} \cdot \$2800 = \frac{\$2800}{4} = \$700$, Choice **C**.

Choice **A** results if you make a calculation error. Choice **B** results if you solve the problem incorrectly by finding 12.5% of $2,800. Choice **D** results if you solve the problem incorrectly by finding 37.5% of $2,800.

41. **D.** Choice **D** is the correct response. You should eliminate Choice **C** immediately because probabilities cannot be greater than 1. Probabilities are always greater than or equal to 0 and less than or equal to 1. This is an independent events probability problem because the outcome of the first spin has no effect on the outcome of the second spin. To find the probability of spinning red on the first spin and green on the second spin will take three steps: First, find the probability of red on the 1st spin; next, find the probability of green on the 2nd spin; and then multiply the probabilities of these two events: P(red on 1st spin) · P(green on 2nd spin).

Step 1. Find the probability of spinning red on the 1st spin.

There are 4 red sections on the spinner, out of a total of 10 sections: $P(\text{red}) = \frac{4}{10} = \frac{2}{5}$

Step 2. Find the probability of spinning green on the 2nd spin.

There is 1 green section on the spinner, out of a total of 10 sections: $P(\text{green on 2}^{nd}\text{spin}) = \frac{1}{10}$

Step 3. To find the probability of spinning red on the 1st spin and green on the 2nd spin, multiply the probabilities:

$$P(\text{red on 1}^{st}\text{ spin}) \cdot P(\text{green on 2}^{nd}\text{ spin}) = \frac{2}{5} \cdot \frac{1}{10} = \frac{2}{50} = \frac{1}{25}$$

The probability of spinning red on the first spin and green on the 2nd spin is $\frac{1}{25}$, Choice **D**.

Did I answer the question? Yes, I found the probability of spinning red on the first spin and green on the second spin. ✓

Does my answer make sense? Yes. ✓

Is the answer stated in the correct units? No units are required for the answer. ✓

Choice **A** results if you multiply the two probabilities incorrectly. Choice **B** results if you make the mistake of adding the probabilities together instead of multiplying them.

42. **D.** Choice **D** is the correct response. Read the problem carefully. What is the question?—*What is the lowest grade the student can make on the fourth test and still receive a B in the course?* Devise a plan. The average of the student's four test grades must be at least 80. This means the sum of the four test grades divided by 4 must be at least 80.

Method 1: You can find the answer by writing and solving an equation.

Let x = the lowest grade the student can make on the fourth test and still have at least an 80 average.

$$\frac{\text{sum of 4 test grades}}{4} = \frac{78 + 91 + 75 + x}{4}$$

Solve $\frac{78 + 91 + 75 + x}{4} = 80$ for x

$$\frac{244 + x}{4} = 80 \qquad \text{Simplify the numerator.}$$

$$\frac{4}{1} \cdot \frac{244 + x}{4} = 80 \cdot \frac{4}{1} \qquad \text{Multiply both sides of the equation by 4 to remove the fraction.}$$

$$244 + x = 320$$

$$244 + x - 244 = 320 - 244 \qquad \text{Subtract 244 from both sides of the equation.}$$

$$x = 76$$

The lowest grade that will yield an average of at least 80 is 76, Choice **D**.

Did I answer the question? Yes, I found the lowest grade the student can make on the fourth test and still receive a B in the course. ✓

Does my answer make sense? Yes. ✓

Is the answer stated in the correct units? No units are required for the answer. ✓

Method 2: Another way to work this problem is to check the answer choices—a smart test-taking strategy for multiple-choice math tests. However, be careful with this problem. Because you have to find the *lowest* test score that will work, you must check all the answer choices even if you find an answer choice that gives an average in the 80s.

Checking **A:** $\frac{\text{sum of 4 test grades}}{4} = \frac{78 + 91 + 75 + 99}{4} = 85.75$

Checking **B:** $\frac{\text{sum of 4 test grades}}{4} = \frac{78 + 91 + 75 + 82}{4} = 81.5$

Checking **C:** $\frac{\text{sum of 4 test grades}}{4} = \frac{78 + 91 + 75 + 80}{4} = 81.0$

Checking **D:** $\frac{\text{sum of 4 test grades}}{4} = \frac{78 + 91 + 75 + 76}{4} = 80.0$, correct because 76 is the *lowest* grade needed.

The other answer choices are too high.

43. **B.** Choice **B** is the correct response. In an ordered set of numbers, the median is the middle number if there is a middle number; otherwise, the median is the arithmetic average of the two middle numbers. Determining the median of a set of numbers is a two-step process.

Step 1. Put the running times in order from least to greatest.

61, 63, 64, 64, 66, 68, 69, 73

Step 2. Find the middle number. If there is no single middle number, average the two middle numbers.

Since there is no single middle number, average the two running times, 64 and 66, that are in the middle of the list (omitting the units for convenience).

$$\frac{64+66}{2} = \frac{130}{2} = 65$$

Mario's median running time is 65 s, Choice **B**.

Did I answer the question? Yes, I found Mario's median running time. ✓

Does my answer make sense? Yes. ✓

Is the answer stated in the correct units? Yes, the units are seconds, which is correct. ✓

Choice **A** is the mode running time. Choice **C** is the mean running time. Choice **D** results if you forget to put the running times in order first.

44. D. Choice **D** is the correct response. This problem is a counting problem. First, decide on how many tasks are involved. The students have three tasks to perform. The first task is to choose a sandwich. After that task, the second task is to select a drink. After that, the third task is to make a chip selection. The number of ways each task can occur does not depend on the outcome of the other tasks. To find the possible combinations for the three tasks, multiply the number of ways the first task can occur by the number of ways the second task can occur by the number of ways the third task can occur.

Total number of possible combinations =

(number of ways students can select a sandwich) · (number of ways students can select a drink) · (number of ways students can make a chip selection) = $4 \cdot 2 \cdot 3 = 24$ ways.

The students can select from 24 different combinations consisting of one sandwich, one drink, and one bag of chips for lunch, Choice **D**.

Did I answer the question? Yes, I found the number of possible combinations that the students can choose from for lunch. ✓

Does my answer make sense? Yes. ✓

Is the answer stated in the correct units? No units are required for the answer. ✓

Choice **A** is the number of combination consisting of one sandwich and one drink without including the chip selection. Choice **B** occurs if you add the number of ways each task can occur, instead of multiplying. Choice **C** occurs if you multiply incorrectly.

45. A. Choice **A** is the correct response. Check each answer choice to determine which statement is true.

Checking **A**: To decide which set of grades has greater variability, you can look at the range of the two sets. The range of a set of data equals the greatest value minus the least value in the set. The range in the English class is $92 - 56 = 36$. The range in the French class is $84 - 75 = 9$. Since $36 > 9$, Choice **A** is a correct statement.

You would not have to continue checking since you know that **A** is true.

Checking **B**: This choice is incorrect because 9 is not greater than 36.

Checking **C**: You have to calculate the means in the two classes.

The mean in the English class is

$$\frac{78+89+67+56+92}{5} = \frac{379}{5} = 75.8$$

The mean in the French class is

$$\frac{75+78+83+84+80+77}{6} = \frac{477}{6} = 79.5$$

Choice **C** is incorrect because the mean in the English class is not higher than the mean in the French class.

Checking **D**: This choice is incorrect because the means in the two classes are not equal.

Reading Skills

1. **A.** Choice **A** is the correct response. This passage is focused on the topic of *appropriate literature for young readers*. Choice **B** is incorrect because this topic is too general to describe the focus of this passage. Choice **C** is incorrect because it disagrees with the intent of the passage, which is to point out that young people should be encouraged to read books written specifically for young readers. Choice **D** is incorrect because this topic is too narrow to describe the focus of this passage.

2. **C.** Choice **C** is the correct response. In the third paragraph, the passage states that all humans need to escape from their everyday lives. Thus, by implication, teenagers need to escape from their everyday lives (Choice **C**). None of the other answer choices are implied in this passage.

3. **D.** Choice **D** is the correct response. In the first paragraph, the word *travail* most nearly means *tribulation* (Choice **D**), meaning "a trial of one's ability to overcome adversity." The words in the other answer choices do not mean the same as the word *travail.*

4. **B.** Choice **B** is the correct response. The main idea of the third paragraph is given by the statement in Choice **B**: *Many good books written for young readers are available.* The information in Choice **A** is given in the last sentence of the third paragraph, but it is not the main idea of the paragraph. The statement in Choice **C** could be inferred from the second sentence of the third paragraph—particularly, when considered in the context of the whole passage—however, it is not the main idea of the third paragraph. The statement in Choice **D** disagrees with the last sentence of paragraph three, so it is not the main idea of the paragraph.

5. **B.** Choice **B** is the correct response. According to this passage, Judy Blume is the author of *Are You There God? It's Me, Margaret.* (Choice **B**). The other answer choices are incorrect because according to this passage, Paula Danziger is the author of *The Cat Ate My Gymsuit* (Choice **A**), S. E. Hinton is the author of *The Outsiders* (Choice **C**), and Robert Cormier is the author of *The Chocolate War* (Choice **D**).

6. **C.** Choice **C** is the correct response. According to the passage, one way in which teenagers can be motivated to read is to provide them with high-interest, young-adult novels. This is the main idea of the reading passage. Choice **A** is incorrect because the author emphatically states that introducing nonreaders to only classical literature can be counterproductive. Choice **B** is incorrect because although the author mentions television watching as a high interest for young people, the author does not advocate television watching as a substitute for reading. Choice **D** is incorrect because the author does not discuss the value of providing teenagers with nonfiction.

7. **A.** Choice **A** is the correct response. As used in the third paragraph, the phrase "escapist fare cloaked in realistic language" best describes *fiction books.* The author of this passage is advocating that young people read books that allow them to escape into both real and imaginary worlds filled with characters and language that is intimately familiar to their own lives. Of all the answer choices, Choice **A**, *fiction books,* is the best choice. Nonfiction books (Choice **B**) are not considered "escapist fare" because nonfiction books are considered stories about actual persons, places, or events. Textbooks (Choice **C**) are not considered escapist fare, nor are autobiographies (Choice **D**). Both are incorrect choices.

8. **D.** Choice **D** is the correct response. The tone of this passage can best be described as *subjective.* The author provides a passionate yet practical argument for the use of young adult literature with adolescents. Choice **A** is incorrect because the author's tone is not caustic, meaning "biting and harsh." Choice **B** is incorrect because the author's tone is not optimistic, meaning "expectant." Choice **C** is incorrect because the author is not objective, meaning the author is "without opinion."

9. **A.** Choice **A** is the correct response. The main idea of the passage is best expressed in the sentence *young adults should be given literature that speaks to their developmental interests.* Clearly, the main idea of this narrative is that adolescents should be reading books that deal with issues and characters that relate to their age and interests. Choice **B** is incorrect because the author does not imply that the purpose of literature for young people is only to inspire good citizenship. Choice **C** is incorrect because the author does not say that young people should read books that discuss traditional family values. Choice **D** is incorrect because the author does not say young people should read only books that are universally recognized as good books.

10. A. Choice **A** is the correct response. The relationship between the two sentences in the second paragraph ("To entice young people . . . , Well intentioned as these informed advocates are . . . ") is that the second sentence clearly expands upon the material presented in the first. Choice **B** is incorrect because the second sentence clarifies the first and does not contradict it. Choice **C** is incorrect because the second sentence does not illustrate the first by providing clear examples of what young adult literature is—the names of specific examples, and so on. Choice **D** is incorrect because the second sentence does not ignore the first, but clarifies it.

11. A. Choice **A** is the correct response. A statement that is implied in the first paragraph is the statement given in Choice **A**: *Religion is an important part of people's lives.* The reader can infer this statement from the third sentence (*For the first two questions, the reasons for humankind's existence and its noble purpose, people of all races and creeds have turned to religion.*) and fourth sentence (*There, amidst ancient myths and modern realities, individuals have found great comfort and joy in the teachings and practices of many of the world's most ancient and revered religious traditions.*) of the first paragraph. The other answer choices are not supported by the information given in the first paragraph.

12. C. Choice **C** is the correct response. An opinion expressed in this passage is the statement given in Choice **C**: *We are fortunate to live in an age of intense exploration.* The word *fortunate* is a judgment word reflecting the author's opinion about living in an age of intense exploration. The word *intense* to describe the level of space exploration might also be debatable. Choice **A** is a statement of fact given in the third paragraph. Choice **B** is a statement of fact given in the third paragraph. Choice **D** is a statement of fact given in the last paragraph.

13. A. Choice **A** is the correct response. In the second paragraph, the word *unprecedented* most nearly means *unparalleled* (Choice **A**), meaning "unmatched or never achieved before." The words in the other answer choices have meanings that are opposite that of *unprecedented.*

14. B. Choice **B** is the correct response. The Challenger disaster occurred in *January 1986* (Choice **B**). This information is given in the last paragraph. The dates in the other answer choices are incorrect.

15. A. Choice **A** is the correct response. According to information given in this passage, *people seek answers to the reasons for humankind's existence* (Choice **A**). This information is given in the first paragraph of the passage. Choices **B** and **C** are incorrect because, even though these are true statements, this information is not given in the passage. Tip: Do not select answer choices based on your personal knowledge that goes beyond the information given in the passage. Choice **D** is incorrect because it disagrees with information given in the last paragraph.

16. B. Choice **B** is the correct response. In this narrative, the author speaks of *two shuttle disasters*. They occurred in 1986 and 2003. Choices **A**, **C**, and **D** are incorrect.

17. A. Choice **A** is the correct response. According to the passage, since the dawn of human history, individuals have been fascinated with exploration because of *mankind's natural inquisitiveness about the universe*. This piece speaks directly about the desire of human beings to explore the vast reaches of the universe—earth, sea, and outer space—simply because it is there. Choice **B** is incorrect because the narrative does not address the need for individuals to become powerful world leaders and rule vast stretches of the universe. Choice **C** is incorrect because this narrative addresses just the opposite, mankind's desire to connect with others in the quest to understand and explore. Choice **D** is incorrect because the narrative does not address mankind's need to bring civilization to the uncivilized universe.

18. B. Choice **B** is the correct response. The author would probably agree that *exploring unknown regions of the world is necessary for human development*. The thrust of this piece is how discovering the riches of the world is a part of the human desire to understand the world. Choice **A** is incorrect because the author stresses that scientific exploration is anything but risk-free; instead, it is filled with real and ever-present dangers. Choice **C** is incorrect because the author suggests that individuals feel the urge to explore all the time and not just in times of trouble or despair. Choice **D** is incorrect because the author implies that searching for the unknown is the province of all, regardless of wealth, status, or ambition.

19. **D.** Choice **D** is the correct response. In this narrative, the following statement is NOT implied: *Tragedy has extinguished America's exploratory spirit*. In fact, as the narrative mentions, tragedy, such as the shuttle disasters, has only fueled America's interest to continue on the path of space exploration. Choice **A** is incorrect because the narrative specifically implies that today, for many once undreamed-of inventions and events, the unimaginable has become reality. Choice **B** is incorrect because the narrative does imply that space exploration has had a positive impact in America. Choice **C** is incorrect because the narrative does imply that America is a leader in space exploration.

20. **C.** Choice **C** is the correct response. The word or phrase when substituted for "Instead" in the fourth paragraph that would maintain the same relationship between the last two sentences is the word *rather*. *Rather* is a word that means the same as *instead* or *besides*. Choice **A** is incorrect because the word *therefore* implies a concluding remark to follow the sentence before. Choice **B** is incorrect because the words *in addition* imply that the sentence which follows is an added thought or conclusion to the preceding sentence. Choice **D** is incorrect because the word *obviously* implies something that is understood by many and, in this narrative's section, the logical conclusion to this paragraph is not something generally assumed.

21. **D.** Choice **D** is the correct response. According to this passage, Maria Montessori was born in *Italy* in 1870 (Choice **D**). The other answer choices do not give the correct country of Montessori's birth.

22. **D.** Choice **D** is the correct response. A statement that is implied in this passage is the statement given in Choice **D**: *Maria Montessori was well-educated.* Although this statement is not explicitly stated in this passage, from the first sentence of the second paragraph, which states that Montessori had a "strong academic record" and that she became "the first female certified physician in Italy," the reader can infer that Montessori was well-educated. Choice **A** is incorrect because the statement in this answer choice disagrees with the third sentence of the first paragraph. Choice **B** is incorrect because the statement in this answer choice disagrees with the information given in the second paragraph. Choice **C** is incorrect because it disagrees with Montessori's ideas about teaching children given in this passage.

23. **A.** Choice **A** is the correct response. An opinion about Maria Montessori expressed in this passage is the statement given in Choice **A**: *She revolutionized the teaching profession.* The word *revolutionized* is a judgment word reflecting the author's opinion about Montessori's impact on the teaching profession. Choice **B** is a statement of fact given in the third paragraph. Choice **C** is a statement of fact derived from information given in the fourth paragraph. Choice **D** is a statement of fact given in the last paragraph.

24. **A.** Choice **A** is the correct response. In the sixth paragraph, this passage states that Maria Montessori *advocated age-appropriate learning activities* (Choice **A**). Choices **B** and **C** are incorrect because these answer choices disagree with information given in the passage. Choice **D** is incorrect because in the last paragraph you learn that Montessori was *nominated* for the Nobel Peace Prize in 1951, but the passage does not tell you that she actually *won* the Nobel Peace Prize in that year.

25. **B.** Choice **B** is the correct response. According to the sixth paragraph, Maria Montessori's teaching ideas *gained attention world-wide during her lifetime* (Choice **B**). Choice **A** is incorrect because this statement is neither stated nor implied by the passage. Choice **C** is incorrect because it disagrees with information given in the last paragraph. Choice **D** is incorrect because there is no information in the passage to support it.

26. **B.** Choice **B** is the correct response. According to this passage, the best word to describe Maria Montessori is *progressive*. As this passage both implies and states, Maria Montessori was a woman who clearly accomplished goals that were unheard of by a woman in the early twentieth century. She was a true revolutionary leader. Choice **A** is incorrect because Maria Montessori was hardly *passive; passive* implies not reacting to the events or ideas that are happening around you. Choice **C** is incorrect because there is no indication in this passage that Maria Montessori was *cynical,* meaning "sharply negative." Choice **D** is incorrect because although Maria Montessori was *active,* the best word to describe her behavior from the list presented is the word *progressive,* meaning "forward-thinking."

27. **C.** Choice **C** is the correct response. According to this passage, Maria Montessori revolutionized the education profession because *she respected the emotional experiences that young people brought to their learning.* As mentioned in the narrative, Montessori was a strong advocate for nurturing children's emotional well-being and made it an intimate part of their learning. Choice **A** is incorrect because this passage is more concerned with emotional rather than academic needs. Choice **B** is incorrect because in this

passage there is no mention of Montessori's stand on the need for standardized assessment in order to understand the academic or subject matter knowledge of young children. Choice **D** is incorrect because even though Montessori likely would have been a strong advocate for individualized reading preferences, there is no mention of this interest or desire in this passage.

28. **A.** Choice **A** is the correct response. According to this passage, Maria Montessori's philosophy is *learning by doing ordinary work* (Choice **A**). This passage mentions that Montessori was interested in the ordinary, everyday lives of young children and incorporating these activities into their learning. Choice **B** is incorrect because no mention is made of learning by memorization. Choice **C** is incorrect because no mention is made of learning by objectives. Choice **D** is incorrect because no mention is made of learning by competition.

29. **D.** Choice **D** is the correct response. According to the ideas in this passage, the choice that best demonstrates active, involved learners who are capable of making independent choices, is a *seven-year-old who plays dress-up enthusiastically* (Choice **D**). The joyous enthusiasm indicates a free spirit and an emotionally healthy child. The situations in Choices **A**, **B**, and **C** are instances of young people operating under distress and without free choice, something Montessori would not have advocated, according to ideas in the passage.

30. **C.** Choice **C** is the correct response. As used in the fifth paragraph, the word *self-reliance* most nearly means *autonomy* (Choice **C**). *Self-reliance* refers to an ability to rely on no one but yourself to accomplish your goals. Choice **A**, *dependence,* implies just the opposite—to rely on someone else to achieve your objectives. Choice **B**, *persistence*, implies that you are aggressive toward achieving your desires, but not necessarily self-reliant or solely in control. Choice **D**, *caution,* implies that you are hesitant about achieving your goals, which does not mean the same as being actively involved in achieving your objectives independently.

31. **D.** Choice **D** is the correct response. The tone of this passage is best described as *factual* (Choice **D**). The author does not show a disbelieving, skeptical tone (Choice **A**); an amusing, humorous tone (Choice **B**); or a mocking, sarcastic tone (Choice **C**).

32. **A.** Choice **A** is the correct response. A statement that is a fact about tropical rain forests that is given in the first paragraph is the statement in Choice **A**: *Tropical rain forests are found near the equator.* The statements in the other answer choices are statements of opinion by the author.

33. **B.** Choice **B** is the correct response. In the second paragraph, the passage states that rain forests occupy only *6 to 7 percent of the Earth's surface* (Choice **B**). The percents in the other answer choices are either too small or too great.

34. **C.** Choice **C** is the correct response. In the fourth paragraph, the passage states that *large industrial companies, desiring to clear land for logging, farming, and mining projects,* threaten the rain forests (Choice **C**). Choice **A** is incorrect because, although from information given in the sixth paragraph, you might assume that the statement in Choice **A** is accurate, this passage does not state this information. Choice **B** is incorrect because the statement in this answer choice disagrees with information given in the last paragraph. Choice **D** is incorrect because, even though this is a fact that you might know, this information is not given in the passage. Remember, do not select answer choices based on your personal knowledge that goes beyond the information given in the passage.

35. **C.** Choice **C** is the correct response. In paragraph three, the author uses the word *mine* in the context of *extracting from plants* (Choice **C**). The author is describing the extraction of substances from plants. Choice **A** is incorrect because the word *mine* is not used in the sense of digging in the Earth. Choice **B** is incorrect because no mention is made of chemicals in the paragraph. Choice **D** is incorrect because, while mining might help increase the supply of new medicines, the verb *to mine* does not mean *to supply*.

36. **C.** Choice **C** is the correct response. A statement about rain forests that is neither stated nor implied in this passage is *They provide unique treasures for self-defined explorers* (Choice **C**). Although this passage mentions the many treasures to be found in the rain forests, this passage does not advocate the use of the rain forests as a place to explore for personal gain. Indeed, this passage advocates the opposite—that any riches to be found in these regions are to be shared under regulation by governments and appropriate organizations. The statements in Choices **A**, **B**, and **D** are stated or implied in the passage. The rain forests do provide a safe haven for indigenous people, serve as a prime source for modern medicines, and act as a rich resource for scientific exploration.

37. **B.** Choice **B** is the correct response. The primary purpose of this passage is to *inform readers about the plight of the rain forests* (Choice **B**). This piece speaks in a detailed voice about the natural beauty of the world's rain forests and how commercial interests threaten to destroy this lush and rich vegetative community. Choice **A** is incorrect because although this passage does mention that rare plants and species are found in the rain forests, this is not the primary purpose of this passage. In this passage the author speaks in an advocacy voice for the preservation of the rain forests. Choice **C** is incorrect because the author expresses concern about indiscriminate logging of the rain forests. Instead, this piece calls for a more responsible approach toward logging in the rain forests. Choice **D** is incorrect because although this piece does underline the importance of scientific exploration in the rain forests, this passage concentrates on how the rain forests can contribute to society in a multitude of ways besides scientific discovery.

38. **D.** Choice **D** is the correct response. Deforestation is a major, not a minor, problem in today's rain forest environment. The statements in the other answer choices are true according to the passage.

39. **C.** Choice **C** is the correct response. According to this passage, the millions of *indigenous* people who live in the rain forests are called by the word *indigenous* because they *are native to the land in which they live*. *Indigenous* is a term that defines a group of people who inhabit a land long before they are discovered by others; they belong to the land because they were born there and usually are not prepared to live anywhere else. Choice **A** is incorrect because *indigenous* implies permanent residents and not transitory migrants who are known to travel from place to place seeking work and shelter. Choice **B** is incorrect because *indigenous* people do not own, in the economic sense, the property on which they live; instead, they own the land because they were born to the land and have lived there for all their natural lives. Choice **D** is incorrect because although *indigenous* people do work the land on which they live, that alone does not make them an indigenous people.

40. **D.** Choice **D** is the correct response. The author's claim that "the rain forests will continue to survive as one of the Earth's most vital and precious resources" *is a reasonable statement given previous remarks* (Choice **D**). The author provides a realistic yet hopeful presentation of the facts surrounding the preservation of the rain forests and their chance for continual renewal despite many competing, often self-serving interests. Choice **A** is incorrect because the author's nonobjectionable, reasoned statement is based on evidence, not, as the answer states, a flimsy, unsubstantiated response. Choice **B** is incorrect because the author's optimistic statement is aligned with the passage's remarks and is not contradictory to the author's thesis or subsequent narrative. Choice **C** is incorrect because the author's optimistic remarks are not objectionable or biased, but a reasonable corollary given the thrust of this author's remarks about the condition and continuation of the world's rain forests.

General Knowledge Practice Test 2

Answer Sheet

(Remove This Sheet and Use It To Mark Your Answers)

Diagnostic General Knowledge Test: Essay

Write your essay on lined paper.

General Knowledge Test: English Language Skills

1 Ⓐ Ⓑ Ⓒ Ⓓ	11 Ⓐ Ⓑ Ⓒ Ⓓ	21 Ⓐ Ⓑ Ⓒ Ⓓ	31 Ⓐ Ⓑ Ⓒ Ⓓ
2 Ⓐ Ⓑ Ⓒ Ⓓ	12 Ⓐ Ⓑ Ⓒ Ⓓ	22 Ⓐ Ⓑ Ⓒ Ⓓ	32 Ⓐ Ⓑ Ⓒ Ⓓ
3 Ⓐ Ⓑ Ⓒ Ⓓ	13 Ⓐ Ⓑ Ⓒ Ⓓ	23 Ⓐ Ⓑ Ⓒ Ⓓ	33 Ⓐ Ⓑ Ⓒ Ⓓ
4 Ⓐ Ⓑ Ⓒ Ⓓ	14 Ⓐ Ⓑ Ⓒ Ⓓ	24 Ⓐ Ⓑ Ⓒ Ⓓ	34 Ⓐ Ⓑ Ⓒ Ⓓ
5 Ⓐ Ⓑ Ⓒ Ⓓ	15 Ⓐ Ⓑ Ⓒ Ⓓ	25 Ⓐ Ⓑ Ⓒ Ⓓ	35 Ⓐ Ⓑ Ⓒ Ⓓ
6 Ⓐ Ⓑ Ⓒ Ⓓ	16 Ⓐ Ⓑ Ⓒ Ⓓ	26 Ⓐ Ⓑ Ⓒ Ⓓ	36 Ⓐ Ⓑ Ⓒ Ⓓ
7 Ⓐ Ⓑ Ⓒ Ⓓ	17 Ⓐ Ⓑ Ⓒ Ⓓ	27 Ⓐ Ⓑ Ⓒ Ⓓ	37 Ⓐ Ⓑ Ⓒ Ⓓ
8 Ⓐ Ⓑ Ⓒ Ⓓ	18 Ⓐ Ⓑ Ⓒ Ⓓ	28 Ⓐ Ⓑ Ⓒ Ⓓ	38 Ⓐ Ⓑ Ⓒ Ⓓ
9 Ⓐ Ⓑ Ⓒ Ⓓ	19 Ⓐ Ⓑ Ⓒ Ⓓ	29 Ⓐ Ⓑ Ⓒ Ⓓ	39 Ⓐ Ⓑ Ⓒ Ⓓ
10 Ⓐ Ⓑ Ⓒ Ⓓ	20 Ⓐ Ⓑ Ⓒ Ⓓ	30 Ⓐ Ⓑ Ⓒ Ⓓ	40 Ⓐ Ⓑ Ⓒ Ⓓ

General Knowledge Test: Mathematics

1 Ⓐ Ⓑ Ⓒ Ⓓ	11 Ⓐ Ⓑ Ⓒ Ⓓ	21 Ⓐ Ⓑ Ⓒ Ⓓ	31 Ⓐ Ⓑ Ⓒ Ⓓ	41 Ⓐ Ⓑ Ⓒ Ⓓ
2 Ⓐ Ⓑ Ⓒ Ⓓ	12 Ⓐ Ⓑ Ⓒ Ⓓ	22 Ⓐ Ⓑ Ⓒ Ⓓ	32 Ⓐ Ⓑ Ⓒ Ⓓ	42 Ⓐ Ⓑ Ⓒ Ⓓ
3 Ⓐ Ⓑ Ⓒ Ⓓ	13 Ⓐ Ⓑ Ⓒ Ⓓ	23 Ⓐ Ⓑ Ⓒ Ⓓ	33 Ⓐ Ⓑ Ⓒ Ⓓ	43 Ⓐ Ⓑ Ⓒ Ⓓ
4 Ⓐ Ⓑ Ⓒ Ⓓ	14 Ⓐ Ⓑ Ⓒ Ⓓ	24 Ⓐ Ⓑ Ⓒ Ⓓ	34 Ⓐ Ⓑ Ⓒ Ⓓ	44 Ⓐ Ⓑ Ⓒ Ⓓ
5 Ⓐ Ⓑ Ⓒ Ⓓ	15 Ⓐ Ⓑ Ⓒ Ⓓ	25 Ⓐ Ⓑ Ⓒ Ⓓ	35 Ⓐ Ⓑ Ⓒ Ⓓ	45 Ⓐ Ⓑ Ⓒ Ⓓ
6 Ⓐ Ⓑ Ⓒ Ⓓ	16 Ⓐ Ⓑ Ⓒ Ⓓ	26 Ⓐ Ⓑ Ⓒ Ⓓ	36 Ⓐ Ⓑ Ⓒ Ⓓ	
7 Ⓐ Ⓑ Ⓒ Ⓓ	17 Ⓐ Ⓑ Ⓒ Ⓓ	27 Ⓐ Ⓑ Ⓒ Ⓓ	37 Ⓐ Ⓑ Ⓒ Ⓓ	
8 Ⓐ Ⓑ Ⓒ Ⓓ	18 Ⓐ Ⓑ Ⓒ Ⓓ	28 Ⓐ Ⓑ Ⓒ Ⓓ	38 Ⓐ Ⓑ Ⓒ Ⓓ	
9 Ⓐ Ⓑ Ⓒ Ⓓ	19 Ⓐ Ⓑ Ⓒ Ⓓ	29 Ⓐ Ⓑ Ⓒ Ⓓ	39 Ⓐ Ⓑ Ⓒ Ⓓ	
10 Ⓐ Ⓑ Ⓒ Ⓓ	20 Ⓐ Ⓑ Ⓒ Ⓓ	30 Ⓐ Ⓑ Ⓒ Ⓓ	40 Ⓐ Ⓑ Ⓒ Ⓓ	

General Knowledge Test: Reading

1 Ⓐ Ⓑ Ⓒ Ⓓ	11 Ⓐ Ⓑ Ⓒ Ⓓ	21 Ⓐ Ⓑ Ⓒ Ⓓ	31 Ⓐ Ⓑ Ⓒ Ⓓ
2 Ⓐ Ⓑ Ⓒ Ⓓ	12 Ⓐ Ⓑ Ⓒ Ⓓ	22 Ⓐ Ⓑ Ⓒ Ⓓ	32 Ⓐ Ⓑ Ⓒ Ⓓ
3 Ⓐ Ⓑ Ⓒ Ⓓ	13 Ⓐ Ⓑ Ⓒ Ⓓ	23 Ⓐ Ⓑ Ⓒ Ⓓ	33 Ⓐ Ⓑ Ⓒ Ⓓ
4 Ⓐ Ⓑ Ⓒ Ⓓ	14 Ⓐ Ⓑ Ⓒ Ⓓ	24 Ⓐ Ⓑ Ⓒ Ⓓ	34 Ⓐ Ⓑ Ⓒ Ⓓ
5 Ⓐ Ⓑ Ⓒ Ⓓ	15 Ⓐ Ⓑ Ⓒ Ⓓ	25 Ⓐ Ⓑ Ⓒ Ⓓ	35 Ⓐ Ⓑ Ⓒ Ⓓ
6 Ⓐ Ⓑ Ⓒ Ⓓ	16 Ⓐ Ⓑ Ⓒ Ⓓ	26 Ⓐ Ⓑ Ⓒ Ⓓ	36 Ⓐ Ⓑ Ⓒ Ⓓ
7 Ⓐ Ⓑ Ⓒ Ⓓ	17 Ⓐ Ⓑ Ⓒ Ⓓ	27 Ⓐ Ⓑ Ⓒ Ⓓ	37 Ⓐ Ⓑ Ⓒ Ⓓ
8 Ⓐ Ⓑ Ⓒ Ⓓ	18 Ⓐ Ⓑ Ⓒ Ⓓ	28 Ⓐ Ⓑ Ⓒ Ⓓ	38 Ⓐ Ⓑ Ⓒ Ⓓ
9 Ⓐ Ⓑ Ⓒ Ⓓ	19 Ⓐ Ⓑ Ⓒ Ⓓ	29 Ⓐ Ⓑ Ⓒ Ⓓ	39 Ⓐ Ⓑ Ⓒ Ⓓ
10 Ⓐ Ⓑ Ⓒ Ⓓ	20 Ⓐ Ⓑ Ⓒ Ⓓ	30 Ⓐ Ⓑ Ⓒ Ⓓ	40 Ⓐ Ⓑ Ⓒ Ⓓ

CUT HERE

CUT HERE

General Knowledge Practice Test 2: Essay

Time: 50 minutes

Directions: This section of the examination involves a written assignment. You are to prepare a written response for *one of the two topics* presented below. Select one of these two topics and prepare a 300- to 600-word response. Be sure to read both topics very carefully to make sure that you understand the topic for which you are preparing a written response. Use your allotted time to plan, write, review, and edit what you have written for the assignment.

Topic 1

My favorite hobbies

Topic 2

A historical figure who changed the world

Be sure to read the two topics again before attempting to write your response. Your essay must be on only one of the topics presented, and it must address the topic completely.

Your essay is graded holistically, meaning only one score is assigned for your writing—taking into consideration both mechanics and organization. *You are not scored on the nature of the content or opinions expressed in your work*. Instead, you are graded on your ability to write complete sentences, to express and support your opinions, and to organize your work.

At least two evaluators will review your work and assign it a score. Special attention is paid to the following specific indicators of good writing:

- Does your writing demonstrate a strong definitive purpose?
- Is there a clear thesis or statement of a main idea?
- Are your ideas organized?
- Do you support your thesis with clear details?
- Are effective transitions present?
- Do you demonstrate an effective use of language?
- Are a variety of sentence patterns present?
- Is there a consistent point-of-view?
- Are the conventions of Standard American English used?

Before you begin, be sure you plan what you want to say. Organize your thoughts and carefully construct your ideas. This should be your original work, written in your own voice.

As you write your piece, you may revise or add information as necessary.

General Knowledge Practice Test 2: English Language Skills

Time: 40 minutes
40 questions

Directions: For questions 1–4, read the entire passage carefully and then answer the questions. Please note that intentional errors have been included in this passage. The passages are designed to measure your identification of logical order and irrelevant sentences in a written passage.

The passage for questions 1 and 2 reads as follows:

(1) The outside shell is one of the most important parts of an organism. (2) Shells grow on the outside of living things. (3) Many plants and animals, from tiny nuts to huge alligators, have a shell to protect them at least one time in their life cycles. (4) Some shells are as tiny as a grain of sand. (5) Many people collect shells as a hobby. (6) Shells also vary in color, helping to protect the organism inside from possible predators. (7) They also serve as a necessary protection from the elements. (8) Plants and animals with shells are usually the most vulnerable of living things without their shells. (9) The shell functions as protective outerwear. (10) Shells are nature's way of protecting creatures that otherwise likely would perish.

1. Select the arrangement of sentences 1, 2, and 3 that provides the most logical sequence of ideas and supporting details in the paragraph. If no change is needed, select Choice A.

   A. The outside shell is one of the most important parts of an organism. Shells grow on the outside of living things. Many plants and animals, from tiny nuts to huge alligators, have a shell to protect them at least one time in their life cycles.
   B. Shells grow on the outside of living things. The outside shell is one of the most important parts of an organism. Many plants and animals, from tiny nuts to huge alligators, have a shell to protect them at least one time in their life cycles.
   C. Many plants and animals, from tiny nuts to huge alligators, have a shell to protect them at least one time in their life cycles. Shells grow on the outside of living things. The outside shell is one of the most important parts of an organism.
   D. The outside shell is one of the most important parts of an organism. Many plants and animals, from tiny nuts to huge alligators, have a shell to protect them at least one time in their life cycles. Shells grow on the outside of living things.

2. Which numbered sentence is LEAST relevant to the passage?

   A. Sentence 3
   B. Sentence 4
   C. Sentence 5
   D. Sentence 6

The passage for questions 3–4 reads as follows:

(1) Students whose home language is other than English must learn to function in schools where the main language is English. (2) Today, most urban school districts have an amalgamation of students who speak different languages. (3) Families from all over the world settle in primarily large metropolitan school districts and bring with them their languages, culture, and customs. (4) Learning in a new language is a difficult and serious concern for all involved—teachers, parents, and students. (5) School districts are taking steps to ensure that all eager and eligible learners can participate in classroom lessons. (6) Faced with a diverse population of learners, teachers must learn to adapt their lessons. (7) They must take special courses to learn how to work with students whose first language is not English. (8) Also, administrators must rethink discipline policies for students who are unfamiliar with American lifestyle and traditional norms. (9) These measures should help ensure success for students who speak English as a second language. (10) With the burgeoning ethnic population in our nation's cities, new specialty foods are being introduced into society.

3. Select the arrangement of sentences 1, 2, and 3 that provides the most logical sequence of ideas and supporting details in the paragraph. If no change is needed, select Choice A.

A. Students whose home language is other than English must learn to function in schools where the main language is English. Today, most urban school districts have an amalgamation of students who speak different languages. Families from all over the world settle in primarily large metropolitan school districts and bring with them their languages, culture, and customs.

B. Families from all over the world settle in primarily large metropolitan school districts and bring with them their languages, culture, and customs. Students whose home language is other than English must learn to function in schools where the main language is English. Today, most urban school districts have an amalgamation of students who speak different languages.

C. Today, most urban school districts have an amalgamation of students who speak different languages. Families from all over the world settle in primarily large metropolitan school districts and bring with them their languages, culture, and customs. Students whose home language is other than English must learn to function in schools where the main language is English.

D. Students whose home language is other than English must learn to function in schools where the main language is English. Families from all over the world settle in primarily large metropolitan school districts and bring with them their languages, culture, and customs. Today, most urban school districts have an amalgamation of students who speak different languages.

4. Which numbered sentence is LEAST relevant to the passage?

A. Sentence 7
B. Sentence 8
C. Sentence 9
D. Sentence 10

Directions: For questions 5–37, select the answer choice that corrects an error in the underlined portion. If there is no error, choose D indicating "No change is necessary."

5. All the actors, <u>accept</u> Martha and John, were
   _A

   <u>allowed</u> <u>to eat</u> in the cafeteria.
   _B _C
   A. except
   B. aloud
   C. to have eaten
   D. No change is necessary.

6. The children on the school bus <u>are wearing</u>
   _A

   brand <u>new</u> t-shirts from <u>Coach Henderson</u>.
   _B   _C
   A. was wearing
   B. knew
   C. coach Henderson
   D. No change is necessary.

7. We encouraged our visitors <u>too</u> <u>formally</u>
   _A _B

   introduce <u>themselves</u> to our neighbors.
   _C
   A. to
   B. formerly
   C. theirselves
   D. No change is necessary.

8. After school, I <u>read</u> my <u>french</u> textbook to
   _A   _B

   prepare for <u>tomorrow's</u> quiz.
   _C
   A. red
   B. French
   C. tommorrow
   D. No change is necessary.

9. Repeatedly, the cheerleaders <u>have went</u> to the
   _A

   <u>all-American</u> championship to represent <u>their</u>
   _B   _C
   high school.

   A. have gone
   B. all-american
   C. there
   D. No change is necessary.

10. Police officer Lance Jones <u>sat</u> <u>among</u> Janice
    _A _B

    and me at the <u>awards</u> ceremony.
    _C
    A. set
    B. between
    C. Awards
    D. No change is necessary.

11. Mark is <u>deep</u> in love with Maria despite <u>their</u>
    _A   _B

    <u>considerable differences</u> in age and interest.
    _C
    A. deeply
    B. there
    C. considerably different
    D. No change is necessary.

12. After the umpire cried <u>fowl</u>, all my teammates
    _A

    protested <u>loudly</u> in <u>disbelief</u>.
    _B   _C
    A. foul
    B. loud
    C. disbelieve
    D. No change is necessary.

13. <u>Unfortunately</u>, the tennis team <u>had</u> lost more
    _A   _B

    tournaments <u>then</u> they ever had before.
    _C
    A. Unfortunate
    B. have
    C. than
    D. No change is necessary.

14. My uncle's <u>surprising</u> musical talents <u>masks</u> <u>his</u>
    _A   _B _C
    inability to read.

    A. surprisingly
    B. mask
    C. his own
    D. No change is necessary.

15. Among the three sisters, only me and Nancy
       A   B
    are tall.
       C
    A. Between
    B. Nancy and I
    C. the tallest
    D. No change is necessary.

16. Despite the heavy reign, we found a dry spot
                 A   B
    where we could eat our lunch.
             C
    A. rain
    B. had found
    C. have eaten
    D. No change is necessary.

17. The students, who seldom were consulted
         A   B
    about issues by the administration, quickly
    seen they must speak up about the injustice
     C
    of the situation.
    A. students'
    B. whom
    C. saw
    D. No change is necessary.

18. The teacher was explaining to the class that
                                A
    scientists are really careful when they take
             B   C
    measurements.
    A. how
    B. real
    C. he or she
    D. No change is necessary.

19. When the students performed the
     A   B
    experiment they were amazed that the
            C
    liquid turned a dazzling green.
    A. Whenever
    B. students'
    C. experiment, they
    D. No change is necessary.

20. Dustin is happy that his new cell phone
            A
    number is more easier to remember than his
             B   C
    previous number.
    A. happier
    B. easier
    C. remember, than
    D. No change is necessary.

21. The boys' mother asked them whether they felt
    badly about breaking her new Tiffany lamp
     A   B
    when they were playing with the ball in
             C
    the house.
    A. bad
    B. tiffany
    C. was
    D. No change is necessary.

22. Last November Ms. Villa's history class went
                       A   B
    on a field trip to Washington, D.C., the
    nation's capitol.
          C
    A. History
    B. had went
    C. capital
    D. No change is necessary.

23. The girls' mother asked them to water the
       A
    plants and feed the dog after they finished
       B
    there homework.
     C
    A. girl's
    B. plants, and
    C. their
    D. No change is necessary.

24. When they arrived at the mall, the children
     A
    had run into the toy store to find the most
      B
    recent edition of their favorite trading cards.
                C
    A. Whenever
    B. ran
    C. thier
    D. No change is necessary.

25. It is hard for me to believe that we <u>cannot</u>
    _A
    resolve the problems between you and <u>I</u> after
    _B
    all these <u>years</u> of trying.
    _C
    A. can not
    B. me
    C. years'
    D. No change is necessary.

26. My daughter and my son <u>are</u> both taller than
    _A
    <u>me</u>, but they still mind what I <u>say when</u> I
    _B   _C
    correct their behavior.
    A. were
    B. I
    C. say, when
    D. No change is necessary.

27. I was anxious during my first semester at the
    new <u>school because</u> the <u>principal</u> told me she
    _A   _B
    would be strict with <u>whomever</u> broke the rules.
    _C
    A. school, because
    B. principle
    C. whoever
    D. No change is necessary.

28. Only one of the contestants <u>who</u> participated
    _A
    in the race <u>want</u> the winner to be disqualified
    _B
    for being <u>too</u> young.
    _C
    A. which
    B. wants
    C. to
    D. No change is necessary.

29. Just before Caleb <u>left, he</u> told me he <u>didn't</u>
    _A   _B
    think he did very <u>good</u> on his geometry test.
    _C
    A. left he
    B. don't
    C. well
    D. No change is necessary.

30. <u>Me</u> graduating from college <u>has</u> been a dream
    _A   _B
    of my parents, neither of <u>whom</u> ever finished
    _C
    high school.
    A. My
    B. have
    C. who
    D. No change is necessary.

31. The contributors to the fundraiser were
    pleased to <u>see that</u> every one of the children
    _A
    <u>were</u> wearing a <u>brand new</u> outfit.
    _B   _C
    A. see, that
    B. was
    C. brand-new
    D. No change is necessary.

32. The <u>couple's</u> teenage sons had outgrown their
    _A
    board <u>games, so</u> the couple donated <u>them</u> to
    _B   _C
    the local charter school.
    A. couples'
    B. games so
    C. the board games
    D. No change is necessary.

33. Donna, <u>who</u> never seeks recognition, <u>recieved</u>
    _A   _B
    the outstanding teacher <u>award at</u> her school
    _C
    this year.
    A. whom
    B. received
    C. award, at
    D. No change is necessary.

34. Austin, Ricardo's <u>most nicest</u> <u>friend,</u> comes
    _A   _B
    over to Ricardo's house <u>every day</u> after school
    _C
    to play.
    A. nicest
    B. freind
    C. everyday
    D. No change is necessary.

35. When you meet the two girls, you will find it difficult to tell which one is <u>oldest</u>.

   A. the oldest
   B. older
   C. more old
   D. No change is necessary.

36. Because the students were going to be gone all day on the field trip to the park, they <u>should have took</u> a lunch.

   A. should of took
   B. should have taken
   C. should of taken
   D. No change is necessary.

37. As the sun <u>sets</u>, the horizon glowed a bright orange.

   A. had set
   B. has been setting
   C. set
   D. No change is necessary.

38. **Directions:** Choose the option that is punctuated correctly.

   A. When you broke your promise, I was extremely upset, I hope that I will be able to trust you in the future.
   B. When you broke your promise I was extremely upset I hope that I will be able to trust you in the future.
   C. When you broke your promise, I was extremely upset. I hope that I will be able to trust you in the future.
   D. When you broke your promise I was extremely upset. I hope that I will be able to trust you in the future.

39. **Directions:** Choose the option that is punctuated correctly.

   A. Having been raised in our household from a puppy, our family's trusted canine is a spoiled pooch.
   B. Having been raised in our household from a puppy, our familys' trusted canine is a spoiled pooch.
   C. Having been raised in our household from a puppy. Our family's trusted canine is a spoiled pooch.
   D. Having been raised in our household from a puppy our family's trusted canine is a spoiled pooch.

40. **Directions:** Choose the sentence in which the modifiers are placed correctly.

   A. Driving through the neighborhood, the woman waved to a child playing with his dog on the sidewalk.
   B. Playing with his dog on the sidewalk, the woman waved to a child driving through the neighborhood.
   C. The woman waved to a child playing with his dog on the sidewalk driving through the neighborhood.
   D. The woman waved to a child driving through the neighborhood playing on the sidewalk with his dog.

General Knowledge Practice Test 2

IF YOU FINISH BEFORE TIME IS CALLED, CHECK YOUR WORK ON THIS SECTION ONLY. DO NOT WORK ON ANY OTHER SECTION IN THE TEST.

General Knowledge Practice Test 2: Mathematics

Time: **100 minutes**
45 questions

Mathematics Reference Sheet

Area

Triangle $A = \frac{1}{2}bh$

Key	
b = base	d = diameter
h = height	r = radius
l = length	A = area
w = width	C = circumference
S.A. = surface area	V = volume
	B = area of base
Use $\pi = 3.14$ or $\frac{22}{7}$	

Rectangle $A = lw$

Trapezoid $A = \frac{1}{2}h(b_1 + b_2)$

Parallelogram $A = bh$

Circle $A = \pi r^2 \quad C = \pi d = 2\pi r$

CUT HERE

Surface Area

1. Surface area of a prism or pyramid = the sum of the areas of all faces of the figure.
2. Surface area of a cylinder = the sum of the areas of the two bases + the area of its rectangular wrap.

 $S.A. = 2(\pi r^2) + (2\pi r)h$

3. Surface area of a sphere: $S.A. = 4\pi r^2$

Volume

1. Volume of a prism or cylinder equals (Area of the Base) times (height): $V = Bh$
2. Volume of a pyramid or cone equals $\frac{1}{3}$ times (Area of the Base) times (height): $V = \frac{1}{3}Bh$
3. Volume of a sphere: $V = \frac{4}{3}\pi r^3$

General Knowledge Practice Test 2

Mathematics Reference Sheet, continued

Pythagorean Theorem: $a^2 + b^2 = c^2$

Simple Interest Formula: $I = prt$

I = simple interest, p = principal, r = rate, t = time

Distance Formula: $d = rt$

d = distance, r = rate, t = time

Given a line containing points (x_1, y_1) and (x_2, y_2),

- Slope of line = $\dfrac{y_2 - y_1}{x_2 - x_1}$
- Distance between two points = $\sqrt{(x_2 - x_1)^2 + (y_2 - y_1)^2}$
- Midpoint between two points = $\left(\dfrac{x_1 + x_2}{2}, \dfrac{y_1 + y_2}{2}\right)$

Conversions	
1 yard = 3 feet = 36 inches	1 cup = 8 fluid ounces
1 mile = 1,760 yards = 5,280 feet	1 pint = 2 cups
1 acre = 43,560 square feet	1 quart = 2 pints
1 hour = 60 minutes	1 gallon = 4 quarts
1 minute = 60 seconds	1 pound = 16 ounces
	1 ton = 2,000 pounds
1 liter = 1000 milliliters = 1000 cubic centimeters	
1 meter = 100 centimeters = 1000 millimeters	
1 kilometer = 1000 meters	
1 gram = 1000 milligrams	
1 kilogram = 1000 grams	

Note: Metric numbers with four digits are written without a comma (e.g., 2543 grams).

For metric numbers with more than four digits, a space is used instead of a comma (e.g., 24 300 liters).

CUT HERE

Directions: Read each question and select the best answer choice.

1. Find the greatest common factor of 30 and 45.

   A. 2
   B. 3
   C. 5
   D. 15

2. In scientific notation, the distance from Venus to the Sun is approximately $1.082 \cdot 10^8$ kilometers. How is this distance expressed in standard notation?

   A. 10,820,000,000 km
   B. 1,082,000,000 km
   C. 108,200,000 km
   D. 0.00000001082 km

3. In triangle ABC shown below, segment $\overline{CE}$ has length 200 meters and segment $\overline{EA}$ has length 100 meters. In triangle ADE, segment $\overline{DE}$ has length 50 meters. What is the area of triangle ABC?

   A. 7,500 m²
   B. 15,000 m²
   C. 22,500 m²
   D. 45,000 m²

4. Simplify $7 + 3(4^2) - 8$.

   A. 23
   B. 32
   C. 47
   D. 152

5. The whole number y is exactly three times the whole number x. The whole number z is the sum of x and y. Which of the following CANNOT be the value of z?

   A. 314
   B. 416
   C. 524
   D. 1,032

6. Justin bought a souvenir while vacationing in a Texas town where the sales tax rate is $8\frac{1}{4}\%$. What is this tax rate expressed as a decimal?

   A. 8.25
   B. 0.825
   C. 0.0825
   D. 0.0814

7. The following Fahrenheit temperatures were the lowest recorded in February for the past five years in a particular city.

   $$2°, 0°, -6°, 4°, -8°$$

   Which list shows the temperatures in order from coldest to warmest?

   A. 0°, 2°, 4°, -6°, -8°
   B. 4°, 2°, 0°, -6°, -8°
   C. -6°, -8°, 0°, 2°, 4°
   D. -8°, -6°, 0°, 2°, 4°

8. If 30% of a monthly salary of $2,400 is budgeted for rent, how much money is budgeted for rent?

   A. $72
   B. $168
   C. $720
   D. $1,680

9. A runner ran a 1500-meter race. How many kilometers did the runner run in the race?

   A. 1.5 km
   B. 15 km
   C. 150 km
   D. 1,500,000 km

10. What is the temperature to the nearest degree?

   A. 33°
   B. 35°
   C. 36°
   D. 34°

11. If the surface area of a sphere is 144π cm², what is the volume of the sphere? Use $\pi = 3.14$.

   A. 36 cm³
   B. 288 cm³
   C. 216π cm³
   D. 288π cm³

12. If a circular flower garden has a diameter of 3 feet, what is the approximate area of the garden? Use $\pi = 3.14$.

   A. 4.71 ft²
   B. 7.07 ft²
   C. 28.26 ft²
   D. 9.42 ft²

13. How many cubic feet of cement are in a rectangular cement slab that is 0.5 feet thick and measures 20 feet long and 10 feet wide?

   A. 100 ft³
   B. 30.5 ft³
   C. 300 ft³
   D. 1,000 ft³

14. A box that has the shape of a cube and measures 10 cm on a side is cut open to form the flattened figure shown here.

10 cm

What is the surface area of the box?

   A. 30 cm²
   B. 100 cm²
   C. 600 cm²
   D. 3,600 cm²

15. A car travels 221 miles in 3 hours 15 minutes. How many miles per hour did the car travel?

   A. 165.75 mph
   B. 70.1 mph
   C. 73.7 mph
   D. 68 mph

16. A nutrition expert recommends that healthy adults drink 64 ounces of water each day. At this rate, how many gallons of water will be consumed in a week by a person who follows the recommendation?

    A. 0.5 gallons
    B. 3.5 gallons
    C. 14 gallons
    D. 16 gallons

17. On a map, the distance between two landmarks is 9.5 inches. If $\frac{1}{2}$ inch represents 10 miles, how far, in miles, is it between the two landmarks (to the nearest mile)?

    A. 0.475 miles
    B. 19 miles
    C. 85 miles
    D. 190 miles

18. How much will it cost, without including tax, to carpet a large classroom that measures 18 feet by 15 feet if the cost of the carpet, including installation, is $25.75 per square yard?

    A. $30.00
    B. $772.50
    C. $2,317.50
    D. $6,952.50

19. Which of the following is the most specific name for the figure shown here?

    A. pentagon
    B. rhombus
    C. hexagon
    D. trapezoid

20. A length of cable is attached to the top of a 16-foot pole. The cable is anchored 12 feet from the base of the pole. What is the length of the cable?

    A. 20 ft
    B. 28 ft
    C. 200 ft
    D. 400 ft

21. A square is also a

    A. cube.
    B. prism.
    C. rhombus.
    D. trapezoid.

22. Which of the following figures contains a correctly drawn line of symmetry?

A.	B.	C.	D.

23. In the drawing shown, right triangle *ABC* is similar to right triangle *DEF*. What is the length of the hypotenuse in triangle *ABC*?

- A. 4 m
- B. 25 m
- C. 28 m
- D. 30 m

24. Which figure below contains an interior obtuse angle?

A.	B.	C.	D.

25. Trapezoid A' on the grid that follows represents what kind of transformation of trapezoid A?

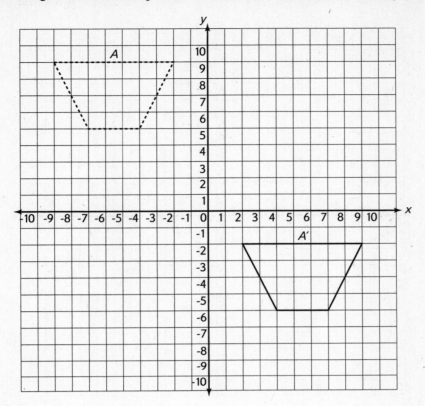

   A.   translation
   B.   reflection
   C.   rotation
   D.   dilation

26. Which point has coordinates (–8, 3)?

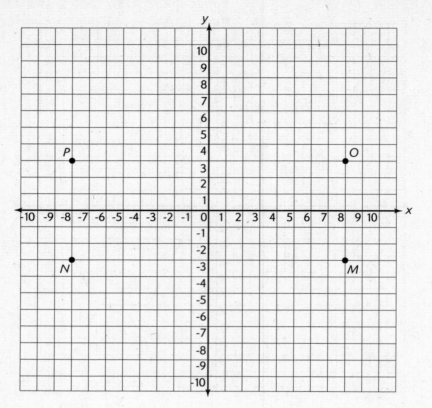

A. M
B. N
C. O
D. P

27. Find the slope of the line that passes through the points (–4, 1) and (2, 3).

A. –3

B. $-\dfrac{1}{3}$

C. $\dfrac{1}{3}$

D. 3

28. Find the missing number in the following sequence.

$$2, \underline{\hphantom{xxx}}, 8, -16, 32$$

A. –4
B. 4
C. 5
D. –6

29. The area of a trapezoid is $A = \frac{1}{2}h(b_1 + b_2)$ where h is the height of the trapezoid and b_1 and b_2 are the lengths of its two bases. Which of the following is the most accurate translation of the expression $A = \frac{1}{2}h(b_1 + b_2)$ into words?

   A. one-half the product of h times b_1 plus b_2
   B. the product of one-half the height times b_1 plus b_2
   C. one-half the height times one-half the sum of the bases
   D. the sum of b_1 and b_2 times one-half of h

30. Simplify $4 + 2(3x + 1)$.

   A. ^-12x
   B. $6x + 5$
   C. $6x + 6$
   D. $18x + 6$

31. If $x = 10$ and $y = -4$, then $2x - y$ has what value?

   A. -24
   B. -16
   C. 16
   D. 24

32. Solve for x.

$$3(x - 6) = 21$$

   A. 1
   B. 5
   C. 9
   D. 13

33. Determine which of the following ordered pairs satisfies the given system.

$$2x - y = -7$$
$$x + 3y = -7$$

   A. $(-4, -1)$
   B. $(-4, 1)$
   C. $(4, -1)$
   D. $(4, 1)$

34. If $x = -5$, which of the following statements is true?

   A. $\frac{1}{x} > -x$
   B. $3x < 2x$
   C. $-x < 0$
   D. $x - 6 > x + 6$

35. Solve $-2x + 5 < 7$.

   A. $x < -1$
   B. $x < -6$
   C. $x > -1$
   D. $x > -6$

36. Find the missing number in the following sequence.

$$15, \underline{\quad}, -5, -15, -25$$

   A. -5
   B. 5
   C. 25
   D. 45

37. The following graph represents the monthly average low and high temperatures in the city of Townville for 4 months of the year. In which month was the difference in the average low and high temperatures the greatest?

A. January
B. February
C. March
D. April

38. Given are eight students' scores on a history test. What is the median of the set of scores?

Student	Score
1	96
2	42
3	56
4	88
5	69
6	73
7	67
8	88

A. 71
B. 72
C. 72.375
D. 88

39. Given is a box of 50 marbles, all identical except for color. The box contains 20 blue, 10 red, 14 green, and 6 yellow marbles. If a person picks out a single marble from the box without looking, what is the probability that the marble will be yellow or blue?

A. $\frac{2}{5}$

B. $\frac{3}{25}$

C. $\frac{6}{125}$

D. $\frac{13}{25}$

40. A girl is making a sandwich for lunch. She has a choice of three kinds of bread (white, whole wheat, or rye) and four sandwich fillings (ham, turkey, sliced beef, or pimiento cheese). How many different sandwiches can she make if she chooses one type of bread and one kind of sandwich filling?

A. 7
B. 9
C. 12
D. 16

41. A library surveys 200 young readers to ask what kind of books they read most often from among adventure, nature, science fiction, and biography or historical books. The results are recorded in the pie graph shown that follows. According to the graph, how many young readers surveyed read science fiction books most often?

Book Type Survey

A. 34
B. 36
C. 46
D. 84

42. A student received the following grades on six science quizzes: 100, 96, 70, 96, 86, and 80. What is the range of the student's grades?

A. 30
B. 88
C. 91
D. 96

43. Which of the following sets of prices has a median of $10.24?

A. $10.29, $9.87, $11.99, $8.45, $10.60, $10.25
B. $7.50, $12.98, $8.25, $10.89, $11.05, $10.67
C. $11.98, $10.50, $9.98, $8.50, $12.95, $9.98
D. $11.05, $12.98, $8.25, $9.55, $7.50, $10.67

44. Which of the following sets of scores has a mode of 87?

A. 90, 87, 96, 96, 87, 96
B. 99, 87, 93, 94, 87, 90
C. 91, 92, 89, 97, 84, 84
D. 92, 91, 85, 87, 88, 95

45. A box contains 40 tiles, all of identical shape and size, numbered 1 through 40. If a person picks out a single tile from the box without looking, what is the probability that the number on the tile will be a prime number?

A. $\frac{1}{4}$

B. $\frac{3}{10}$

C. $\frac{13}{40}$

D. $\frac{27}{40}$

IF YOU FINISH BEFORE TIME IS CALLED, CHECK YOUR WORK ON THIS SECTION ONLY. DO NOT WORK ON ANY OTHER SECTION IN THE TEST.

General Knowledge Practice Test 2: Reading

Time: 40 minutes

40 questions

Directions: Please read the following passages carefully. Each passage in this section is followed by questions based on the passage's content. After reading each passage, answer the questions by choosing the best answer from among the four choices given. Be sure to base your answers on what is *implied* or *stated* in the passage.

Passage 1

Baseball: America's National Pastime

(1) If you want to know the spirit of America, you need to know the role of baseball in American life. Loved by millions, played by thousands, baseball, since its first introduction into American life, has become the hallmark of all that is good and right about our country. Unlike football or basketball, baseball evokes a bygone era of American independence, openness, and simplicity. Perhaps, because it is played outside in the fresh air and beneath America's clear blue skies or, perhaps, because it is such a civil and simple game, it evokes nostalgia and happiness whenever people, young and old alike, gather to watch this homegrown sport played out on our nation's amateur and professional fields.

(2) Patterned after a game in England, baseball has its roots in America's colonies. Early settlers played "rounders," a game that involved hitting a ball with a bat and advancing around bases. One big difference from the traditional English rounders, though, in this early colonial game is that players were counted out when another threw the ball and hit the man advancing. The practice was known as "plugging" or "soaking" runners. Fortunately, this practice of literally "striking" runners was changed to a simple "tagging" of runners, thereby beginning the game of baseball as we know it today. In fact, by the mid 1800s, baseball was played in America very similar to the way it is played today—a baseball diamond, two teams, three outs, nine innings, and whichever team has the most runs batted in wins.

(3) Although myth has it that Abner Doubleday invented modern baseball, it is most often credited to Alexander Cartwright, a New York City sportsman. In 1845, he started a club, "The Knickerbocker Base Ball Club of New York,"

whose sole purpose was to play baseball. Beginning with a dream and a desire, Cartwright wrote many of the rules that baseball follows today. Shortly after Cartwright's New York team was formed, others followed. Ironically enough, the Civil War (1861–1865) helped spread baseball across the United States. For recreation, Union troops played the game to the amusement of onlookers from both sides of America's great conflict. After the war, Northerners and Southerners were playing this popular game, and gradually its popularity grew from state to state.

(4) With popularity came commercialism, and soon baseball became a professional sport. Major American cities—Boston, New York, Philadelphia, Detroit, and others—sported a major league baseball club to rival competing teams. Americans, eager to watch this new sport and cheer their respective home teams, began flocking to makeshift baseball stadiums in the early 1900s, ensuring the success of the country's first professional sports franchise system.

(5) Success meant more competition. Fans followed their favorite teams, hoping for championship seasons. Soon, star players became local and national heroes, and baseball enthusiasts knew the statistics of every player. Baseball became America's national pastime. With each passing game, teams and their players added more to its historical lore and contemporary allure.

(6) Of all of America's obsessions, baseball is one of pure passion. To fans of the game, nothing exemplifies America's spirit, independence, and competitiveness more than an exciting game of baseball. And, fans feel that nothing has come along to compete with the feeling of sitting outdoors, soaking in the warm summer sun, and enjoying a favorite team at play in a leisurely and orderly game of baseball. Perhaps, these reasons explain why baseball has so long endured.

1. This passage indicates that

   A. baseball should be played outside and on grass.
   B. "plugging" is not a part of modern baseball.
   C. Abner Doubleday invented baseball.
   D. Alexander Cartwright was an American patriot.

2. According to this passage, "rounders" is a game that

   A. was imported from England.
   B. had nine innings.
   C. was played by Civil War soldiers.
   D. was never popular in America.

3. In the first paragraph, the word *evokes* means

   A. deters.
   B. entices.
   C. projects.
   D. elicits.

4. According to this passage, the Knickerbocker Base Ball Club was formed in the city of

   A. Boston.
   B. Detroit.
   C. New York.
   D. Philadelphia.

5. Which of the following is an opinion expressed in this passage?

   A. Early settlers played "rounders."
   B. Alexander Cartwright wrote many of the rules that baseball follows today.
   C. Professional baseball teams were formed by the 1900s.
   D. Baseball has become the hallmark of all that is good and right about our country.

6. According to the passage, why is baseball considered America's favorite pastime?

   A. It provides interested individuals with a casual diversion.
   B. It engages sports enthusiasts in a fast-paced spectator sport.
   C. It is played casually without rules.
   D. It occurs at a leisurely pace in a pastoral setting.

7. As used in the final paragraph, the word *exemplifies* means to

   A. define by definition.
   B. illustrate by example.
   C. organize by listing.
   D. delineate by detailing.

8. The narrative style of this passage can best be described as

   A. derisive.
   B. cynical.
   C. subjective.
   D. pessimistic.

9. Which sentence best states the main idea of this passage?

   A. Baseball is a sport that is elitist in tone and style.
   B. Baseball evokes an era of a simpler life and pace.
   C. Baseball reflects the simplicity of all competitive sports.
   D. Baseball inspires youngsters to become competitive athletes.

10. Identify the relationship between the following three sentences in the final paragraph.

    "Of all of America's obsessions, baseball is one of pure passion. To fans of the game, nothing exemplifies America's spirit, independence, and competitiveness more than an exciting game of baseball. And, fans feel that nothing has come along to compete with the feeling of sitting outdoors, soaking in the warm summer sun, and enjoying a favorite team at play in a leisurely and orderly game of baseball."

    The second and third sentences

    A. dispute the first sentence.
    B. contradict the first sentence.
    C. explain the first sentence.
    D. ignore the first sentence.

Passage 2

Dancing: One Person's Lament

(1)   Do you know how to dance? I mean, really dance? Most people know how to "shake, rattle, and roll"; and many can do a fairly good imitation of an individual in the "throes of a demonic possession," but very few of us can actually dance well. We might know how to twist and shout, but how many of us can cha-cha, rhumba, or waltz? I know I can't. I have (to repeat a time-honored phrase) two left feet and have tried on numerous occasions to learn to really dance; but have always ended up in the arms of someone desperate enough to be kind, but not quite assertive enough to say, "Stick to walking."

(2)   Dancing, to be sure, is among the oldest of human art forms. Traditionally, it has been a most immediate form of self-expression. Ancient rituals were (and still are to this day) celebrated in dance, as the dance symbolizes a form of prayer. Dancing for rain, good fortune, fertility of crops, and for success in war or hunting was common. Often, elaborate costumes and props were incorporated in these highly ritualistic endeavors as well.

(3)   Ritualistic dancing eventually gave rise to social dancing. Instead of being used to strengthen religious connections, dancing became a prime means for social bonding as people gathered for celebrations and used their love for movement and song to unite their heads and hearts. Social dancing became the mechanism through which individuals discovered common bonds and together affirmed their sense of common identity or belonging.

(4)   As dance evolved, it naturally took on a life of its own. Soon, formal dancing emerged. In formal dancing, the steps involved are more complicated in design than dancing that is self-willed and free-wheeling. Instead of simple and impulsive movements, the participants learn exact steps that require time, diligence, and a certain special nimbleness to master.

(5)   I have never had the patience to master formal moves, but I envy all who really know how to dance well—those who have perfected both the art and skill of masterful movement to music and who can cha-cha and tango expertly. Blessed with the gift of mimicry, these strong and able dancers rival professional sports athletes in their dexterity, agility, and nimbleness. Indeed, their expertise lies in making the difficult and strenuous look easy and joyous. In this way, the universal language of dance invites its watchers and participants—even those as seemingly hopeless as I—to engage in an activity that is part seduction, part mystery, and part unifier, and that expresses the whole range of human emotions.

11. According to this passage, the author believes that dancing is

    A. detrimental to one's health and well-being.
    B. always free-willed and free-wheeling.
    C. a waste of time and energy.
    D. a joyous expression of movement to music.

12. The author's claim that "I have two left feet" (paragraph 1) is

    A. questionable because of the author's love for dance.
    B. a narrative technique to engage the reader.
    C. full proof that the author dislikes dancing.
    D. an argumentative style to disarm the reader.

13. This passage is an example of a

    A. narrative portrayal of a positive experience.
    B. cynical perspective on the human condition.
    C. valedictory speech regarding a dying art form.
    D. descriptive narration of an obscure obsession.

14. In the fifth paragraph, the phrase "Blessed with the gift of mimicry" best means being able to

   A. deceive.
   B. reinvent.
   C. imitate.
   D. circumvent.

15. According to this narrative, dancing is universally enjoyed because it

   A. is an ancient and mysterious ritual.
   B. speaks to human emotions.
   C. is compelling and consequential.
   D. revels in the known and factual.

16. Which of the following statements is implied in the first paragraph?

   A. Most people know how to shake, rattle, and roll.
   B. The waltz is an easy dance to master.
   C. The cha-cha, rhumba, and waltz are types of dances.
   D. Few people can actually dance well.

17. Which of the following is an opinion expressed in this passage?

   A. Ancient rituals were celebrated in dance.
   B. Ritualistic dancing gave rise to social dancing.
   C. Dancing has been a most human form of self-expression.
   D. In formal dancing, the participants learn exact steps.

18. In the first paragraph, the word *assertive* means

   A. hesitant.
   B. ambiguous.
   C. bold.
   D. inhibited.

19. This passage states that

   A. Gene Kelly was a good dancer.
   B. ritualistic dancing is no longer practiced.
   C. dancing is an art form.
   D. only expert dancers can learn to cha-cha.

20. According to information given in this passage,

   A. people have an inborn desire to want to learn to dance.
   B. ritualistic dancing is very similar to social dancing.
   C. Native Americans performed ritualistic dances for success in hunting.
   D. formal dancing is difficult and strenuous.

Passage 3

Jean Piaget: The Beginning of Educational Thought

(1)   Jean Piaget's (1896–1980) major contribution to the history of educational thought and the study of cognitive science is that he proposed that children pass through four stages of mental development. Each stage, he believed, lasted for a specified period of time and must be followed in a designated order. He felt that this defined order accounted for why young children perceived the world as they do and why they make their respective choices. Piaget's work is seminal to understanding modern child development and integral to defining his subsequent impact on everything that followed his early findings.

(2)   Piaget's four stages of cognitive development in children are the *sensorimotor period* (birth to 2 years old), the *preoperational period* (2 to 7 years old), the *period of concrete operations* (7 to 11 years old), and the *period of formal operations* (11 to 15 years old). Each stage has its own defined characteristics, and each must be lived or traversed in the chronological order in which it appears. The *sensorimotor period* is the time when infants and toddlers obtain their basic knowledge of the world through their senses. Next, the *preoperational period* is when young children develop such skills as language and drawing ability. In the period of *concrete operations*, older children begin to think logically. Gradually, they begin to take on the ability to organize their knowledge, classify objects, and do thought problems. Finally, during the period of *formal operations*, young people or teenagers begin to think conceptually, applying rational and abstract reasoning to their burgeoning thought processes. Piaget knew, though, that if young children got stuck in a particular stage of mental development, their world would be forever defined by that mental stage. Thus, if young people gradually grow into the final

developmental stage—the *period of formal operations*—they, more than likely, will have a promising intellectual future. To be stuck in an earlier stage, though, means a life of limited intellectual abilities.

(3)   Before we discuss Piaget's work any further, it is best to know about his life. Born in 1896 in Neufchatel, Switzerland, Jean Piaget was soon recognized by his family, teachers, and peers as an exceptionally bright and inquisitive child. Not satisfied with simple explanations, Piaget spent hours researching whatever scientific principle or theory caught his interest. At the age of 10 (or some say 11), his innate curiosity and deep-seated drive led him to publish his first scientific paper on an albino sparrow. This accomplishment was followed by a number of articles on mollusks at the age of 15.

(4)   Naturally, this precocious child excelled in school; and by 1918, at the early age of 22, he received his doctorate in the natural sciences. Not content to know just the physical world, Piaget began studying psychology, hoping to uncover the mysteries of the human mind. Retreating in 1921 to the world-famed Institute J. J. Rousseau in Geneva, Piaget embarked on a career that eventually led to his breakthrough discoveries in human cognition. From 1933 to 1971, Piaget served as the co-director of this famed institute and as the director of the International Bureau of Education (1929–1967). Always busy and engaged, Piaget was also a professor of psychology at the University of Geneva from 1929 until his death in 1980, at age 94.

(5)   Piaget's most significant contribution to the world of scientific thought about human cognition is the results of his studies of young children, primarily his own children–Jacqueline, Lucienne, and Laurent. From their infancy, Piaget recorded their every move and nuance, crystallizing his observations into his renowned scientific theories. And his lasting contribution, though commonplace today, was radical for its time—that children think differently than adults.

(6)   Both a qualitative and a quantitative researcher, Piaget studied human growth and development from a holistic perspective, always trying to integrate disparate elements of information into a cohesive and recognizable human whole. His research on how knowledge grows systematically, that it is a progressive construction of logically embedded structures superseding one another, transformed the manner in which psychologists think of young

people. No longer are they thought of as miniature adults. Instead, Piaget's seminal work recognized that children's logic and modes of thinking were entirely their own. His thinking radically transformed the world of cognitive science and led to the formation of the field of developmental psychology. Simply, by studying his own children, Piaget introduced us to the world of all children.

21. In this narrative, the author suggests that Piaget was

    A. a curious and prodigious thinker.
    B. an effete intellectual and disciplinarian.
    C. a raucous and caustic intellectual.
    D. a cautious and solitary scientist.

22. As thinking about human cognition has evolved, one principle, according to this passage, has remained constant:

    A. Human beings need to reconcile the absurd.
    B. Human beings need to understand the misunderstood.
    C. Human beings need to develop mentally in defined stages.
    D. Human beings need to rediscover ancient truths.

23. The author of this passage would probably agree that

    A. developmental psychology has its origins in ritualistic thinking.
    B. studying cognitive thinking reveals human behavior patterns.
    C. understanding abstract thinking parallels nutritional habits.
    D. searching for the unknown is the province of only religious thinkers.

24. Which of the following statements is NOT supported by the passage?

    A. Psychology is the study of human developmental growth patterns.
    B. Piaget's developmental theories were the result of a small sample size.
    C. Developmental thinking can be classified into specified age groups.
    D. Cognitive psychology relies on the suspension of disbelief.

25. In the fourth paragraph, the phrase, "Not content to know just the physical world," implies that Piaget

    A. was a literal scientific researcher.
    B. understood only the human body.
    C. engaged in quantitative research.
    D. intended to explore mental functions.

26. According to this passage, Jean Piaget was born in

    A. France.
    B. England.
    C. Italy.
    D. Switzerland.

27. Which of the following is the topic of the second paragraph?

    A. Piaget's four stages of cognitive development.
    B. Piaget's views on teaching and learning.
    C. Piaget's ideas about rational thought.
    D. Piaget's theories on how infants perceive the world.

28. Which of the following is an opinion about Jean Piaget expressed in this passage?

    A. His work is seminal to understanding modern child development.
    B. He received a doctorate degree in natural sciences.
    C. He studied his own children.
    D. He published his first paper before he was 12 years old.

29. This passage states that Jean Piaget

    A. advocated developmentally appropriate learning activities.
    B. made breakthrough discoveries in human cognition.
    C. received a number of honorary degrees in his lifetime.
    D. died before his theories were generally accepted.

30. The tone of this passage is best described as

    A. doubtful.
    B. mocking.
    C. persuasive.
    D. serious.

Passage 4

Whales: Special Mammals Indeed

(1)   Many people think whales are a type of fish because whales live in the water. Whales, however, are not fish; they are mammals and have much in common with human beings. It is hard to believe, but it is true. Whales, monkeys, dogs, and people all belong to the same class, and like these mammals, whales have a highly developed brain and are among the most behaviorally complex of all animals.

(2)   Whales differ from fish in multiple ways. For instance, whales have different tails than fish. Fish tails are vertical—they move sideways; whale tails are horizontal—they move up and down. Also, fish breathe through gills, taking in dissolved oxygen from water. Whales, on the other hand, have lungs and must come to the surface to breathe. But, for some whales, the trip to the surface for oxygen can be delayed quite a while; in fact, the sperm whale can hold its breath for up to two hours.

(3)   Gestation and birth are another example of how fish and whales differ. Fish lay eggs and do not feed their offspring. Whales, though, have the "mothering instinct" of mammals. Like apes, dogs, and cats, they give birth to live young and proceed to feed them with milk from the mother's body. Fish are emotionally detached from their offspring; whereas, for a whale, the mothering instinct remains strong throughout a lifetime.

(4)   Another major difference between fish and whales is that fish are cold-blooded and whales are warm-blooded. As a cold-blooded creature, a fish's body temperature changes with the water's temperature. When the water is cold, the fish is cold. A whale, on the other hand, remains warm regardless of the temperature of the surrounding water.

(5)   Adaptation has played a major role in the evolving of whales. Yes, they are considered mammals; but unlike most mammals, they do not have much hair nor do they have legs or much neck mobility. Through centuries of change and adaptability, whales have developed streamlined, compact, and compressed body frames that allow them to carry enormous weight and still manage to swim through the sea with great ease. In fact, scientists believe their front legs developed into flippers, allowing them to steer and keep their balance.

(6)   Today, many whales are an endangered species, and some, especially the blue and humpback whales, are in danger of extinction

because of unregulated hunting. For years, whalers were permitted to kill whales, like the blue and humpback, for their meat and byproducts. The result is that whales of all kinds slowly disappeared from our oceans. Yet, thanks to environmental laws and public awareness, the significance of whales as one of the oldest and most distinct mammals is readily recognized by scientists and citizens alike. Once again, they populate our oceans and add to our knowledge about these unique marine mammals.

31. One thing that this narrative makes clear is that whales have more in common with

- **A.** mammals than with fish.
- **B.** reptiles than with mammals.
- **C.** amphibians than with fish.
- **D.** fish than with mammals.

32. According to the passage, whales are unique in the animal kingdom because whales

- **A.** are indigenous only to the northern hemisphere.
- **B.** can carry enormous weight without much effort.
- **C.** are nonmaternal and indifferent to their offspring.
- **D.** rely on protective fish clans for self-preservation.

33. The author of this passage implies that whales are

- **A.** timid.
- **B.** aggressive.
- **C.** intelligent.
- **D.** unintelligent.

34. Which of the following statements can be inferred from the passage?

- **A.** Whales are creatures that have experienced successful adaptations.
- **B.** Whales are ponderous creatures with a sluggish metabolism.
- **C.** Whales are a species timid in scale and singular in design.
- **D.** Whales are an anomaly on the scale of biological diversity.

35. In the fifth paragraph, the word *Adaptation* can best be defined as

- **A.** modification.
- **B.** skillfulness.
- **C.** awareness.
- **D.** immutability.

36. The tone of this passage is best described as

- **A.** skeptical.
- **B.** humorous.
- **C.** sarcastic.
- **D.** factual.

37. Which of the following is a fact about whales that is given in this passage?

- **A.** Whales are a type of fish.
- **B.** Whales have lungs.
- **C.** The blue whale is extinct.
- **D.** Blubber comes from whales.

38. Which of the following statements about whales is implied in this passage?

- **A.** They are cold-blooded creatures.
- **B.** They cannot take in oxygen when underwater.
- **C.** They have gills.
- **D.** They have nothing in common with humans.

39. This passage states that the sperm whale can hold its breath for

- **A.** no more than 30 minutes.
- **B.** up to 2 hours.
- **C.** at least 3 hours.
- **D.** well over 4 hours.

40. According to the passage, whales

- **A.** are the world's largest animal.
- **B.** nurture their young.
- **C.** have difficulty swimming.
- **D.** are of little concern to environmentalists.

IF YOU FINISH BEFORE TIME IS CALLED, CHECK YOUR WORK ON THIS SECTION ONLY. DO NOT WORK ON ANY OTHER SECTION IN THE TEST.

Answer Key

English Language Skills

1. B	15. B	29. C
2. C	16. A	30. A
3. C	17. C	31. B
4. D	18. D	32. C
5. A	19. C	33. B
6. D	20. B	34. A
7. A	21. A	35. B
8. B	22. C	36. B
9. A	23. C	37. C
10. B	24. B	38. C
11. A	25. B	39. A
12. A	26. B	40. A
13. C	27. C	
14. B	28. B	

Mathematics

1. D	16. B	31. D
2. C	17. D	32. D
3. C	18. B	33. A
4. C	19. A	34. B
5. A	20. A	35. C
6. C	21. C	36. B
7. D	22. D	37. D
8. C	23. B	38. A
9. A	24. D	39. D
10. C	25. A	40. C
11. D	26. D	41. C
12. B	27. C	42. A
13. A	28. A	43. C
14. C	29. D	44. B
15. D	30. C	45. B

Reading

1. B	15. B	29. B
2. A	16. C	30. D
3. D	17. C	31. A
4. C	18. C	32. B
5. D	19. C	33. C
6. D	20. D	34. A
7. B	21. A	35. A
8. C	22. C	36. D
9. B	23. B	37. B
10. C	24. D	38. B
11. D	25. D	39. B
12. B	26. D	40. B
13. A	27. A	
14. C	28. A	

Answer Explanations

Sample Essays

In this section of the examination, you were asked to prepare a written assignment on one of two topics.

Topic 1

My favorite hobbies

Topic 2

A historical figure who changed the world

You were asked to write a 300- to 600-word response that would be well-written, organized, and defined. You were also informed that your writing would be graded holistically, taking into consideration both mechanics and organization.

What follows are examples of a weak and strong response to both prompts.

Topic 1—My Favorite Hobbies

Weak Response

My favorite hobbies are many. In fact, I have so many favorite hobbies that I have difficulty listing them all in one sitting. I like to swim, read, play tennis, and even collect stamps. I know that stamp collecting is not a very popular hobby anymore, but I really like it, I really do! Don't you? I also like bike riding. In fact, I think bike riding is my favorite thing to do. I just love going out on a sunny afternoon, feeling the brisk cool air at my back and just letting myself go on my bicycle. I ride everywhere, smiling at all I meet and waving to all who I see. Then, when I am really anxious, I love to do crossword puzzles. Thinking real hard about the right word calms me down and gets my juices flowing. I have to stop and think about what word would fit in a particular space—and that requires great skill. But, then again, sometimes I just give up and just sit and stare into space, and that's fun too.

Strong Response

Human beings can be many things. We can be parents, friends, lovers, workers, caregivers, cooks, handymen, and tired souls. Yet, despite the responsibilities of our various roles, an activity that we often enjoy the most is one we do just for ourselves. Such an activity is called a hobby. We find a diversion that appeals to us very much and despite everything else—bills, problems, and even illness—we find time to pursue our enjoyment. I know. I have three hobbies that I enjoy no matter what.

First, I enjoy reading. For me, reading is a luxury that I try to enjoy at every opportunity. Wherever I go, I carry something to read. Sometimes, it is a book that I just can't put down—so when no one is looking or there is a lull at work, I sneak in a few seconds to read just a little bit more of what I am presently enjoying. And there is no limit to my reading preferences. I enjoy everything from mysteries to political biographies. I find each fascinating and intriguing. Each genre—comedy, mystery, romance, thriller, or biography—provides a new insight into the human condition and, of course, whets my appetite for more.

Second, I enjoy eating. Now, I know eating is not considered a typical hobby, but when you are a connoisseur of fine food like I am, then eating is considered your hobby. Often, my spouse and I will go miles just to try out a new restaurant—no matter how obscure or famous it might portend to be. We enjoy trying new dishes—comparing our culinary adventures to climbing Mount Everest or floating down the Nile—we never know what to expect. Sometimes, we hit a real gem with great dishes, breads, and wines. Other times, well, let's just say, we don't finish our plates. But, despite all, I never tire of eating.

Third, I enjoy laughing. Laughing, you say? Is laughing really a hobby? It is if you laugh like I do. I laugh loud and long and hard. And I constantly look for things to amuse me. I enjoy good jokes (preferably clean and clever), funny books, musical comedies, and silly movies. Each—when done well—tickles my ribs like nothing else possible. Does that mean that I don't like sad things? Sure, I do; but I figure, why cry when laughing is so much more pleasurable? Besides, evoking laughter is harder to execute. Making someone laugh—even a pushover like me—is a skill in and of itself.

Thus, my hobbies are personal and unique. While many adults enjoy tennis and jogging, I prefer reading, eating, and laughing. I know that likely I won't end up looking like the famous athletes I see on television, but, I will have fun pursuing my passion—just like they do. And what more could I ask?

Topic 2—A Historical Figure Who Changed the World

Weak Response

To be sure, there are many historical figure who have had a major impact on world events. Everyone from four start general to great explorers have impacted the way the world events have and continue to unfold. No person, though, in my mind, has had a greater impact on world events than Franklin Delano Roosevelt. Elected to an unprecedented four terms in political office, Roosevelt literally changed the face of the globe with his far-reaching goals and programs. He lifted—singlehandedly—people out of poverty and defeated Nazism with one fell swoop. His reach is felt to this day as his political programs and ideas are still being implemented in the halls of American government and foreign countries. His far-reaching social programs were just the tonic needed for a downtrodden and desperate American people. And his great courage to defeat a worldwide enemy despite his own personal pain and hardship is much to be admired. Indeed, he is a truly remarkable historical figure.

Strong Response

President Franklin D. Roosevelt is truly a historical figure who changed the world. The only president to be elected to four consecutive terms in office, Roosevelt led the United States through its worst depression and its worst war. In his personal life, he showed courage and great strength of character in overcoming hardships. Stricken by polio in mid-life, he refused to give up his career of public service. In fact, even after being stricken with polio, Roosevelt was elected to the presidency. It was this strength of determination in the face of insurmountable difficulty and pain that helped him to successfully lead the country through very difficult times.

In the prime of his life, Roosevelt became paralyzed from the waist down. Polio left him immobile, but not downtrodden. For the rest of his life, he fought desperately to overcome his disability; and from the comfort of his wheelchair, he continued his political career. He loved public service and relished the attention that it brought him. He also wanted to prove to himself and the world that any hardship could be overcome with sheer determination. With this in mind, he ran for public office. He was elected governor of New York, and then later became president of the United States.

When Roosevelt became president, America was experiencing an unprecedented social upheaval; a serious economic depression was occurring and millions of people were unemployed. Immediately, Roosevelt and his administration began the difficult work of trying to solve the country's social and economic problems. Quickly, he set up numerous government agencies to provide relief for the jobless and to stabilize the country's economy. He also supplied banks in good financial condition with money so that they would reopen and return the country to a healthy financial condition. Finally, he passed laws to protect the investments of those who held stocks and bonds. All these actions were taken to ensure the economic viability of a country and a people who were desperate for help.

At the beginning of Roosevelt's third term in office, the United States entered the Second World War. Shortly after the attack of the Japanese on Pearl Harbor, The U.S. Congress declared war on Japan. Three days later, Germany and Italy declared war on the United States. America then declared war on those countries. Under Roosevelt's leadership, the United States together with its allies prevailed over the enemy. America's citizens firmly supported Roosevelt during the difficult war years, but unfortunately, he was never to see the final victory. He died suddenly at his favorite spa for the treatment for his polio, Warm Springs, Georgia, just before the surrender of the German army.

Truly, Roosevelt was a remarkable historical figure. Despite crippling pain, he managed to achieve political greatness and monumental significance by imposing his own physical and intellectual will onto the American people. Overcoming tremendous odds both at home and abroad, Roosevelt raised the economic conditions of the American people while simultaneously helping to liberate the world from oppression and tyranny. In so doing, he was instrumental in changing the course of history and demonstrated the power of the human spirit.

English Language Skills

1. **B.** Choice **B** is the correct response. This arrangement provides the most logical sequence of ideas and supporting details in this paragraph. Choices **A, C,** and **D** do not represent a logical arrangement of the possible sentence combinations.

2. **C.** Choice **C** is the correct response. The passage is discussing shells as a protective covering, not about collecting them.

3. **C.** Choice **C** is the correct response. This arrangement provides the most logical sequence of ideas and supporting details in the paragraph. Choices **A, B,** and **D** do not represent a logical arrangement of the possible sentence combinations.

4. **D.** Choice **D** is the correct response. The passage is discussing the challenge of language diversity in schools, not ethnic foods.

5. **A.** Choice **A** is the correct response. The word *accept* is used incorrectly in this sentence. The correction is *except*. The word *accept* means "to receive something." The word *except* means "excluding"; it is an indication that something is not included in the general whole. The word *allowed* at **B** is the correct spelling and used properly. The infinitive *to eat* at **C** is also the proper usage.

6. **D.** Choice **D** is the correct response. No change is necessary. The sentence is correct as written.

7. **A.** Choice **A** is the correct response. The word *too* is used incorrectly in this sentence. The correction is *to*. The word *too* means "also" or "in addition." The word *to* is a preposition used to connect two thoughts together in a sentence. The words *formally* at **B** and *themselves* at **C** are both the correct word choices for this sentence.

8. **B.** Choice **B** is the correct response. The word *french* is presented incorrectly in this sentence. The correction is *French*. A language—English, French, Spanish, German, and so on—is considered a proper noun and, hence, is capitalized. The words *read* at **A** and *tomorrow's* at **C** are spelled and used correctly in this sentence.

9. **A.** Choice **A** is the correct response. *Have went* is incorrect. The correction is *have gone*. The word *all-American* at **B** is properly capitalized. The word *their* at **C** is properly used as a possessive pronoun.

10. **B.** Choice **B** is the correct response. The word *among* is used incorrectly in this sentence. The correction is *between*. *Among* is used when you are referring to three or more objects; *between* is used when you are referring to only two objects. The verb *sat* at **A** is correctly used in this sentence. The word *awards* at **C** does not require capitalization.

11. **A.** Choice **A** is the correct response. The word *deep* is used incorrectly in this sentence. The correction is *deeply*. The word *deep* is used here as an adverb and, thus, should be replaced with *deeply*. The word *their* at **B** is the correct word choice because it is showing possession. The phrase *considerable differences* at **C** is an appropriate word choice for this sentence.

12. **A.** Choice **A** is the correct response. The word *fowl* is the wrong word choice in this sentence. The correction is *foul*. The word *fowl* is another word for bird. As used in this sentence, the word *foul* refers to an infringement of the rules in a game of play. The word *loudly* at **B** is an adverb modifying *protested* and is used correctly in this sentence. The word *disbelief* at **C** is spelled correctly.

13. **C.** Choice **C** is the correct response. The word *then* is the wrong word choice in this sentence. The correction is *than*. The word *than* is used when making a comparison, as is the case in this sentence. The word *then* refers to time. In this sentence, the word *unfortunately* at **A** is used correctly to modify the action of the tennis team. The auxiliary verb *had* at **B** is used correctly in this sentence.

14. **B.** Choice **B** is the correct response. The word *masks* is the wrong verb choice in this sentence. The correction is *mask*. The verb *mask* is used because the subject of the sentence is the plural noun *talents*. In this sentence, the adjective *surprising* at **A** is used correctly to modify the noun *talents*. The possessive form *his* at **C** is used correctly in this sentence.

15. **B.** Choice **B** is the correct response. The phrase *me and Nancy* is the wrong choice for this sentence. The correction is *Nancy and I*. The parts of a compound subject of a sentence are always in the subjective case. The word *among* at **A** is the correct word choice because it refers to more than two sisters. The word *tall* at **C** is correct as used in this sentence.

16. **A.** Choice **A** is the correct response. The word *reign* is the wrong word choice in this sentence. The correction is *rain*. The verbs *found* at **B** and *eat* at **C** are used correctly in this sentence.

17. **C.** Choice **C** is the correct response. The sentence should be in the past tense, so *saw* is the correct verb at **C**. Keep in mind that the verb *seen* cannot stand alone; it requires an auxiliary verb. The word *students* at **A** does not show possession, so no apostrophe is needed. The word *who* at **B** is correct because it serves as the subject of the nonrestrictive clause it introduces.

18. **D.** Choice **D** is the correct response. The word *that* at **A** introducing the subordinate clause, which identifies what is being talked about, is correct. The word *really* at **B** is also correct because it is an adverb modifying the adjective *careful*. The plural pronoun *they* at **C** is correct because it agrees with its antecedent *scientists*.

19. **C.** Choice **C** is the correct response. A comma is needed at **C** to separate the introductory subordinate clause from the rest of the sentence. The word *when* at **A** is correct and makes sense in the sentence. The word *students* at **B** does not show possession, so no apostrophe is needed.

20. **B.** Choice **B** is the correct response. The phrase *more easier* at **B** is a faulty comparison of two things. The correct comparative form of *easy* is *easier*. The word *happy* at **A** is correct because it is an adjective referring to one thing. Placing a comma at **C** would be incorrect.

21. **A.** Choice **A** is the correct response. In this sentence, the word following the verb *felt* at **A** modifies its subject, the pronoun *they*. The word *badly* is an adverb, however, and should not be used to modify a pronoun. The adjective *bad* should be used instead. The word *Tiffany* at **B** is a proper noun, so it should be capitalized. The plural verb *were* at **C** agrees with its plural subject *they*.

22. **C.** Choice **C** is the correct response. The word *capitol* refers to a building, not to a city. Change *capitol* to *capital*, which refers to a seat of government, to make the sentence grammatically correct. The word *history* at **A** is not a proper noun, so it should not be capitalized. The sentence is in the past tense, so *went* is the correct verb at **B**.

23. **C.** Choice **C** is the correct response. The word *there* at **C** should be changed to the plural third-person pronoun *their* to make the sentence grammatically correct. The possessive form *girls'* of the plural noun *girls* at **A** is correctly formed. To form the possessive of a plural noun that ends in *s*, add an apostrophe after the *s*. Inserting a comma at **B** would be incorrect. No comma should be placed between two items joined by the word *and*.

24. **B.** Choice **B** is the correct response. The sentence is in the past tense; *ran* is the correct verb instead of *had run*. The word *when* at **A** is correct and makes sense in the sentence. The word *their* at **C** is spelled correctly.

25. **B.** Choice **B** is the correct response. The word *between* is a preposition. The object of a preposition should be in the objective case. Change *I* at **B** to *me* to make the sentence grammatically correct. The word *cannot* at **A** is spelled correctly. The word *years* at **C** is not showing ownership, so it should not be in the possessive case.

26. **B.** Choice **B** is the correct response. The word at **B** is the subject of the verb *am* (which is understood) and thus, should be in the subjective case. Change *me* to *I* to make the sentence grammatically correct. The sentence is in the present tense, so *are* at **A** is correct. Inserting a comma at **C** would be incorrect.

27. **C.** Choice **C** is the correct response. The word at **C** should be in the subjective case because it is the subject of the subordinate clause it introduces. Change *whomever* to *whoever* to make the sentence grammatically correct. Inserting a comma at **A** would be incorrect. The word *principal,* referring to the person who is the building supervisor of the school, at **B** is the correct word choice.

28. **B.** Choice **B** is the correct response. The singular pronoun *one* is the subject of the verb at **B,** so change *want* to *wants* to make the verb agree with its singular subject. The relative pronoun *who* at **A** is correct because it is the subject of the relative clause it introduces. The word *too* at **C** is spelled correctly.

29. **C.** Choice **C** is the correct response. The word *good* at **C** modifies the verb *did,* so it should be an adverb. Change *good* to *well* to make the sentence grammatically correct. The comma at **A** following the introductory clause is correct. The verb *didn't* at **B** agrees with its singular subject *he.*

30. **A.** Choice **A** is the correct response. The pronoun at **A** modifies the gerund noun *graduating,* which is the subject of the main clause; hence you should use the possessive pronoun *My* instead of *Me* to make the sentence grammatically correct. The singular verb *has* at **B** agrees with its singular subject *graduating.* The relative pronoun *whom* at **C** is the object of the preposition *of,* so it should be in the objective case.

31. **B.** Choice **B** is the correct response. The singular pronoun *one* is the subject of the verb at **B,** so change *were* to *was* to make the verb agree with its singular subject. Inserting a comma at **A** would be incorrect. No hyphen is needed at **C.**

32. **C.** Choice **C** is the correct response. Does *them* at **C** refer to *sons* or *board games*? Change *them* to *the board games* to avoid ambiguity. The word *couple's* at **A** is the correct possessive form of *couple.* The comma at **B** is needed to separate the two independent clauses.

33. **B.** Choice **B** is the correct response. The word at **B** should be spelled *received.* The relative pronoun *who* at **A** is correct because it is the subject of the clause it introduces. Inserting a comma at **C** would be incorrect.

34. **A.** Choice **A** is the correct response. At **A** the superlative form of *nice* is *nicest,* not *most nicest.* The word *friend* at **B** is spelled correctly. The noun phrase *every day* at **C** should not be replaced with the adjective *everyday,* which means "common" or "used daily."

35. **B.** Choice **B** is the correct response. The correct comparative form of *old* is *older.* The comparative form is used when two things are compared.

36. **B.** Choice **B** is the correct response. The past participle for the verb *to take* is *taken.* Note that *should of* in **A** and **C** is an error for *should have.*

37. **C.** Choice **C** is the correct response. The tense of the verb in **C** relates logically to the verb in the main clause because both verbs are in the past tense. The verb tenses in **A** and **B** do not relate logically to the verb in the main clause.

38. **C.** Choice **C** is the correct response. All punctuation in Choice **C** is correct. Choice **A** is incorrect because it is a run-on sentence. It is two complete sentences connected by only a comma. Choice **B** is also a run-on sentence. It is two complete sentences joined without a word to connect them or a proper punctuation mark to separate them. The first sentence in Choice **D** needs a comma after the word *promise.*

39. **A.** Choice **A** is the correct response. All punctuation in Choice **A** is correct. In Choice **B,** the word *familys'* is incorrect. To form the possessive of a noun (either singular or plural) that does not end in *s*, add an apostrophe and *s*. Choice **C** is incorrect because it contains a fragment. (*Having been raised in our household from a puppy.*) A comma is needed in Choice **D** to separate the introductory participial phrase from the rest of the sentence.

40. A. Choice **A** is the correct response. The modifiers in sentence **A** are placed correctly. The participial phrase *driving through the neighborhood* modifies *woman* and should be close to it. In Choices **B** and **C**, *driving through the neighborhood* is separated from the noun *woman*, resulting in ambiguity. Additionally, the participial phrase *playing with his dog* modifies the noun *child* and should be close to it. In Choice **D**, the participial phrase *playing with his dog* is separated from the noun *child*, resulting in ambiguity.

Mathematics

1. D. Choice **D** is the correct response. The greatest common factor of 30 and 45 is the largest number that will divide into both 30 and 45 evenly. The numbers that will divide evenly into 30 are 1, 2, 3, 5, 6, 10, 15, and 30. The numbers that will divide evenly into 45 are 1, 3, 5, 9, 15, and 45. Looking at the two sets of divisors, you can see that 15 is the largest number that will divide into both 30 and 45 evenly. Thus, GCF (30, 45) = 15. Choice **A** is incorrect because 2 is not a common factor of 30 and 45. Choices **B** and **C** are incorrect because 3 and 5 are common factors of 30 and 45, but both are less than 15, so neither is the greatest common factor.

2. C. Choice **C** is the correct response. $1.082 \cdot 10^8 = 1.082 \cdot 100,000,000 = 108,200,000$, which is equivalent to moving the decimal point 8 places to the right. Choice **A** is the result of moving the decimal point 10 places to the right. Choice **B** is the result of moving the decimal point 9 places to the right. Choice **D** is the result of moving the decimal point 8 places to the left.

3. C. Choice **C** is the correct response. Analyze the problem. From the figure, you can see that triangles ABC and ADE are right triangles. To find the area of right triangle ABC, you find $\frac{1}{2}$ the product of the lengths of its two legs. You can determine the length of leg $\overline{CA}$ by adding the lengths of the two segments, $\overline{CE}$ and $\overline{EA}$. Since right triangles ABC and ADE have two congruent right angles and an acute angle in common, namely angle A, they are similar triangles. Thus, the length of $\overline{BC}$ can be determined by using properties of similar triangles. Devise a plan. To find the area of triangle ABC will take three steps. First, find the length of leg $\overline{CA}$ by adding the lengths of the two segments, $\overline{CE}$ and $\overline{EA}$. Next, find the length of leg $\overline{BC}$ by using the proportionality of the corresponding sides of the similar triangles ABC and ADE. Then, find the area of triangle ABC by calculating $\frac{1}{2}bh = \frac{1}{2}$(length of $\overline{CA}$) (length of $\overline{BC}$). Carry out the plan.

Step 1. Find the length of leg $\overline{CA}$: $\overline{CA}$ = 200 m + 100 m = 300 m

Step 2. Find the length of $\overline{BC}$, call it x:

$$\frac{x}{300 \text{ m}} = \frac{50 \text{ m}}{100 \text{ m}}$$

$$x = \frac{50 \cdot 300 \text{ m}}{100} = 150 \text{ m}$$ Find a cross product you can calculate, and then divide by the other number.

Step 3. Find the area of triangle ABC: area = $\frac{1}{2}bh = \frac{1}{2}(300 \text{ m})(150 \text{ m}) = 22,500 \text{ m}^2$.

The area of triangle ABC is 22500 m², Choice **C**.

Did I answer the question? Yes, I found the area of triangle ABC. ✓

Does my answer make sense? Yes. ✓

Is the answer stated in the correct units? Yes, the units are square meters, which is correct. ✓

4. C. Choice **C** is the correct response. To simplify the expression $7 + 3(4^2) - 8$, follow the order of operations using the mnemonic "<u>P</u>lease <u>E</u>xcuse <u>M</u>y <u>D</u>ear <u>A</u>unt <u>S</u>ally."

$7 + 3(4^2) - 8 = 7 + 3(16) - 8$ First, do the exponentiation inside the parentheses.

$= 7 + 48 - 8$ Next, add and subtract.

$= 47$, Choice C

Choice **A** results if you evaluate 4^2 incorrectly as $4 \times 2 = 8$. Choice **B** results if you add and subtract before multiplying. Choice **D** results if, after you do the exponentiation in the first step, you continue by simplifying from left to right without regard for the order of operations.

5. A. Choice **A** is the correct response. Analyze the problem. Since x and $y = 3x$ are whole numbers and $z = x + y = x + 3x = 4x$, then z is a multiple of 4. Therefore, z represents a whole number that is divisible by 4. A number is divisible by 4 if and only if the last two digits form a number that is divisible by 4. Looking at the answer choices, you can see that only Choice **A** fails the test for divisibility by 4—because the last two digits of 314 are 14, which is not divisible by 4.

6. C. Choice **C** is the correct response. To change $8\frac{1}{4}\%$ to a decimal, first rewrite it as 8.25%. Then move the decimal point two places to the left and drop the percent sign to obtain 0.0825. Choices **A** and **B** result if you drop the percent sign but fail to move the decimal point two places to the left. Choice **D** results if you convert $8\frac{1}{4}$ to a decimal representation incorrectly.

7. D. Choice **D** is the correct response. To list the temperatures in order from coldest to warmest, list them in order from lowest to highest. Start with the positive temperatures: $2° < 4°$. You know that $0°$ is less than the positive temperatures and greater than the negative temperatures, so you have this: negative temperatures $< 0° < 2° < 4°$. To compare $-6°$ and $-8°$, sketch a number line:

From the number line, you can see that -6 is greater than -8 because it lies to the right of -8, so you end up with $-8° < -6° < 0° < 2° < 4°$, Choice **D**. Choice **A** results if you list the temperatures in order as if all were nonnegative. Choice **B** results if you list the temperatures from warmest to coldest. Choice **C** results if you make the mistake of thinking $-6° < -8°$.

8. C. Choice **C** is the correct response. To find the amount budgeted for rent, you will need to answer the question: What is 30% of $2,400?

Method 1: To solve the problem, identify the elements of the percent problem, plug the values into the percent proportion, and solve the proportion:

Step 1. Identify the elements.

$$r = 30$$

$$\text{part} = ?$$

$$\text{whole} = \$2{,}400$$

Step 2. Plug into the percent proportion (omitting the units for convenience).

$$\frac{r}{100} = \frac{\text{part}}{\text{whole}}$$

$$\frac{30}{100} = \frac{x}{2400}$$

Step 3. Solve the proportion.

30×2400	Find a cross product you can calculate. You don't know the value of x, so the only cross product you can calculate is 30 times 2,400.
$\dfrac{30 \times 2400}{100} = 720$	Divide by 100, the numerical term you didn't use.
$x = 720$	

The amount budgeted for rent is $720, Choice **C**.

Did I answer the question? Yes, I found the amount budgeted for rent. ✓

Does my answer make sense? Yes. ✓

Is the answer stated in the correct units? Yes, the units are dollars, which is correct. ✓

Method 2: Change 30% to a decimal fraction or common fraction and multiply:

30% of $2,400 = 0.30 × $2,400 = $720.00

Or 30% of $2,400 = $\frac{3}{1\cancel{0}} \times \frac{$240\cancel{0}}{1} = 3 \times $240 = 720

Choice **A** results if you make a decimal point error. Choice **B** results if you solve the problem incorrectly by finding 70% of $2,400, and you make a decimal point error. Choice **D** results if you solve the problem incorrectly by finding 70% of $2,400.

9. **A.** Choice **A** is the correct response.

Method 1: The conversion fractions are $\frac{1\text{ km}}{1000\text{ m}}$ and $\frac{1000\text{ m}}{1\text{ km}}$.

Write your measurement as a fraction with denominator 1 and let unit analysis tell you whether to multiply by $\frac{1\text{ km}}{1000\text{ m}}$ or $\frac{1000\text{ m}}{1\text{ km}}$. Since you want the meters to divide out, multiply by $\frac{1\text{ km}}{1000\text{ m}}$.

$\frac{1500\ \cancel{m}}{1} \cdot \frac{1\text{ km}}{1000\ \cancel{m}} = \frac{1500\text{ km}}{1000} = 1.5\text{ km}$

The runner ran 1.5 kilometers in the race, Choice **A**.

Choices **B** and **C** occur if you make a mistake in placing the decimal point in your answer. Choice **D** results if you multiply by 1000 to convert.

Method 2: Use "**K**ing **H**enry **D**oesn't **U**sually **D**rink **C**hocolate **M**ilk," which is a mnemonic for remembering the following metric prefixes: kilo-, hecto-, deca-, unit measurement, deci-, centi-, milli-.

In this problem, the unit measurement is meters. You are going from meters to kilometers. Since to go from meters to kilometers you move left three times on the list above, you will divide by 10 three times to convert meters to kilometers. Of course, dividing by 10 three times is equivalent to dividing by 1000 one time. Therefore,

1500 m = 1500 ÷ 1000 (3 moves left) = 1.5 km

The runner ran 1.5 kilometers in the race, Choice **A**.

10. **C.** Choice **C** is the correct response. The thermometer is reading between 30° and 40°. The difference between these two points is 40° − 30° = 10°. It takes five marks to go from 30° up to 40°. Divide the difference between the two points by 5: 10° ÷ 5 = 2°. Therefore, each mark on the thermometer represents 2°. The thermometer is reading three marks or 6° above 30°, which is 36° (Choice **C**). Choice **A** results if you mistakenly determine that each mark represents 1°. Choice **B** results if you mistakenly determine that the reading is at 35°. Choice **D** results if you read down from 40° instead of up from 30°.

11. **D.** Choice **D** is the correct response. Analyze the problem. From the Mathematics Reference Sheet, you have that the formula for the surface area of a sphere is $S.A. = 4\pi r^2$ and the formula for the volume of a sphere is $V = \frac{4}{3}\pi r^3$. Devise a plan. To find the volume of the sphere will take two steps. First, find the radius of the sphere by using the formula for the surface area of the sphere. Next, use the radius obtained to find the volume. Carry out the plan.

Step 1. Find the radius of the sphere:

Surface area $S.A. = 4\pi r^2 = 144\pi \text{ cm}^2$

$\qquad \frac{4\pi r^2}{4\pi} = \frac{144\pi \text{ cm}^2}{4\pi}$ Divide both sides by 4π to solve for r^2.

$\qquad\qquad r^2 = 36 \text{ cm}^2$

Because $r^2 = 36 \text{ cm}^2$, you know that r is the square root of 36 cm^2; that is,

$\qquad r = \sqrt{36 \text{ cm}^2}$

$\qquad r = 6 \text{ cm}$

Note: From the list of square roots given in the section titled "Numeration and Operations" in Chapter 3, you know that $\sqrt{36} = 6$.

Step 2. Find the volume:

$$\text{Volume } V = \frac{4}{3}\pi r^3 = \frac{4}{3}\pi (6 \text{ cm})^3 = \frac{4}{3}\pi (216 \text{ cm}^3) = 288\pi \text{ cm}^3, \text{ Choice } \mathbf{D}.$$

Did I answer the question? Yes, I found the volume of the sphere. ✓

Does my answer make sense? Yes. ✓

Is the answer stated in the correct units? Yes, the units are cubic centimeters, which is correct. ✓

12. **B.** Choice **B** is the correct response.

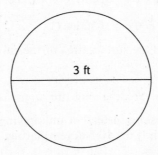

3 ft

The Mathematics Reference Sheet gives the formula of a circle as $A = \pi r^2$. To find the area of the circular garden, find the radius, and then plug in to the formula.

Step 1. The radius is half the diameter = 3 ft ÷ 2 = 1.5 ft.

Step 2. Plug into the formula, using $\pi = 3.14$.

$$A = \pi r^2 = A = 3.14(1.5 \text{ ft})^2 = 3.14(2.25 \text{ ft}^2) = 7.07 \text{ ft}^2$$

The area of the circular garden is 7.07 ft², Choice **B**.

Did I answer the question? Yes, I found the area of the circular garden. ✓

Does my answer make sense? Yes. ✓

Is the answer stated in the correct units? Yes, the units are square feet, which is correct. ✓

Choice **A** results if you find the radius but do not square it. Choice **C** results if you use the diameter in the area formula instead of the radius. Choice **D** results if you find the circumference instead of the area, and you disregard that the units do not work out to be square feet when you make this mistake.

13. **A.** Choice **A** is the correct response. First, sketch a diagram to illustrate the problem:

10 ft

0.5 ft

20 ft

Analyze the problem. Cubic feet are units of volume. The amount of cement in the slab is equal to the volume of the slab, which is a rectangular prism. The Mathematics Reference Sheet gives the formula for the volume of a rectangular prism as $V = Bh$, where B is the area of the base. Thus, $V = lwh$ for a rectangular prism. To find the amount of cement, plug the dimensions into the formula.

$$V = lwh = 20 \text{ ft} \cdot 10 \text{ ft} \cdot 0.5 \text{ ft} = 100 \text{ ft}^3$$

There are 100 ft³ of cement in the slab, Choice **A**.

Did I answer the question? Yes, I found how many cubic feet of cement are in the slab. ✓

Is the answer stated in the correct units? Yes, the units are cubic feet, which is correct. ✓

Choice **B** results if you add the dimensions instead of multiplying. Choice **C** results if you multiply the volume by 3. Choice **D** results if you place the decimal point incorrectly when computing the volume.

14. **C.** Choice **C** is the correct response. Analyze the problem. The surface area of a cube is the sum of the areas of the faces of the cube. The cube in this problem has six congruent faces, each of which is a 10-cm square. To find the surface area of the cube, multiply 6 times the area of one face.

$$\text{Surface area} = 6 \times (10 \text{ cm})^2 = 6 \times 100 \text{ cm}^2 = 600 \text{ cm}^2$$

The surface area of the 10-cm cube is 600 cm², Choice **C**.

Did I answer the question? Yes, I found the surface area of the cube. ✓

Does my answer make sense? Yes. ✓

Is the answer stated in the correct units? Yes, the units are square centimeters, which is correct. ✓

Choice **A** results if you add the dimensions instead of multiplying. Choice **B** is the area of only one of the six faces. Choice **D** results if you multiply 6×10 before squaring.

15. **D.** Choice **D** is the correct response. To solve this problem requires two steps. First, convert 3 hours 15 minutes to hours. Then, divide 221 miles by the result.

Step 1. Convert 3 hours 15 minutes to hours. The two conversion fractions are $\frac{1 \text{ hour}}{60 \text{ min}}$ and $\frac{60 \text{ min}}{1 \text{ hour}}$. Write 15 minutes as a fraction with denominator 1 and let unit analysis tell you whether to multiply by $\frac{1 \text{ hour}}{60 \text{ min}}$ or $\frac{60 \text{ min}}{1 \text{ hour}}$. Since you want the minutes to divide out, multiply by $\frac{1 \text{ hour}}{60 \text{ min}}$.

$$\frac{15 \text{ min}}{1} \times \frac{1 \text{ hour}}{60 \text{ min}} = \frac{\overset{1}{\cancel{15} \text{ min}}}{1} \times \frac{1 \text{ hour}}{\underset{4}{\cancel{60}} \text{ min}} = \frac{1}{4} \text{ hour} = 0.25 \text{ h}$$

Thus, 3 hours 15 minutes = 3.25 hours.

Step 2. To obtain miles per hour, divide 221 miles by 3.25 hours: $\frac{221 \text{ mi}}{3.25 \text{ hour}} = 68 \frac{\text{mi}}{\text{hour}} = 68 \text{ mph}$

The car traveled at the rate of 68 mph, Choice **D**.

Did I answer the question? Yes, I found the rate of travel in miles per hour. ✓

Does my answer make sense? Yes. ✓

Is the answer stated in the correct units? Yes, the units are miles per hour, which is correct. ✓

Choice **A** results if you divide incorrectly. Choices **B** and **C** result if you convert 3 hours 15 minutes to hours incorrectly.

16. **B.** Choice **B** is the correct response. To determine how many gallons are consumed per week, find how many gallons are consumed per day. Then multiply the result by 7 days per week $\left(\frac{7\text{d}}{\text{wk}} \right)$.

Step 1. Find how many gallons are consumed per day.

The Mathematics Reference Sheet provides the following information:

1 cup = 8 fluid ounces

1 pint = 2 cups

1 quart = 2 pints

1 gallon = 4 quarts

These conversion facts yield 8 conversion fractions=: $\frac{1\ c}{8\ oz}$ and $\frac{8\ oz}{1\ c}$, $\frac{1\ pt}{2\ c}$ and $\frac{2\ c}{pt}$, $\frac{1\ qt}{2\ pt}$ and $\frac{2\ pt}{1\ qt}$, $\frac{1\ gal}{4\ qt}$ and $\frac{4\ qt}{1\ gal}$. Write 64 ounces per day as a fraction. Then, using unit analysis, multiply a "chain" of conversion fractions that will result in gallons as the final unit.

$$\frac{64\ oz}{d}\cdot\frac{1\ c}{8\ oz}\cdot\frac{1\ pt}{2\ c}\cdot\frac{1\ qt}{2\ pt}\cdot\frac{1\ gal}{4\ qt}=\frac{64\ \cancel{oz}}{1}\cdot\frac{1\ \cancel{c}}{8\ \cancel{oz}}\cdot\frac{1\ \cancel{pt}}{2\ \cancel{c}}\cdot\frac{1\ \cancel{qt}}{2\ \cancel{pt}}\cdot\frac{1\ gal}{4\ \cancel{qt}}=\frac{0.5\ gal}{d}$$

Step 2. Multiply by 7 days per week $\left(\frac{7d}{wk}\right)$:

$$\frac{0.5\ gal}{d}\cdot\frac{7d}{wk}=\frac{0.5\ gal}{\cancel{d}}\cdot\frac{7\ \cancel{d}}{wk}=\frac{3.5\ gal}{wk}$$

The person will consume 3.5 gallons of water per week, Choice **B**.

Did I answer the question? Yes, I found the number of gallons consumed per week. ✓

Does my answer make sense? Yes. ✓

Is the answer stated in the correct units? Yes, the units are gallons per week, which is correct. ✓

Choice **A** results if you fail to multiply by 7 days per week. Choices **C** and **D** result if you convert 64 ounces to gallons incorrectly by omitting one or more of the conversion fractions.

17. **D.** Choice **D** is the correct response. This problem is a proportion problem involving a map scale. To solve the problem, determine the ratios being compared, being sure to compare corresponding quantities in the same order; write a proportion using the two ratios; and use cross products to solve the proportion.

Step 1. Determine the ratios being compared.

Let d be the actual distance in miles between the two landmarks. The first sentence gives the first ratio: $\frac{d\ (in\ miles)}{9.5\ in.}$. The second sentence gives you the second ratio: $\frac{10\ miles}{\frac{1}{2}\ in.}$. (Notice, you put miles in the numerator in the second ratio because you have miles in the numerator in the first ratio.)

Step 2. Write a proportion using the two ratios.

$$\frac{d\ (in\ miles)}{9.5\ in.}=\frac{10\ miles}{\frac{1}{2}\ in.}$$

For ease of calculation, change $\frac{1}{2}$ to 0.5.

$$\frac{d\ (in\ miles)}{9.5\ in.}=\frac{10\ miles}{0.5\ in.}$$

Step 3. Use cross products to solve the proportion (omitting the units for convenience).

9.5×10 Find a cross product you can calculate. You don't know the value of d, so the only cross product you can calculate is 9.5 times 10.

$d=\frac{9.5\times10}{0.5}=190$ Divide by 0.5, the numerical term you didn't use.

Key the calculation into the calculator like this: $9.5\times10\div0.5=190$

$d=190$ miles

The actual distance in miles between the two landmarks is 190 miles, Choice **D**.

Did I answer the question? Yes, I found the actual distance in miles between the two landmarks. ✓

Does my answer make sense? Yes. ✓

Is the answer stated in the correct units? Yes, the units are miles, which is correct. ✓

Choice **A** results if you set up the proportion incorrectly. Choice **B** results if you make a mistake in placing the decimal point in the answer. Choice **C** results if you deal with the $\frac{1}{2}$ in the proportion incorrectly.

18. **B.** Choice **B** is the correct response. First, sketch a diagram to illustrate the problem:

Analyze the problem. Square yards are units of area. The number of square yards of carpet needed will be the area of the rectangular room. The Mathematics Reference Sheet gives the formula for the area of a rectangle as $A = lw$. The cost of the carpet is $25.75 per square yard. You will need to find the area of the room in square yards. To find the cost of the carpet will take three steps: First, convert the dimensions of the room to yards; next, find the area of the room in square yards; then, multiply the number of square yards by the cost per square yard.

Step 1. Convert the dimensions of the room to yards.

The two conversion fractions are $\frac{1 \text{ yd}}{3 \text{ ft}}$ and $\frac{3 \text{ ft}}{1 \text{ yd}}$. Write each dimension of the room as a fraction with denominator 1, and let unit analysis tell you which conversion fraction to use. Since you want the feet to divide out, use $\frac{1 \text{ yd}}{3 \text{ ft}}$.

$$\frac{18 \text{ ft}}{1} \cdot \frac{1 \text{ yd}}{3 \text{ ft}} = \frac{\overset{6}{\cancel{18}} \cancel{\text{ft}}}{1} \cdot \frac{1 \text{ yd}}{\underset{1}{\cancel{3}} \cancel{\text{ft}}} = 6 \text{ yd}$$

$$\frac{15 \text{ ft}}{1} \cdot \frac{1 \text{ yd}}{3 \text{ ft}} = \frac{\overset{5}{\cancel{15}} \cancel{\text{ft}}}{1} \cdot \frac{1 \text{ yd}}{\underset{1}{\cancel{3}} \cancel{\text{ft}}} = 5 \text{ yd}$$

Step 2. Find the area of the room in square yards. Plug into the formula.

$A = lw = 6 \text{ yd} \cdot 5 \text{ yd} = 30 \text{ yd}^2$

Step 3. Multiply the number of square yards by the cost per square yard.

$$\frac{30 \text{ yd}^2}{1} \cdot \frac{\$25.75}{\text{yd}^2} = \frac{30 \ \cancel{\text{yd}^2}}{1} \cdot \frac{\$25.75}{\cancel{\text{yd}^2}} = \$772.50$$

Not including tax, it will cost $772.50 to carpet the room, Choice **B**.

Did I answer the question? Yes, I found the cost of carpeting the room. ✓

Does my answer make sense? Yes. ✓

Is the answer stated in the correct units? Yes, the units are dollars, which is correct. ✓

Choice **A** results if you fail to multiply by the cost of the carpet, and you disregard that the units do not work out to be dollars when you make this mistake. Choice **C** results if you find the area in square feet and divide this result by 3 to convert to square yards. This approach is incorrect because 1 yd² = 3 ft × 3 ft = 9 ft², not 3 ft². Choice **D** is the result of finding the area in square feet and then multiplying by the cost per square yard.

19. **A.** Choice **A** is the correct response. The figure is a polygon that has exactly five sides, so it is a pentagon. Choice **B** is incorrect because a rhombus is a parallelogram that has exactly four congruent sides. Choice **C**

is incorrect because a hexagon is a polygon that has exactly six sides. Choice **D** is incorrect because a trapezoid is a quadrilateral that has exactly one pair of opposite sides parallel.

20. A. First, sketch a diagram to illustrate the problem:

Analyze the problem. The pole and the cable form a right triangle. From the diagram, you can see that the length of the cable is the hypotenuse of the right triangle that has legs of 16 feet and 12 feet. Plug into the formula:

c = hypotenuse = ?, a = 16, and b = 12

$c^2 = a^2 + b^2 = (16)^2 + (12)^2 = 256^2 + 144^2 = 400^2$

Because $c^2 = 400^2$, you know that $c = \sqrt{400^2}$. From the list of square roots given in the section titled "Numeration and Operations" in Chapter 3, you have $\sqrt{400} = 20$, so $c = 20$. The length of the cable is 20 feet, Choice **A**.

Did I answer the question? Yes, I found the length of the cable. ✓

Does my answer make sense? Yes. ✓

Is the answer stated in the correct units? Yes, the units are feet, which is correct. ✓

Choice **B** results if you mistakenly decide to solve the problem by adding the lengths of the two legs to find the length of the hypotenuse. Choice **C** results if you make the mistake of dividing 400 by 2 to find its square root. Choice **D** results if you fail to find the square root of 400.

21. C. Choice **C** is the correct response. A square is a parallelogram that has exactly four congruent sides and four right angles. A rhombus is a parallelogram that has exactly four congruent sides. Therefore, a square is a special type of rhombus that has four right angles. Choices **A** and **B** are incorrect because cubes and prisms are three-dimensional figures, but a square is a two-dimensional figure. Choice **D** is incorrect because a trapezoid has exactly one pair of opposite sides parallel, but a square has two pairs of opposite sides parallel.

22. D. Choice **D** is the correct response. Only the figure for Choice D has a correctly drawn line of symmetry that cuts the figure into two congruent halves. The lines in the figures for Choices **A**, **B**, and **C** do not cut the figures into two congruent halves.

23. B. Choice **B** is the correct response. The corresponding sides of similar triangles are proportional. Side $\overline{AB}$ is the hypotenuse of triangle ABC. Its corresponding side is $\overline{DE}$, which is the hypotenuse of triangle DEF. The corresponding side for side $\overline{AC}$ is $\overline{DF}$. Let h = length of $\overline{AB}$. Set up a proportion and solve it.

$$\frac{\text{length of } \overline{AB}}{\text{length of } \overline{DE}} = \frac{\text{length of } \overline{AC}}{\text{length of } \overline{DF}}$$ *Hint:* Made sure you keep corresponding sides in the same order.

$$\frac{h}{10 \text{ m}} = \frac{20 \text{ m}}{8 \text{ m}}$$

Use cross products to solve the proportion (omitting the units for convenience).

10×20 Find a cross product you can calculate. You don't know the value of h, so the only cross product you can calculate is 10 times 20.

$\dfrac{10 \times 20}{8} = 25$ Divide by 8, the numerical term you didn't use.

Key the calculation into the calculator like this: $10 \times 20 \div 8 = 25$

$h = 25$ meters

The length of the hypotenuse of triangle *ABC* is 25 meters.

Did I answer the question? Yes, I found the length of the hypotenuse of triangle *ABC*. ✓

Does my answer make sense? Yes. ✓

Is the answer stated in the correct units? Yes, the units are meters, which is correct. ✓

Choices **A, C,** and **D** result if you set up the proportion incorrectly.

24. **D.** Choice **D** is the correct response. An obtuse angle measures between 90° and 180°. All of the interior angles of the octagon in Choice **D** are obtuse angles. All of the interior angles in the triangle in Choice **A** are acute angles. All of the interior angles in Choice **B** are either right angles or 270°. The right triangle in Choice **C** contains one interior right angle and two interior acute angles.

25. **A.** Choice **A** is the correct response. Trapezoid *A'* represents a translation (slide) of 11 units to the right and 11 units down of trapezoid *A*. Choice **B** is incorrect because trapezoid *A'* does not represent a flip of trapezoid *A*. Choice **C** is incorrect because trapezoid *A'* does not represent a turn of trapezoid *A*. Choice **D** is incorrect because trapezoid *A'* does not represent an enlarging or shrinking of trapezoid *A*.

26. **D.** Choice **D** is the correct response. The point P is located 8 units to the left and 3 units up from the origin, so it has coordinates (–8, 3). Choice **A** is incorrect because point M is located at (8,–3). Choice **B** is incorrect because point N is located at (–8,–3). Choice **C** is incorrect because point O is located at (8, 3).

27. **C.** Choice **C** is the correct response.

Step 1. Sketch a diagram and label it.

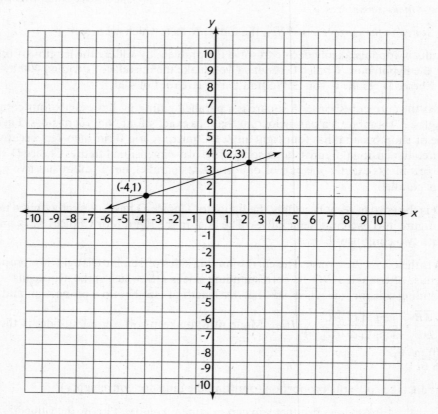

From your sketch, you can see that the line slopes upward from left to right, indicating that the slope is positive; therefore, you can eliminate Choices **A** and **B**.

Step 2. Specify (x_1, y_1) and (x_2, y_2).

Let $(x_1, y_1) = (-4, 1)$ and $(x_2, y_2) = (2, 3)$. Then $x_1 = -4$, $y_1 = 1$, $x_2 = 2$, and $y_2 = 3$.

Step 3. Plug into the formula. (*Hint:* Enclose negative values in parentheses.)

$$\text{slope} = \frac{y_2 - y_1}{x_2 - x_1} = \frac{3 - 1}{2 - (-4)} = \frac{3 - 1}{2 + 4} = \frac{2}{6} = \frac{1}{3}$$

The line through the points $(-4, 1)$ and $(2, 3)$ has slope $\frac{1}{3}$, Choice **C**.

Choice **A** results if you invert the slope formula and make a sign error. Choice **B** results if you make a sign error. Choice **D** results if you invert the slope formula.

28. **A.** Choice **A** is the correct response. Check for an arithmetic sequence by subtracting consecutive terms listed from the terms that follow them:

$-16 - 8 = -24$

$32 - (-16) = 32 + 16 = 48$

No common difference is found. Next, check for a geometric sequence by dividing consecutive terms listed by the terms that follow them:

$-16 \div 8 = -2$

$32 \div -16 = -2$

You get -2 as the quotient both times, so the sequence is geometric with a common ratio of -2. Multiply 2 by -2 (the common ratio) to obtain the missing term: $2 \times -2 = -4$, Choice **A**.

Choice **B** results if you multiply 2×-2 incorrectly. Choice **C** results if you mistakenly conclude that the next number is halfway between 2 and 8. Choice **D** results if you mistakenly conclude the sequence is arithmetic with a common difference of -8.

29. **D.** Choice **D** is the correct response. This expression is a product of three terms: $\frac{1}{2}$, h, and $(b_1 + b_2)$. Notice that the sum $b_1 + b_2$ is in parentheses, so it must be treated as a quantity. Using the order of operations, this sum would be computed first, and then multiplied by the product of $\frac{1}{2}$ and h. Choices **A** and **B** are incorrect because neither treats $b_1 + b_2$ as a quantity. Choice **C** is incorrect because $\frac{1}{2}$ is a factor only once, not twice, in the expression.

30. **C.** Choice **C** is the correct response.

$4 + 2(3x + 1) = 4 + 2(3x) + 2(1) = 4 + 6x + 2$ Using the distributive property, multiply each term in the parentheses by 2.

$= 6x + 4 + 2 = 6x + 6$, Choice **C**   Simplify, using the commutative and associative properties.

Choice **A** results if you make the mistake of combining the coefficients after you obtain $6x + 6$. Choice **B** results if you fail to use the distributive property correctly. Choice **D** results if you make the mistake of adding 4 and 2 before applying the distributive property.

31. **D.** Choice **D** is the correct response. Substitute into the expression, being sure to enclose the substituted values in parentheses:

$2x - y = 2(10) - (-4) = 20 + 4 = 24$, Choice **D**.

Choice **A** occurs if you make a sign error. Choices **B** and **C** result if you deal with the subtraction incorrectly.

32. D. Choice **D** is the correct response.

Method 1: Solve using the steps for solving an equation:

Solve $3(x - 6) = 21$

$3x - 18 = 21$	Use the distributive property to remove parentheses.
$3x - 18 + 18 = 21 + 18$	18 is subtracted from the variable term, so add 18 to both sides of the equation.
$3x = 39$	Then simplify.
$\dfrac{3x}{3} = \dfrac{39}{3}$	You want the coefficient of x to be 1, so divide both sides by 3.
$x = 13$	

Choice **A** results if you subtract 18 from both sides instead of adding 18. Choices **B** and **C** result if you fail to use the distributive property correctly.

Method 2: Check each answer choice by plugging the value into the equation:

Checking **A:** $3(x - 6) = 3(1 - 6) = 3(-5) = -15 \neq 21$. Choice **A** is incorrect because $x = 1$ does not satisfy $3(x - 6) = 21$.

Checking **B:** $3(x - 6) = 3(5 - 6) = 3(-1) = -3 \neq 21$. Choice **B** is incorrect because $x = 5$ does not satisfy $3(x - 6) = 21$.

Checking **C:** $3(x - 6) = 3(9 - 6) = 3(3) = 9 \neq 21$. Choice **C** is incorrect because $x = 9$ does not satisfy $3(x - 6) = 21$.

Checking **D:** $3(x - 6) = 3(13 - 6) = 3(7) = 21$ ✓. Choice **D** is correct because $x = 13$ makes $3(x - 6) = 21$ a true statement.

33. A. Choice **A** is the correct response. To determine which ordered pair satisfies the system, you will need to find the ordered pair that satisfies *both* equations. Check each ordered pair by plugging the x and y values into the two equations, being careful to enclose in parentheses the values you put in.

Checking **A:** $2x - y = 2(-4) - (-1) = -8 + 1 = -7$ ✓.

Since $(-4, -1)$ works in the first equation, try it in the second equation. $x + 3y = (-4) + 3(-1) = -4 + -3 = -7$ ✓. Choice **A** is correct because the ordered pair $(-4, -1)$ satisfies both equations in the system.

In a test situation, you should go on to the next question since you have obtained the correct answer. Here are the other checks:

Checking **B:** $2x - y = 2(-4) - (1) = -8 + -1 = -9 \neq -7$. Choice **B** is incorrect because $(-4, 1)$ does not satisfy $2x - y = -7$.

Checking **C:** $2x - y = 2(4) - (-1) = 8 + 1 = 9 \neq -7$. Choice **C** is incorrect because $(4, -1)$ does not satisfy $2x - y = -7$.

Checking **D:** $2x - y = 2(4) - (1) = 8 + -1 = 7 \neq -7$. Choice **D** is incorrect because $(4, 1)$ does not satisfy $2x - y = -7$.

34. B. Choice **B** is the correct response. Check each response by replacing x with -5 in the statement.

Checking **A:** When $x = -5$, $\dfrac{1}{x} > -x$ becomes $\dfrac{1}{-5} > -(-5)$. When you simplify both sides, this statement becomes $-\dfrac{1}{5} > 5$, which is false because 5 is to the right of $-\dfrac{1}{5}$ on the number line.

Checking **B:** When $x = -5$, $3x < 2x$ becomes $3(-5) < 2(-5)$. When you simplify both sides, this statement becomes $-15 < -10$, which is true because -10 is to the right of -15 on the number line.

In a test situation, you should go on to the next question since you have obtained the correct answer.

Checking the remaining choices, you would find:

Checking **C:** When $x = -5$, $-x < 0$ becomes $-(-5) < 0$. When you simplify both sides, this statement becomes $5 < 0$, which is false because 5 is to the right of 0 on the number line.

Checking **D:** When $x = -5$, $x - 6 > x + 6$ becomes $(-5) - 6 > (-5) + 6$. When you simplify both sides, this statement becomes $-11 > 1$, which is false because 1 is to the right of -11 on the number line.

35. **C.** Choice **C** is the correct response.

$$-2x + 5 < 7$$

$-2x + 5 - 5 < 7 - 5$ 5 is added to the variable term, so subtract 5 from both sides of the inequality.

$-2x < 2$ Then simplify.

$\dfrac{-2x}{-2} > \dfrac{2}{-2}$ You want the coefficient of x to be 1, so divide both sides by -2 and reverse the inequality because you divided both sides by a negative number.

$x > -1$ Then simplify.

$x > -1$, Choice **C**.

Choice **A** results if you fail to reverse the inequality. Choice **B** results if you add 5 to both sides of the inequality instead of subtracting 5. Choice **D** results if you add 5 to both sides of the inequality instead of subtracting 5, and you fail to reverse the inequality.

36. **B.** Choice **B** is the correct response. Check for an arithmetic sequence by subtracting consecutive terms listed from the terms that follow them:

$$-15 - (-5) = -15 + 5 = -10$$

$$-25 - (-15) = -25 + 15 = -10$$

You get -10 as the common difference both times, so the sequence is arithmetic with a common difference of -10. Add -10 to 15 to obtain the missing term: $15 + -10 = 5$, Choice **B**.

Choice **A** results if you make a sign error. Choice **C** results if you add 10 instead of -10 as the common difference. Choice **D** results if you mistakenly conclude the sequence is geometric with a common ratio of 3.

37. **D.** Choice **D** is the correct response. From the graph, you can see that the greatest gap between the average low and high temperature lines occurs in April, Choice **D**. The gaps for Choices **A, B,** and **C** are not as great.

38. **A.** Choice **A** is the correct response. To find the median, do the following:

Step 1. Put the scores in order from least to greatest.

42, 56, 67, 69, 73, 88, 88, 96

Step 2. Find the middle score. The median is the average of the two middle scores, 69 and 73.

The median $= \dfrac{69 + 73}{2} = 71$

Choice **B** results if you fail to order the scores and mistakenly decide to average 56 and 88 to find the median. Choice **C** is the mean, not the median. Choice **D** is the mode, not the median.

39. **D.** Choice **D** is the correct response. This problem is a straightforward probability problem. To solve the problem, find the number of total outcomes possible, find the number of favorable outcomes, and then plug into the probability formula.

There are 50 total possible outcomes. There are 26 favorable outcomes—6 yellow marbles and 20 blue marbles. The probability of drawing a yellow or a blue marble is $\dfrac{\text{number of favorable outcomes}}{\text{number of possible outcomes}} = \dfrac{26}{50} = \dfrac{13}{25}$

The probability of drawing a yellow or blue marble is $\dfrac{13}{25}$, Choice **D**.

Did I answer the question? Yes, I found the probability of drawing a yellow or blue marble from the box. ✓

Does my answer make sense? Yes. ✓

Is the answer stated in the correct units? No units are required for the answer. ✓

Choice **A** is the probability of drawing a blue marble. Choice **B** is the probability of drawing a yellow marble. Choice **C** results if you multiply the probability of drawing a yellow marble times the probability of drawing a blue marble.

40. **C.** Choice **C** is the correct response. This problem is a counting problem. To solve the problem, multiply the number of ways the girl can select a bread by the number of ways she can select a sandwich filling.

    Total number of possible different sandwiches =

    (number of ways to select a bread type) × (number of ways to select a sandwich filling) =

    $3 \times 4 = 12$ possible different sandwiches.

Did I answer the question? Yes, I found the number of possible different sandwiches. ✓

Does my answer make sense? Yes. ✓

Is the answer stated in the correct units? No units are required for the answer. ✓

Choice **A** results if you add instead of multiply in the problem. Choices **B** and **D** result if you count or compute incorrectly.

41. **C.** Choice **C** is the correct response. From the pie chart, you can see that 23% of the young readers surveyed responded they read science fiction books most often. To answer the question, you must find 23% of 200.

    Method 1: To solve the problem, identify the elements of the percent problem, plug the values into the percent proportion, and solve the proportion:

    Step 1. Identify the elements.

    $r = 23$

    part = ?

    whole = 200

    Step 2. Plug into the percent proportion (omitting the units for convenience).

    $$\frac{r}{100} = \frac{\text{part}}{\text{whole}}$$

    $$\frac{23}{100} = \frac{x}{200}$$

    Step 3. Solve the proportion.

    23×200 Find a cross product you can calculate. You don't know the value of x, so the only cross product you can calculate is 23 times 200.

    $x = \frac{23 \times 200}{100} = 46$ Divide by 100, the numerical term you didn't use.

    $x = 46$

    The number of young readers surveyed who responded they read science fiction books most often is 46, Choice **C**.

Did I answer the question? Yes, I found the number of young readers surveyed who responded they read science fiction books most often. ✓

Does my answer make sense? Yes. ✓

Is the answer stated in the correct units? No units are required for the answer. ✓

Method 2: Change 23% to a decimal fraction or common fraction and multiply:

23% of 200 = $0.23 \times 200 = 46$. Or 23% of 200 $= \frac{23}{100} \cdot \frac{200}{1} = \frac{23}{1\cancel{00}} \cdot \frac{2\cancel{00}}{1} = 46$.

Choice **A** is the number of young readers surveyed who responded they read biography or historical books most often. Choice **B** is the number of young readers surveyed who responded they read nature books most often. Choice **D** is the number of young readers surveyed who responded they read adventure books most often.

42. **A.** Choice **A** is the correct response. The range is the difference between the greatest and the least score.

range = greatest score – least score = 100 – 70 = 30, Choice **A.**

Choice **B** is the mean score, not the range. Choice **C** is the median score, not the range. Choice **D** is the mode score, not the range.

43. **C.** Choice **C** is the correct response. To answer the question, find the median for each answer choice.

Choice **A**: $10.29, $9.87, $11.99, $8.45, $10.60, $10.25

Step 1. Put the prices in order from least to greatest.

$8.45, $9.87, $10.25, $10.29, $10.60, $11.99

Step 2. Since there are six values, the median is the average of the two middle values, $10.25 and $10.29. You can eliminate **A** at this point because you can see that the average of these two prices is greater than $10.24. Just so you know, the median $= \dfrac{\$10.25 + \$10.29}{2} = \$10.27$.

Choice **B**: $7.50, $12.98, $8.25, $10.89, $11.05, $10.67

Step 1. Put the prices in order from least to greatest.

$7.50, $8.25, $10.67, $10.89, $11.05, $12.98

Step 2. Since there are six values, the median is the average of the two middle values, $10.67 and $10.89. You can eliminate **B** at this point because you can see that the average of these two prices is greater than $10.24. Just so you know, the median $= \dfrac{\$10.67 + \$10.89}{2} = \$10.78$.

Choice **C**: $11.98, $10.50, $9.98, $8.50, $12.95, $9.98

Step 1. Put the prices in order from least to greatest.

$8.50, $9.98, $9.98, $10.50, $11.98, $12.95

Step 2. Since there are six values, the median is the average of the two middle values, $9.98 and $10.50. $\dfrac{\$9.98 + \$10.50}{2} = \$10.24$. Choice **C** is the correct response.

In a test situation, you should go on to the next question since you have obtained the correct answer. Just so you know, the median for Choice **D** is $10.11.

44. **B.** Choice **B** is the correct response. To answer the question, find the mode for each answer choice.

Choice **A** is incorrect. The mode is 96 because it occurs three times.

Choice **B** is correct. The mode is 87 because it occurs two times.

Choice **C** is incorrect. The mode is 84 because it occurs two times.

Choice **D** is incorrect. There is no mode because each score occurs the same number of times.

45. **B.** Choice **B** is the correct response. This is a straightforward probability problem. To solve the problem, find the number of total outcomes possible, find the number of favorable outcomes, and then plug into the probability formula.

There are 40 total possible outcomes. The primes between 1 and 40 are 2, 3, 5, 7, 11, 13, 17, 19, 23, 29, 31, and 37. Thus, there are 12 favorable outcomes. The probability of drawing a tile numbered with a prime number is

$$\frac{\text{number of favorable outcomes}}{\text{number of possible outcomes}} = \frac{12}{40} = \frac{3}{10}$$

The probability of drawing a prime-numbered tile is $\frac{3}{10}$, Choice **B**.

Did I answer the question? Yes, I found the probability of drawing a prime-numbered tile. ✓

Does my answer make sense? Yes. ✓

Is the answer stated in the correct units? No units are required for the answer. ✓

Choice **A** is the result of mistakenly determining that there are 10 favorable outcomes. Choice **C** is the result of including 1 as a prime number. The number 1 is neither prime nor composite. Choice **D** is the probability of drawing a composite-numbered tile.

Reading Skills Answers and Explanations

1. **B.** Choice **B** is the correct response. This passage indicates that *"plugging" is not a part of modern baseball.* This information is given in the second paragraph. None of the other answer choices are indicated in this passage.

2. **A.** Choice **A** is the correct response. According to this passage, rounders is a game that *was imported from England.* Although this information is not stated explicitly in this passage, it can be inferred from the information given in the second paragraph. The other answer choices are not supported by the passage.

3. **D.** Choice **D** is the correct response. In the first paragraph, the word *evokes* most nearly means *elicits,* "to draw forth." The words in the other answer choices do not mean the same as the word *evokes.*

4. **C.** Choice **C** is the correct response. According to this passage, the Knickerbockers baseball club was formed in the city of *New York*. The cities in the other answer choices are incorrect locations.

5. **D.** Choice **D** is the correct response. An opinion expressed in this passage is the statement given in Choice **D**: *Baseball has become the hallmark of all that is good and right about our country.* The description of baseball as *the hallmark of all that is good and right about our country* is a view, not a fact, expressed by the author, reflecting the author's opinion about baseball. Choice **A** is a statement of fact given in the second paragraph. Choice **B** is a statement of fact given in the third paragraph. Choice **C** is a statement of fact that can be determined from the information given in the fourth paragraph.

6. **D.** Choice **D** is the correct response. According to the passage, baseball is considered America's pastime because *it occurs at a leisurely pace in a pastoral setting.* Remember, the question reads "according to this passage," and this reference to "baseball and its natural allure to wide open spaces," is exactly the description the reader needs to select Choice **D**. Choice **A** is incorrect because as the passage implies, baseball provides interested individuals with more than a "casual diversion." It provides a dramatic confrontation of a competitive sport in which fans can cheer for their respective teams and watch the game leisurely unfold before them. Choice **B** is incorrect because it is not supported by the passage. Choice **C** is incorrect because the passage indicates baseball has rules.

7. **B.** Choice **B** is the correct response. As used in the final paragraph, the word *exemplifies* best means *to illustrate by example.* Choices **A**, **C**, and **D** are incorrect meanings of the word *exemplifies* and, thus, are incorrect choices.

8. **C.** Choice **C** is the correct response. The narrative style of this passage can best be described as *subjective.* The author provides a passionate, yet practical analysis of the reasons that baseball is regarded as America's favorite pastime. Choice **A** is incorrect because the author is not *derisive,* meaning "mocking or sarcastic." Choice **B** is incorrect because the author is not *cynical,* meaning "pessimistic or scornful." Choice **D** is incorrect because the author is not *pessimistic,* meaning "doubtful or gloomy."

9. **B.** Choice **B** is the correct response. The sentence that best states the main idea of this passage is *baseball evokes an era of a simpler life and pace.* The author expresses this view in the first paragraph with the statement: "[B]aseball evokes a bygone era of American independence, openness, and simplicity." Choice **A** is incorrect because the passage does not indicate that baseball is a sport that is elitist in tone and style. Choice **C** is incorrect because the passage describes baseball as simple in design and pace. Choice **D** is incorrect because although watching professional baseball might inspire youngsters to become competitive athletes, this thought is not expressed in this narrative about baseball.

10. **C.** Choice **C** is the correct response. In the final paragraph, the second and third sentences *explain the first sentence.* The two sentences that follow the first sentence explain by illustration what the author means by *Of all of America's obsessions, baseball is one of pure passion.* Choice **A** is incorrect because the second and third sentences do not dispute or disagree with the first sentence, and do not modify it. Choice **B** is incorrect because the second and third sentences support the first sentence. Choice **D** is incorrect because the second and third sentences relate to the first sentence, and do not ignore it.

11. **D.** Choice **D** is the correct response. The author of this passage believes that dancing *is a joyous expression of movement to music.* The passage demonstrates the author's fondness for dancing as a form of self-expression. Choice **A** is incorrect because the passage does not portray dancing as detrimental to one's health and well-being. Choice **B** is incorrect because the author says that formal dancing is not self-willed and free-wheeling. Choice **C** is incorrect because nowhere in the passage does the author imply that dancing is a waste of time and energy.

12. **B.** Choice **B** is the correct response. The author's claim that "I have two left feet," meaning that the author is a poor dancer, is clearly *a narrative technique to engage the reader.* The author uses the technique of self-deprecating humor to lure the reader into a discussion of dance and the many forms it has taken throughout human history. Choice **A** is incorrect because even though the author is writing positively about dancing, the author might truly be a poor dancer. Choice **C** is incorrect because the self-deprecating humor is no indication that the author does not like dance; indeed, it is an indication of the contrary. Choice **D** is incorrect because the author does not engage in an argumentative style; instead, the author uses a self-deprecating style to entice and tease the reader into the discussion about dance.

13. **A.** Choice **A** is the correct response. This passage is an example of *a narrative portrayal of a positive experience.* The author writes in a clear and optimistic voice about the power of dance to transform the lives of all who participate in it or observe it. Choice **B** is incorrect because the author does not provide a cynical perspective on the human condition in this passage. Choice **C** is incorrect because the author does not see dance as a dying art form—it is something that lives from generation to generation—and thus, this narrative is not a valedictory speech. Choice **D** is incorrect because the author points out that dancing is universally enjoyed and, thus, is not an obscure obsession.

14. **C.** Choice **C** is the correct response. In the fifth paragraph, the phrase *Blessed with the gift of mimicry* best means *being able to imitate.* Choices **A**, **B**, and **D** are incorrect meanings of the word *mimicry* and, thus, are incorrect choices.

15. **B.** Choice **B** is the correct response. According to information given in the fifth paragraph, dancing is universally enjoyed because *it speaks to human emotions.* Choices **A**, **C**, and **D** are not supported by the passage.

16. **C.** Choice **C** is the correct response. A statement that is implied in the first paragraph is the statement given in Choice **C**: *The cha-cha, rhumba, and waltz are types of dance.* The author never states explicitly that these are types of dances, but the reader can draw this conclusion based on the topic of the paragraph. Even though you may disagree with the statements in choices **A** and **D**, these statements are explicit in the first paragraph. The statement given in Choice **B** is neither stated nor implied in the first paragraph.

17. **C.** Choice **C** is the correct response. An opinion expressed in this passage is the statement given in Choice **C**: *Dancing has been a most human form of self-expression.* The description of dancing as *a most human form of self-expression* is a view, not a fact, expressed by the author, reflecting the author's opinion about dancing. Choice **A** is a statement of fact given in the second paragraph. Choice **B** is a statement of fact given in the third paragraph. Choice **D** is a statement of fact given in the fourth paragraph.

18. **C.** Choice **C** is the correct response. In the second paragraph, the word *assertive,* meaning aggressively self-confident, most nearly means *bold.* The words in the other answer choices have a meaning opposite to that of *assertive.*

19. **C.** Choice **C** is the correct response. This passage states that *dancing is an art form.* This information is given in the second paragraph. The statement in Choice **A** is neither stated nor implied in the passage. Choice **B** disagrees with information given in the second paragraph. Choice **D** is implied, but not stated, in the first paragraph.

20. **D.** Choice **D** is the correct response. According to information given in this passage, formal dancing is difficult and strenuous. This determination can be inferred from the third sentence in the last paragraph, "their [referring to those who do formal dancing] expertise lies in making the difficult and strenuous look easy and joyous." Choices **A** and **B** are not supported by the passage. Neither is Choice **C** supported by the passage. Even though this is a true statement, this information is not given in the passage. Tip: Do not select answer choices based on your personal knowledge that goes beyond the information given in the passage.

21. **A.** Choice **A** is the correct response. In this narrative, the author's description of Piaget and his work suggests that Piaget was *a curious and prodigious thinker.* As the narrative indicates, from a very early age, Piaget showed signs of the intense intellectual curiosity that served him well all his life. Choices **B**, **C**, and **D** are not supported by the passage.

22. **C.** Choice **C** is the correct response. As thinking about human cognition has evolved, one principle, according to the passage, has remained constant—*Human beings need to develop in defined stages.* Piaget defined human cognitive development as a series of well-defined stages of growth and maturity. Each stage defined a different thinking process and learning perspective. Choices **A**, **B**, and **D** are not supported by the passage.

23. **B.** Choice **B** is the correct response. The author would probably agree that *studying cognitive thinking reveals human behavior patterns.* The thrust of this piece is how Piaget's investigations of cognitive thinking led him to define human behavior into recognizable patterns of development. None of the other answer choices are supported by this passage.

24. **D.** Choice **D** is the correct response. In this narrative, the following statement is NOT supported: *cognitive psychology relies on the suspension of disbelief.* In fact, as the narrative mentions, cognitive psychology relies on validated truths or things that you can actually see. Choice **A** is incorrect because the narrative specifically implies that psychology is the study of the mind and its mental and emotional processes. Choice **B** is incorrect because Piaget's developmental theories were the result of a small sample size. Choice **C** is incorrect because developmental thinking can be classified into specified age groups.

25. **D.** Choice **D** is the correct response. In the fourth paragraph, the phrase, *Not content to know just the physical world,* implies that Piaget *intended to explore mental functions.* The paragraph goes on to discuss Piaget's pursuit of psychology. Choice **A** is incorrect because Piaget was much more than a literal or "just the facts" scientific researcher. Choice **B** is incorrect because Piaget understood more than the human body when he explained his theories. Choice **C** is incorrect because Piaget engaged in more than quantitative or "numbers only" research; instead, he relied on qualitative or observed characteristics as well.

26. **D.** Choice **D** is the correct response. According to this passage Jean Piaget was born in *Switzerland* in 1896. The other answer choices do not give the correct country of Piaget's birth.

27. **A.** Choice **A** is the correct response. The topic of the second paragraph is *Piaget's four stages of cognitive development.* The topic in Choice **B** is too broad to describe the information in the second paragraph. The topics in choices **C** and **D** are too narrow to describe the information in the second paragraph.

28. **A.** Choice **A** is the correct response. An opinion about Jean Piaget expressed in this passage is the statement given in Choice **A**: *His work is seminal to understanding modern child development.* The word *seminal* is a judgment word reflecting the author's opinion about Piaget's impact on the field of child development. Choice **B** is a statement of fact given in the fourth paragraph. Choice **C** is a statement of fact given in the fifth paragraph. Choice **D** is a statement of fact established in the third paragraph.

29. **B.** Choice **B** is the correct response. In the fourth paragraph, this passage states that Jean Piaget embarked on a career that led to *breakthrough discoveries in human cognition.* Choices **A** and **C** are incorrect because, although these are true statements (as you may know), this information is not given in this passage. Remember, you must not select answer choices based on your personal knowledge that goes beyond the information given in the passage. Choice **D** is not supported by the passage.

30. **D.** Choice **D** is the correct response. The tone of this passage is best described as *serious.* The author does not show a disbelieving, doubtful tone (Choice **A**); a sarcastic, mocking tone (Choice **B**); or a convincing, persuasive tone (Choice **C**).

31. **A.** Choice **A** is the correct response. One thing that this narrative makes clear is that whales have more in common with *mammals than with fish.* The central thesis of this passage is that whales belong to the class of mammals, although most people think of them as fish. Choices **B, C,** and **D** are not supported by the passage.

32. **B.** Choice **B** is the correct response. According to this passage, whales are a unique creature in the animal kingdom because *whales can carry enormous weight without much effort.* They are the largest sea creatures, yet their bodies are structured so that they can glide through the ocean without much difficulty or effort. Choice **A** is incorrect because the passage makes no mention of this. Choice **C** is incorrect because whales are very maternal and, like all mammals, nurture their offspring. Choice **D** is incorrect because the passage makes no mention of this.

33. **C.** Choice **C** is the correct response. The author of this passage implies that whales are intelligent. The author of this passage states that whales have a highly developed brain from which can be inferred that they are intelligent. Choices **A, B,** and **D** are not supported by the passage.

34. **A.** Choice **A** is the correct response. After reading this passage, the following statement can be inferred as true: *whales are creatures that have experienced successful adaptations.* Clearly, this passage implies that the adaptations whales have experienced have helped them survive. The other answer choices are not supported by the passage.

35. **A.** Choice **A** is the correct response. In the fifth paragraph, the word *Adaptation* can best be defined as *modification.* As the passage states, whales have grown into the successful creatures they are because their bodies have adapted to life in the sea. The other answer choices are not accurate definitions for *adaptation.*

36. **D.** Choice **D** is the correct response. The tone of this passage is best described as *factual.* The author does not show a disbelieving, skeptical tone (Choice **A**); an amusing, humorous tone (Choice **B**); or a mocking, sarcastic tone (Choice **C**).

37. **B.** Choice **B** is the correct response. A statement that is a fact about whales that is given in the first paragraph is the statement in Choice **B**: *Whales have lungs.* The statements in choices **A** and **C** disagree with information given in the passage. Neither is Choice **D** supported by the passage. Even though this is a true statement, this information is not given in the passage. Tip: Do not select answer choices based on your personal knowledge that goes beyond the information given in the passage.

38. **B.** Choice **B** is the correct response. A statement about whales that is implied in this passage is given in Choice **B**: *They cannot take in oxygen when underwater.* This statement can be inferred from information given in the second paragraph. The statements about whales given in the other answer choices disagree with information given in this passage.

39. **B.** Choice **B** is the correct response. In the second paragraph, this passage states that *the sperm whale can hold its breath for up to two hours.* The timeframes given in the other answer choices disagree with information in this passage.

40. **B.** Choice **B** is the correct response. According to information given in the third paragraph of this passage, *whales nurture their young.* Choice **A** is a true statement, but this information is not given in this passage. As stated earlier, do not select answer choices based on your personal knowledge that goes beyond the information given in the passage. Choice **C** is incorrect because it disagrees with information given in the fifth paragraph. Choice **D** is incorrect because it disagrees with information given in the first paragraph.

6. Remedies.

  (a) WPI's entire liability and your exclusive remedy for defects in materials and workmanship shall be limited to replacement of the Software Media, which may be returned to WPI with a copy of your receipt at the following address: Software Media Fulfillment Department, Attn.: *CliffsNotes® FTCE General Knowledge Test with CD-ROM, 2nd Edition,* John Wiley & Sons, Inc., 10475 Crosspoint Blvd., Indianapolis, IN 46256, or call 1-877-762-2974. Please allow four to six weeks for delivery. This Limited Warranty is void if failure of the Software Media has resulted from accident, abuse, or misapplication. Any replacement Software Media will be warranted for the remainder of the original warranty period or thirty (30) days, whichever is longer.

  (b) In no event shall WPI or the author be liable for any damages whatsoever (including without limitation damages for loss of business profits, business interruption, loss of business information, or any other pecuniary loss) arising from the use of or inability to use the Book or the Software, even if WPI has been advised of the possibility of such damages.

  (c) Because some jurisdictions do not allow the exclusion or limitation of liability for consequential or incidental damages, the above limitation or exclusion may not apply to you.

7. U.S. Government Restricted Rights. Use, duplication, or disclosure of the Software for or on behalf of the United States of America, its agencies and/or instrumentalities "U.S. Government" is subject to restrictions as stated in paragraph (c)(1)(ii) of the Rights in Technical Data and Computer Software clause of DFARS 252.227-7013, or subparagraphs (c) (1) and (2) of the Commercial Computer Software - Restricted Rights clause at FAR 52.227-19, and in similar clauses in the NASA FAR supplement, as applicable.

8. General. This Agreement constitutes the entire understanding of the parties and revokes and supersedes all prior agreements, oral or written, between them and may not be modified or amended except in a writing signed by both parties hereto that specifically refers to this Agreement. This Agreement shall take precedence over any other documents that may be in conflict herewith. If any one or more provisions contained in this Agreement are held by any court or tribunal to be invalid, illegal, or otherwise unenforceable, each and every other provision shall remain in full force and effect.